AMERICAN DECORATIVE ARTS

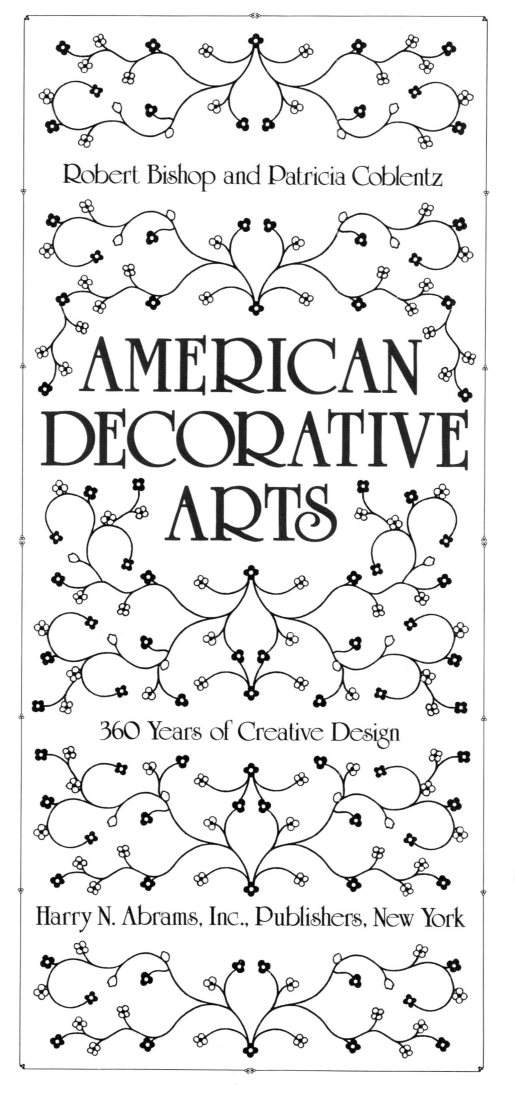

Robert Bishop and Patricia Coblentz

AMERICAN DECORATIVE ARTS

360 Years of Creative Design

Harry N. Abrams, Inc., Publishers, New York

*Frontispiece: Pearl Room of William Henry Vanderbilt House,
New York City. See plate 314*

Project Director: Darlene Geis
Editor: Reginald Gay
Designer: Judith Michael
Motifs and borders: Lydia Gershey

LIBRARY OF CONGRESS CATALOGING IN PUBLICATION DATA

Bishop, Robert Charles.
American decorative arts.

Bibliography: p.
Includes index.
1. Decoration and ornament—United States—History.
I. Coblentz, Patricia, joint author. II. Title.
NK1403.B57   745′.0973   80–39631
ISBN 0–8109–0692–9

Illustrations © 1982 by Harry N. Abrams, Inc.

Printed and bound in Japan

Contents

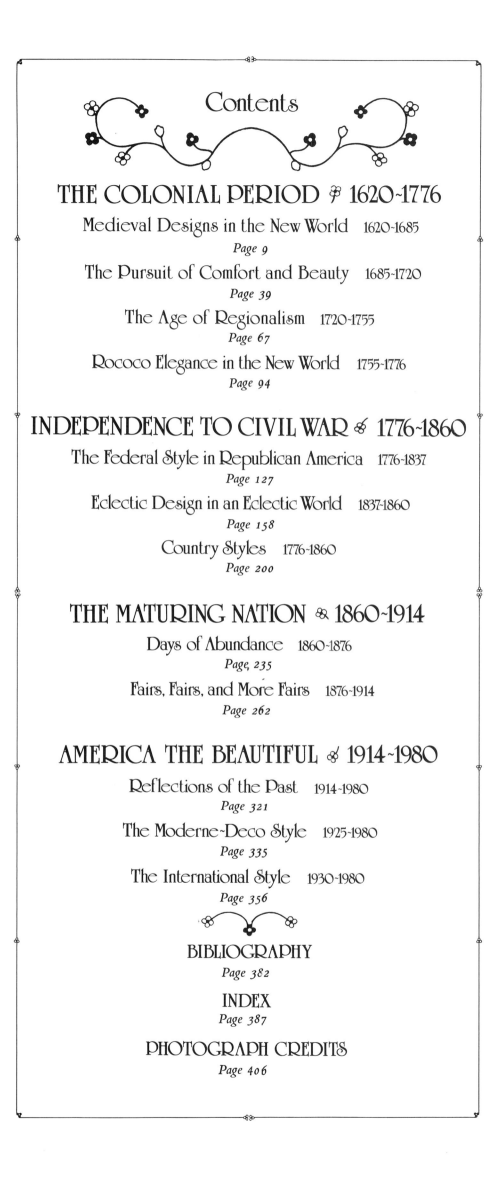

THE COLONIAL PERIOD
1620-1776

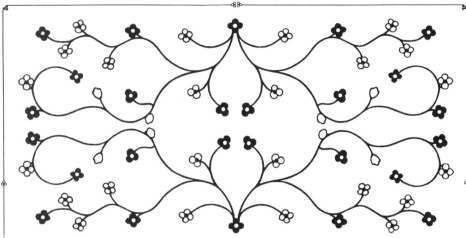

itting in a comfortable easy chair in front of an ornamental fireplace in a centrally heated, air-conditioned room, with carpeting underfoot and all of the amenities of physical comfort at hand, no one living in America today can readily comprehend the austere life endured by the early colonists. Survival itself was tenuous. Food, a dwelling that was warm and dry, and security against hostile Indians were the primary concerns of every colonist. Experimentation in the design of home furnishings—the decorative arts—took many years to develop in the culturally isolated seaboard hamlets and towns that dotted the Atlantic coast during the seventeenth century.

Until about 1680, design in colonial America was for the most part borrowed from England, where the simple, crude styles of the Middle Ages still prevailed. The Italian Renaissance had led to the development of a more gracious way of life throughout much of continental Europe, but the influence had yet to leap the Channel and affect England. For the colonists, whatever London dictated was followed in America. By the end of the seventeenth century, international commerce had brought increased wealth and a new awareness of comfort and beauty to the colonies, inspiring a taste for foreign fashions introduced via England from India, Spain, Holland, and the Orient. These foreign fashions served as a catalyst for the American craftsman—the cabinetmaker, silversmith, glassblower, and needleworker.

At the beginning of the second quarter of the eighteenth century, a new style—the Queen Anne—was introduced from the English court. With its graciously curved forms, the Queen Anne mode replaced the uncompromising straight lines and massive forms of medieval English pieces that still dominated colonial styles, and it was freely adapted by American craftsmen working in the sizable cities that the infant settlements had now become. Distinct schools of cabinetmaking emerged, each with its own method of construction, and regional variations in all of the decorative arts were not difficult to discern.

By mid-century, another style rose to prominence. It was based on the designs of the English cabinetmaker Thomas Chippendale, transmitted to American shores in his 1754 guide, *The Gentleman and Cabinet-Maker's Director,* an English interpretation of the French rococo, itself an exquisitely refined and sinuous adaptation of the Italian baroque.

Throughout the colonial period Americans were engrossed in the latest English and European styles as they attempted to approximate in the New World the mode of living they had left behind in the Old.

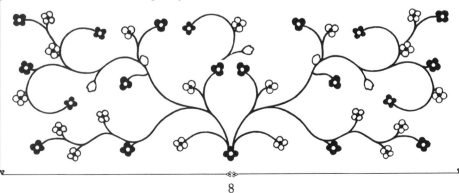

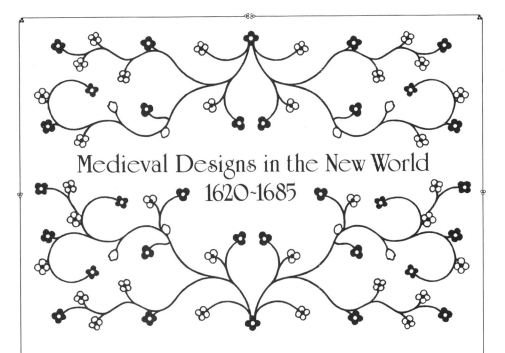

Medieval Designs in the New World
1620-1685

John Smith, the English adventurer who encouraged colonization in America, was seeking the excitement of new discoveries as well as financial gain in the New World. An investor in the London Company, he was one of the members of the 1607 expedition that established what is now Jamestown, Virginia, the first permanent English settlement in America. Twenty-eight-year-old Smith traded with the Indians for provisions and led exploratory journeys that enabled him to map the surrounding region. He was president of the governing council of Jamestown from 1608 to 1609, and it was his resourcefulness that permitted the colony to survive those difficult early years. He returned to England in 1609 to recuperate from injuries received in an explosion of gunpowder.

Smith journeyed across the sea several times and on each occasion he explored and attempted to map the geographic characteristics of the regions he visited (plate 1). It was he who first used the name New England for the coastal land he charted from Penobscot Bay to Cape Cod. Eventually returning to England for good, Smith recorded his impressions and experiences in the New World in numerous publications, and it was his writings that provided the primary impetus for the great surge of colonization throughout the seventeenth century.

1. Map of New England. Printed by James Reeve. London, England. 1635. Engraving, 12¼ × 14″. Greenfield Village and Henry Ford Museum, Dearborn, Michigan

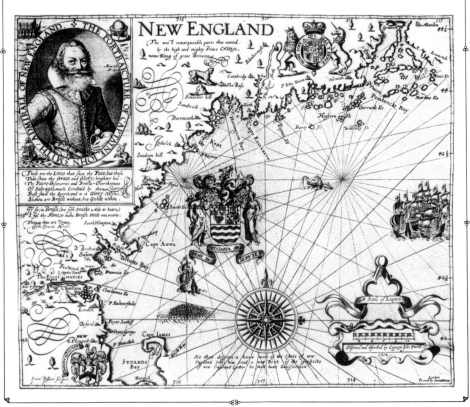

This is the ninth state of the first labeled map of New England. Minor changes were made after the first state, which Simon Passaeus engraved in 1616 on the basis of information gathered by Captain John Smith, whose portrait the map bears. It was first published in Smith's A Description of New England *(London, 1616).*

2. Cradle. Maker unknown. Holland. c. 1620. Wicker and oak, length 29½". Pilgrim Society, Plymouth, Massachusetts

This was the cradle of Peregrine White, son of William and Susannah White, who was born on the Mayflower *in Provincetown Harbor in 1620. Peregrine was the first European child born in New England. Children's furniture in both Holland and England was often fashioned from wicker, and an occasional diary entry indicates that Americans used it for large chairs as well.*

During much of the first century of permanent settlement in the New World, medieval European traditions dominated popular taste. This is not surprising since colonists often attempted to re-create the social patterns, the cultural styles, and the homes they had left behind in their native land. Most settlers did not wish to deny their past but hoped to enrich their future, not only by establishing the religious freedom that was often unobtainable in the Old World but also by exploiting the economic opportunity offered in the form of free or inexpensive land. The zealous adventurers brave enough to risk the long, arduous sea voyage had little understanding of what life would be like in their strange new country.

The Reverend Francis Higginson, first minister at Salem, Massachusetts, sent many encouraging descriptions of New England to investors in London, tempered with advice to those considering migrating to the new land:

Before you come, be careful to be strongly instructed what things are fittest to bring with you for your more comfortable passage at sea, as also for your husbandry occasions when you come to the land. For when you are once parted with England you shall meete neither markets nor fayres to buy what you want. Therefore be sure to furnish yourselves with things fittest to be had before you come: as meale for bread, malt for drinke, woolen and linnen cloath, and leather for shoes, and all manner of carpenters tools, and a great deale of iron and steele to make nails, and locks for houses, and furni-

3. Cotswold Cottage. Builder unknown. Chedworth, England. Early seventeenth century. Greenfield Village and Henry Ford Museum, Dearborn, Michigan

The cottage was originally built in the seventeenth century at Chedworth, Gloucestershire. Henry Ford purchased this two-family limestone dwelling—which he then had moved stone by stone to his great outdoor museum and village at Dearborn—because it was a notable example of the Old World origins of America's earliest New England colonists.

4. *Parlor of Cotswold Cottage. English furnishings. Seventeenth century. Greenfield Village and Henry Ford Museum, Dearborn, Michigan*

5. *Museum installation. Puritan Keeping Room. New England. Seventeenth century. American Museum in Britain, Bath, England*

A wooden trencher and a burl bowl on the top of the gateleg table, and the leather blackjack, or pitcher, on the cupboard are appointments commonly found in a colonial interior, similar to this restoration of one of the rooms of the Cotswold Cottage (see plate 3). The brass English lantern clock is a luxurious item for such a simple room. The windows of leaded glass are the casement type, which open outward rather than divide in the center as windows do today.

This room was constructed using beams and floorboards from a house at Wrentham, Massachusetts, dating from the late seventeenth century. The furnishings are all from the middle and late seventeenth century and are typical of New England's best pieces of the period. A brass lantern clock on the wall and a lighting stand with betty lamps on the center table are refinements that very few settlers of the period could have afforded.

OVERLEAF:

6. *Interior of Plympton House. New England. Seventeenth century. Greenfield Village and Henry Ford Museum, Dearborn, Michigan*

The house was originally built by Thomas Plympton at South Sudbury, Massachusetts. Plympton, a founder of the Puritan settlement of Sudbury Plantation in 1638, was an indentured servant and his home was of unpretentious, simple construction. The furnishings reflected the stark simplicity of seventeenth-century New England life. Many of the accessories, such as the English clock on the wall, the pewter in the cupboard, the imported delft, the brass bedwarmer hanging on the fireplace, would have been beyond the means of a man like Plympton.

ture for ploughs and carts, and glasse for windows, and many other things which were better for you to think of there than to want them here.

Food, shelter, and personal safety were luxuries that few enjoyed in the tiny settlements the colonists established along the eastern seaboard. Survival was difficult and many of the earliest Pilgrims in the Massachusetts Bay Colony were forced to burrow into the earth under a hillside for their first shelter.

In the South and the Southwest, the Spanish had experienced many of the same hardships when they attempted to set up permanent settlements during the 1530s and 1540s. None of the sixteenth-century colonies survived; however, in 1609 a building was raised at Santa Fe as a residence for the royal governor. This adobe structure, with its dirt floor, was typical of most domestic architecture in that area for several centuries to follow.

In Virginia, after a difficult beginning that included struggles with the Indians and disastrous fires, the settlement at Jamestown took root. In 1619 the first representative assembly in America convened there, and in the same year the first African slaves were introduced into the colonies. Jamestown served as the capital of the colony in Virginia until 1699.

This building, almost medieval in design with oak frame and pine boards, has a second story that projects over the first. Leaded-glass casement windows and many gables are conspicuous features of homes built by the wealthier colonists.

A similar pattern is discernible for each new settlement. During the first few years the inhabitants were forced to concern themselves with the construction of permanent homes to replace rude temporary shelters; crops were planted, raised, and harvested; and peace in varying degrees was negotiated with the surrounding native American tribes. In Massachusetts the practical Reverend Higginson added to his advice the strong recommendation that future colonists set out for the new land with appropriate armor, a long piece, a sword bandolier, and sufficient ammunition. Breastplates—like the one hanging on the wall of the Puritan Keeping Room (plate 5)—and helmets were familiar sights in nearly every colony, and Captain Smith, sailing from Jamestown in 1609, noted the incongruity of there being more protective armor in the colony than there were men who could readily make use of it. By the end of the seventeenth century colonists were aware that such heavy protection was thoroughly impractical in battles with the Indians, whose methods of warfare were totally different from those of the Europeans.

Many of the furnishings in the first settlements were transported from the Old World by the colonists. The wicker cradle (plate 2) arrived at Plymouth, Massachusetts, with the Pilgrims on the *Mayflower*. In those early decades few

In many of the colonial homes a room that was special and refined in character—the best room, or parlor—was set aside for family conversation or the entertainment of guests. This gracious room, the parlor of the Susquehanna House (see plate 9), is furnished with elegant English oak furniture from the seventeenth century and reflects the comfort occasionally achieved by English settlers in the New World. A beadwork box is one of the many decorative accessories that well-to-do colonists imported for their homes. One of the oldest pieces of furniture in the Susquehanna House is the wainscot chair placed next to the tall-case clock. This elaborately carved oak piece is dated 1626.

settlers were affluent enough to concern themselves with furniture and purely decorative accessories. William Wood, writing in 1634 from the fourteen-year-old Massachusetts Bay Colony, sent out a plea for an "ingenious Carpenter, a cunning Joyner, a handie Cooper, such a one as can make strong ware for the use of the countrie." Utility was the prime consideration and every object had to be functional. Even so, society measured an individual not only by his social or political position but more concretely by the quantity and quality of furniture, pewter, silver, and other household objects in his possession.

The transition from a clearing in the woods to a permanent settlement and then to a fully organized town often did not require a long span of time. Edward Johnson, a professional cabinetmaker, or "joyner" (the term of the period), observed in 1642: "The Lord hath been pleased to turn all the wigwams, huts, and hovels the English dwelt in at their first coming, into orderly, fair, and well-built houses, well furnished many of them."

A history of Dedham, Massachusetts, compiled in 1827 by Erastus Worthington, portrays a perfect example of the dramatic growth of a New England town. Dedham, settled in 1635, was incorporated originally under the name of Contentment in 1636.

11. Bedchamber of Cotswold Cottage. English furnishings. Seventeenth century. Greenfield Village and Henry Ford Museum, Dearborn, Michigan

The carved oak bed in the bedchamber of Cotswold Cottage (see plate 3) has a linsey-woolsey cover as well as printed fabrics that serve as curtains. These curtains could be closed on cold, windy nights, keeping out drafts and retaining at least some heat within the sleeping area.

In 1664, ninety-five small houses near each other were situated within a short distance of the place where the new court house now stands; the greater part of them east of that place, and around Dwight's brook. A row of houses stood on the north side of High Street. . . . The greatest number of these houses were built soon after the first settlement commenced. There were then very few carpenters, joiners or masons in the colony. There was no saw mill in the settlement for many years. The only boards which could be procured at first, were those which were sawed by hand. The saw pits, now seen, denote that boards were sawed in the woods. . . . Around these houses nothing was seen but stumps, clumsy fences of poles, and an uneven and unsubdued soil; such as all the first settlements in New England present. The native forest trees were not suitable shades for a door yard. A shady tree was not then such an agreeable object as it now is, because it could form no agreeable contrast with cleared grounds. Where the meeting house of the first parish now stands, there stood for more than 30 years a low building, thirty-six feet

12. Chest. Thomas Dennis (attr.). Ipswich, Massachusetts. c. 1675. Oak, height 29¾". Metropolitan Museum of Art, New York City. Gift of Mrs. Russell Sage, 1909

The elaborate carving on this chest confirms its relationship to several other pieces that descended through the Dennis family. The top lifts up and reveals a storage well. It should be noted that the carving is only on the face of the chest, where it would certainly be most evident.

long and twenty wide, twelve feet high, with a thatched roof, and a large ladder resting on it for fire protection. This was the first meeting house. Near by was the school house standing on an area of 18 feet by 14, and rising to three stories. The third story however was a watch house of small dimensions. The watch house was beside the ample stone chimney. The spectator elevated on the little box called the watch house might view this plain, on which a part of the present village stands, then a common plough field, containing about two hundred acres of cleared land, partially subdued.

Dedham was the location of Fairbanks House, erected in 1636 and generally believed to be the oldest frame house in America. The town schoolhouse, mentioned above, was the nation's first free public school; established in 1645, it was supported by a general tax of the citizens.

A reminder of the Old World origins of many of New England's earliest settlers is the English limestone Cotswold Cottage (plate 3), with its walled garden, barnyard, dovecote, and forge. This stone structure was built in the early seventeenth century at Chedworth, Gloucestershire, in southwestern England and was the home of a family of sheepherders. Working farms represented by the Cotswold cluster of buildings often had their own forge. The forge that accompanies the Cotswold Cottage was set up about 1620 and was operated for almost three hundred years by members of the family who built the house. Wrought-iron farm tools, household utensils such as lighting devices, and building materials including nails, latches, and hinges were fashioned by the smith. The English Tudor and Jacobean oak furniture throughout the

The room, which is from the second floor of a house built by Thomas Hart at Ipswich, is furnished with massive oak furniture, including a court cupboard—an important utilitarian item in every prosperous colonial home. Imported ceramics, candlesticks, and tankards serve as decorative accessories. An imported rug is spread over the tabletop, a common practice of the period since textiles were too costly to withstand heavy use on the floor. Several items in this room reveal an interest in making seating pieces more comfortable: the stool is fitted with a red cushion with gold braid, the two turned chairs against the wall have leather seats and backs, and the wainscot armchair in front of the fireplace also has a cushion.

15. *Museum installation. Hart Room. Ipswich, Massachusetts. c. 1670. Henry Francis du Pont Winterthur Museum, Winterthur, Delaware*

house (plate 4) has been blackened by the smoke from roaring fires in the massive stone fireplaces. The Cotswold buildings were brought to America in 1930 by Henry Ford and are now a part of Greenfield Village, his restoration of an early American village at Dearborn, Michigan.

The Puritan Keeping Room (plate 5), part of the American Museum in Britain at Bath, England, is constructed with beams and floorboards from a house at Wrentham, Massachusetts, and is furnished with seventeenth-century American pieces, including a four-slat ladder-back chair with mushroom ter-

16. *Press cupboard. Maker unknown. Essex County, Massachusetts. c. 1680. Oak with pine top and ebonized maple balusters, height 61". Greenfield Village and Henry Ford Museum, Dearborn, Michigan*

Both the design and the use of turned pendant drops, where the upper section overhangs the lower, are reminiscent of the treatment of the overhangs on the Ironmaster's House (see plate 7).

17. Turned armchair. Maker unknown. New England. Second half of seventeenth century. Maple and hickory, height 53½". Table. Maker unknown. New England. Second half of seventeenth century. Oak and maple, width 36½". Bible box. Maker unknown. New England. Second half of seventeenth century. Oak, width 20". All Greenfield Village and Henry Ford Museum, Dearborn, Michigan

The armchair is of the turned type named after Governor John Carver. Like a chair that he owned, it was constructed without the addition of spindles under the arms and seat. This impressive example with bobbin turned sloping arms and mushroom-capped front posts retains much of its original red paint. The table fashioned in the up-and-down stretcher style is Cromwellian, typified by the turned bobbins incorporated into its design. The Bible box is decorated with carved lunettes and the corners are chip-carved.

minals on the front posts, a trestle table, a paneled one-drawer chest with applied spindles, and a paneled wainscot chair. This room, like many present-day restorations, is obviously overfurnished, for diaries from the early seventeenth century describe a sparseness of furniture. Heating and lighting were elementary at best, the fireplace providing the only source of warmth. Simple fire tools, when they existed, were forged from iron by local blacksmiths. More elaborate types would have been imported.

The colonists' first homes were constructed from rough-hewn timbers and frequently had chimneys of wood and wattle smeared with clay to retard burning. The roofs of these rude one-room structures were usually covered with thatch. These elementary homes were replaced with more refined, comfortable

18. Chest of drawers. Thomas Dennis (attr.). Ipswich, Massachusetts. Dated 1678. Red oak, poplar, maple, and walnut, width 44¾". Henry Francis du Pont Winterthur Museum, Winterthur, Delaware

Three methods of decoration were used to embellish this distinctive chest of drawers—painting, carving, and the application of split turnings.

buildings as soon as was feasible. A one-room house (plate 6) typical of New England colonial architecture in its earliest phase was built by Thomas Plympton at South Sudbury, Massachusetts. Plympton arrived in America as an indentured servant and was one of the founders of the Puritan settlement of Sudbury Plantation in 1638. The Plympton House has simple sheathed walls, an open raftered ceiling, and a central summer beam. Unusual features are a freestanding fireplace built within the room to provide heat on all four sides and a convenient inside covered well, visible to the left of the ladder. This well enabled the residents to conceal themselves from hostile Indians and the wild animals that roamed the land. The chair-table, which is placed in the middle of the room and is of somewhat later vintage, is of special interest; this piece has a top that flips so that it becomes the back of the chair. The open cupboard with its array of pewter plates would have represented a substantial asset, for utensils of this type were not within the means of most of the general population. In fact pewter objects were so valued that many colonists included them among the few household pieces they brought from England; when Miles Standish arrived at Plymouth Colony, he had among his effects a pewter charger (plate 30). Iron cooking pots were also highly valued and they too were imported in large quantities during the early years of settlement.

The Ironmaster's House (plate 7), erected at Saugus, Massachusetts, between 1650 and 1670, is typical of the dwellings built by the more affluent members of the upper class. It has nearly every architectural detail and feature of a fine New England house of the period. The second story projects over the lower story and the overhang is emphasized with ornate decorative carvings at the corners. The casement windows are fitted with diamond-shaped leaded glass. The solid front door was constructed with two layers of boards studded with a decorative pattern of large hand-fashioned rosehead nails to provide durability and security. John Winthrop, Jr., had the house built as a residence for the ironmaster of his ironworks. Unfortunately the works soon went bankrupt because of the high costs of production, insufficient capital, and Winthrop's inability—in spite of his evident consideration for their living conditions—to attract skilled laborers. Houses with some pretension to grandness, like this one, boasted several rooms, including a parlor that contained the best furnishings and was reserved for festive occasions such as the entertainment of travelers or guests. Frequently this room served as a bedchamber for the owner and his wife. For the most part domestic life in every home, regardless of its size or sumptuousness, was centered around the fireplace. Besides the warmth and light the fire provided, the hearth was used for cooking.

During this period fireplaces were usually made from random-sized fieldstones, but in areas where clay was plentiful handmade bricks were used. Baking ovens were frequently built into the back of the fireplace, which was attached to the chimney, a massive tower of bricks. Many years after the Ironmaster's House was constructed, Reverend Leonard Withington—a descendant of a Dorchester, Massachusetts, resident—wrote in *The Puritan: A Series of Essays* a description of his grandfather's house, a building similar to the Ironmaster's House. It was an "old mansion, with every story jutting out, contrary to all the rules of modern architecture, wider at the top than at the foundation," and had a "kitchen, with its vast fireplace, an apartment in itself, collected in which the family was wont to huddle in a cold winter evening."

The fireplaces (plate 8) in the six-room Susquehanna House of Tidewater, Maryland, are more refined and are probably closer to contemporary English examples of the period. Maryland was also considerably warmer than the New England area and consequently the fireplaces could be smaller and were less prominent features of the interior. Susquehanna House (plate 9) was occupied shortly after 1650 by Christopher Rousby, tax collector for the royal crown. This one-and-a-half-story home, built one room deep, is furnished chiefly with English and American pieces of the seventeenth and eighteenth centuries. The Rousbys, as well as their rich planter neighbors in the South, could afford important furnishings. Probably the brass chandelier over the table would have

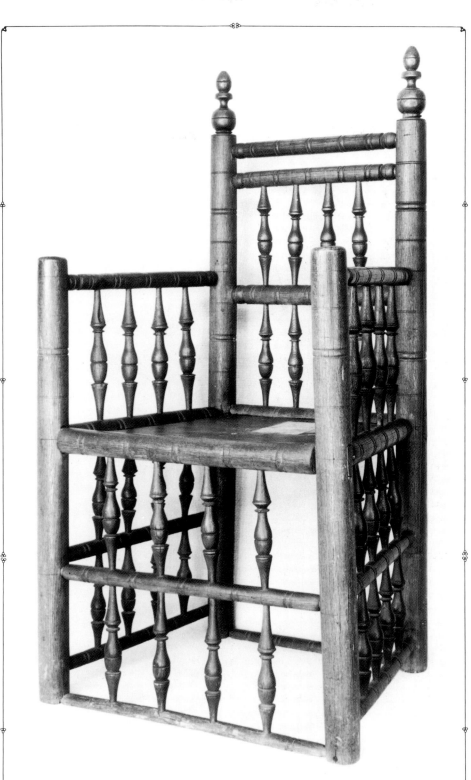

19. *Turned chair. Maker unknown. Plymouth Colony, Massachusetts. c. 1640. Ash, height 45¼". Pilgrim Society, Plymouth, Massachusetts*

This chair was an heirloom that descended in the family of William Bradford and is believed to have been among his personal possessions. Bradford, governor of Plymouth Colony for thirty years, probably sat in it while writing his invaluable history of the Pilgrim venture. When Bradford died, the inventory of his estate listed six chairs, an exceedingly large number for the time. This type of seating piece is generally called a Brewster chair, because the Elder William Brewster owned a similar armchair.

been their most prized possession, for its cost would have been high even for the king's tax collector.

American furniture was made by joiners like Edward Johnson, who were jacks-of-all-trades. They not only framed ships, houses, and churches—such as the Old Ship Meeting House (plate 10) erected at Hingham, Massachusetts, in 1681—but they also crafted pieces of furniture such as tables, benches, stools, and case pieces. The joiner used the mortise and tenon method of construction, in which a tenon, or protrusion, of one piece of wood was fitted into a mortise, or groove, in another. Although this technique was widely used, it is a mistaken belief that all early furniture was joined and pegged and that screws and nails indicate either that the construction was poor or that the piece was of a later date. (Even early Egyptian furniture was constructed with nails, and occasionally screws were used.) Another common misconception is that the drawers of all early furniture were dovetailed—connected at the corners with wedge-shaped mortise and tenon joints. The use of dovetailing as it is known today did not become popular until the seventeenth century, when craft guilds encouraged members to develop refinements in furniture production that would bolster the idea of specialization and add significantly to the cost of a piece of furniture.

Throughout the colonial period imported goods were always considered

20. Wainscot chair. Thomas Dennis (attr.). Essex County, Massachusetts. Second half of seventeenth century. Oak, height 45". Essex Institute, Salem, Massachusetts

The carving on this wainscot chair is of superior quality. The three urnlike finials surrounding and topping the crest rail are late and inaccurate restorations. The style of the carving on this piece may be compared with that on the chest (see plate 12) and on the chest of drawers (see plate 18).

infinitely superior to anything that could be made in the new land. Lieutenant Colonel William Fitzhugh of Virginia wrote to his London agent in 1681 requesting a "feather bed & furniture, curtains & vallens. The furniture, curtains & vallens I would have new, but the bed at second hand, because I am informed new ones are very full of dust." The bed when finally delivered might well have been fitted with hangings similar to those on the carved-oak seventeenth-century example in the bedchamber of Cotswold Cottage (plate 11).

The style of furniture from the period 1620 to 1700 is often designated Jacobean, derived from the Latin *Jacobus,* referring to James I, the reigning English king at the time Jamestown and Plymouth were settled. Generally furniture was constructed of native oak, which was frequently carved (plates 12, 18, 20), decorated with paint (plates 14, 18), and, in the case of the finest pieces, additionally embellished by the application of spindles and bosses (plates 16, 18, 26).

As rooms in the colonial period developed more specialized purposes, they became progressively more comfortable and convenient, especially those reserved for privacy, such as bedrooms. Specialization was gradual and it was not unusual for the bedroom also to serve as a dining room, when space and circumstances dictated, or to do double duty as a storage room. Because the houses tended to be small and families large, the colonists were quick to make use of dual-function pieces similar to those developed during the late Middle Ages in continental Europe. When many people were forced to live, eat, and sleep in a single room, tables that could be put up and taken down quickly (plate 13) or turned into chairs (plates 6, 25), benches that converted into beds, and folding beds that were raised against the walls when not in use were especially popular due to their space-saving practicality.

21. High-back settle. Maker unknown. Probably New England. Late seventeenth century. Pine, height 63½". Metropolitan Museum of Art, New York City. Gift of Mrs. Russell Sage, 1909

The projecting sides and hood on this settle were intended to protect its occupant from drafts during inclement weather. This is the simplest form of settle known. More elaborate, framed types could be upholstered, and some had storage wells under the seat, which could be pulled out for sleeping, thus serving a dual purpose.

The most frequently encountered furniture forms included chests with lift tops for storage, chests with drawers below, richly carved boxes, settles, stools, benches, chairs, tables, beds, and cradles. No furniture form was as prevalent as the easily crafted six-board chest (plate 14). The deep well hidden beneath the lift top provided ample storage. Six-board chests were also utilized as seats and could be pulled out into the room or placed at a table. The evolution from a six-board chest to a chest with several drawers was a natural one, and it is easy to see why the chest of drawers with its increased storage space became so popular.

The court cupboard and the press cupboard were the most important pieces of furniture in every prosperous colonial home. The court cupboard (plate 15) had a shelf for the display of silver, pewter, or other precious possessions, and it included a closed section for the storage of utensils for everyday use. The press cupboard (plate 16) usually had a closed section at the top and was fitted with several drawers below, a more practical arrangement since it provided much-needed protective storage space for clothing and linens. Most press and court cupboards were constructed of oak and were architectural in form: their general configuration, with a typical overhanging upper section, was similar to the exterior of the houses built in the same period. These "architectural" display pieces were made even richer by the application of split bosses, spindles, and elaborately turned drops at the corners of the overhang.

Boxes, today called Bible boxes (plate 17), were used mainly to store precious books and other personal items of great value. Many of them were fitted with a lock.

The early colonists have been erroneously portrayed as a drab, deeply religious people who suffered through cold, arduous winters and long, humid summers. To be sure, the colonists were religious and the environment was difficult, but the men and women certainly were not colorless, either in dress or in the decoration of their homes. Even that most forbidding personage, the devout William Brewster, sported a violet-colored coat, a bright blue suit, and green drawers.

Furniture, too, was enhanced with a surprising array of colors. During the seventeenth century, stains, paints, and glazes became widely used in Europe. A taste for vibrant-hued furniture led the colonists to wax, oil, varnish, and paint protective surfaces on their wooden pieces. Stains were derived from vegetable coloring dissolved in oil. Pigments for paints, though very expensive, were imported from England and ground into an oil base before being applied. Little of the American furniture created during the first century of settlement retains its original painted finish. Most of the few surviving examples come from Massachusetts, the Connecticut River valley, and the Hudson River valley.

Several furniture decorators or schools of decorative painters of the seventeenth century have now been identified, and some of the history of these artist-craftsmen has been reconstructed from surviving journals and community records of the time. Of special interest are the pieces crafted by the famed seventeenth-century joiner Thomas Dennis, including a framed chest of drawers (plate 18) that featured carved and painted decoration and was further adorned by the application of turned split spindles. Another great example of Massachusetts decorated furniture is the press cupboard (plate 40) made for Hannah Barnard in the second decade of the next century. Several other surviving pieces with the same geometric designs, including chests of drawers at the Henry Francis du Pont Winterthur Museum in Winterthur, Delaware, and at the Pocumtuck Valley Memorial Association in Deerfield, Massachusetts, appear to have been decorated by the same skilled hand.

Seating, except in the most affluent homes, was confined to simple benches and stools (plates 8, 15, 26). In general few families could boast a chair among their furnishings. In fact the term "chairman" stems from the reservation of such an important piece of furniture for the man of the house or a distinguished guest.

Most of the earliest chairs appear to have been of the turned variety (plates 5, 6, 17, 19, 22). Turned furniture was crafted on a hand-powered wheel, or lathe. There are two distinct types of turned chairs. The Brewster chair (plate 19) is named after Elder William Brewster, the Puritan leader of the Pilgrims at Plymouth Colony, who owned a piece of this type, now in the collection of Pilgrim Hall in Plymouth, Massachusetts. These chairs have banks of turnings in the back and below the arms and seat rails and are decorative as well as imposing. Carver chairs (plate 17), named for John Carver, first governor of Plymouth Colony, were generally simpler than Brewster chairs. Decorative turnings on these chairs are confined to positions above the seat.

Another esteemed type was the wainscot chair (plate 20), which because of its rich carving and impressive profile was preferred by those in positions of authority. This majestic oak form, essentially of Renaissance design, took its

OPPOSITE:

22. Side chair. Maker unknown. Probably Connecticut. 1650–75. Oak, height 37″. Metropolitan Museum of Art, New York City. Bequest of Mrs. J. Insley Blair, 1952

This chair in the Cromwellian style retains its original turkeywork cover. The seat and back were stuffed with marsh grass. It was not until the nineteenth century that chairs were upholstered with coil springs.

name from the Dutch word *wagonschot,* meaning a fine grade of oak board. The American wainscot chair was architectural in concept. Elaborate monumental examples, much like the chair associated with the name of Thomas Dennis, provided a prototype for less ambitious chairmakers whose modest adaptations seldom achieved the artistic integrity of the original design. Dennis was born in England and received his training there prior to emigrating to Portsmouth, New Hampshire, in 1663. In 1668 he is known to have been working at

23. *Candlestand. Maker unknown. Connecticut. 1660–80. Oak, height 24¼". Current whereabouts unknown*

Few candlestands of such an early date survive. The simplicity of craftsmanship does not suggest the various forms of candlestands that became common in the seventeenth century.

Ipswich, Massachusetts, where a wainscot chair, Bible boxes, chests, and even a tape loom—all crisply carved with guilloche, foliated S-scrolls, arcading palmette panels, and strapwork—are testimony to the wide range of his abilities.

The ladder-back, or slat-back, chair (plate 5) was also in common use. Many ladder-back chairs exhibit a high degree of sophistication in terms of design and balance, while others are more modest and purely functional in nature. Early ladder-back chairs typically have large front posts, and often their back posts are connected to the front posts by turned sloping arms. Some were constructed from oak; most, however, were turned from maple, fitted with hickory, ash, or oak slats, and finished with a splint or rush seat. Splint was made by slicing supple young trees lengthwise. These strips were soaked in water to make them flexible and then woven into basketlike seats whose resiliency proved to be infinitely more comfortable than the unyielding plank seats typical of wainscot chairs. Rush, derived from wild marsh plants, was also soaked and then twisted into long strands and woven. Because it was demonstrated that rush was extremely durable, its use increased in succeeding years.

Most settles (plate 21) were simple constructions of flat boards nailed to-

24. Folding table. Maker unknown. Essex County, Massachusetts. 1675–90. Oak and maple, height 27″, diameter of top 36″. Metropolitan Museum of Art, New York City. Gift of Mrs. J. Insley Blair, 1951

This piece may be unique. A swinging gateleg in the back supports the upper leaf when it is open. The top of the table is decorated with smoke graining, perhaps an attempt to approximate the look of marble.

gether to form a bench with a back. Some were given projecting hoods and closed-in sides that shielded the sitter from the inevitable drafts when the house was buffeted by winter winds. Others were of framed construction allowing the seat and back to be upholstered in leather. Though less durable, this type of settle was far more comfortable than the wooden variety. Occasionally settles were constructed with a bed under the seat which could be folded out for sleeping. Historical records reveal that William Brewster owned two such space-saving devices.

Interest in upholstered furniture developed during the Cromwellian period, but the style that evolved during this period flourished in America only after the early 1670s. The designs that inspired American Cromwellian furniture originated in England in the middle of the seventeenth century. With the failure of Oliver Cromwell's Commonwealth and the restoration of the Stuart monarchy in 1660, Charles II returned to England from exile in France and took the Portuguese princess, Catherine of Braganza, as his queen. Despite Catherine's personal disadvantages—she lacked charm, was plain in appearance, and had scant education—she was the ideal bride in an age when marriages were arranged for financial benefits, bringing with her the richest dowry Europe had ever known. Her homeland was a vital trading partner with the Orient and she introduced into the plainness of post-Cromwellian England Chinese and Indian curiosities—colorful porcelains, lacquers, and other exotic wares. She also popularized tea drinking, a custom that eventually became an absolute rage, for it enabled fashionable women to indulge in a ceremony that demonstrated their wealth and stylishness. Her dowry included a large retinue of craftsmen who grafted onto English decorative arts a new gracefulness that was almost immediately in vogue.

It was during the reign of Charles and Catherine that the Cromwellian style, based upon bobbin and ball-and-ring turnings (plate 17), at last reached America and found favor in the seaboard colonies. The immensely popular rope-twisted turnings of the English Cromwellian period, evident on the gate-leg table (plate 4), were not used extensively by American joiners. When

25. Chair-table. Maker unknown. Probably Connecticut. 1650–75. Oak, height 30", diameter of table 42". Smithsonian Institution, Washington, D.C. Greenwood Collection

This dual-function piece was popular in homes with limited space. The stretchers uniting the four legs of the base supply extra sturdiness.

rope turnings do occur on American pieces, they are generally found on furniture from New York, New Jersey, or the South. Cromwellian chairs were often covered in leather held in place by imported brass nails. Although leather was costly, it was not nearly as expensive as the rich textile covering known as turkeywork (plates 22, 60). Turkeywork is a coarse needlework upholstery originally in imitation of the design and texture of oriental rugs. During the sixteenth and seventeenth centuries this oriental-style textile was produced in great quantity by English needleworkers. Because it was so much in demand, exporters attempted to include it in any shipment destined for the New World.

26. Museum installation. Best
room. New England. Seventeenth
century. Henry Francis du Pont
Winterthur Museum, Winterthur,
Delaware

This low-ceilinged seventeenth-
century installation was created
with wood salvaged from a house
built about 1684 at Essex,
Massachusetts, by Seth Story. The
maple Carver armchairs on either
side of the fireplace were assembled
from pieces shaped on a great
wheel. An extremely rare wall
cupboard hangs to the right of the
fireplace. Below it is a small
tuckaway table with a large double-
handled burl bowl. The top of the
court cupboard has a fabric runner,
a popular custom at the time. A
pine bench stands next to the
stretcher base table. Wooden
plates, a burl bowl, and a pewter
dish attributed to the Boston
silversmith John Dolbeare are
placed on the tabletop.

Both leather and turkeywork were common as upholstery materials over a long period of time. Existing records indicate that in 1691 John Bowles's parlor at Roxbury, Massachusetts, in addition to several other pieces of furniture, contained thirteen chairs covered with leather, six with turkeywork, and four stools with needlework covers. The chairs, according to prevalent European custom, were probably placed in rows against the walls.

Trestle tables (plate 13), candlestands (plate 23), small occasional tables such as tuckaways (plate 24), and tables that could be converted into chairs by swinging the top up (plate 25) enjoyed wide popularity. Chair-tables are known to have been used in the colonies as early as the 1630s. Several extant examples are fitted with a storage drawer under the seat, and later versions sometimes have a bank of drawers that extends from the seat to the floor. Some tables had a specific function and were situated permanently in the rooms where they were needed. Generally these were tables of the framed type and they often had turned legs connected by turned stretchers (plate 27) or by boxlike ones (plate 26). The purpose of the stretchers was to provide additional strength for the table, but

27. Table. Maker unknown. New England. 1640–60. Pecan, hickory, and poplar, length 42''. Collection A. F. Hewitt

According to tradition, this table was owned by Hannah Brewster, one of the first children born in America from a family that came over on the Mayflower. Her grandfather was Elder William Brewster.

they made it difficult for someone sitting at the table to get close enough to be comfortable. In an effort to resolve this problem, joiners began to construct tables with large overhangs so that the tabletop extended well beyond the frame. Stools were fashioned in much the same way. Ordinarily they also had turned legs connected by stretchers. A stool was an especially useful piece of furniture that could easily be tucked under the table or in an out-of-the-way corner and brought out as needed.

The modern homemaker would be appalled at the paucity of kitchen equipment available in the seventeenth century. An iron pot was practically the only cooking utensil in most homes. Cranes and similar devices simplified moving heavy boiling pots in and out of a fireplace. One way of adding substantially to the heating effectiveness of a fireplace was to place a cast-iron fireback (plate 66) in the rear of the opening. Many of these devices were embellished with decorative motifs that reflected the popular taste of the period. The fireback absorbed and retained the fire's heat and radiated it into the room for several hours after the fire had burned out. These iron plaques also served as protectors for chimney masonry.

The kitchen repertory was limited in other ways. Eating utensils were rare indeed. Wooden trenchers and other treen objects, or small utensils made of wood (plates 4, 26), were the most commonplace. Forks were unknown; a person ate with his fingers or speared his meat with a knife. Animal horns, sliced into sections and fitted with a bottom, served as drinking glasses and other receptacles. Since glassware was not successfully produced in the colonies until the middle of the seventeenth century and such imported items were expensive to acquire, the blackjack (plates 4, 28)—a vessel originally made of tanned, tar-coated leather—was used as a pitcher for beer and ale.

Some settlements, such as Jamestown, were fortunate enough to attract potters who set up kilns. They supplied utilitarian objects—bowls, pans, jugs, and lighting vessels like the grease lamp (plate 35). In this period a great deal of

28. Blackjack. Maker unknown. Probably England. Seventeenth century. Leather with metal mounts, height 26". Greenfield Village and Henry Ford Museum, Dearborn, Michigan

Because glass pitchers were difficult to make and expensive to acquire, most colonists used pitchers and other vessels made from tanned leather.

pottery was imported, and lading bills abound with records of large shipments of ceramics from the Old World to the New. Excavations at early colonial sites disclose that ceramics from England, Holland, Portugal, Spain, and the Rhineland, as well as from the Orient, found their way to American shores. Delft (plates 29, 61), a tin-glazed, white-bodied earthenware that was sometimes decorated in various shades of blue, was the most desirable. This attractive, brilliantly colored earthenware furnished American homes of the well-to-do with an approximation of the costly chinaware or porcelain that was imported into Europe from the Far East at this time.

Utilitarian pieces shaped from precious metals such as silver and gold were among the most highly cherished of all possessions. They were the owners' wealth transformed into useful objects and displayed for everyone to admire. A piece could be engraved with initials and inscriptions that positively identified it if it were stolen. Pewter forms were not unlike the shape and design of works made of silver and gold. Pewter (plate 30), although far less precious, could be polished to a very high luster and, when frequently buffed, had the visual impact of silver.

29. Standing salt dish. Maker unknown. London, England, probably Lambeth. 1640–60. Tin-glazed earthenware, height 4½". Henry Francis du Pont Winterthur Museum, Winterthur, Delaware

In a colonial home the guest of honor sat "above the salt" and near the host, who was "chairman of the board," so-called because of the scarcity of chairs and the simplicity of tables, which were made of planks or boards. The reservoir of this delft standing salt dish held precious imported salt. Despite efforts by the younger John Winthrop and many other colonists to produce salt in quantity from evaporated sea water, the condiment continued to be imported throughout the colonial era.

Almost all surviving silver and gold objects from the early colonial period were made in Boston and New York. Forms were limited to ceremonial pieces for the church and drinking and eating utensils for the home. Throughout the colonial period many philanthropic parishioners presented their churches with fine pieces of pewter, silver, and gold which were used during the celebration of the religious sacraments. In the Dutch Reform churches of New Jersey and

30. Platter. Maker unknown. England. Seventeenth century. Pewter, diameter 16½". Pilgrim Society, Plymouth, Massachusetts

Miles Standish brought this pewter charger with him to the Plymouth Colony upon his arrival in 1620. It is recorded that among his possessions he also carried an iron cooking pot, a highly valued utensil at the time.

31. *Two-handled caudle cup.*
Robert Sanderson. Boston,
Massachusetts. 1656–76. Silver,
height 5″, diameter of top 4¾″.
Henry Francis du Pont Winterthur
Museum, Winterthur, Delaware

Elaborate cast handles and repoussé
decoration, including the native
American turkey as a design motif,
establish this early cup as a major
work of the silversmith's art.

New York the usual gifts were tall beakers. In Philadelphia and farther south objects of European origin were frequently given; whereas in the North communion vessels as well as candlesticks were not uncommon presents.

The Massachusetts Bay Colony set up a mint in Boston in 1652, to establish a standardized currency, and John Hull, who was named mintmaster, chose Robert Sanderson as his partner. Their partnership, which included the shaping

32. *Porringer. John Hull and*
Robert Sanderson. Boston,
Massachusetts. c. 1655. Silver,
diameter 4¼″. Museum of Fine
Arts, Boston, Massachusetts.
P. L. Spalding Collection

This is the earliest surviving
American porringer. The
techniques used for its shaping
would have been identical to those
illustrated in the frontispiece to
A Touch-Stone for Gold and
Silver Wares (see plate 33).

This illustration includes every step in the production of fine metal pieces. Three workmen in the lower section (number 11) are forging a plate, while the gentleman in the shop, in the upper section (number 20), is weighing the final product.

of silver objects, lasted until Hull's death in 1683. In 1651 Hull, working with Sanderson, had fashioned the earliest known piece of colonial silver—a tiny dram cup less than three inches in diameter fitted with handles of twisted silver wire and decorated with the initials R B and simple floral motifs. "Dram" was the common seventeenth-century term for distilled liquor, and it was the prevailing notion that a sip of liquor would raise the spirits of the sickly. The cup is a small and simple relative of the two-handled caudle cup (plate 31) shaped by Sanderson working alone in 1656. This cup, with delicately cast caryatid handles, is engraved with the initials S/TA on the base and probably was made for Thomas and Ann (Tyng) Shepherd of Charlestown, Massachusetts. Its elaborate repoussé decoration includes the unusual portrait of a native American turkey and conventionalized foliage and flowers.

Porringers and spoons were the most common household utensils made of precious metals. About 1655 Hull and Sanderson crafted the earliest known American porringer (plate 32), in honor of the marriage of Arthur and Johanna Mason.

New York silver of this period, as might be expected, borrowed from

Dutch prototypes, and many of the forms duplicated seventeenth-century
examples from Holland. After the middle of the seventeenth century, some
New York goldsmiths began to forge oversized tankards (plate 71) for their
more convivial customers. The lids were often ornately engraved with
decorated monograms and coats of arms. American silversmiths, probably following many of the techniques described in *A Touch-Stone for Gold and Silver
Wares* (plate 33), also fashioned candlesticks of elaborate design and great beauty.
A unique pair (plate 34), each with an engaged shaft of clustered columns, was
made by the Boston silversmith and engraver Jeremiah Dummer in the mid-
1680s. The sticks probably commemorated the marriage of the first owners,
David and Elizabeth Jeffries. Besides being one of the finest silversmiths in
colonial New England, Dummer, it is generally believed, was one of the first
native-born portrait painters in colonial America.

Most houses were lighted by far simpler, almost crude wrought-iron devices (plate 35). During the very earliest colonial period, lamps, sometimes
fueled with fat or grease, their design practically unmodified from those found
in ancient Egypt, Greece, and Rome, were in common use. American versions of metal lamps incorporating multiple wicks and spouts, similar to those
that had appeared in the ancient world by the third century of the modern era,
were the most effective weapons the colonists had against the darkness. Writing
in 1621, Edward Winslow advised future settlers to bring cotton yarn for use
as wicks in their spout lamps. The Reverend Higginson observed that although

splints—the tiny slices of thin wood held in iron holders—burned "clear as a torch," they were bothersome because of the sooty smoke which left a deposit of a "pitchy kind of substance" when they were used. The colonists cut rush in the summer or early autumn while it was still green and stripped it to a small spine, which they then dried. Subsequent immersion in tallow converted it to an illuminant.

Rush could be burned successfully only at an angle of approximately forty-five degrees. Most holders for rush and splint were, like the hanging betty lamp or the grease lamp, fashioned of iron. Short lighting devices were placed on tables, fireplace mantels, or specially designed stools. Tall standing lamps were less common because metal, even in its basest form, was precious. Thus wall sconces and hanging lamps augmented low devices, providing additional light from above.

The candle, like the rushlight, was based upon the principle of a wick coated with a solid fuel. Candles in seventeenth-century America were extremely expensive and it is safe to presume that the early settlers kept hours dictated by the sun for practical rather than moral reasons.

Textiles added color and softness to simple interior settings. Bed hangings that provided privacy and kept out drafts (plates 11, 36), curtains, and upholstery fabrics were produced domestically; foreign imports, however, were the materials that every housewife dreamed of adding to her home. One of the first textiles imported in any significant quantity was the coverlet known in the seventeenth and eighteenth centuries as a "bed rugg," a coarse, thick bedcovering fashioned by pulling strands of wool through a heavy canvas to make a looped or clipped pile. In 1630 Governor John Winthrop wrote from Massachusetts to his son in England "to bring a store of Coarse Rugges, bothe to use and to sell." Six years later the ship *William and John* sailed to Massachusetts from England carrying 240 yards of rugs for beds. Bed rugs remained popular throughout the seventeenth and most of the eighteenth centuries, and the earliest surviving example is in the collection of the Essex Institute at Salem, Massachusetts. This coverlet is initialed M A, for Mary Avery of North Andover, and is dated 1722.

Linen, wool, and linsey-woolsey, a coarse blend of linen and wool, were the most common domestically produced textiles. Rich bedcovers like the deep-blue linsey-woolsey on the carved bed (plate 11) in the Cotswold Cottage bedchamber were sewn by ambitious homemakers when their busy hands were free from other essential domestic chores. With the increase of population and wealth in the New World the market for foreign goods expanded. Ships arriving at colonial docks were stocked with silks and damasks from France and Italy, brocades and velvets from Spain, and painted and printed chintzes from England and India. The colorful cotton hanging (plate 36) was painted and dyed in the second half of the seventeenth century in western India. The desire to own printed fabrics, which were extremely fashionable in London, became so great in the colonies that the demand could not begin to be satisfied. Inventories of the estates of leading colonists frequently list fabrics, indicating the great value placed upon them.

Glass furnaces were rare in the New World, and nearly all glass items had to be imported from abroad. Twice in the early seventeenth century attempts were made to set up glassmaking facilities at Jamestown, but both of these were short-lived: in 1608 eight German and Polish workmen sponsored by the London Company produced pieces for nearly a year; again in 1621 Italian glassblowers spent fourteen months attempting to craft utilitarian pieces, but they were no more successful than their predecessors. Several other glass factories existed for short periods later in the century—at Salem, New Amsterdam, and Philadelphia—but all failed to produce works of consequence, and in any case none of the earliest domestic glass has survived intact.

Life in America before 1685 was an arduous adventure, death often occurring relatively early. Almost simultaneously with the settling of the community was the establishment of a burying ground. Grave markers and monuments

37. Mrs. Elizabeth Freake and
Baby Mary. *Artist unknown.
Massachusetts. c. 1674. Oil on
canvas, 42½″ × 36¾″. Worcester
Art Museum, Worcester,
Massachusetts. Gift of Mr. and
Mrs. Albert W. Rice*

*This portrait of mother and child
is one of the most celebrated
seventeenth-century American
paintings. Colonial portraits, when
not inspired by the copying of
prints, place equal emphasis on
every detail of the background,
costume, and face. The results are
flat, bright-colored, and shaded
forms with rich, elaborate designs
reminiscent of portraiture in
medieval Europe.*

are the earliest dated American sculpture. The designs of these funerary sculptural pieces most often depicted death extinguishing human life, while Father Time
gazed passively on; death was symbolized by an entire skeleton. Funeral
customs surrounding burials furthered the careers of many artists. The family
of important citizens observed elaborate ceremonies in which hatchments
bearing the coat of arms of the deceased were painted on the sides of family
coaches.

Personal luxuries and refinements in the early communities were rare,
and the fine arts were practiced on the simplest level. The only sculpture was
found in graveyards, and painting, other than the hatchment panels on coaches,
centered around portraiture, which appears to have flourished in New England.
One of the most distinctive paintings of the early colonial period is that of
Mrs. Elizabeth Freake and Baby Mary (plate 37). Mrs. Freake, the daughter of
Thomas Clarke, married John Freake of Boston in 1661 and Elisha Hutchinson
in 1677. In this portrait of a mother and child the figures are as stiff as dolls. But
the artist has painted their clothing with meticulous detail, displaying the rich,
sumptuous fabrics available to those who could afford them. Most colonials,
however, dressed rather simply in coarse homespun cloth. Toward the end of
the seventeenth century, the colonists in the established towns on the eastern
seaboard began to re-create the comforts and amenities of the Old World in the
New. Family portraits were the first and most popular paintings, and not until
many years later did landscape painting and other pictorial art flourish.

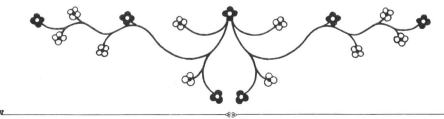

The Pursuit of Comfort and Beauty
1685~1720

During the last decades of the seventeenth century, the official representatives of the crown stationed in America, as well as affluent colonists, mimicked the ever-changing European court styles, especially those of England. Ponderous postmedieval designs, which had been lightened by craftsmen serving the English court during the austere rule of Oliver Cromwell, all but disappeared at the lively court of Charles II, the "Merry Monarch." New concepts of taste once again were introduced into the English court, this time by Prince William of Orange, the Dutch ruler who in 1689 was persuaded to ascend the throne of England with Mary Stuart as his queen.

Under the aggressive leadership of William and Mary, the nation developed into a truly important shipping and trading empire, rivaling Spain and other more established mercantile countries. This newfound strength by England greatly affected life in the English colonies throughout the world. In America commercial ties with London were bolstered, and a substantial increase in the importation of goods enabled traders with the mother country to offer the general population many of the everyday amenities enjoyed abroad.

William brought with him to the English court countless craftsmen who infused the still moderately conservative court with an innovative style that

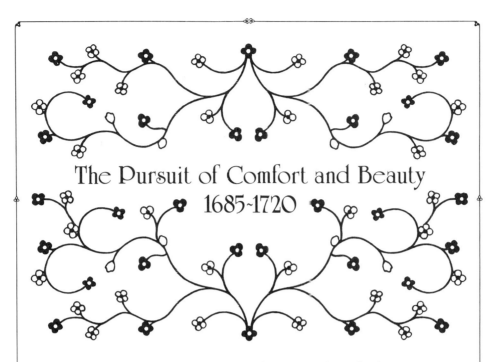

38. Map of New Netherland, New England, New Jersey, Pennsylvania, and Maryland. Nicholas Visscher. Amsterdam, Netherlands. c. 1685. Engraving, 22⅝ × 26⅞". Greenfield Village and Henry Ford Museum, Dearborn, Michigan

Based on a 1635 prototype by Willem Janszoon Blaeu, this map is replete with pictorial details of early American life. The town view in the lower right-hand corner is the earliest known depiction of New York while it was still called New Amsterdam.

now bears the names of the co-rulers, William and Mary. Daniel Marot, a French Huguenot seeking relief from religious persecution in his homeland, had served William in Holland as court designer and architect. He moved to London when William did and became one of the leading tastemakers for all of England. Marot's opulent designs contributed significantly to European styles of decoration in the late seventeenth and early eighteenth centuries, and his elaborate engravings are excellent records of the current fashions, particularly as they illustrate the incipient European interest in oriental motifs. The William and Mary style prevailed over a long period of time and in America survived long after newer fashions had superseded it in England.

The American colonists considered themselves Englishmen, both politically and socially. Their way of life, their homes, their furnishings, and even their clothing were reflections of this attitude. A traveler in New England during the early years of the eighteenth century commented in a self-congrat-

39. Macpheadris-Warner House. John Drew (attr.). Portsmouth, New Hampshire. c. 1716. Warner House Association, Portsmouth, New Hampshire

Built for Captain Archibald Macpheadris about 1716, the house was later remodeled, probably in the middle of the eighteenth century. The design of this New England Queen Anne brick house is strikingly reminiscent of English country houses of the same period. It was commissioned by a man who enjoyed great prosperity from the fur trade in a seaport town where the economy was gradually turning away from dependency on the land to the sea and where community leadership was passing from religious elder to merchant trader.

ulatory manner that a "Gentleman from *London* would almost think himself at home at *Boston* when he observes the Numbers of People, their Houses, their Furniture, their Tables, their Dress and Conversation, which perhaps is as splendid and showy, as that of the most considerable Tradesman in *London*. . . . There is no Fashion in *London* but in three or four Months is to be seen at *Boston*."

Initially the major cities had developed in the northern colonies (plate 38), but during the second half of the seventeenth century several other centers of commerce and industry emerged. Charleston, South Carolina, founded in 1670 as Charles Towne, was noted for its citizens of considerable wealth and taste. Philadelphia (plate 74), established in 1681, had by 1720 become "full of all Country business and Sea affairs." With respect to commerce, this city far outshone all its other colonial rivals—except for Boston. New cities continued to spring up and rural boundaries expanded as the dramatic increase in population was augmented by a steady influx of immigrants.

Throughout the remainder of the colonial period, fine houses with handsome architectural detail became the standard for domestic building. Sliding sashes, classical moldings and details, elaborate framed and carved doorways emphasized a new graciousness of style. Rooms increased in number and began to serve specific functions, the kitchen operating as a separate entity in larger

40. Press cupboard. Maker unknown. Area of Hadley, Massachusetts. c. 1715. Oak and pine, height 61⅛". Greenfield Village and Henry Ford Museum, Dearborn, Michigan

Hannah Barnard, whose name appears on the front of this press cupboard, was born at Hadley, Massachusetts, on June 8, 1684. She married John Marsh in 1715 and died in 1717. Polychrome and black geometric designs on this early eighteenth-century piece show a connection to other decorated furniture originating in the Connecticut River valley. The cupboard was probably a wedding present.

homes. Many architects and craftsmen immigrated to America to participate in the building boom. In 1710 the earl of Clarendon shrewdly reported on the opportunities in the New World in a letter to Lord Dartmouth:

41. Chest with single drawer. Maker unknown. Connecticut. c. 1715. Oak, tulipwood, and chestnut, height 34¼". Greenfield Village and Henry Ford Museum, Dearborn, Michigan

In and around Guilford and Old Saybrook, Connecticut, many examples of furniture in a similar style were constructed and painted sometime between 1700 and 1725. Charles Gillam has often been credited with the decoration on these distinctive pieces. Painted partridges in flight appear on the raised panels forming the sides of this chest, and decoration inspired by the traditional fleur-de-lis and thistle and rose motif adorns the front.

42. Tulip and sunflower chest.
Maker unknown. Connecticut.
c. 1680. Oak, pine, and maple,
width 48″. Greenfield Village
and Henry Ford Museum,
Dearborn, Michigan

*The storage well is covered by a
hinged top. The two full-length
drawers are suspended on runners
—they do not slide on their
bottoms, but on strips of wood
that fit into slots in the sides of
the drawer. Three methods of
decoration were employed to
embellish this piece: carved panels,
applied turned and split spindles
and bosses, and paint.*

It is most certain that no person that has his Limbs, and will work, can starve in that Country [the American colonies], every Man or Woman above 15 years of age may earn two shillings and three pence New York Money (which is eighteen pence Sterling) every day in the year except Sundays. Handicraftsmen, such as Smiths, Joyners, Carpenters, Masons & Bricklayers may earn at least Five Shillings New York Money every day they will work, so that nothing can bring those people into the danger of starving but willful laziness.

The Macpheadris-Warner House at Portsmouth, New Hampshire, typifies the elegance and solidity of early Queen Anne architecture in America (plate 39). This brick structure was built about 1716 by Captain Archibald Macpheadris, a Scottish fur trader who became a member of Governor John Winthrop's council and married the governor's daughter Sarah. The well-balanced facade is enriched with fluted Corinthian columns and an arch pediment that frame and crown the central doorway. Horizontal brick belt courses and a low-pitched gambrel roof with balustrade and cupola are features directly harking back to English houses of the Restoration period. The house represents a regional ex-

*43. Box. Maker unknown.
Massachusetts. 1680–1700. Pine
with oak front, width 25⅞″.
Greenfield Village and Henry
Ford Museum, Dearborn,
Michigan*

*The stylized floral and leaf motif
reveals the kinship of this box to
the famed Hadley chests first
discovered in the area of Hadley,
Massachusetts, and popular in the
Connecticut River valley.*

THE BOOK OF JOB.

CHAP. I.

1 The holineſſe, riches, and religious care of Job for his children. 6 Satan appearing before God, by calumniation obtaineth leave to tempt Job. 13 Underſtanding of the loſſe of his goods and children, in his mourning he bleſſeth Go D.

Satan anſwered the L O R D, and ſaid, From going to and fro in the *earth, and from walking up and down in it.

8 And the L O R D ſaid unto Satan, † Haſt thou conſidered my ſervant Job, that there is none like him in the earth, a perfect and an upright man, one that feareth God, and eſcheweth evil?

9 Then Satan anſwered the L O R D, and ſaid, Doth Job fear

*1 Pet.5.8.

† Heb. haſt thou ſet thy heart on?

Here was a man in the land of Uz, whoſename was Job, and

44. Chapter headpiece. King James Bible. London, England. 1611. Woodcut. Greenfield Village and Henry Ford Museum, Dearborn, Michigan

The traditional fleur-de-lis and thistle and rose motif appears to have been the influence for decoration on many of the Guilford –Saybrook chests (see plate 41).

ample of the prevailing interest in classicism. The paired windows, which contribute to the overall unity, reflect this concern for classical design. The house, which cost the staggering sum of six thousand pounds to build, has interior walls adorned with murals. Two of the murals on the stairwell are life-sized representations of Iroquois sachems, who caused an unprecedented furor when they were presented in 1710 at the court of Queen Anne by Captain Peter Schuyler.

While fashionable homes were being erected in major seaboard cities, most country houses were built with rural simplicity and furnished with solid, rustic furniture. Carving, which had been an important element of decoration in earlier periods, continued to be used extensively on chests, boxes, and chairs by craftsmen in inland areas such as Hartford, Connecticut. The ornately carved and decorated tulip and sunflower chest (plate 42) and the simple unadorned box from Massachusetts (plate 43) are typical of these pieces. Sunflower chests were often painted and further adorned with applied ornamentation in the form of turned spindles and bosses. This applied decoration was almost always painted black, perhaps to simulate ebony, a very costly imported wood. The carving on the sunflower chest and on the box was relatively shallow but was made more dramatic by the application of bright shades of paint.

Other medieval forms, including court and press cupboards, continued to be produced. The press cupboard (plate 40) made for Hannah Barnard of Hadley, Massachusetts, and the chest-over-drawer (plate 41) from the Guilford–Saybrook area of Connecticut exemplify furniture of this type. The press cupboard is believed to have been constructed at the time of Barnard's marriage to

45. Designs for lacquered furniture. John Stalker (and George Parker). England. 1688. Engraving from A Treatise of Japaning and Varnishing, Being a Compleat Discovery of Those Arts (Oxford, 1688). Art and Architecture Division, New York Public Library, Astor, Lenox and Tilden Foundations, New York City

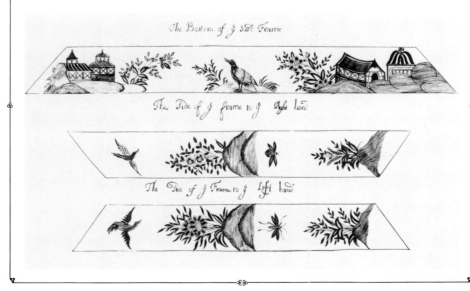

The taste in America for lacquered furniture based on oriental techniques and styles became dominant in the 1670s and lasted for over a century. Stalker and Parker's influential treatise contained twenty-four pages of copperplate engravings which featured oriental motifs.

46. Shop sign. Maker unknown. Boston, Massachusetts. 1697 (dated 1701). Wood, carved and painted, height 35". Bostonian Society, Old State House, Boston, Massachusetts

Thomas Child, a professional painter-stainer, acquired this sign and changed its date when he purchased property in Boston. The sign displays the coat of arms of the Honourable Company of Painters-Stainers of London, an organization, founded in the sixteenth century, of which Child was a member.

John Marsh in 1715, when she was thirty-one years old. The dazzling polychromed piece is engraved with black geometric designs, including hearts and vines. The raised front panel on the Guilford–Saybrook chest is decorated with a rose, a fleur-de-lis, a thistle, and a crown—all motifs associated with the British royal arms and used extensively by generations of decorative painters both in Europe and America. This overall stylized design can be traced directly to an illustration in the 1611 King James Version of the Bible in which it appears as a headpiece from the Book of Job (plate 44). Like many pieces of rural furniture, the Guilford–Saybrook chest has straight legs that are extensions of the side posts.

The painting of furniture appears to have been practiced by professionals like Thomas Child, who came to Massachusetts before 1688, the year he married Katherine Masters. Child was born about 1658 in Middlesex, England, and became a freeman of the Honourable Company of Painters-Stainers of London in 1679. He acquired his elaborately carved sign (plate 46) presumably in 1701 when he purchased property in Boston and transferred his shop there from Roxbury. The upper part of the sign was broken off and Child repaired the piece, including his own initials as well as those of his wife and changing the date of the sign from 1697 to the date of his acquisition. Child—as did all painter-stainers—refined oils, made and sold brushes, stained furniture, and executed interior decorative designs. It is believed that he also painted portraits. When he died in 1706, Samuel Sewall, a Boston businessman and judge who was a noted diarist as well, jotted down the entry "This morning Tom Child the Painter died," and then added a short poem lamenting his passing:

> Tom Child had often painted Death,
> But never to the Life, before:
> Doing it now, he's out of Breath;
> He paints it once, and paints no more.

The interest in painted ornamentation from earlier times continued, and many of the best American decorators developed a style that approximated japanning, a technique of decorating an object with colored shellac. Japanese

OPPOSITE:

47. High chest of drawers. Maker unknown. New England. 1700–20. Maple case with burl walnut veneer, height 61⅞". Greenfield Village and Henry Ford Museum, Dearborn, Michigan

This superb chest once belonged to Mary Ball Washington, mother of George Washington. It was exhibited at the 1893 World's Columbian Exposition in Chicago, where it sparked a keen interest in collecting colonial furniture and household accessories.

A stone structure built in 1762 overlooking Rondout Creek, near Kerhonkson, New York, the house consisted of a kitchen, a parlor, and a bedroom. The original woodwork from the bedroom now forms part of a museum installation at the Henry Francis du Pont Winterthur Museum. Except for the New England table on the left, traditional furnishings of the Hudson Valley are displayed in this interior, including the typical fiddle-back armchair with a seat worked in flamestitch. The grisaille-painted kas, or two-door cupboard, was common in New York and New Jersey, and its pendant fruit motifs executed in a trompe-l'oeil style are similar to painting found in Dutch houses of the seventeenth century.

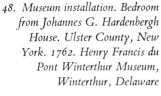

48. Museum installation. Bedroom from Johannes G. Hardenbergh House. Ulster County, New York. 1762. Henry Francis du Pont Winterthur Museum, Winterthur, Delaware

furniture first appeared in the Western world during the early seventeenth century, when Portuguese and Dutch traders brought small pieces of oriental lacquer furniture to London and other large European cities. During the period of the English Restoration, the Dutch East India Company secured trading rights with the Orient and large quantities of lacquer furniture reached the Western market. Despite the increased supply of oriental furniture, it could not begin to meet the demand. Ambitious artisans tried to approximate the expertise of their oriental counterparts, and in copying lacquer they substituted available varnishes and stains for unknown Far Eastern ingredients. In 1688 the Englishmen John Stalker and George Parker published at Oxford a book of techniques and sample designs for those who wished to imitate oriental lacquer work (plate 45). Stalker and Parker in their elaborately titled book, *A Treatise of Japaning and Varnishing Being a Compleat Discovery of Those Arts, With the best*

49. Dressing table. Maker unknown. New England. 1700–20. Walnut with walnut veneer, width 34''. Greenfield Village and Henry Ford Museum, Dearborn, Michigan

On much of the furniture in the William and Mary style the decorative veneer is confined to the top and front of the case. The legs on most of these case pieces are united by flat stretchers, a device that provided additional strength.

Way of making all sorts of Varnish for Japan, Wood, Paints, Plate, or Pictures, offered what was purported to be seldom-revealed information regarding the "Method of Guilding, Burnishing and Lackering, . . . the Art of Guilding, Seperating, and Refining Metals, and the most Curious way of Painting on Glass." It presented various ways of "Counterfeiting Tortoise-Shell, and Marble, and for Staining or Dying Wood, Ivory &c." The book was familiar to American craftsmen and in 1789 was included in the catalog of the Library Company of Philadelphia.

Stalker and Parker's book included twenty-four plates of recommended patterns and drawings, featuring almost one hundred designs, and it advertised itself as depicting exact imitations of oriental "Buildings, Towers, and Steeples, Figures, Rocks and the like, according to the Patterns which the best workmen amongst them have afforded us on their Cabinets, Screens, Boxes, &c." The authors felt that they may have improved on the original models, "where they were lame or defective," and justified the fact of having altered them by rendering them "more pleasant" but simultaneously preserving the character of "true genuine Indian work."

In authentic japanned furniture, visually important aspects of the decoration are built up by first applying several layers of a plaster and glue mixture, today known as gesso. These raised designs are then covered with paint or gold leaf and finally varnished. The background color most frequently used was black; other colors—which must have been more difficult to apply since they are considerably more rare—were white, red, green, chestnut, and a soft-hued blue.

Japanned furniture was especially popular in Boston and in New York where various schools of decorators plied their trade in order to satisfy the great demand. A seventeenth-century New York advertisement of Gerardus Duyckinck offered "Looking glasses—frames plain, Japan'd or flowered."

The taste for japanned furniture in America lasted from about 1675 through the 1780s and underwent three distinct phases. At first japanning was a conscious attempt at the imitation and glorification of Chinese decoration and culture. In its second phase it caricatured Chinese style in a humorous way, and in the final phase Chinese and European rococo designs were synthesized to the extent that pure whimsy dominated the works decorated in this manner.

The use of paint as a method of decoration varied greatly from region to region. The Dutch in the Hudson River valley preferred grisaille—a monochromatic painting in neutral grays or beiges only, designed to produce a sculptured relief effect. Grisaille painting was frequently applied on large wardrobes embellished with depictions of abundant fruit and flower motifs that were nearly identical to carved decoration found on similar furniture in Holland. Undoubtedly it was faster and less expensive to execute these motifs in paint than it would have been to carve or apply them. Properly called a kas, the wardrobe (plate 47) was a simple but large cabinet with broad projecting moldings at the top and massive turned bun feet, usually painted black. Stored on top of a kas, imported blue and white oriental pottery, as well as porcelain jars, jugs, and vases, added a colorful note. The kas was the proud possession of the traditional Dutch colonial family in America.

During the William and Mary period several new furniture forms appeared. The tall chest, or highboy (plate 48), and matching dressing table, or lowboy (plate 49), are perhaps the most significant. Fashioned with a flat top, the highboy (plate 50) of this period was really nothing more than a chest of drawers set upon a base with trumpet or cup turned legs usually united by flat stretchers and supported by ball or bun feet. Teardrop brass drawer pulls, a common feature of highboys, were imported. American foundries had not yet developed sufficient technology to produce fine brass hardware of this type.

Another new furniture form that emerged in the colonies was the bureau-desk (plate 51), essentially a bureau with hinged desk equipment added. It is not surprising that such forms evolved, for a prodigious amount of writing flowed from the pens of famous diarists of the day, such as Samuel Sewall

50. Highboy. Maker unknown. Probably Boston, Massachusetts. Late seventeenth or early eighteenth century. Pine, height 52″. Metropolitan Museum of Art, New York City. Gift of Mrs. Russell Sage, 1910

Birds and decorative floral motifs painted in various hues of red on a black background on this highboy, or tall chest, in the William and Mary style simulate the more expensive japanned decoration popular in New England and New York at the time that this piece was crafted. The drop brasses and pierced escutcheons would have been imported.

51. Fall-front bureau-desk. Maker unknown. Probably New York. 1690–1720. Cedar with beechwood and walnut inlay, height 66¾″. Museum of the City of New York, New York City. Gift of Mrs. Elon Huntington Hooker

and William Byrd II, and ecclesiastical writers like Cotton Mather, and it is safe to presume that all of those who could, wrote—and wrote voluminously. Essentially a chest-on-chest with ball feet, the upper section of the bureau-desk was fitted with a fall front that became a writing surface when opened. The case contained small pigeonholes, numerous drawers, and a cupboard that could be securely locked to protect valuable documents. Elaborate inlaid floral and vine motifs formed a decorative pattern similar to those achieved in the very best European cabinetmaking shops specializing in marquetry and parquetry. Prior to the early 1700s, inlay as a method of decoration was almost unknown in the colonies; in the next few decades it was used often, but seldom as successfully as on this desk.

An increase in literacy also led to the development of the fall-front desk (plate 52). Many desks of this type were veneered only on those surfaces that would show—fronts of drawers, the face of the fall front, and the top. Veneering became especially popular, for a craftsman could take a simple piece of case furniture and make it exceedingly beautiful. Inlay was also occasionally used in conjunction with veneer, a fine example being the eight-pointed star centered on the fall front of the desk. The sides of case pieces were usually cut from maple and the drawer interiors from secondary woods, such as pine.

During the period from 1685 to 1720, after the hardships of the earlier years, American homemakers became obsessed with the pursuit of comfort. Upholstered furniture, indicative of a softer life, provided a graciousness that inspired the development of new forms. The easy chair (plates 53, 55), today generally called a wing chair, reached a maturity of design during this period. The upholstered stool (plate 54), although never quite as popular as in England, became a common appointment in many households. The daybed (plate 58),

This handsome piece with inlay of flowers and scrolls was handed down through eight generations of the Joris Dircksen Brinckerhoff family, which was established in America in 1638. The secretary was mentioned in the wills of the family for a period of nearly two hundred years and was referred to, in every case, either as the "chest of drawers" or the "drawers." A similar piece but without the inlay was constructed by Edward Evans in Philadelphia in 1707 and is in the Raleigh Tavern at Colonial Williamsburg, Virginia.

52. Fall-front desk. Maker
unknown. Massachusetts.
1700–20. Maple with walnut
veneer and pine secondary woods,
height 38''. Greenfield Village
and Henry Ford Museum,
Dearborn, Michigan

As is true of much early William
and Mary style of furniture, only
the parts that would show were
embellished with richly grained
veneer. The top, the fall front,
and the drawer fronts are faced
with beautiful burl walnut veneer.
The sides were cut from simple
maple and stained to look like
walnut. An unusual feature is the
inlaid star centering the fall front.
This diminutive piece sits on
turnip feet, typical of the William
and Mary style.

often with a caned back and seat covered with a cushion, and the impressive
leather upholstered armchair (plate 57) have crest rails and pierced stretchers
incorporating the new C-scroll motif.

Beautifully carved, elegant tall-back chairs included in their design deeply
cut and pierced Flemish S-scrolls and C-scrolls and were finished with such East
Indian–influenced curiosities as caning. The fashionable English ladies in an
early-eighteenth-century print, *The Tea-Table* (plate 59), sit in tall caned-back
chairs. They wear modish dresses cut from printed calico, possibly imported from
India, while celebrating the new social ritual of taking tea. This print also
demonstrates that carpets had moved from the table to the floor and that the

53. Museum installation. Murphy
Room. New England. First half of
eighteenth century. Museum of
Fine Arts, Houston, Texas.
Bayou Bend Collection

This installation at Bayou Bend,
the American decorative arts
branch of the Houston Museum of
Fine Arts, is based architecturally
on a room given by an eminent
collector of early Americana,
Katherine Prentis Murphy, to the
New Hampshire Historical
Society. The design of the Queen
Anne paneling is based on
woodwork from a Connecticut
house of the 1730s. The floor is
painted and stenciled in a geometric
pattern, a common method of floor
decoration in the well-to-do homes
of the late seventeenth and early
eighteenth centuries. The Murphy
Room and its contents were
assembled by Ima Hogg, donor
of the Bayou Bend Collection,
and named in honor of Mrs.
Murphy.

well-appointed home boasted cupboards in which fine porcelains and utensils for making and serving tea could be displayed for all to see. American versions of the tall caned-back chair were less ornate. Because cane was fragile, the practical colonists frequently upholstered the seats and backs of their chairs in leather.

Banister-back chairs (plates 56, 57) with pierced crest rails, large vase-and-ring turned front stretchers, and ornate outward-flaring arms ending in ram's-head terminals have a distinctly American character, both more vigorous and more dramatic than similar contemporary forms abroad. The banisters in the backs of the chairs were crafted in an interesting manner—a foretaste of the vaunted "Yankee ingenuity." Two pieces of wood were glued together, turned on a great wheel, and then separated, providing two uprights identical in shape and design.

54. Footstool. Maker unknown. Found in New Hampshire. 1710–20. Maple, height 18¼". New Hampshire Historical Society, Concord, New Hampshire. Prentis Collection

Flamestitch embroidery embellishes the seat on this stool in the William and Mary style. Upholstered stools appeared in England as early as 1600, but they were never common in America in any period. In the colonies they probably were first esteemed as articles of great luxury but soon were outmoded as the backstool, or side chair, became increasingly popular.

Tables increased in size and consequently were no longer moved about from place to place. Although some carpets were now being used on floors, the most prized turkeywork carpets (plate 60) were primarily decorative coverings for these fine tables. The legs on gateleg tables could be swung out to support drop leaves when raised, affording tabletop flexibility of a sort; the tables were practical space-savers as well. The legs and stretchers, which were embellished with turnings, added to the gracefulness of these tables.

The Spanish, or paintbrush, foot appeared around 1700 and was used for approximately twenty years in urban cabinetmaking shops, until it was finally superseded by the pad foot strongly associated with the Queen Anne style. In rural areas, however, where fashion lagged, the Spanish foot continued to enjoy great popularity throughout much of the eighteenth century. During those twenty years, and even later in country cabinetwork, the legs on highboys, easy chairs (plate 55), corner chairs (plate 64), banister-back chairs, stools (plate 54), daybeds, gateleg tables, and many other forms of furniture terminated in this ornately carved device.

56. Dining room. New England. Eighteenth century. Lillian Blankley Cogan, Farmington, Connecticut

During the eighteenth century there was a conscious movement toward comfort and graciousness. Furniture became more rounded, designed to fit the human body. Like most seventeenth-century chairs, the black banister-backs in this interior of a private home have the pronounced vertical architectural quality typical of the period. The two butterfly tables are of different designs; one has a rectangular top when opened, the other is oval. The window treatment consists of plain straight curtains hung from a simple wooden rod.

OPPOSITE:

55. Easy chair. Maker unknown. Eastern Massachusetts. c. 1700. Walnut and maple, dimensions unavailable. Watercolor rendering by Rolland Livingstone, New York City Project. Index of American Design, National Gallery of Art, Washington, D.C.

The cabriole legs of this chair in a transitional William and Mary–Queen Anne style terminate with Spanish paintbrush feet, a design motif popular at the close of the seventeenth century. The vase-and-ring turned stretchers uniting the legs were also just coming into vogue.

57. *Banister-back armchair. Maker unknown. New England. c. 1690. Curly maple, height 55½".*
Gateleg table. Maker unknown. New England. 1695–1720. Mahogany, width when open 77¾".
Armchair. Maker unknown. Massachusetts. c. 1690. Maple with leather upholstery, height 52".
All Greenfield Village and Henry Ford Museum, Dearborn, Michigan

This museum installation at the Henry Ford Museum features two chairs and a gateleg table all in the William and Mary style. The grand proportions and beautiful design of the truly distinctive banister-back chair place it in a class of its own. The crest rail is ornately carved with scrolls and is made from one piece of wood. The banisters, or spindles, in the back were created by gluing two pieces of wood together, turning them on a great wheel, and then separating them. Especially large examples of gateleg tables were constructed with two swinging gates to support each drop leaf. Vase-and-ring turnings on the knees on the lower gate and on the stretchers are especially crisp and beautiful. The carving of the Flemish C-scroll and pierced top rail on the armchair is matched by that on the front stretcher. This leather-upholstered chair once belonged to a distinguished early New Yorker, Colonel Peter Schuyler, who became the first mayor of Albany.

58. *Daybed. Maker unknown. New England. Late seventeenth century. Maple with cane seat and back, length 60". Metropolitan Museum of Art, New York City. Gift of Mrs. Russell Sage, 1909*

American furniture made of beech in this period has always been an object of controversy, most scholars insisting that beech furniture is of English construction. Recent investigation, however, has advanced arguments rejecting this claim, and many pieces once assigned a European provenance are now considered of American origin. The pierced S-scrolls and C-scrolls, adorning the side stretchers of this daybed in the William and Mary style, are also found on caned-back chairs. Chairs were often made en suite with daybeds, and in 1719 Chief Justice Samuel Sewall of Massachusetts ordered from England, for his daughter Judith, a "Duzen of good black Walnut chairs, fine Cane, with a Couch."

The TEA-TABLE

59. The Tea-Table. *Artist unknown. England. c. 1710. Engraving, including type* $8\frac{1}{8} \times 6\frac{1}{4}''$. *Department of Prints and Drawings, British Museum, London, England*

The stylish women at the tea party sit in typical English tall cane-backed chairs at what appears to be a gateleg table. The furniture in the center of the room is placed on a carpet, an amenity few Americans could afford during this period. In this seventeenth-century satirical print Envy is driving Justice and Truth out the door, while two men at the open window eavesdrop on the women's conversation. Below the illustration there is a long poem describing women's proclivity to scandal and envy—"How see we Scandal (for our Sex too base) | Seat its dread Empire in the Female Race"—which may seem offensive to modern sensibilities.

Clocks and other timepieces remained beyond the means of most colonists. Since few homes could boast a timepiece, it was important for the business and political life of the community to have large clocks installed in the steeples of public buildings such as town halls or churches. These tower clocks had a bell or chimes that sounded the hour, and many had only a single hand that rarely specified a time shorter than a quarter of an hour. Miniature brass sundials placed

60. The Bermuda Group. *John Smibert. America. 1729. Oil on canvas,* $69\frac{1}{2} \times 93''$. *Yale University Art Gallery, New Haven, Connecticut. Gift of Isaac Lothrop*

The English painter John Smibert arrived in America in 1729. He was accompanied by George Berkeley, dean of Derry and bishop of Cloyne, on his so-called romantic design to travel to the West Indies, New York, or the Bermudas to lay the foundation of a college devoted to studies on the Bermudas and to instruct European and Indian children. In this painting of Dean Berkeley and his wife and family the subjects gather at a table covered with a turkeywork carpet. In many homes carpets were still too expensive and valuable to be used for floor coverings. Smibert included his self-portrait in this picture as the gentleman in the left foreground sitting in a Queen Anne–style chair.

61. *Delft vases. Maker unknown. Holland. c. 1695. Tin-glazed earthenware, dimensions unavailable. Current whereabouts unknown*

During the seventeenth and eighteenth centuries colonial inventories abound with references to Dutch and English glazed earthenware known as delft. Oriental decoration ensured popularity for these pieces in the New World, where fashion-conscious colonials were eager to boast their awareness of current European taste.

in gardens or yards offered a more private method of determining time, and sundials are recorded in many of the diaries and inventories of America's fashionable families. These inevitably were imported from England, Holland, and other European countries.

62. *Posset pot. Maker unknown. Lambeth, England. 1690–1710. Tin-glazed earthenware, height 10″. Henry Francis du Pont Winterthur Museum, Winterthur, Delaware*

This form was duplicated in metal by American craftsmen well into the eighteenth century.

Blue and white delft vases (plate 61) and tiles, originally produced in Holland but also made in England, enriched interiors; the tiles were commonly used to surround fireplace openings. The fireplace took on importance as the focal point of a room, and imported andirons and fire tools were crafted with an eye to design, serving as an embellishment as well as a utilitarian necessity. Pots, teakettles, and other cooking utensils made of brass were especially popular with the Dutch, for they could be highly polished, giving a sense of elegance and beauty while also attesting to the housekeeping proficiency of the owner.

Almost as soon as colonial settlements in New England developed out of the rude outposts in the wilderness, churches were built in an attempt to save man from the damnation of hell; at the same time taverns sprang up where he could be eased down a primrose path leading to that very destination. It is a well-documented fact that male churchgoers were also taverngoers. Occasionally even the parson himself dropped in for a libation, whether to keep an eye on his wandering flock or to quench a parched throat following a rousing sermon has not been thoroughly demonstrated.

63. Monteith. Maker unknown. Japan. 1750–75. Porcelain with American-made silver rim, diameter 9⅞". Philadelphia Museum of Art, Philadelphia, Pennsylvania. Ozeas, Ramborger, Keehmle Fund

In the eighteenth century both the French and the English collected oriental porcelains that were fitted with ornate rococo ormolu, gold, or silver mounts. The upper rim on this unusual monteith, produced for export to America, is somewhat similar in design.

The General Court of Massachusetts, quick to discover a source of revenue, passed its first law governing tavern activities in 1633. "Strong waters" were available only from those who had secured a vendor's permit from the governor or the deputy governor. In spite of such restrictive laws, taverns flourished and tavern signs became a familiar part of both town and country landscapes. One of the drinks popular in the late seventeenth century was posset, a hot drink of spiced and sweetened milk curdled with wine or ale. The imported delft posset pot (plate 62) would have been made specifically for serving this warmly appreciated beverage. Punch and wine were also fashionable alcoholic drinks, and the handsome porcelain monteith with silver fittings (plate 63) had a special purpose in the service of these beverages. It held ice or chilled water in which the bowls of blown glasses were suspended while the foot of the glass was supported by the indentations in the curvatures of the rim.

Between 1710 and 1730 there was a distinct blending of styles. The typical characteristics of the William and Mary style began to yield gradually to those of the Queen Anne. Both the corner, or roundabout, chair (plate 64)—with its Spanish foot in front and ball feet on three legs, its vase-and-ring turned stretchers, and its solid splats in the back—and the double butterfly table (plate 65) are medleys of the William and Mary and Queen Anne styles and reflect this period of transition. Increasingly, native woods such as maple and walnut were employed, and oak, extremely popular in the earlier periods, all but disappeared from cabinetmaking shops.

In spite of the fact that the new style was replacing the old, earlier pieces remained in use in even the most fashionable parlors. The joint stool (plate 66) may seem incongruous in an up-to-date interior that exulted in upholstered chairs, a veneered highboy, and a rope turned gateleg table. Samuel Sewall mentioned such a joint stool in one of his diary entries for 1697, when he described a fine dinner: "Had first Butter, Honey, Curds and Cream. For Dinner, very good Rost Lamb, Turkey, Fowls, Applepy. After Dinner sung the 121 Psalm. Note. A Glass of spirits my Wife sent stood upon a Joint-Stool which, Simon W. jogging, it fell down and broke all to shivers: I said twas a lively Emblem of our Fragility and Mortality."

The simple splendor of early-eighteenth-century American homes is suggested by the handsome Flock Room (plate 66), which derives its name from the gray and green flocked canvas wall covering that simulates cut velvet. Flocked wall covering was produced by adhering cut-up wool to a stenciled design of shells and leaves on canvas. Traces of the original blue paint remain on much of the woodwork, which was removed from Morattico Hall, built about 1715 on the Rappahannock River at Morattico on a promitory formerly in Richmond County, Virginia. As with most interiors of this period, the room is dominated by the paneled fireplace wall, which includes a sensitively painted landscape overmantel. The window hangings were inspired by the elaborate and opulent designs published by Daniel Marot. Throughout much of the colonial period, lighting remained unchanged. The brass chandelier and brass candlesticks probably were imported.

In the first quarter of the eighteenth century affluent colonists were in a position to commission metalsmiths to handcraft ornate candlesticks and accessories like the beautifully designed silver stick and snuffer stand (plate 67) made around 1705 by Cornelius Kierstede. The bases of the stick and snuffer stand are engraved with tiny oriental figures in exotic landscapes. Today it would seem undeniable that the atmosphere created by candlelight is a pleasant one—but the fact is that odorless wick-consuming candles are a modern invention, and the charm of colonial candlelight was not unqualified. Candleholders in the past required proper equipment, including snuffers and stands, and these were designed with great ingenuity and style.

One of America's most distinguished statesmen first worked in the chandler business, making tallow and soap. According to Benjamin Franklin—as recorded in his *Autobiography*—his father, Josiah, felt no hesitation about teaching his young son the trade:

I was the youngest Son and the youngest Child but two, and was born in Boston, N. England. . . .

At Ten Years old, I was taken home to assist my Father in his Business, which was that of a Tallow Chandler and Sope-Boiler. A Business he was not bred to, but had assumed on his Arrival in New England and on finding his Dying Trade would not maintain his Family, being in little Request. Accordingly I was employed in cutting Wick for the Candles, filling the Dipping Mold, and the Molds for cast Candles, attending the Shop, going of Errands, &c. I dislik'd the Trade and had a strong Inclination for the Sea.

Candles, which provided little light, were not altogether satisfactory, particularly for skilled craftsmen who did close work. Those who required more intense illumination resorted to water refractors (plate 68). The blown-glass balls, filled with water, intensified the light generated by a candle placed in the midst of the refractors. Devices of this type were used as early as the sixteenth century in Europe, and what they lacked in elegance of workmanship or richness of material they made up for in practicality.

One of the most ornate forms of American silver is the sweetmeat, or sugar, box. Edward Winslow, a successful Boston silversmith, fashioned an elaborate example (plate 69) about 1702 for William Partridge, who presented it to Daniel

64. Corner chair. Maker unknown.
Rhode Island. 1710–25. Maple,
height 29⅜". Greenfield Village
and Henry Ford Museum,
Dearborn, Michigan

The legs and stretchers of this chair show remnants of the William and Mary period, while the splats and curved top rail are characteristics of the Queen Anne style. The corner chair, also known as the roundabout chair, is not indigenous to America but first appeared here at the close of the seventeenth century. It was frequently used as a desk chair, and some examples were constructed with deep, broad seats that concealed a commode, an amenity much desired in a period before indoor plumbing was introduced.

and Elizabeth (Belcher) Oliver. Peter Oliver, a Tory descendant of Daniel Oliver, took the small object to England during the Revolution. This repoussé box is further enhanced by a hasp that depicts the figure of a knight on horse-back. Winslow was one of the most illustrious silversmiths working in New England in the first half of the eighteenth century. Silversmiths were prominent members of their communities and often held public office or were the town bankers. Winslow was no exception; by the time of his death at the age of eighty-four, he had served in numerous community offices.

65. Double butterfly drop-leaf
table. Maker unknown. Connecticut.
1690–1720. Cherry, length 66⅝".
Greenfield Village and Henry
Ford Museum, Dearborn,
Michigan

For many years historians of the decorative arts believed that the butterfly table was an original American furniture form. This was recently disproved when both English and Dutch oak examples dating from the third quarter of the seventeenth century were discovered. This table is especially important because it is one of the very few extant pieces with double butterfly supports. The turned legs are splayed, providing a distinctive profile.

*66. Museum installation. Flock
Room. Virginia. c. 1715. Henry
Francis du Pont Winterthur
Museum, Winterthur, Delaware*

*The room takes its name from the
flocked canvas wall covering,
which simulates cut velvet. The
woodwork was found in Morattico
Hall, built in Richmond County,
Virginia, about 1715. The
unusual overmantel painting, the
plasticity of the paneling, and the
ample scale of the room make it
one of the truly gracious examples
of the period. Several of the New
England chairs are upholstered in
leather and the easy chair next to
the fireplace is finished in gold
silk brocatelle. The large Queen
Anne looking glass is veneered
and has an outsized pierced crest.
Few American homes at the time
were as sumptuous.*

The silver chocolate pot (plate 70) was crafted by Winslow around 1700, and it is nearly as rich in design as the sweetmeat box. Chocolate was introduced into Europe by the conquistadores on their return from Mexico. Montezuma, the Aztec emperor, drank "chocolatl" as a daily ritual and cocoa beans were so valued that they were commonly used in Aztec Mexico as a form of currency. The drinking of chocolate became popular in England in the last decades of the seventeenth century and immediately found favor among the affluent in the colonies. Samuel Sewall, who was particularly fond of rich foods and frequently wrote about them, mentions a savory pot of "chockalette" that he shared at breakfast in Boston with Lieutenant Governor William Stoughton.

The tankard, an immensely popular drinking vessel for beer and ale, displayed regional variations as did furniture forms. Essentially the tankard was a canlike vessel with a handle; some were fitted with covers. The silver tankard by Jeremiah Dummer (plate 71) is embellished with a finely tooled handle and sensitively worked lid. Dummer had been apprenticed to Hull and Sanderson in Boston, makers of the porringer (plate 32). In 1692 Dummer shaped the earliest known colonial punchbowl, a form developed to accommodate the brewing of punch, a practice brought to America from India in the middle of the seventeenth century. It is commonly thought that Dummer trained Edward Winslow. Besides his great skill as an artisan, Dummer prospered in many areas. Not only was he county treasurer, captain of his artillery company, and a judge, he was also one of Boston's richest shipowners. Colonial silversmiths almost always signed their work. A silversmith's mark, which included his initials and sometimes a small personal device, guaranteed the purity of the silver as well as the quality of workmanship of each piece. Dummer marked his pieces with his initials and a small lily set in a heart.

Textiles continued to be among the colonists' most esteemed possessions, and when a suit of clothing could no longer be mended and patched, the

67. Candlestick and snuffer stand. Cornelius Kierstede. New York. 1700–15. Silver, height of candlestick 11½". Metropolitan Museum of Art, New York City. Gift of Mr. and Mrs. William A. Moore, 1923, and gift of Robert L. Cammann, 1957

American-made candlesticks from the late seventeenth and early eighteenth centuries are extremely rare. This example is one of the most ornate and sophisticated known and was made for Elizabeth and John Schuyler, members of a socially and politically active New York family. Whimsical exotic oriental figures and animals embellish the base of the stick and the stand. They represent a very early example of chinoiserie taste in the New World. The stick was molded from wrought sheets of silver, and producing it involved highly skilled knowledge of an array of techniques: casting, engraving or chasing, repoussé gadrooning, punching and stippling, drawn molding, and applying meander wire.

68. *Water refractors. Maker
unknown. America. Seventeenth
or early eighteenth century.
Wood and glass, dimensions
unavailable. Current whereabouts
unknown*

*Water refractors were developed
in Europe and were used by
lacemakers, cobblers, and
watchmakers to intensify
candlelight. The hollow blown-
glass balls were filled with
water, and when a lighted candle was
placed in the center of the stand,
illumination was greatly increased.
American women found them
particularly useful when doing
fine needlework since the light from
a roaring fire often was the only
other source of illumination.*

69. Sugar box. Edward Winslow. Boston, Massachusetts. c. 1702. Silver, height 5''. Henry Francis du Pont Winterthur Museum, Winterthur, Delaware

The sugar, or sweetmeat, box is one of the rarest and finest forms of American silver. This example, with its dazzling repoussé and cast hasp, was found in England, taken there during the Revolution by the Tory Peter Oliver. During the seventeenth century sugar represented a great luxury, and it was not until the eighteenth century that the general use of tea and coffee made it a food staple in most homes.

70. Chocolate pot. Edward Winslow. Boston, Massachusetts. c. 1700. Silver with wooden handle, height 9⅛''. Metropolitan Museum of Art, New York City. Bequest of A. T. Clearwater, 1933

Since silver conducts heat, metal objects designed to hold hot beverages were nearly always fitted with wooden handles to make them more comfortable and easy to hold.

71. Tankard. Jeremiah Dummer. Boston, Massachusetts. c. 1675. Silver, height 7''. Metropolitan Museum of Art, New York City. Anonymous gift, 1934

In order to guarantee both workmanship and the purity of the silver, most colonial silversmiths marked their pieces with a cypher that was their own. Dummer used his initials and a small lily set in a heart. Dummer, who was well known as a silversmith, was chosen by the governor of the Colony of Connecticut to engrave and print currency in 1709. He executed 6,550 sheets of bills, having a value of ten thousand pounds.

72. *Pieced quilt. Maker unknown. Probably Massachusetts. Nineteenth century. Brocaded silk and velvet and other fabrics, 75 × 82". Essex Institute, Salem, Massachusetts*

It was once believed that this quilt was stitched by Sarah Sedgwick Leverett and her daughter, Elizabeth, in Massachusetts in 1704. Since recent research has revealed that the bedcover includes nineteenth-century brocaded silks and velvets as well as many eighteenth-century fabrics, an early-eighteenth-century assignment would be impossible. It is unusual to find a quilt incorporating eighteenth-century fabrics in such good condition.

73. Portrait of Peter Schuyler.
Nehemiah Partridge (attr.).
Albany, New York Province.
c. 1718. Oil on canvas, 87¾ ×
51″. Collection City of
Albany, Albany, New York

The high standard of portraiture
that was reached in Holland in the
seventeenth century—with extreme
faithfulness and literal resemblance
to the subject the prevailing
fashion—influenced painting in this
genre in the American colonies.
Peter Schuyler was appointed the
first mayor of Albany, thus
becoming head of the commission
of Indian affairs for New York.
He maintained a remarkable and
positive influence over the New
York Iroquois.

74. The South East Prospect of
The City of Philadelphia. *Peter*
Cooper. Pennsylvania. c. 1720.
Oil on canvas, 20¼ × 87″.
Library Company of Philadelphia,
Philadelphia, Pennsylvania

This painting is the earliest known
American panoramic cityscape
executed in oil. It clearly portrays
Philadelphia, a rapidly growing
city in 1720, as already lined
with "brave brick houses."
Despite the polyglot nature of
William Penn's capital city,
Philadelphia remained primarily
English in character.

remnants were carefully washed and saved by thrifty housekeepers, who stitched the pieces into bedcovers. During the seventeenth and eighteenth centuries most quilts were made from salvaged fabrics. A woman of means could augment her bits of woolen material and linen homespun culled from the ragbag with exotic toiles, brocades, damasks, and printed cottons imported from France, Italy, Sweden, England, and India. A December 17, 1651, inventory of the estate of the Boston shopkeeper Henry Landis lists over forty fabrics purchasable at the time; they included such items as "black Turky tamet, linsie woolsey, broadcloth, tamy cheny, adretto, herico Italiano, sad hair coloured Italiano, say, red satinesco tufted Holland, broad dowlas, white calico."

The brocaded silk and velvet quilt with its geometric framed center (plate 72), once considered the oldest surviving pieced quilt, was traditionally assigned the date 1704 and attributed to Sarah Sedgwick Leverett and her daughter, Elizabeth. Recent research indicates that this bedcovering is made from nineteenth-century silks and velvets as well as many eighteenth-century fabrics, making the earlier eighteenth-century date impossible.

During the first half of the eighteenth century, portraiture flourished in the Hudson Valley between New York City and Albany. The Dutch immigrants in the New World lived comfortably and surrounded themselves with refinements not affordable in many of the other colonies. In 1730 a Captain Dean, lumber merchant and sloop captain, owned thirteen pictures, as well as a tea table, a looking glass, a mahogany table, extensive silver, and many books. Interest in paintings, especially portraits (plate 73), was inherited from the Old World, where during the seventeenth century canvases by skilled artists were sold in open-air markets in nearly every city in Holland.

There was a growing interest in paintings of the New World. American cities were developing at an astonishing rate during the early eighteenth century, with streets and buildings spreading out from their centers in a short time. *The South East Prospect of The City of Philadelphia* (plate 74), executed by Peter Cooper about 1720, depicts a well-ordered town with large public and private buildings. The growth of Philadelphia, which was organized by an agent of William Penn in 1681 and laid out in 1682, was quite dramatic.

Transportation in colonial cities like Philadelphia was generally confined to horses or horse-drawn coaches. Coachmakers turned out handsomely crafted vehicles for the gentry. Many of these were emblazoned with the coats of arms of their owners, following European custom. Americans loved to travel and many viewed a trip home to England and a visit to the royal court as an essential accomplishment within a lifetime. Upon their return to the colonies, they brought back many of the latest vogues, both in stylish dress and in the decorative arts.

With the passing of the William and Mary style new concepts of design and comfort rose to prominence. The rectilinear, vertical, architectural nature of furniture gave way to the sumptuous curves and the oriental-influenced contours apparent in the Queen Anne period. As went the style in London, so it followed in the American colonies.

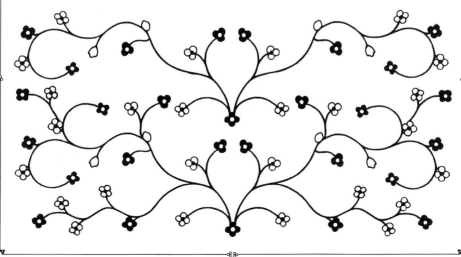

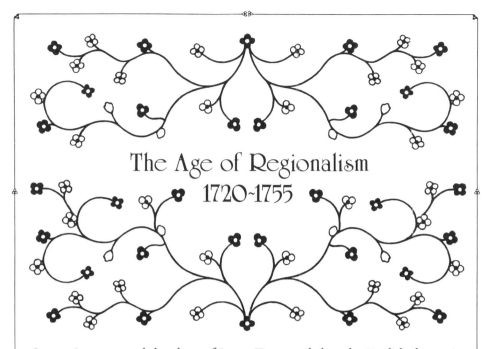

The Age of Regionalism
1720~1755

Queen Anne, second daughter of James II, succeeded to the English throne in 1702. She was the last of the Stuart monarchs and her reign, a brief one, lasted but twelve years. In those few years England replaced Spain as the most consequential international power, especially in the economic strength resulting from its vast mercantile activities. The Treaty of Utrecht, signed in 1713, signaled the end of the War of the Spanish Succession and brought new prominence to England. The nation's rising prestige spread the influence of English customs and English social patterns into virtually every country in the world. Increased trade with the colonies resulted in burgeoning expansion and created new wealth for an ever-growing number of merchant princes. England, in its position as the mother country, exploited its economic relationship with the colonies, exporting great quantities of English textiles and household furnishings and frequently introducing new laws to curb local production by colonial craftsmen that was in direct competition with those goods.

On the American shores the growth within the colonies of village or hamlet to small town to larger town to major city was steady and persistent. Because the various colonies had often been settled by diverse ethnic groups, differences in taste and design from town to town began to emerge in a distinctive and noticeable way.

At the close of the seventeenth century the power of the clergy was beginning to dissipate. A merchant class developed into the American aristocracy. Ships heavily laden with imports and exports cleared America's major harbors on a

75. Thomas Hancock House. *Artist unknown. America. Eighteenth century. Engraving, dimensions unavailable. Current whereabouts unknown*

In 1737 Thomas Hancock began the construction of his distinctive home on Beacon Hill in Boston; it stood just outside the settled part of the city, overlooking the Boston Common. The design for the Georgian-style structure was obviously derived from English architectural books. The glass for the windows was ordered from London as well as three marble hearths and twenty dozen blue and white delft tiles to frame the fireplace. Hancock sent a pattern of his own design for wallpaper with instructions to his agent to have it made "as Cheap as Possible, & if they can make it more Beautifull by adding more Birds flying here & there, with Some Landskip at the Bottom I should Like it well."

76. Museum installation. Paneled sitting room. Furnishings New England and Philadelphia. Second and third quarters of eighteenth century. Museum of Fine Arts, Houston, Texas. Bayou Bend Collection

Fine period examples of native and imported furnishings grace this exquisite Queen Anne sitting room. The rare accordion-action game table with its original embroidered top was crafted in Boston for merchant Peter Faneuil; the side chairs accompanying it and the open armchair to the left come from Philadelphia. The flat stretcher arrangement at the bottom of the side chairs is typical of Philadelphia cabinetmaking. Dutch aubergine delft tiles with biblical scenes surround the fireplace opening, and English and Dutch delft ware are displayed on the mantel and in the cupboard at the right. The pastel by John Singleton Copley above the mantel and the oil by Boston portraitist Joseph Badger, as well as the superb Kuba carpet, add to the elegance sought by affluent families in this mature period of decorative arts in the American colonies.

77. *Museum installation. Parlor. Maryland. 1733. Henry Francis du Pont Winterthur Museum, Winterthur, Delaware*

This handsome parlor was originally in a house built in 1733 near Centreville, Maryland. The corner fireplace, in what is considered the first mansion in the colony, is enhanced by bolection molding and seventeenth-century Dutch tiles surrounding the opening. The fully paneled walls are a pale gray-white. The furnishings in the room include a Philadelphia Queen Anne easy chair with scrolled arms dating from the 1730s. Other pieces are Philadelphia chairs with shell-carved crest rails, an elaborately decorated New York tea table with claw-and-ball feet, and a handsomely decorated japanned highboy. The silver candle branches on the sconces were executed by Jacob Hurd of Boston. The portrait over the fireplace is by John Wollaston.

regular basis. Furniture, such as the Boston chair, as it is now called, was exported from that New England center of cabinetmaking to other colonies and to the West Indies, where cargoes of sugar and molasses were loaded aboard in its place to be shipped to the colonies. By 1728, regularly scheduled packet service united New York and Boston, facilitating the trade of provisions between the two cities. Despite improved communications, schools of cabinetmaking that reflected popular regional taste became discernible. Boston, Newport, New York, Philadelphia, and to a lesser degree Williamsburg emerged as the major design centers in the Queen Anne period. Although the queen died in 1714, the style that bears her name flourished in America well into the middle of the century, long after her death.

By the mid-1730s it was not uncommon for a family to own its own carriage. Transportation and communications between the several colonies increased steadily throughout the eighteenth century. *The Vade Mecum for America,* the first American guide for travelers, was published in Boston in 1732

78. Dining room of Secretary Pearson House. New Hampshire. Middle of eighteenth century. Greenfield Village and Henry Ford Museum, Dearborn, Michigan

Originally the home of John Giddings, a prosperous merchant, trader, and shipbuilder, the home was built at Exeter in the 1750s but was purchased during the 1790s by Joseph Pearson, the first secretary of state of New Hampshire. Five years after he had acquired the house, Pearson married Dorothy Giddings, the daughter of the original builder and owner. The Pearson house was built in a modified Georgian style of architecture which originally developed in England during the early eighteenth century. An existing inventory taken at the time of Joseph Pearson's death in 1823 made it possible to furnish the home much as it was when Pearson and his wife resided there.

by Daniel Henchman, and it provided precise information about highways and taverns from Maine to Virginia. Residents in either Boston or Newport had the advantage of stage travel after coach routes linked the two cities in 1736.

America's natural resources proved to be of great economic value. Timbers felled from virgin forests supplied the royal navy with masts for its ships and builders with lumber for the construction of homes.

American gentlemen of means who felt insecure in matters of design sought assistance in the construction of their great houses from a new professional class of architects. In 1724 the Carpenters' Company of the City and County of Philadelphia was formed. This was the first builders guild in America and was created not only to teach architectural skills but also to protect members involved in accidents or in need of assistance, and to give support to the widows and minor children of members. In order to establish a standard remuneration for their services, the Carpenters' Company published a book of prices; it also issued a manual of construction details and architectural designs. Many of America's best craftsmen learned their trade by the apprenticeship system, and excerpts from Benjamin Franklin's *Life and Essays* detail colonial attitudes toward this practice:

In the old long-settled countries of Europe, all arts, trades, and professions, farms, &c. are so full, that it is difficult for a poor man who has children to place them where they may

80. Secretary. Maker unknown. Connecticut. 1730–50. Cherry and pine, height 87¼". Greenfield Village and Henry Ford Museum, Dearborn, Michigan

The sunburst flower-and-leaf carving on a punched ground is reminiscent of that found on early doorways throughout the Connecticut River valley and on Pilgrim chests. The short, bandy legs terminating in pad feet, the shaped skirt, and the arched panel, or tombstone, doors are typical Queen Anne characteristics. The rich interior is comprised of document partitions, drawers, and a small center cupboard with an ornate shell on the door.

79. Linen press. Ebenezer Hartshorne. Charlestown, Massachusetts. c. 1735. Walnut, inlaid with satinwood and rosewood, and oak, height 89¼". Greenfield Village and Henry Ford Museum, Dearborn, Michigan. Gift of Mrs. Edsel B. Ford in memory of Robert Hudson Tannahill

This unique architectural linen press in the Queen Anne style descended in the family of John Marston, a member of the Sons of Liberty, a lieutenant during the American Revolution, and proprietor of both the Golden Ball Tavern and the Bunch of Grapes Tavern in Boston. The linen press is an attractive combination of inlay and carving. Line inlay surrounds the drawers, and the bonnet is inlaid with compass stars. The carved block-front base is flanked by freestanding classical columns repeated on the upper section. Between the upper and lower sections is a full-width pullout slide for small linens.

gain, or learn to gain, a decent livelihood. The artisans, who fear creating future rivals in business, refuse to take apprentices, but upon conditions of money, maintenance, or the like, which the parents are unable to comply with. Hence the youth are dragged up in ignorance of every gainful art, and obliged to become soldiers, or servants, or thieves, for a subsistence. In America, the rapid increase of inhabitants takes away that fear of rivalship, and artisans willingly receive apprentices from the hope of profit by their labor, during the remainder of the time stipulated, after they shall be instructed. Hence it is easy for poor families to get their children instructed; for the artisans are so desirous of apprentices, that many of them will even give money to the parents, to have boys from ten to fifteen years of age bound apprentices to them, till the age of twenty-one; and many poor parents have, by that means, on their arrival in the country, raised money enough to buy land sufficient to establish themselves, and to subsist the rest of their family by agriculture. These contracts for apprentices are made before a magistrate, who regulates the agreement according to reason and justice; and, having in view the formation of a future useful citizen, obliges the master to engage by a written indenture, not only that, during the time of service stipulated, the apprentice shall be duly provided with meat, drink, apparel, washing, and lodging, and at its expiration with a complete new suit of clothes, but also, that he shall be taught to read, write, and cast accounts; and that he shall be well instructed in the art or profession of his master, or some other, by which he may afterward gain a livelihood, and be able in his turn to raise a family.

Numerous English publications such as William Kent's *The Designs of Inigo Jones* and William Salmon's *Palladio Londinensis,* both printed in 1727, made European architectural designs available to an ever upwardly mobile middle class eager to build their colonial mansions in the latest taste. Architectural manuals were imported in vast numbers, and many contemporary diaries record the countless hours learned men spent poring over these publications. The new interest in architecture led to an increased emphasis on furniture that was somewhat massive and formal in nature. Furniture with carved ornamental columns in a classical mode (plates 79, 80) was a natural choice for elegant houses surrounded by meticulously kept gardens and well-preserved outbuildings.

The Thomas Hancock House (plate 75), built 1737–40 on Beacon Hill in Boston, became a prototype of these new dwellings. Hancock, an eminently successful merchant, ordered quantities of seeds and fruit trees from England so that he might properly landscape the grounds of his fine new home. The Georgian-style structure was obviously derived from designs in English architectural books. Characteristics of the Georgian style are a centrally located door and balanced windows on either side. Hancock even investigated the cost of having the house's Corinthian capitals executed in England.

House interiors also became more luxurious during this period. An increasing number of fireplaces were adorned with the popular delft tiles or in some instances even with marble facing. Walls with decorative raised panels (plates 76, 77) and windows with sliding shutters (plate 78) all reflect a conscious effort to construct bigger and more showy homes. The height of the ceilings in the finest homes was increased from approximately six feet to between ten and twelve feet; thus the scale of case pieces increased proportionately. Linen presses (plate 79), tall-case clocks, secretaries (plate 80), and grand imported mirrors did much to fill this new interior spaciousness gracefully.

England remained the arbiter of taste for most Americans. Furniture forms paralleled design concepts introduced into the English court by Daniel Marot. These opulent designs, executed by court craftsmen, inspired the general acceptance of the Queen Anne style. Anne's reign was important in the history of American decorative arts, for it was during this period that the earlier influences of foreign excesses were domesticated and totally nationalized into a cohesive style.

Increased travel and commercial trade with the Orient brought about novel changes in the decorative arts. The outline of vaselike solid splats in the backs of Queen Anne chairs (plates 81, 82) are comparable to the profiles of oriental porcelains imported into the English court by the Dutch East India Company. Claw-and-ball feet (plates 83, 84), offered by some innovative chair-

82. Armchair. John Gaines
(attr.). Portsmouth, New
Hampshire. 1710–40. Maple,
height approximately 43″.
Current whereabouts unknown

Although the full-blown Queen
Anne style was evident on early
eighteenth-century American chairs
with bold cabriole legs and large
pad feet, rural versions using
elements from the William and
Mary period continued to be made
well into the century. This
transitional example, with its
pierced crest rail and paintbrush
feet of William and Mary style,
has a solid splat and shaped back
associated with the Queen Anne.

81. Side chair. Maker unknown.
Boston, Massachusetts. 1730–60.
Walnut and maple, height 40″.
Historic Deerfield, Inc.,
Deerfield, Massachusetts

This side chair in the Queen Anne
style is one of six known chairs
that descended in the Winthrop–
Blanchard families of
Massachusetts. According to
tradition, they were sent to China
and decorated there about 1795,
but it seems more reasonable to
assume that these pieces were
actually decorated in America
around 1810, because both the
motifs and the method of execution
are very similar to japanning of
that period. The center of the front
seat rail is embellished with
Samuel Pickering Gardner's coat
of arms. Gardner's great-niece
Eliza Blanchard married Robert
Winthrop in 1832.

83. Lowboy. Job Townsend (attr.). Newport, Rhode Island. 1740–60. Mahogany, width 33¼". Side chair. Maker unknown. Rhode Island. 1740–60. Walnut, height 38⅜". Both Greenfield Village and Henry Ford Museum, Dearborn, Michigan

The slipper foot was especially popular in Rhode Island during the years 1730–80, when it was produced by Quaker cabinetmakers. The inverted carved shell on this lowboy in the Queen Anne style is also typical of Rhode Island pieces of the period. The side chair is transitional in style from the Queen Anne to the Chippendale periods. Evidence of the new style is the claw-and-ball foot. The balloon-shaped slip seat is covered in white and green antique moquette. The four legs are united by block and turned stretchers, a prevalent feature on furniture from New England, where both strength and form were much admired.

makers on their pieces, apparently were based on earlier Chinese carvings of dragons' claws clutching a pearl. The craze in London throughout the second half of the seventeenth century for oriental furniture continued unabated into the eighteenth, and it explains the collecting of treasured pieces of oriental porcelain and other Eastern trinkets as a pastime for those colonials who could afford such faddish indulgences.

The greater concern for comfort—manifested by the development of the easy chair (plate 101) and the daybed, or couch, in the last decades of the seventeenth century—became even more evident during the first half of the eighteenth century. Many new forms such as settees (plate 85) and open armchairs (plates 76, 86) reflected the continuing interest in upholstered furniture.

No decorative element was more popular than the carved shell, and it appeared with great frequency on furniture of every type imaginable. There is abundant testimony to the obsessive preoccupation with this baroque design motif in American furniture: chairs with shells in the center of seat rails or on crest rails (plates 83, 84) or on the carved leg, highboys with shells on the drawer fronts (plate 87), lowboys (plate 83) and secretaries (plate 80) with shells centered on the skirts, and settees with shells on the knees (plate 85).

Another popular decorative theme incorporated into American design schemes was the carved acanthus leaf, a classical architectural element of the Greeks and the Romans that was revived during the Italian Renaissance. Acanthus leaves frequently appeared on the crest rails of chairs and the fronts of chair legs (plate 84). Following English precedent, walnut was the most popular wood in the early eighteenth century; by the 1720s or 1730s America's best furniture was being crafted from mahogany especially imported for the purpose.

The period abounds with new furniture forms. The dish-top candlestand with tripod base and birdcage attachment (plate 88), the rectangular mixing table (plate 89), and the card table with its folding top (plate 102) are the most notable examples. Earlier forms that were modified include the highboy, which during this period attained its most characteristic form with a scrolled pediment and beautifully carved shells on upper and lower drawers (plate 87); the secretary was now fitted with a broken scrolled pediment (plate 80). One of the most revolutionary forms was the drop-leaf table with swinging cabriole legs that supported the open leaves (plates 78, 90). Upholstered settees (plate 85) and sofas apparently were not plentiful; perhaps the expense of upholstery fabrics, which were nearly always imported, made this form a luxury too costly for most households.

In the cosmopolitan city of Boston cabinetmakers were strongly influenced by English fashions; yet inherent New England restraint was everywhere evident and pieces were spare and delicate. Slender cabriole table legs terminating in pad or cushioned pad feet were very much in vogue. The pad-footed tiletop mixing table (plate 89) is fitted with twenty blue and white delft squares decorated with biblical scenes from the Old and New Testaments. This table indicates how eagerly colonials used imported objects, such as Dutch and English tiles, where they could be easily noticed.

A cabinetmaking dynasty of two Quaker families evolved during this period in Newport, Rhode Island, a major center of American furniture craftsmanship. From the shops of Job Townsend and John Goddard and their many relatives came a prodigious outpouring of exquisite pieces with elaborate shell carvings (plate 83). Newport's strategic geographic location, with its deep natural harbor, provided local furniture makers with an international market to which they could ship the products they skillfully fashioned from native walnut and imported mahogany. Because of its great strength, chestnut, which grew in abundance locally, was used as a secondary wood on most Rhode Island furniture.

In Connecticut shops warm-hued cherrywood, which seemed to be in inexhaustible supply, served as a good substitute for the more expensive imported

84. Side chair. Maker unknown. Philadelphia, Pennsylvania. 1750–60. Walnut, height 40⅝". Henry Francis du Pont Winterthur Museum, Winterthur, Delaware

Philadelphia Queen Anne furniture was elaborate, richly carved, and beautifully conceived. This piece retains the horseshoe-shaped seat and the top rail of the Queen Anne period and introduces rococo detail, common to the Chippendale style, on the pierced splat and carved knees. As with most Philadelphia chairs of this type, the seat rail is mortised through the back legs, a feature rarely encountered in chairs produced in other areas. The needlework seat is original and was executed in varicolored crewels in a conventional floral design.

85. Settee. Maker unknown. Philadelphia, Pennsylvania. c. 1740. Walnut, height 48". Metropolitan Museum of Art, New York City. Rogers Fund, 1925

This settee in the Queen Anne style was designed for James Logan, governor of Pennsylvania, and is believed to have been part of the furnishings of Stenton, Logan's country house in Germantown. An inventory completed in 1776 of the estate of William Logan, James's son, includes a walnut settee in the parlor of the family house on Second Street. The central front leg, missing for years, has been restored, and a retaining edge was added to the front seat rail. These restorations are appropriate and desirable in such an important piece.

mahogany (plate 80). Because of the colony's relative isolation, Connecticut craftsmen tended to be more conservative than their contemporaries in other

86. Open armchair. Maker unknown. New England. 1740–60. Walnut and maple, height 41". Greenfield Village and Henry Ford Museum, Dearborn, Michigan

The high curved back and the open arms make this a rare form in the Queen Anne style. There is an added cushion under the generous pad foot. The chair is perhaps a forerunner of the familiar Martha Washington open armchair of the late eighteenth century.

OPPOSITE:

87. Highboy. Made by John Pimm; japanned perhaps by Thomas Johnson. Boston, Massachusetts. 1740–50. Maple and pine, height 95¾". Henry Francis du Pont Winterthur Museum, Winterthur, Delaware

This japanned highboy in the Queen Anne style was made for Commodore Joshua Loring. It has a tortoiseshell background, produced by streaking vermilion with lampblack, and raised figures that have been gilded. In the early eighteenth century Boston and New York became the centers of domestic production for japanned furniture, although it was popular in other colonies as well. The highboy is signed with the maker's name, an unusual practice at the time.

colonies. A style might come into vogue in Newport, flourish there for a period of several years, and then fade as a new style was introduced from Europe. In Connecticut the Queen Anne style, once firmly established, was prominent throughout the entire eighteenth and well into the nineteenth century.

Although Dutch rule in New Amsterdam had ended in 1664—when the English, under the duke of York, deposed the doughty peg-legged Peter Stuyvesant and the Dutch West India Company and renamed the city New York— the colonists remained faithful to their Dutch heritage. Despite the polyglot nature of New York's population, Dutch traditions and concepts of design continued to dominate daily life in the growing colony. So pervasive was Dutch

88. *Candlestand. Maker unknown. Philadelphia, Pennsylvania. c. 1745. Mahogany, diameter 18⅝″. Greenfield Village and Henry Ford Museum, Dearborn, Michigan*

This candlestand in the Queen Anne style has a dished top. The combination of the suppressed ball turning and the slender tapering post is a distinctive variation of a familiar Philadelphia form. The table has a birdcage device under the top that enables it to be tilted to a vertical position and swiveled so that it can be placed close to a wall.

culture that the Swedish naturalist Peter Kalm during his travels in North America made the following observations about the inhabitants of the city of Albany in 1749: "They speak Dutch . . . their manners are likewise Dutch; their dress, however, is like that of the English."

In New York, halfway between conservative New England and flamboyant Philadelphia, cabinetmakers used a blend of construction techniques. The New England tradition of uniting the four legs of chairs with stretchers was sometimes followed (plate 81). Yet many seating pieces were influenced by Philadelphia design and were constructed without supporting stretchers (plate

Mixing tables were designed specifically for the mixing of drinks and had marble, slate, or tile tops to withstand damage from hot liquids or prevent stains in general. Of the three or four tables of this type extant, this is the largest. This Queen Anne–style piece, which is painted black, includes twenty eighteenth-century blue and white Holland delft tiles, depicting stylized scenes from the Old and New Testaments, set into the top.

84). In New York City walnut and then mahogany were the preferred woods for the most expensive furniture. Farther up the Hudson, native woods such as maple, hickory, and ash were used in the construction of the less sophisticated furniture for the great stone houses like the one shown in the wooden Van Bergen overmantel (plate 91), painted by an unknown artist about 1735. This overmantel is one of the earliest American landscapes extant. Originally it was a panel above the fireplace in the parlor of the Van Bergen homestead in Greene County, New York. Rich in detail, the picture provides a document for the study of Hudson Valley architecture of the period. The artist, in typical genre fashion, included nearly everything he saw. The hay barracks, peculiar to this area, were constructed so that the roof and floors could be raised and lowered to protect the hay. Prototypes for this ingenious device are known in Europe. The Van Bergen stone house was built with a tile roof over the main structure and shingles over the kitchen wing. Small dormers and a wooden gutter, a front stoop, and windows with solid wooden blinds further illustrate Dutch architec-

90. Drop-leaf table. Maker unknown. New York. 1730–40. Mahogany and pine with oak gates, height 21⅝". Greenfield Village and Henry Ford Museum, Dearborn, Michigan

This table in the Queen Anne style has eight legs, four of which swing out to support the wide, heavy leaves when they are raised. The legs terminate in pointed, slipper feet. Similar New York drop-leaf tables were passed on from generation to generation in the prominent Beekman and Schuyler families.

91. *Van Bergen overmantel. Artist unknown. New York. c. 1735. Oil on wood, 15¼ × 87⅝". New York State Historical Association, Cooperstown, New York*

This painting, one of the earliest Hudson Valley genre pictures, was executed by an unknown artist on a farm owned by Marten Van Bergen at Leeds in Greene County, New York. It served as an overmantel in the Van Bergen house until the structure was demolished, and was remounted in the house that replaced the original Van Bergen home. Appearing in the painting are numerous members of the Van Bergen household, including three adults, nine young people, four black slaves, two white servants, and two Indians (of either the Catskill or the Esopus tribe). Slaveholding in the valley was occasionally encountered during the period, and it has been documented that Mrs. Van Bergen received a slave as a wedding present from her father. It is believed that one of the black servants depicted is that woman.

92. Cockerel weathervane. Shem Drowne. Boston, Massachusetts. 1721. Copper, length 60". First Church in Cambridge Congregational, Cambridge, Massachusetts

The exact date of the first American weathervane is probably unrecorded. Early American vanes were perhaps direct copies of European imports; artisan blacksmiths, however, were soon creating their own designs, which displayed a vigor that prompted many art historians to regard the weathervane as the first significant American native sculpture.

ture of the Hudson Valley. The overmantel offers a comprehensive view of the Van Bergen farm, its owner and his family and slaves, Indians, livestock, representative farming activities, and the natural landscape.

Slaves were owned extensively in the North, and Peter Kalm details one of their many duties:

At this time of year [October] since it was beginning to grow cold, it was customary for the women, all of them, even maidens, servants and little girls, to put live coals into small iron pans which were in turn placed in a small stool resembling somewhat a footstool, but with a bottom . . . upon which the pan was set. The top of the pan was full of holes through which the heat came. They placed this stool with the warming pan under their skirts so that the heat therefrom might go up to the *regiones superiores* and to all parts of the body which the skirts covered. As soon as the coals grew black they were thrown away and replaced by live coals and treated as above. It was almost painful to see all this changing and trouble in order that no part should freeze or fare badly. The women had however spoiled themselves, for they could not do without this heat. . . .

93. Museum installation. Millbach Kitchen. Pennsylvania. 1752. Philadelphia Museum of Art, Philadelphia, Pennsylvania

This room from a house built in 1752 by George Muller at Millbach in Lebanon County, Pennsylvania, is furnished with many primitive reminders of the early Pennsylvania German country life, including a walnut chair, a trestle table, a corner cupboard, pewter and pottery platters, and numerous iron and brass cooking utensils hanging in the soot-blackened fireplace and sitting on the hearth.

The negroes or their other servants accompanied them to church mornings carrying the warming pans. When the minister had finished his sermon and the last hymn had been sung, the same negroes, etc. came and removed the warming pans and carried them home. . . .

In a house where there were four women present it was well nigh impossible to glance in the direction of the fire without seeing at least one of them busily engaged in replacing the coals in her warming pan. Even their negro women had acquired this habit, and if time allowed, they also kept warming pans under their skirt.

In this period Philadelphia furniture, more than that from the other colonies, resembles contemporary English examples. The similarities are so striking in both form and construction that even present-day experts disagree on the origins of many of these pieces. Techniques for making chairs were much like those employed by English furniture makers. Side rails extended through the rear legs and were pegged in place. Front legs were doweled into the underside of the seat rail. This procedure contrasts sharply with the New England practice of mortising the front rail into the front legs.

Southern furniture, owned by wealthy planters isolated by rural plantation life, was for the most part modest. From the beginning, settlers in the South, who considered themselves Englishmen and accepted London as the major center of commerce and trade, rarely were interested in furniture of domestic origin. Despite this strong preference for imported objects, at least thirteen

94. *Speaker's Chair. Maker unknown. Virginia. c. 1753. Walnut, tulipwood, and pine, height 97½". Colonial Williamsburg Foundation, Williamsburg, Virginia*

A chair described in a requisition dated 1703 as a "large Armed Chair for the Speaker to sit in, and a cushion stuft with hair Suitable to it" was intended for the hall at the House of Burgesses. This Queen Anne chair probably replaced the earlier one. Few Queen Anne pieces are as architectural in form as this example.

cabinetmakers lived and worked in Williamsburg, Virginia, during the eighteenth century. The Speaker's Chair (plate 94), from the House of Burgesses in Williamsburg and once believed to be of English construction, has now been authenticated as a local piece.

American japanned furniture, first appearing in the William and Mary period, was popular throughout the Queen Anne period. One of the most impressive examples is a shell-carved highboy (plate 87) made between 1740 and 1752 for Commodore Joshua Loring by John Pimm of Boston in his Fleet Street shop. The background decoration on the highboy is in a tortoise-shell design produced by streaking vermilion with lampblack.

While seaboard communities and their environs boasted proud homes in the latest fashion, isolated rural farming towns, populated by closely related immigrant families, retained building styles that went back to earlier European prototypes. The prosperous Dutch in the Hudson Valley, with their stone dwellings and rich farmsteads (plate 91), and the sturdy Germans in Pennsylvania, with their simple agrarian way of life, continued an existence almost untouched by more modern influences. In 1752 George Muller built a house (plate 93) at Millbach in Lebanon County, Pennsylvania, which, while typical of the houses of that time and place, was still medieval in its conception. The large stone fireplace topped by a heavy molded wooden mantel is used for the prominent display of pewterware, a pottery plate, and a Kentucky rifle. The fireplace equipment includes an array of brass and iron items—cooking pots, a waffle iron, a frying pan, and several small utensils. The walnut raised-panel chair and the X-shaped trestle table are typical of the solid Pennsylvania German pieces of the first half of the eighteenth century.

It was the responsibility of the colonial blacksmith to forge an extensive variety of household items. Few were as graceful or beautiful as the practical weathervanes that topped both public and private buildings as early as the mid-seventeenth century. The exact date of the first vane made in America is unrecorded, but several are known to have existed in the middle of the century since cityscapes depicted in the margins of early maps clearly show them silhouetted above the rooftops.

95. Jamb stove plate. Christien Furnace. French Creek, Chester County, Pennsylvania. Dated 1748. Cast iron, width 28". Greenfield Village and Henry Ford Museum, Dearborn, Michigan

The architectural columns united by semicircular arches on this stove plate evoke the painted motifs found on traditional Pennsylvania German painted chests. Stoves of the jamb type were usually decorated with religious scenes. This example is inscribed with the verse "Gotes Brynlein hat Waser die Fyle" (Psalms 65:10), which translates in the King James Bible as "Thou waterest the ridges thereof abundantly."

Some makers of weathervanes were famous in their own time. Shem Drowne, who was born at Kittery, Maine, in 1683 and died in 1774, has deservedly received more attention than any other American vane maker. In 1692 Drowne's family moved to Boston, where he became one of the leading metalsmiths in that growing seaport. In 1716, when the Peter Sargent mansion —which had been built in 1679—became the residence of the royal governor of the province of Massachusetts, Drowne fashioned a glass-eyed Indian with bow and arrow for it. Numerous other vanes by his master hand also survive. His golden cockerel (plate 92), hammered out of two large old copper kettles and then gilded, was ordered for the New Brick Church on Hanover Street, built by a congregation that had seceded from the older North Church on Market Square. Put in place in 1721, it weighs 172 pounds and is more than one foot thick. Through the years the golden cockerel was taken down several times for repairs and given a new coat of gold leaf. In 1779, when the New Brick Society united with the Second Church, the weathervane was placed on a different church. During a violent storm in 1869 the steeple was blown to the ground with such force that the cockerel flew through the air, landing in a nearby house where supper was being served. It was again repaired and in 1873 the First Church in Cambridge bought the cockerel for their new Garden Street church, where it has perched ever since.

96. *Master bedchamber of Secretary Pearson House. New Hampshire. Middle of eighteenth century. Greenfield Village and Henry Ford Museum, Dearborn, Michigan*

The eighteenth-century New England pencil-post bed has an early linsey-woolsey bedcover which is quilted. The walnut Queen Anne dressing table displays accessories appropriate for a woman's toilet, including a looking glass, a curling iron, and a scent bottle.

Drowne billed Christ Church for a "blew ball and banner" vane on August 15, 1740; the church—more commonly known as Old North Church, famous for the two lanterns that signaled Paul Revere's moonlit ride—still supports Drowne's weathervane, which twice survived the toppling of the church steeple. His most noted vane is the green-eyed grasshopper wrought for Peter Faneuil's famous Faneuil Hall in Boston; it was placed in position by the craftsman himself in 1749. These four weathervanes by Drowne are still extant, and two of them, the green-eyed grasshopper and the Old North Church vanes, are the only ones still blowing in the wind on the buildings for which they were originally created.

The heating of rooms was a major problem before the introduction of modern central heating systems. In Europe the open hearth had been replaced by the fireplace in the late Middle Ages. In America, following the early temporary shelters of underground burrows where a makeshift fire burned against the earth at the higher end, the colonists constructed their homes centering around massive chimneys with wide fireplaces. Especially in the North, with its harsh, bitter winters, the hearth was the center of the house. In the early eighteenth century various improvements added to the effectiveness of heating the American colonial household. Benjamin Franklin, who developed an efficient cast-iron fireplace, recorded the results of his efforts in his *Account of the New Invented Pennsylvania Fire-Places,* printed and published by Franklin in 1744 in Philadelphia. The fireback, another heating aid, was not only common in city homes, it was found in country dwellings as well. Traditional Pennsylvania German decorative motifs such as geometric stylized flowers are evident on the

97. Bed furnishings. Mary Swett Bulman. York, Maine. c. 1745. Woolen crewel yarns on unbleached linen, length of head curtain 77". Old Gaol Museum Collection, York, Maine. Gift of Anna Everett

Very few complete sets of early American bed furnishings exist. Valances, because they suffered less wear, are more frequently encountered than the hanging curtains—which were sometimes fitted so that they could be drawn at night as protection from drafts—and the bedcovering, which probably was the first to wear out.

cast-iron jamb stove plate (plate 95), manufactured in 1748 at Christien Furnace in Pennsylvania. Jamb stoves were constructed of five cast-iron plates bolted together to form a box left open at the back. They were built into the wall of one room, the open end protruding into a fireplace in an adjoining room. This opening, through which fuel could be supplied to the stove, served as an exhaust path, allowing the smoke and fumes of the stove to reach the fireplace chimney, an ingenious and practical arrangement.

While men dealt in hard materials, women spent their spare time creating objects of softer substances. Although few women in the eighteenth century had the advantage of a college education, a young woman might be sent to a local academy, usually maintained by a single instructress, to learn the rudiments of reading and writing. Working a sampler provided an easy way of familiarizing her with the alphabet and numbers while it gave her practical experience in handling a needle. Many talented women turned their skills into domestic works of art, creating beautiful embroidered pictures like the English example (plate 96) in the Secretary Pearson House master bedchamber, and showy bedhangings such as the remarkable curtains, valances, and spread (plates 97, 98) executed about 1745 by Mary Swett Bulman of York, Maine.

Ever since Jacobean times the designs in English crewel were generally stiff and executed in dark colors, combining influences from Persia, India, and China with the English love for family crests, scrolls, and symbolic animals. American women used the same stitches but their designs were freer, with an airiness of space surrounding the motifs, and were not confined within borders. American crewel was frequently embroidered on a linen homespun that was

*98. Counterpane. Mary Swett
Bulman. York, Maine. c. 1745.
Woolen crewel yarns on
unbleached linen, 79 × 73½".
Old Gaol Museum Collection,
York, Maine. Gift of Anna
Everett*

*Because there is a unity to the
design of both the counterpane and
the rest of the bed furnishings
(see plate 97), it is assumed that
Mary Bulman designed and
executed all parts of this unique
masterpiece by herself.*

not too fine. The earliest examples were probably worked in various shades of blue. Other colors were developed when it was discovered that natural dyes could be obtained by boiling herbs and barks in water. Mary Bulman's dramatic bed furnishings are unequaled for their complexity of design and dazzling beauty. All of the valances are embroidered with the poem "Meditation in a Grove" (published in 1706 in *Horae Lyricae*) by the English minister and hymnist Isaac Watts, which concludes with the following verses:

I'll carve our passion on the bark,
And every wounded tree
Shall drop and bear some mystic mark
That Jesus dy'd for me
The swains shall wonder when they read,
Inscribed on all the grove
That heaven itself came down and bled
To win a mortal's love.

99. Candle sconce. Artist unknown. New England. 1730–50. Quillwork with pine, height 26¼". Greenfield Village and Henry Ford Museum, Dearborn, Michigan

Quillwork was comprised of tightly rolled strips of paper arranged in an elaborate pattern. Incorporated into the design were painted shells, silver and gold filigree, and delicate mica flowers. This sconce is an example of the occasional American taste for elegance in household decor and might well have been made by a young woman at a fashionable finishing school where such arts and skills were taught to the daughters of well-to-do families.

It is believed that she designed and embroidered these furnishings while her husband was serving as a surgeon under the American colonial merchant and politician Sir William Pepperrell at the siege of the French fortress of Louisbourg on Cape Breton Island in present Nova Scotia. The verses testify to her loneliness following her husband's death in 1745.

Besides being taught the refined techniques of needlework in the finishing schools, young women of fashion also learned the technique of making quillwork (plate 99), which consisted of tightly rolled, multicolored strips of paper arranged in decorative patterns or designs, decorated with painted shells, silver filigree, gold filigree, and delicate flowers fashioned out of mica. Quillwork

100. Portrait of a Lady in a Blue Gown. *Artist unknown. America. Dated 1755. Oil on canvas, 20¼ × 15½″. Hirschl and Adler Galleries, Inc., New York City*

The inclusion of a landscape painting in this interior is unusual, since by the middle of the eighteenth century American painting still consisted primarily of portraiture. The unidentified woman sits in a transitional Queen Anne–Chippendale chair with rounded stiles and crest rail. Her sumptuous satin gown and fine lace accessories denote her upper-class social position.

was framed in deep shadow boxes, many of which were fitted with a candle arm, thus functioning as a sconce. Silversmiths were commissioned to execute these brass candle arms; Jacob Hurd of Boston fashioned several which have survived.

The elegant young woman seated in a Queen Anne chair with rounded stiles (plate 100), her arm resting on a stylish tripod-base table, might well have been one of the New England beauties described by Dr. Alexander Hamilton in his narrative of a journey through the Middle Atlantic and New England states in 1744, published in Saint Louis in 1907 as *Hamilton's Itinerarium*:

This town [Newport] is as remarkable for pretty women as Albany is for ugly ones, many of whom one may see sitting in the shops in passing along the street.

I went with Moffatt in the evening to Dr. Keith's, another countryman and acquaintance, where we spent the evening very agreeably in the company of one Dr. (John) Brett, a very facetious old man. I soon found that Keith passed for a man of great gallantry here, being frequently visited by the young ladies in town, who are generally very

101. Easy chair. Maker unknown.
Rhode Island. c. 1725. Walnut
and maple, height 46¾".
Metropolitan Museum of Art,
New York City. Gift of Mrs.
J. Insley Blair, 1950

This dazzling chair in the Queen
Anne style retains its original
flamestitch needlework on the
front and sides and a crewelwork
pastoral scene on the back.
Eighteenth-century upholsterers—
or upholders, as they were known
at the time—supplied everything
from the rough frame for a chair to
the bindings and materials that
would be used to cover it. When
the upholstery was removed for
cleaning, the signature "Gardner
junr/Newport May 1758" was
discovered on the back of the
crest rail.

102. Card table. Maker unknown.
Probably Boston, Massachusetts.
1730–40. Mahogany, height
26¾". Museum of Fine Arts,
Boston, Massachusetts. Anonymous
contribution and William
Nickerson Fund

The slender cabriole leg and
shallow frame are typical of
furniture produced in New
England. The turret ends, or
round corners, were designed to
hold the circular-based candlesticks
of the period. This Queen Anne
card table, with its original
needlework cover, is an extremely
rare form. Card playing developed
into a popular pastime in the
eighteenth century.

*103. Teapot. Jacob Hurd.
Boston, Massachusetts. c. 1750.
Silver with wood, height 6⅛".
Henry Francis du Pont Winterthur
Museum, Winterthur, Delaware*

*The apple-shaped teapot was a
fashionable form during the second
quarter of the eighteenth century.
The wooden knob in the finial
prevented the tea pourer from
burning her fingers. The top of
the pot is engraved with a border
of drapery and plaited baskets
of fruit.*

airy and frolicsome. He showed me a drawer full of the trophies of the fair, which he called his cabinet of curiosities. They consisted of torn fans, fragments of gloves, whims, snuff boxes, girdles, apron-strings, laced shoes and shoe-heels, pin-cushions, hussifs [needlecases], and a deal of other such trumpery.

Most women took great pride in their artistic endeavors. A prime example of the aesthetic quality of their work was included on the beautiful Rhode Island walnut and maple easy chair (plate 101), which retains its original needlework cover. When chairs were designed to be placed in the middle of the room, frequently needlework landscapes were executed on all sides. The back of this

*104. Cream pitcher. Samuel
Casey. South Kingston, Rhode
Island. c. 1750. Silver, height
3¾". Private collection*

*This cream pitcher is beautiful in
form and chaste in its decoration.
In subsequent years Casey, like
most American silversmiths,
succumbed to the French rococo
style, and elaborate embellishment
for its own sake was rampant on
his pieces. Attractive features of
this pitcher are the graceful curves
of the handle and the modified
shell feet.*

105. Flagon. Myer Myers. New York City. c. 1760. Silver, height 10". Greenfield Village and Henry Ford Museum, Dearborn, Michigan

Born in New York of Jewish parents who had emigrated from Holland, Myers crafted ritual silver for both Jewish and Christian congregations in various American cities. This beautifully proportioned piece shows how the best metalsmiths of the period successfully adapted the rococo style to large objects.

106. Salver. Thomas Edwards. Boston, Massachusetts. 1745–55. Silver, diameter 12⅜". Henry Francis du Pont Winterthur Museum, Winterthur, Delaware. Gift of Mrs. Francis B. Crowninshield

Thomas Edwards advertised in The Boston Weekly Newsletter on May 8, 1746, that he was prepared to carry on the goldsmith trade established by his father, John Edwards, following settlement of his father's estate. Delicate engraving surrounds the inside of the salver's rim.

107. Sauceboat. Elias Boudinot. Princeton or Elizabethtown, New Jersey. c. 1760. Silver, length 7½". Philadelphia Museum of Art, Philadelphia, Pennsylvania. Purchase, McIlhenny Fund

An example of late Queen Anne silverwork, the sauceboat was created by Elias Boudinot, a smith who worked in gold and silver in Philadelphia, between 1730 and 1752, and in New Jersey. The mixture of simple hammered work with more elaborate applied decoration reflects a change of direction in this period. The ornamentation of the hoof feet and the eagle-head handle show tendencies soon to be fully exploited in the Chippendale period.

chair has a crewelwork scene that includes a shepherd in a pastoral setting, fanciful wild animals frolicking in the woods, and exotic birds in flight. The chair is notable for its from, proportion, and superior workmanship. Although the cabriole leg and pad foot first came into fashion in the 1720s, it was obviously still a significant design element by the middle of the eighteenth century. In addition to stitching covers for easy chairs, women also worked slip seats for side chairs (plate 83) and covers for gaming tables (plate 102).

Colonial women enthusiastically indulged in the ritual of tea drinking, imported from their English counterparts abroad. Teapots were generally

108. Taperstick. Wistarburgh Glassworks. Alloway, Salem County, New Jersey. 1739–77. Blown glass, height 4⅜". Henry Francis du Pont Winterthur Museum, Winterthur, Delaware

This exceedingly rare blue blown-glass eighteenth-century taperstick is probably typical of the finer products created by the Wistarburgh Glassworks, which specialized in window glass and bottles of various shapes and sizes.

fitted with wooden handles, which prevented the server from burning her hands. Many of the silver pieces derived their beauty from their graceful forms, and they were frequently enriched with elaborate engraving that was a means of positive identification—especially if these valuable objects were stolen. Jacob Hurd created some of the most beautiful teapots of the period. Hurd's apple-shaped teapot (plate 103), the cream pitcher by Samuel Casey (plate 104), the flagon by Myer Myers (plate 105), and the salver by Thomas Edwards (plate 106) are all embellished with decorative engraving. The sauceboat (plate 107) designed and executed by Elias Boudinot is striking for its undulating rim and for the handle in the form of an eagle head adapted from earlier English furniture design. Silver forms, once established, often prevailed for a period of time, for the molds used in the production of the various applied parts were expensive to create and were passed down through successive generations of metalsmiths.

Glassware was still exceedingly rare since glass manufacturing in America was unsuccessful until the second quarter of the eighteenth century. One of the first major glassmaking factories from which documented pieces survive was the Wistarburgh Glassworks established in 1739 on the banks of Alloway's Creek in Salem County, New Jersey, not far from Philadelphia, by Caspar Wistar and his son Richard. Wistar, a German who immigrated to the colonies as a young man, eventually brought over four expert glassmakers from Germany, and consequently German styles had a strong influence on early American blown glass. Window glass and bottles, as well as the globes and tubes used for chemical wares, were the primary products of the Wistarburgh works, and amber and olive green were the favorite colors because they were the hues that could most easily be produced. When Wistar died in 1752, his son continued the business until 1780. The blown-glass taperstick (plate 108), produced between 1739 and 1777, is one of the finest early pieces of blown glass attributed to Wistar.

Although from the beginning the colonists considered themselves fiercely independent, in many instances this independence was simply an involuntary response to a sense of pride in their hard-earned achievements in a new environment. Socially, culturally, and politically the inhabitants of the New World were very much tied to the Old.

When the powerful European nations battled one another, it was often over claims to the lands and to the riches that the colonies offered. From 1744 to 1748 France and Great Britain struggled for mastery of the North American continent during King George's War, which was the American phase of the much wider European conflict known as the War of the Austrian Succession. The two colonial powers were technically at peace between 1713 and 1744, but in fact they experienced recurring differences over the boundaries of Acadia (Nova Scotia) and northern New England and over control of the Ohio Valley. In 1745 the French launched an unsuccessful attack on Port Royal in Nova Scotia. In an effort to protect New England's vast trade network and rich fisheries, Governor William Shirley of Massachusetts organized forces to take over the French fortress of Louisbourg, the "Canadian Gibraltar." The American army was transported to Canada by a fleet of ninety ships and achieved the surrender of the enemy's impressive fortification after a siege of forty-nine days. In the peace treaty negotiated in 1748, however, Louisbourg was returned to the French and the American colonists were again placed at a serious military disadvantage.

The French refused to be contained and systematically began to advance their interests in the Ohio Valley. On July 4, 1754, Lieutenant Colonel George Washington of the Virginia militia was forced to surrender at Fort Necessity and return home in bitter defeat. The French philosopher Voltaire was only one of many intellectuals on both sides of the Atlantic who realized the seriousness of the political situation, and he issued a subtle warning: "Such was the complication of political interests that a cannon shot in America could give the signal that set Europe in a blaze." To offset this precarious state of affairs it is not surprising that some colonial leaders with political foresight began to press for unity among the individual colonies, and in 1754 at the Albany Congress Benjamin Franklin strongly urged colonial representatives to form an association for their mutual defense.

As the Queen Anne period drew to a close, new styles emanating from England once again inspired urban American craftsmen to pursue their work with renewed vigor. Improved transportation and communications, developing technology, and increased wealth provided the impetus for an unprecedented expansion in the following years.

Rococo Elegance in the New World
1755-1776

The Seven Years War, a worldwide struggle fought between 1756 and 1763, chiefly involved two distinct conflicts, one centered in Europe and one in North America. The contest for power in the New World, known as the French and Indian War, was the result of colonial rivalry between France and England. The Treaty of Paris, signed in 1763, effectively ended French control of Canada, with Quebec being ceded to Great Britain. The treaty also secured the Ohio River valley for the British. The colonists were jubilant over the dramatic defeat of France and for the first time felt certain about their own destiny. The colonies became less dependent militarily on England and began to think of themselves as Americans rather than British. This self-confidence was one of the contributing factors that led to the ultimate challenge of British authority and the revolutionary confrontation that resulted in America's independence.

Continued American dependence on England in matters of taste chafed many prominent political and cultural leaders. John Adams was only one who strongly advocated the development and refinement of an indigenous culture. Yet colonial families were still attracted by the prestige of a European education, and contemporary diaries and journals abound in references proving that ambitious parents sent their sons "home" to Britain for advanced schooling. The American Revolution interrupted this pattern only briefly, and when peace was declared, affluent Americans almost immediately embarked for England to take advantage of its educational and cultural opportunities.

109. Drayton Hall. Twentieth-century drawing by Stephen Thomas and Frank E. Seel. Pen and ink, dimensions unavailable. National Trust for Historic Preservation, Washington, D.C.

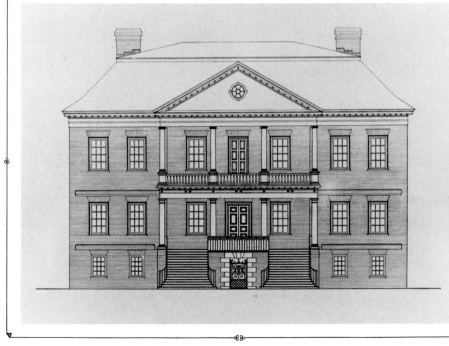

One of the major plantations of South Carolina, Drayton Hall was built on the banks of the Ashley River near Charleston, South Carolina, in 1740. Thomas Drayton constructed the house of bricks and Portland marble imported from his native England at a cost of over $90,000. "The house is an ancient building, but convenient and good," wrote a late-eighteenth-century visitor, "and the garden is better laid out . . . than any I have hitherto seen." The interior boasts elaborately carved mantelpieces and wainscoting from floor to ceiling with frames for pictures set in the mantels.

Although new native materials and the time lag in transmitting styles and tastes from the home country accounted for some examples of highly individual furniture in the middle of the century, the influence of European furniture styles and techniques was still paramount. Countless pattern books issued to instruct cabinetmakers and their clients in the niceties of design were exported to America in great quantities. The London cabinetmaker Thomas Chippendale in his first edition of *The Gentleman and Cabinet-Maker's Director*, published in 1754, offered the most complete up-to-date furniture manual. The *Director* was so successful that a year later it was reissued and in 1762 a revised and enlarged edition was prepared. Chippendale was born in Yorkshire about

110. Side chair. Maker unknown. Charleston, South Carolina. c. 1770. Mahogany, height 39¼". Greenfield Village and Henry Ford Museum, Dearborn, Michigan

This side chair in the Chippendale style is one of a set carved specifically for Drayton Hall (see plate 109); the remainder of the set is still at the mansion. Its carving is comparable in quality and style to that of the house's wainscoting. The airy feeling of the splat, the lush carving overall, and the use of mahogany throughout, including the seat blocks, are proofs of Charleston's close contact with English fashion centers. The legs, terminating in hairy paw feet, feature projecting scrolls at the knees.

1718 into a family of carpenters and furniture makers. In 1753, having resided in London for five years, he married and moved to an exclusive district more appropriate to his financial status. He maintained a prosperous shop in Saint Martin's Lane, and although he never obtained a royal appointment, his furniture designs influenced craftsmen throughout the world during the second half of the eighteenth century. His published drawings were a kind of amalgam of three major elements: Chinese design, borrowed and adapted from imported oriental objects; medieval Gothic style, never completely out of fashion in England; and the exquisite refinement of rococo—rococo apparently being a contraction of the French terms *rocailles* and *coquilles* (rocks and shells), natural forms in the Italian baroque style.

111. Highboy. Maker unknown.
Philadelphia, Pennsylvania.
1760–80. Mahogany, cedar, tulip,
and poplar, height 91½".
Metropolitan Museum of Art,
New York City. Kennedy Fund,
1918

During the 1720s and 1730s
English architecture influenced
English furniture design. It also
influenced American forms at a
later date when ornamental
details were borrowed from the
classical entablature of architrave,
frieze, and cornice. The broken
pediment on this richly carved
baroque piece in the Chippendale
style is accented by carved columns
at the side, which are similar to
the pilasters that flank doorways
and chimney breasts.

112. Lowboy. Maker unknown.
Philadelphia, Pennsylvania.
1760–80. Mahogany, height
31⅞". Museum of Fine Arts,
Boston, Massachusetts. M. and
M. Karolik Collection

Chinese motifs featured in Thomas
Chippendale's Gentleman and
Cabinet-Maker's Director
(1754) might have been the
inspiration for the Chinese
fretwork on the frieze of this
Chippendale-style dressing table.
Floral pendants embellish the inset
columns, and rococo leaflike
designs surround the carved swan.

In his preface to the *Director*, Chippendale made it clear that he was willing to stake his reputation on the clarity and ease with which his patterns and models could be realized:

Upon the whole, I have here given no design but what may be executed with advantage by the hands of a skilful workman, tho' some of the profession have been diligent enough to represent them (especially those after the Gothic and Chinese manner) as so many specious drawings, impossible to be work'd off by any mechanic whatsoever. I will not scruple to attribute this to malice, ignorance and inability: and I am confident I can convince all Noblemen, Gentlemen, or others, who will honour me with their commands, that every design in the book can be improved, both as to beauty and enrichment, in the execution of it, by Their Most Obedient Servant.   THOMAS CHIPPENDALE

The original subscribers to Chippendale's publication are a clear indication of his prominence as a designer. Not only the nobility and men of means but also cabinetmakers, upholsterers, carpenters, joiners, carvers, plasterers, and picture framers hoped to derive, through subscription, benefits from exposure to this talented man's design ideas. Chippendale was not the innovator of the style that bears his name. He was an astute compiler of contemporary taste, gathering together in one place the most current styles promoted by English furniture designers. The naming of a thirty-five-year period of furniture making after this gifted craftsman is testimony to the influence of Chippendale and his publication.

The importance of the *Director* was particularly discernible in Philadelphia, where it inspired a school of cabinetmaking and chairmaking that ultimately developed into the most sophisticated and cohesive furniture design movement in the history of American decorative arts. The Library Company of Philadelphia in its 1769 catalog included the third edition, the revised version of 1762, of Chippendale's *Director*. Thomas Affleck, a distinguished Pennsylvania cabinetmaker, originally from Aberdeen, Scotland, kept a copy of Chippendale's book of designs by his side, and the highly gifted Benjamin Randolph also personally relied upon Chippendale's work extensively.

As in earlier periods, regional variations abounded. Philadelphia craftsmen, following contemporary English taste, were particularly intrigued by the English adaptation of the French rococo (plates 111, 112, 116). Three-dimensional carved motifs laid onto curvilinear frames reflected an elegance never before achieved in American furniture making. The South, with its close ties to England, preferred this robust organic style (plate 110) to the more restrained productions created in New England's centers of cabinetmaking, such as Newport and Boston (plates 122, 125, 126).

During the 1740s, when John Drayton erected his impressive plantation house on the Ashley River at Charleston, South Carolina, he chose to embellish the structure with modern interpretations of the classical style borrowed from the sixteenth-century treatise *The Four Books of Architecture,* of the great Italian Renaissance architect and designer Andrea Palladio, which was translated into English in 1716. The Ionic and Tuscan columns supporting the balcony and pediment of the plantation house facade (plate 109) are derived directly from Palladio's treatise. The interior of this stylish mansion was fully paneled and the fireplaces were ornately carved in patterns freely borrowed from English design books. Many of the furnishings were sumptuous and the seating pieces (plate 110) were decorated with carvings of shells and floral motifs. Carved hairy paw feet, an unusual but not unique feature in American cabinetmaking, terminate the front legs of these chairs.

The claw-and-ball feet on the Philadelphia highboy (plate 111) and lowboy (plate 112) were far more typical of the contemporary style. Finely detailed carvings of rococo leaves and animals, possibly derived from French and English illustrated editions of Aesop's *Fables,* decorate the lower drawers on both of these pieces. The second edition of Chippendale's *Director,* as well as the expanded third edition, included similar sketches from the famous fables. The

OVERLEAF:

113. Museum installation. Chinese Parlor. America. Third quarter of eighteenth century. Henry Francis du Pont Winterthur Museum, Winterthur, Delaware

The Chinese Parlor is so-named because the furniture and accessories depict the influence of Chinese design on Western decorative arts. The walls are covered with Chinese wallpaper, circa 1770, providing an appropriate setting for American Chippendale furniture. Thomas Chippendale was fascinated with all types of oriental design and included in his Director *many drawings for furniture incorporating these motifs.*

highboy is topped with a broken-scroll pediment centered with a carved bust of an elegant woman, perhaps intended to represent the marquise de Pompadour. Pierced brasses on the lowboy give an additional airiness to the design. Both the highboy and lowboy have carved columns at the sides and these are also enhanced by the addition of delicate patterned designs. The American Chippendale highboy, with its tall scrolled pediment and richly carved drawers in the top and bottom, has no parallel in English furniture design. The typical lowboy, with inset quarter columns and shell-carved drawer, is also decidedly American.

Cabinetmakers in this period favored elaborate embellishment, and the marlborough leg on the blocked-foot mahogany and white oak armchair (plate

114. Upholstered open armchair. Thomas Affleck (attr.). Philadelphia, Pennsylvania. 1760–80. Mahogany and white oak, height 42¾". Colonial Williamsburg Foundation, Williamsburg, Virginia

This chair in the Chippendale style is believed to be part of a set originally purchased by Governor John Penn for his home, Lansdowne. The marlborough leg ending in a block foot has a paneled inset of husks and strapwork carved in relief. Upholstered chairs with open arms were based on the French seating form, the fauteuil, and were called French chairs by Chippendale.

114) with its pendant carving down the face of the leg reflects this interest. The straight leg in Chippendale furniture can be traced to sketches made by the English adventurer Sir William Chambers on a trip to China in the 1740s. American furniture with blocked feet usually emanated from Philadelphia; yet Rhode Island examples are known as well.

Although Americans had little direct contact with China until 1784, Chinese goods were imported in vast quantity on English ships after the mid-seventeenth century. Chinese wallpaper was the supreme status symbol in the affluent American home. The walls of the Chinese Parlor (plate 113), covered with soft-hued paper dating from around 1770, depict scenes of daily life in an oriental village. Of special interest in this interior is the easy chair at the right of the

*Chippendale sofas are not
common, and those that do remain
usually have cabriole legs and
claw-and-ball feet. A few,
however, have marlborough legs
and block feet, similar to those
on the upholstered open armchair
(see plate 114).*

fireplace. It is one of a set attributed to the Philadelphia cabinetmaker Benjamin
Randolph, who regularly advertised chairwork in the Chinese and modern
modes. The Newport gaming table in front of the window is surrounded by
chairs attributed to James Gillingham, another Philadelphia chairmaker, who
relied heavily upon Chippendale's *Director* as a guide in fashioning the Gothic
backs of the chairs. In front of the sofa is a carved stand from Charleston, South

*In France and to some extent in
England eighteenth-century rococo
design was willfully asymmetrical.
But in America symmetry, as
exemplified by this Chippendale-
style looking glass, appealed to
cabinetmakers as well as to their
clients; American furniture with
asymmetrical designs is
considerably rarer.*

Carolina, and on it sits a silver teakettle made by Edward Lownes of Philadelphia in the early years of the nineteenth century. Wrought in the rococo style, it shows a lingering interest by silversmiths in Chippendale's designs. Elias Haskett Derby, one of America's richest merchant princes, was among the first to engage in serious trade with China, and the sections of the black and gold lacquer screen were brought to his hometown, Salem, aboard one of his fast sailing ships. The shell cupboard is filled with Chinese export porcelain, or penciled ware as it was known in the period. An impressive English cut-glass chandelier hangs in the center of the room.

While few citizens could afford such luxurious surroundings, Benjamin Franklin's wife, Deborah, described her efforts at redecorating their home in a letter to her husband penned in the fall of 1765, which is striking for its quaint phonetic spelling:

The little Southroom I had papered as the wales was much soyled. In that is a pritey Card tabel and our Chairs that yoused to stand in the parler and orney mental Chaney over the fierplase on the flower a Carpit I bought cheep for the goodnes. It is not quite new. The large Carpit is in the blewroom the fier not maid yit in the room for our friends. The Pickter of the Erel of Bute is hung up and a Glase. This is but a verey imperfeckte a counte.

It is obvious that wallpapers were greatly treasured, for they are mentioned in both published and unpublished sources time and again. In a signed advertisement in the *New Hampshire Gazette and Historical Chronicle* for May 5, 1769, Jonathan Warner made the following plea: "Whereas some evil-minded, malicious Person or Persons, have in a most scandalous Manner abused the house of John Tufton Mason, Esq; under my Care, by breaking the Windows and defacing the Paper Hangings in the Rooms, and very lately stealing away the Brass Knocker from the Front Door, I do hereby offer a Reward of Three Dollars to any one who will discover any Person concerned in said Theft, so that they may be convicted thereof; either as Principals or Accessories."

In the second half of the eighteenth century the city of Charleston, South Carolina, grew at an astonishing rate. The bustling activity involving a burgeoning merchant class stimulated the building of many magnificent homes similar to Drayton Hall, which had been constructed thirty years earlier, and thus talented architects and builders from several colonies were attracted to the area. Much of the furnishing for these homes was imported from England as well as from other colonies, but there were significant items fashioned in local shops like the one maintained by the upholsterer John Linton. In 1780 Linton moved from Charleston to Philadelphia, where he is recorded as an upholder, or upholsterer. His name is chalked onto the frame of the camelback sofa (plate 115). The sofa is one of a pair that would have been made for the kind of ornamental parlor that might have also included the ornate carved looking glass (plate 116), also possibly from Philadelphia.

Chippendale case pieces such as serpentine bureaus or chests of drawers rely upon finely figured and grained woods for their ornamental value. Although relatively simple in construction, a chest of drawers (plate 117) by another Philadelphia cabinetmaker, Jonathan Gostelowe, is a masterpiece of American furniture design. Cabinetmakers were subject to stiff taxes, and in 1783 Thomas Affleck was assessed and had to pay an occupational tax of 250 pounds. This large amount proves his prominence as a leading craftsman, for Gostelowe paid 100 pounds and Thomas Tufft, noted particularly for his chairs, only 50 pounds.

Mahogany was the predominant cabinet wood favored in Philadelphia during the Chippendale period. It was imported from Honduras and Santo Domingo and provided the material for the craftsmen who fashioned the tea table and easy chair (plate 118). There is a delicate and subtle contrast between the richly carved legs and supporting stem of the table and the simple yet beautiful legs of the chair. The candlestick on the tea table is of the Battersea type and

Gostelowe is best known for his chests with serpentine fronts, large molded ogee bracket feet, and carved fluted pilasters on the canted corners. This chest in the Chippendale style bears Gostelowe's label. The ormolu mounts simulate French rococo style.

117. Chest of drawers. Jonathan Gostelowe. Philadelphia, Pennsylvania. c. 1770. Mahogany, height 36¼''. Philadelaphia Museum of Art, Philadelphia, Pennsylvania. Temple Fund

118. Tea table. Maker unknown. Philadelphia, Pennsylvania. 1760–80. Mahogany, diameter 32''.
Footstool. Maker unknown. England. c. 1720. Walnut, height 16½''.
Easy chair. Benjamin Randolph. Philadelphia, Pennsylvania. c. 1760. Mahogany, height 47''. All Greenfield Village and Henry Ford Museum, Dearborn, Michigan

The furnishings of a typical affluent home, exemplified in this museum installation, reflect the taste of the highest social levels of colonial America. As was common in the eighteenth century, many of the fine accessories were imported from England, such as the Battersea enameled copper candlestick, the Staffordshire teapot, and the tea bowls and saucers produced at the Lowestoft Porcelain Factory. The oil portrait of a member of the Van Schenck family was painted circa 1750 in New York City by John Wollaston.

is finished with enamel on copper. This interior represents the achievements in taste of the most affluent social levels from several American colonies, with many of the expensive household accessories still being imported from England.

Chippendale seating pieces were usually equipped with slip seats (plate 119) so that the upholstery could be changed easily to accommodate the color scheme of a room and to suit the mood of the owner. One way of updating an interior without incurring the extreme costs of purchasing new furniture was to reupholster old pieces and acquire new matching curtains or window hangings. The Queen Anne footstool (plate 118) in the midst of Chippendale objects shows an unwillingness to cast aside something that had gone out of style but was still useful. This piece, because it was beautifully crafted, would have had its slip seat refurbished as tastes dictated through the years. Upholstery and upholstering were extremely expensive. Both John and Nicholas Brown of Providence, Rhode Island, ordered easy chairs from Plunket Fleeson in Philadelphia during the 1760s. A 1764 dated invoice to John Brown (now in the John Carter Brown Library, Brown University, Providence) underscores the high costs involved in the acquisition of such a piece. The invoice is tallied in pounds, shillings, and pence, the colonial unit of account, since the U.S. dollar was not established as currency until after the Revolution.

1764	To Plunket Fleeson D[ebto]r
April 13th	
To a Mahogany Easy Chair Frame	£ 2:05:00
To Bottoming 6 chairs @ 5/	1:10:10
To 11 Yds Harateen @ 4/	2:04:00
To 13 Yds Canvas for thee Chair @ 1/6	19:00
To 8 lbs Curled Hair @ 1/10	14:00
To girth & Tax	07:00
To 3⁴ of Feathers @ 3/	10:06
To 1⁴ Yds of Ticken @ 3/6	05:03
To 18 Yds Silk Lace @ 8d	12:00
To Thread Silk & Cord	03.00
To a sett castors	08:00
To making the Easy Chair	1:15:00
	£ 11:13:11

The New York school of cabinetmaking often came up with something grand. The squareness of the claw-and-ball feet on the five-legged card table (plate 120) is typical of the elegance with which pieces from this area were imbued. Equally familiar on New York furniture is the serpentine front and the carved gadrooning on the apron. The slender cabriole legs ending in elongated claw-and-ball feet and the overall undulations of this table distinguish it from the normally solid and less curvilinear objects associated with the New York colony. The design on the eighteenth-century imported tobacco jar placed on the table depicts the native American Indian surrounded by representations of the tobacco leaf.

The chest-on-chest (plate 121) is one of the most elegant examples of Chippendale furniture emanating from Newport, Rhode Island. The blocked drawers in the lower and upper sections are enhanced by nine magnificently carved shells. A well-balanced broken-scroll pediment is centered with and flanked by delicate finials—classical urns with flames. Rhode Island furniture is usually crafted of mahogany; cedar, which grew in great abundance in the area, was utilized as a secondary wood for drawer linings and for chair and table blocks. The drop-leaf table (plate 122), simple in design, is especially noteworthy for its claw-and-ball feet with open talons. Carved open talon feet are nearly always associated with Rhode Island cabinetmaking. The tall-case clock (plate 123), also of Rhode Island origin, has a blocked door that includes a carved convex shell. Although the urn finials vary somewhat from those on the chest-on-chest, they strongly suggest a Newport attribution.

A comparison between the Rhode Island side chair with stop-fluted front legs and pierced splat (plate 124), and the Drayton Hall chair (plate 110) offers succinct evidence that rococo elements were being replaced by classical details of design. Since few documented pieces have been traced to other craftsmen, carved stop fluting as a dominant feature of Rhode Island furniture design is generally attributed to the shops of the Goddards and Townsends. The Quaker Goddard-Townsend dynasty of cabinetmakers, long associated with the elegant furniture produced in Newport, worked in the vicinity of that busy seaport for three generations, covering both the Queen Anne and Chippendale periods.

119. Armchair. Maker unknown. Philadelphia, Pennsylvania. 1755–80. Pine, height 40". H. and R. Sandor, Inc., Philadelphia, Pennsylvania

This representative form was a popular version of the Chippendale chair in Pennsylvania. A carved shell centers both the crest rail and the seat rail. These utilitarian chairs were made more comfortable by the addition of an upholstered removable slip seat.

Toward the end of the eighteenth century the trend toward rectilinear furniture reasserted itself. The fluted pilasters with Ionic capitals that flank the wooden paneled doors on the bombe secretary-desk (plate 125) reflect the new interest in both classicism and rectilinear design. Since furniture of this type was infrequently produced in England, the bombe, or kettle-shaped, base was probably inspired by baroque traditions introduced from Holland and other European countries. American examples are also uncommon. Although the doors in the upper section of bombe secretary-desks are sometimes mirrored, many have solid wooden panels.

New Englanders clung tenaciously to sturdy craftsmanship, and even in the Chippendale period easy chairs and open armchairs (plate 126) continued to

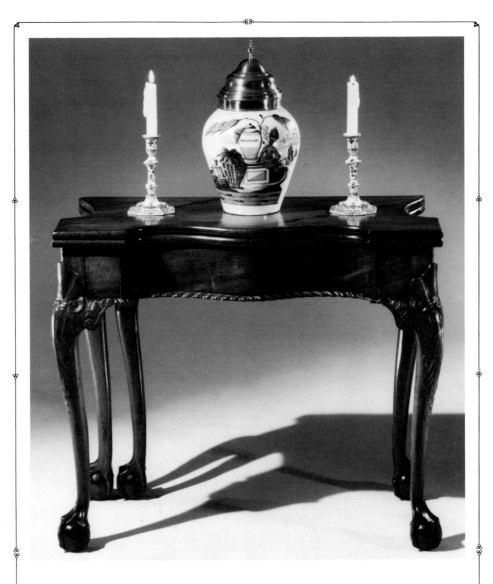

120. Card table. Maker unknown. New York. c. 1770. Mahogany, cherry, and oak, width 34¼''. Greenfield Village and Henry Ford Museum, Dearborn, Michigan

be constructed with legs that were braced by stretchers. With a seat that was ample and close to the floor and a back that was vertical and high, this richly carved chair has arms that terminate in the form of a bird's head and wing.

The Windsor chair (plates 127, 128) had its origins in the Gothic style of fifteenth-century England. Saint Cross Hospital in Winchester owns an ancient chair that is a prototype for adaptations in the sixteenth, seventeenth, and eighteenth centuries. These later versions were in turn the models that inspired colonial craftsmen. The English Windsor chair, while immensely popular, never achieved the acceptance that its American counterpart enjoyed. Thomas Chippendale omitted illusrtrations of the commonplace form in his 1754 *Director*, because it was considered fit only for country folk and for gardens and porches. Yet in America the Windsor was the universal chair of the eighteenth century. The most eminent and prosperous chose to live with Windsors. Thomas Jefferson, while struggling with the first draft of the Declaration of Independence in June 1776, sat in a writing-arm Windsor. Benjamin Franklin and other members of the Continental Congress when voting to secede from the parent country on July 4, 1776, were seated on Windsors in Independence Hall. There are essentially seven basic varieties of Windsor chair design: the comb, fan, bar, arch, loop, rod, and lowback. These forms were made in Philadelphia, the birthplace of the American Windsor, and shipped to other colonies along the eastern seaboard, where they served as guides for local cabinetmakers. These craftsmen, from diverse backgrounds, adapted, refined, and embellished the basic designs and developed countless variants of the Windsor chair (plate 128).

The house illustrated in the wood-panel painting of Moses Marcy (plate 129) might well have included Windsor chairs among its furnishings. Decorative mantels and overmantels often embellished the main rooms of contemporary affluent homes. Marcy, a splendidly dressed New England merchant, is

122. Drop-leaf table. Maker unknown. Rhode Island. c. 1770. Walnut, maple, and pine, width 37¾″. Greenfield Village and Henry Ford Museum, Dearborn, Michigan

This table in the Chippendale style features open talons on the claw-and-ball feet, which support squared cabriole legs. The carved open talon is a feature almost exclusively associated with Rhode Island furniture.

at leisure enjoying his clay pipe and a glass of punch. But near at hand, resting on the table, is another adjunct of the prosperous, financially active gentleman—what appears to be an account book awaiting his attention.

Successful merchants comprised part of a developing upper-class society. The prominent British statesman and political thinker Edmund Burke, writing in 1758, described in detail New York mercantile activity and some of the reasons for its success:

The town has a very flourishing trade, and in which great profits are made. The merchants are wealthy, and the people in general most comfortably provided for, and with a moderate labour. From the year 1749 to 1750 two hundred and thirty-two vessels have been entered in this port, and two hundred and eighty-six cleared outwards. In these vessels were shipped six thousand seven hundred and thirty-one tons of provisions, chiefly flour, and a vast quantity of grain; of which I have no particular account. In the year 1755 the export of flax seed to Ireland amounted to 12,528 hogsheads. The inhabitants are between eighty and an hundred thousand; the lower class easy, the better rich, and hospitable; great freedom of society; and the entry to foreigners made easy by a general toleration of all religious persuasions. In a word, this province yields to no part of America in the healthfulness of its air, and the fertility of its soil. It is much superior in the great convenience of water carriage, which speedily and at the slightest expense carries the product of the remotest farms to a certain and profitable market.

John Dunlap is perhaps the best known craftsman of the Dunlap dynasty of furniture makers from New Hampshire. With his cabinetmaking relatives he created a unique style of country furniture out of the familiar Chippendale vocabulary, fashioning maple chairs (plate 130) during the late eighteenth and early nineteenth centuries. The seat rail and top rail are carved with a depressed fan and the splat is pierced with S-scrolls. Other forms constructed by these gifted craftsmen include highboys, lowboys, and chests-on-chests, as well as a paneled room end with a richly carved corner cupboard, which is now part of the collections at the Henry Francis du Pont Winterthur Museum in Delaware.

Painted or printed bedspreads, or counterpanes, came into vogue in the seventeenth century when English versions of Indian calico, or chintz, were imported extensively. By the middle of the eighteenth century chintz had be-

123. Tall-case clock. Maker unknown. Rhode Island. c. 1785. Mahogany and pine, height 91¾″. Greenfield Village and Henry Ford Museum, Dearborn, Michigan

Blocking, which appears on the front of chests, desks, secretaries, and tables, is a common feature of clocks, such as this one in the Chippendale style. The four freestanding columns on the hood and the urn–and–flame finials demonstrate close links between Philadelphia and Newport cabinetmaking. The blocked door with shell decoration and the stylized rosettes terminating the scrolls on the pediment are proofs of a Rhode Island origin.

come the most sought-after fabric. The eighteenth century introduced copper-plate-printed fabrics and toiles. Benjamin Franklin, writing to his wife in 1758 about a purchase of printed cotton, reveals his customary curiosity about the new technique: "56 Yards of Cotton printed curiously from Copper Plates, a new Invention, to make Bed and Window Curtains; and 7 Yards Chair Bottoms printed in the same Way, very neat; these were my Fancy; but Mrs. Stevenson tells me I did wrong not to buy both of the same Colour. Also 7 Yards of printed Cotton, blue Ground, to make you a Gown; I bought it by Candlelight, and lik'd it then, but not so well afterwards."

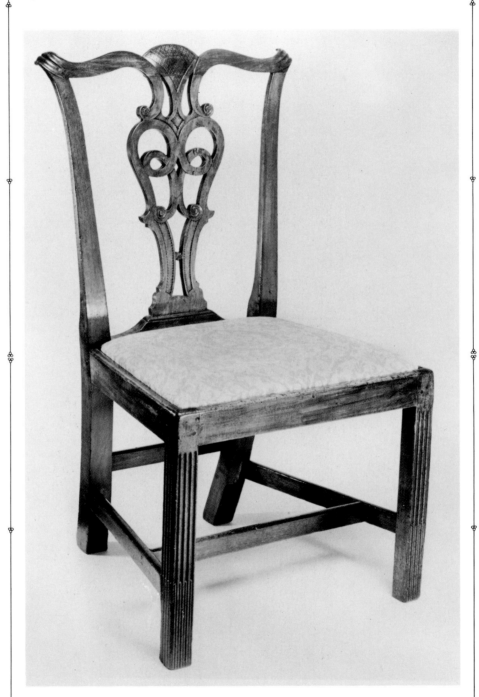

124. Side chair. Maker unknown. Newport, Rhode Island. c. 1780. Walnut, height 37″. Collection Joseph K. Ott

Cross-hatching on the top rail and upper part of the splat and carved stop fluting are features often encountered on Rhode Island furniture. Simplified, less sophisticated versions of this Chippendale-style chair are found in the Hartford, Connecticut, area. The similarity of details on furniture from these two neighboring regions becomes more obvious in the Federal period.

One of the most important eighteenth-century textile printers in America was John Hewson, who worked in Philadelphia after 1773. Hewson, an Englishman who completed his apprenticeship in his native country, came to America at the urging of Benjamin Franklin. The printed cotton spread (plate 131), attributed to Hewson, is a superb example of the great skill with which this man executed his trade. Martha Washington ordered handkerchiefs from him for her husband, George, and his fabrics were esteemed by America's well-to-do families. This spread is a priceless example of eighteenth-century American printed fabric. Only two complete spreads by Hewson are known, but some

125. Secretary-desk. Maker unknown. Boston, Massachusetts. 1760. Mahogany, height 99½″. Museum of Fine Arts, Boston, Massachusetts. Bequest of Charlotte Hazan

The fine imported, beautifully grained mahogany and the superb carving on the base, the pilasters flanking the doors, and the filigree rosette streamers from the scrolled pediment combine to make this Chippendale case piece an exceedingly rich work of art. Few pieces in the bombe style are as elegant.

of the fragments of his printed textiles have been used in pieced quilts of later periods.

The art of needlework continued to serve a kind of utilitarian function in the area of decoration. A fine example is the pole screen (plate 132), which originally belonged to William Samuel Johnson, delegate from Connecticut to the Constitutional Convention and Continental Congress; it has a needlework picture executed by his four daughters. The stem of the stand is carved in a corkscrew device that enables the screen to be adjusted. The pole screen was actually a fire screen that shielded people from the roaring fires necessary to heat colonial homes.

Few porcelain manufacturers were successful in eighteenth-century America, and what was produced in the second half of the century was largely utilitarian compared to the increasingly sophisticated porcelains and other ceramics created in European factories. To satisfy the demand for fine wares, ships arrived almost daily laden with expensive bric-a-brac. The shell cupboard (plate 133) is stocked with specific imported pieces that were included in an advertisement (plate 135) in the *New York Gazette* in 1771. The advertisement announces a load of imported porcelain and other household items to be sold, "wholesale and retale," including plain and copperplated Queen Anne's ware, glass, delft ware, white stoneware, as well as "Collyflower Ware, Tortois Shell, and Agate Ware."

126. Upholstered open armchair. Maker unknown. Massachusetts. c. 1750. Mahogany, height 42¾". Greenfield Village and Henry Ford Museum, Dearborn, Michigan

This fine example in the Chippendale style exhibits a very tall back, a broad seat close to the floor, and typical block and turned stretchers between the legs. It is upholstered in scarlet damask similar to that imported in 1760 from London by the Boston firm of Hunt and Torrey. Carved birds serve as arm terminals.

In an effort to capitalize on the American demand for porcelain, Gousse Bonnin and George Anthony Morris established a factory in Philadelphia in 1770, where they produced the first American soft-paste porcelain that has survived. The factory consisted of three kilns, two furnaces, two mills, two clay vaults, cisterns, engines, and treading room. The two potters hired young English workmen and brought in clay from nearby Delaware. Their pieces are generally decorated in blue and white and many of them are rococo in design. The pierced sides and top of the covered basket (plate 134) are decorated with floral rosettes. The cover is fitted with a floral handle as well.

Metal objects were also greatly in demand. While the extraction of ore from the earth and new refining processes improved the supply of metal substantially, it was not nearly enough to satisfy the citizens' demand for finely

127. Comb-back Windsor writing-arm chair. Maker unknown. New England. 1760–90. Maple, hickory, white pine, and butternut, height 46⅛". Greenfield Village and Henry Ford Museum, Dearborn, Michigan

Shallow, dovetailed, sliding drawers are fitted below the writing-arm surface and the shaped saddle seat. The writing-arm Windsor chair, generally with a comb back, like so many other forms apparently originated in Philadelphia. A resident of that city, writing in the spring of 1763, recorded his order for two such chairs from "Richmonde on Sassafras Street, a joiner of much repute who has come out from the Motherland." This same writer, perhaps sitting with quill and sander in hand in one of the newly acquired chairs, later reported: "Chairs arrived, am so pleased, shall not take them to country."

wrought metal objects. American metalsmiths, even if they worked inordinately long hours, could not provide pieces sufficient for the needs of the rapidly expanding population. The trade card of Boston merchant Lewis Deblois (plate 136), printed in 1757, announced that this ambitious shopkeeper imported twice a year from London a "Great assortment of Iron Mongery Founder's, Brazier's

128. Museum installation. Commons Room. Delaware. Early nineteenth century. Henry Francis du Pont Winterthur Museum, Winterthur, Delaware

The woodwork in the stairway in this interior is from the Red Lion Inn, built in the early nineteenth century at Red Lion, New Castle County, Delaware. A wide variety of eighteenth-century Windsor chair forms and a rare triple-chair-back settee provide the seating for a room furnished with country furniture. Windsors were nearly always painted—the colors being black, red, blue, green, or yellow. Early collectors zealously cleaned their prized Windsors of the original paint and stained them with what they believed to be authentic early American orange varnishes and shellacs. Today museums across the country are stripping these twentieth-century finishes from the Windsors in their collections and repainting them to match the original colors.

129. Overmantel panel. Artist
unknown. Massachusetts. Middle
of eighteenth century. Oil on wood
panel, 41 × 27⅞". Old
Sturbridge Village, Sturbridge,
Massachusetts

*This overmantel painting, which
depicts Moses Marcy standing at a
table in front of his gambrel-
roofed house located at
Southbridge, Massachusetts, is a
splendid document of New England
merchant activity. The book on the
table possibly is an account book
in which the wealthy mill owner
kept a record of his financial
endeavors.*

& Cutlery Ware. Also sundry sorts of English Goods, Spices, Musick Books,
Instruments & Strings; together with a very great Variety of other Kind of
Goods which if enumerated here would be tedious for the Reader." Deblois's
card assured the buyer that his prices were fully competitive with any shop in
Boston and that he was capable of shipping to anyone in the nearby vicinity
who could not conveniently come to town.

In spite of the competition of European goods American silversmiths were
highly successful. Paul Revere, the folk hero of the American Revolution, was
a master silversmith—a craft he learned from his father, a Huguenot refugee
in the New World. A noted portrait of Revere by John Singleton Copley shows
him working on a handsome Queen Anne teakettle with wooden handle (plate
137). The simplicity of the kettle Revere is holding in his left hand contrasts
dramatically with the asymmetrical silver cruet stand with glass casters (plate
138) fashioned in 1765 for the New Jersey Ringgold family by John David of
Philadelphia. The ruffled cartouche and the curvilinear cinquefoil frame exhibit
the very latest taste, with its interest in a combination of European and American interpretation of rococo design. Also expressive of the mature American
rococo style is the silver coffeepot (plate 139) designed by the Philadelphia silversmith Philip Syng, Jr. The cover of the elaborately wrought repoussé pot
is topped by a cast pineapple finial. The New York silversmith Lewis Fueter
was noted for particularly fine and delicate work. Fueter was responsible for the

A nearly identical chair in the Chippendale style, also retaining its original needlework seat, is in the collection of the Henry Francis du Pont Winterthur Museum in Delaware. The top rail of these pieces forms a cupid's bow. Country Chippendale furniture is often eccentric and retains a vertical profile from much earlier periods. This profile contrasts with the sensuous undulating forms popular in the major centers of cabinetmaking like Philadelphia.

130. Side chair. John Dunlap. New Hampshire. c. 1775. Maple, height 44⅞". Metropolitan Museum of Art, New York City. Gift of Mrs. J. Insley Blair, 1943

beautiful silver handles, tiny claw-and-ball feet, and elegant latches on the set of three knife boxes (plate 140), which were originally crafted for the New York Stuyvesant family.

The flagon, covered chalice, and paten (plate 141) were shaped by Johann Christophe Heyne, active in Lancaster, Pennsylvania, in the third quarter of the

131. Bedcover. John Hewson. Probably Philadelphia, Pennsylvania. 1780–1800. Cotton, 106¾ × 103¼". Henry Francis du Pont Winterthur Museum, Winterthur, Delaware

Few examples of American-printed eighteenth-century fabrics can be positively identified as to their maker. This superb spread has been definitely assigned to the highly skilled textile printer John Hewson, who was born in England and worked in Philadelphia. Two complete Hewson spreads are known, and some fragments of his printed fabrics have been appliquéd onto other spreads.

132. *Pole screen. Maker unknown. Probably Connecticut. Third quarter of eighteenth century. Mahogany, height 55½". Private collection*

Pole screens served as shields from the roaring fires that heated colonial homes. This example in the Chippendale style originally belonged to William Samuel Johnson, a distinguished politician and the first president of Columbia University. The floral and vase needlework pattern is attributed to Johnson's daughters.

eighteenth century. Like many other colonial craftsmen, Heyne had his training in Europe before immigrating to America. He crafted these pieces in a style he had learned while training in his native Germany and working in Scandinavia. This communion service was commissioned by the Canadochly Lutheran Church in York County, Pennsylvania.

Until the revolutionary war, pewter was imported from England in great quantities. The few examples of objects made from this alloy in the first half of the eighteenth century proves that colonial craftsmen did not attempt to

133. Corner cupboard (detail). Maker unknown. New England. 1760–70. Pine, overall height 83½". Greenfield Village and Henry Ford Museum, Dearborn, Michigan

This painted pine cupboard has a finely shaped shell and fluted pilasters flanking deeply cut butterfly shelves. The cupboard displays types of English pottery and glass that were being imported in great quantities in the 1760s and 1770s.

equal the range of European forms, concentrating instead on necessities such as basins, plates, and spoons. American pewter styles in the second half of the century were inevitably behind the times. A striking example of this démodé design is the set of cast feet on Heyne's flagon, which are in the form of masks—devices long out of date in major style centers.

The carousing gentlemen at a social gathering, shown in the black ink and wash drawing (plate 142) by George Roupell, sit at a large table appropriately equipped with many of the latest amenities. A punchbowl and ladle and ornate Chippendale candlesticks, probably brass, are in every way up-to-date. The long-stemmed goblets and the decanters and bottles of spirits probably would have been imported. Drinking vessels made of glass were still costly at mid-century, as a brief article in the December 31, 1753, edition of the *New York Gazette, or The Weekly Post Boy* sadly reports:

You must understand, Sir, that I have for some years past borne, with uncommon Patience, the Lashes of an ill-natur'd Husband, who constantly made it a Practice, to stay at a slop-shop till he had drowned his Senses in Rum, his Darling Delight, and then poor I must stand clear; for the merciless Wretch wou'd spare neither my Tea Cups or Saucers to throw at my Head, besides whipping of me; but I must do him the Justice to acknowledge, that he always had Compassion on the Rum Glasses, which stood close by them; and tho' we had but two of those Glasses for these Eight or Ten Years, yet they have liv'd to see as many Dozen of Tea Cups and Saucers broke over my Head; for he says if I can't drink my Tea out of these Glasses, I shall go without; which I had rather do; for I shou'd imagine I was drinking Rum instead of Tea, and I think he need not be so hard upon me, for they never cost him a Penny; but his destroying of 'em has brought me so low, that I have no more Apparel than I at present have on, and I will have Tea Cups and Saucers if I pawn my very Shift: for I must own I love Tea as well as he loves Rum.

Had the gentleman actually thrown his glass, a practical, yet unorthodox suggestion for mending the broken piece was included in *Poor Richard Improved for the Year 1768*, printed in Philadelphia by David Hall as a continuation of Benjamin Franklin's annual "almanack and ephemeris": "An exceeding fine Cement to mend broken China or Glasses. Garlick, stamped in a Stone Mortar, the Juice whereof, when applied to the Pieces to be joined together, is the finest and strongest Cement for that Purpose, and will leave little or no Mark, if done with Care."

By the 1760s several glassmaking factories, at the time known as glasshouses, were in operation in New Jersey and southeastern Pennsylvania, which became an important center of glassmaking between 1763 and 1774. A German

134. *Basket with cover. Bonnin and Morris. Philadelphia, Pennsylvania. c. 1770–72. Soft-paste porcelain, height 3¾". Colonial Williamsburg Foundation, Williamsburg, Virginia*

The factory of Gousse Bonnin and George Anthony Morris is believed to have produced the first American porcelain, but very few examples remain. Of special interest, along with this porcelain basket with blue underglaze decoration, is a sweetmeat dish in the shape of imported shells in the collection of the Brooklyn Museum in New York.

immigrant, Henry William Stiegel, arrived in Philadelphia in 1750. Eight years later not only had this ambitious young man established himself as a partner in the ironworks of Jacob Huber, he had also married Huber's daughter, fathered two daughters, become a widower, remarried, and set up another iron foundry. He was enthralled with glassmaking; in a brief six years he organized three factories—the Elizabeth Furnace in 1763, a glassworks at Manheim in 1765, and a second one at Manheim in 1769—all located in Lancaster County, Pennsylvania. Although he named the second Manheim glassworks facility the American Flint Glass Works, Stiegel staffed it with continental and English craftsmen. Stiegel's artists produced pattern-molded sugar molds, bottles, and saltcellars in various colors including numerous shades of blue, green, and amethyst. In addition to pattern-molded glass, Stiegel's craftsmen produced tableware often enameled with familiar Pennsylvania German motifs such as birds, hearts, and tulips. The mug attributed to Stiegel (plate 143) was formed from white flint glass. Shortly before the Revolution, sales declined, and Stiegel, who had in a few years become so prosperous he was dubbed the Baron, was faced with bankruptcy. The sale of his foundries and numerous other real estate holdings unfortunately was not sufficient to stem the tide, and in 1774 Baron Stiegel was clapped in terns, and hat trimmings, &c. wholesale and retail , ...

JUST IMPORTED,

And to be sold, wholesale and retale, at the west-side of the Exchange, fronting the Great Dock, by

FLORES BANCKER,

A LARGE, neat, and general assortment of glass and earthen ware, consisting of the following particulars,

Copper plated Queen's Ware, viz.

Dishes, plates, tureens, sauce boats, bread baskets, flower pots, coffee pots, tea pots, milk pots, sugar dishes, canisters, bowls, &c.

Plain Queen's Ware, viz.

Dishes, plates, tureens, fruit plates and dishes, bread and fruit baskets, sauce tureens, sauce boats, butter tubs, cream bowls, salts, castors, mustard pots, flower pots, potting pots, chamber pots, coffee pots, tea pots, milk pots, sugar dishes, tea and coffee cups and saucers, bowls, mugs, pitchers, pickle stands and leaves, forms, porrengers, bottles and basons, toys.

White Stone Ware, viz.

Dishes, plates, tureens, bowls, mugs, pitchers, bottles and basons, salts, castors, mustard pots, chamber pots, porrengers, butter tubs, sauce boats, cups and saucers, white, blue and white, and enamelled.

Collyflower Ware, viz.

Tea pots, coffee pots, milk pots, sugar dishes, bowls, mugs, salts, mustard pots, and pickle leaves.

Tortois Shell and Agate Ware, viz.

Tea pots, coffee pots, milk pots, sugar dishes, bowls, mugs, salts, mustard pots cups and saucers.

Delph Ware, viz.

Dishes, plates, tureens, bowls, mugs, bottles and basons, chamber pots, &c.

Glass, viz,

Decanters, wine glasses, pint, half-pint, jill, and half-jill tumblers, ale glasses, jelly glasses, vinegar and oil cruets, salts, mustard pots, sugar dishes, milk pots, mugs, pocket bottles, &c. Red China tea pots.

STOLEN out of the stable of the subscriber, in Horse-Neck, Fairfield county, Connecti- Sunday the 14th ... or strawberry rea...

135. Newspaper advertisement. New York. 1771. From The New York Gazette. *Greenfield Village and Henry Ford Museum, Dearborn, Michigan*

In this advertisement Flores Bancker offered wares for sale that were being imported in great quantity in the third quarter of the eighteenth century. The same types of pottery and glass are displayed in the shell corner cupboard (see plate 133).

136. Trade card. Engraved by T. Johnston. Boston, Massachusetts. 1757. Engraving, $6\frac{1}{4} \times 7\frac{3}{8}$". Henry Francis du Pont Winterthur Museum, Winterthur, Delaware. Joseph Downs Manuscript Collection

Lewis Deblois

At the Golden Eagle on Dock Square Boston,

Imports every Spring and Fall from London

A Great Assortment of Iron Mongery, Founder's Brazier's & Cutlery Ware. Also sundry Sorts of English Goods, Spices, Musick Books, Instruments & Strings; together with a very great Variety of other kind of Goods which if enumerated here would be tedious for the Reader. N.B. As He deals only for Ready Money, will engage to Sell full as Cheap as is sold in any Shop in the TOWN of BOSTON & to such of his Country Customers as does not suit to come to Town, they shall be serv'd equally the same by Letter as if Present themselves.

T. Johnston Sc.

Boston 1757

Bo.t Lewis Deblois

Although American goldsmiths and silversmiths had become increasingly proficient by the middle of the eighteenth century, they were unable to produce a sufficient quantity of metalwork to satisfy the great demand in the new country. Lewis Deblois, located at the Golden Eagle on Dock Square, Boston, imported a large assortment of iron. Quite probably the objects that he offered twice a year were purely utilitarian and might well have been cooking pots, cranes, and other objects indispensable to the kitchen.

*137. Portrait of Paul Revere.
John Singleton Copley.
Massachusetts. 1768–70. Oil
on canvas, 35 × 28½". Museum
of Fine Arts, Boston,
Massachusetts. Gift of Joseph W.,
William B., and Edward H. R.
Revere*

*The hero of the American
Revolution holds a silver teapot,
and the artist has chosen to
illustrate the painting with the
tools of the silversmith's trade,
including a leather hammering
pillow. Revere is shown without
the customary wig of the period
and his hair is unpowdered.*

*138. Cruet stand. John David.
Philadelphia, Pennsylvania.
c. 1763. Silver with silver-capped
glass bottles, height of stand
10¾". Henry Francis du Pont
Winterthur Museum, Winterthur,
Delaware*

*The engraved ruffled cartouche—
bearing the cipher C R—and the
curvilinear cinquefoil frame show a
combination of French rococo
design, which is characteristically
asymmetrical, and American rococo
design, in which symmetry
predominates. Americans were
unwilling to adopt wholeheartedly
the French rococo. The bottles are
contemporary but not original to
the frame. The silver caps bear a
London hallmark.*

*139. Coffeepot. Philip Syng, Jr.
Philadelphia, Pennsylvania.
c. 1760. Silver with wood handle,
height 11⅞". Philadelphia
Museum of Art, Philadelphia,
Pennsylvania. John D. McIlhenny
Fund*

*C-scrolls, S-scrolls, and carefully
worked leafage motifs embellish
this opulent coffeepot. The full-
blown designs of this piece are a
marked contrast to Samuel Casey's
chaste cream pitcher (see plate
104) produced ten years earlier.*

140. Set of knife boxes. Mounts by Lewis Fueter. New York. c. 1770. Mahogany and whitewood with silver mounts, maximum height 13¼". Metropolitan Museum of Art, New York City. Morris K. Jessup Fund, 1954

In the finest English and American homes freestanding knife boxes were deemed the epitome of luxury. When filled with fine handcrafted silver, the value of these sets was extraordinary. This set of knife boxes was originally owned by the Stuyvesant family.

141. Covered chalice, flagon, and paten. Johann Christophe Heyne. Lancaster, Pennsylvania. Dated 1765. Pewter, height of flagon 11¼". Greenfield Village and Henry Ford Museum, Dearborn, Michigan

These three pieces—a communion service made for the Canadochly Lutheran Church in York County, Pennsylvania—are not unlike objects created for domestic use by Heyne and his contemporaries. Pewter, considered a poor man's silver, was seldom purchased by well-to-do congregations, which preferred silver services.

142. Peter Manigault and His Drinking Guests. George Roupell. Charleston, South Carolina. c. 1760. Black ink and wash on paper, 10¼ × 12¼". Henry Francis du Pont Winterthur Museum, Winterthur, Delaware

This drawing depicts Peter Manigault and guests carousing in a fashionably appointed interior. Manigault, a graduate of the Inner Temple in London, was one of the most renowned hosts of Charleston's smart society. Although Charleston was noted for its cultivated gentry, the realities of life in the New World were ever-present. Two of Manigault's guests were ultimately killed by hostile Indians on the nearby frontier.

Table and ornamental wares by
Stiegel are the earliest examples
about which there is anything
definitely known. In general the
shapes were expertly formed, and
the decoration was achieved mainly
through enameling, copper wheel
engraving, and pattern molding.

debtor's prison. Many successful enterprises failed as internal strife between the
Tories, loyal to the English crown, and American citizens, who sought political
and economic freedom from the mother country, began to divide the country.

Polarization between the two factions was given increased impetus when
George III on March 22, 1765, approved the much-hated Stamp Act, which
had passed Parliament with little opposition even though six colonial assem-
blies had registered vehement protests. This direct internal tax imposed by a
remote government without consent or representation of the thirteen colonies
sparked a swift reaction. In New York City an effigy of Cadwallader Colden,
the royal governor, was dumped onto his coach and set ablaze. In Boston a
group of citizens entered and plundered the house of Governor Thomas
Hutchinson. Colonial boycotts put pressure on British merchants everywhere
and the Stamp Act was repealed on March 18, 1766.

Liberty poles were erected throughout the colonies to symbolize freedom
from injurious and improper interference, and patriotic symbols such as the
liberty cap and the eagle appeared in paintings (plate 144), on tavern signs, and
in the design of glassware and textiles. The Bloody Massacre (plate 145), engraved
by Paul Revere in 1770, documented the death of several of Boston's citizens
during an exchange of fire with the British military. The sharp hostility of the
local townspeople toward the British army sent to the northern seaport town to
collect monies for military supplies and provisions was the immediate cause of
the confrontation. The massacre was the dramatic climax of the growing fric-
tion between the English soldiers and the Boston citizenry, and an expression
of anti-British public opinion was at last out in the open and becoming increasingly vociferous.

144. Liberty in the Form of the Goddess of Youth: Giving Support to the Bald Eagle. *Abijah Canfield. Chusetown, Connecticut. Last quarter of eighteenth century. Reverse gouache painting on glass, 24¼ × 18½″. Greenfield Village and Henry Ford Museum, Dearborn, Michigan*

145. The Bloody Massacre. *Engraved by Paul Revere; colored by Christian Remick. Boston, Massachusetts. 1770. Hand-colored engraving, 13 × 11⅞″. Greenfield Village and Henry Ford Museum, Dearborn, Michigan*

Countless prints celebrating the strength and pride of the colonies and the young nation circulated in America and in England before and after the Revolution. Some of the prints reached China aboard merchant ships and were freely copied. Paintings with designs almost identical to this one were executed by oriental artists using the technique of reverse painting on glass. This is one of the very few extant American examples, and the artist acknowledges an engraving by Edward Savage as the source of the design. The taste for reverse paintings on glass increased in the nineteenth century, and by the 1850s many of them were backed with gold or silver foil and referred to as tinsel pictures.

The Bloody Massacre, which occurred on King Street in Boston on March 5, 1770, was the event that triggered open anti-British public actions leading to the American Revolution. This impression of one of Paul Revere's most famous engravings is one of two known copies hand-colored and signed by Remick.

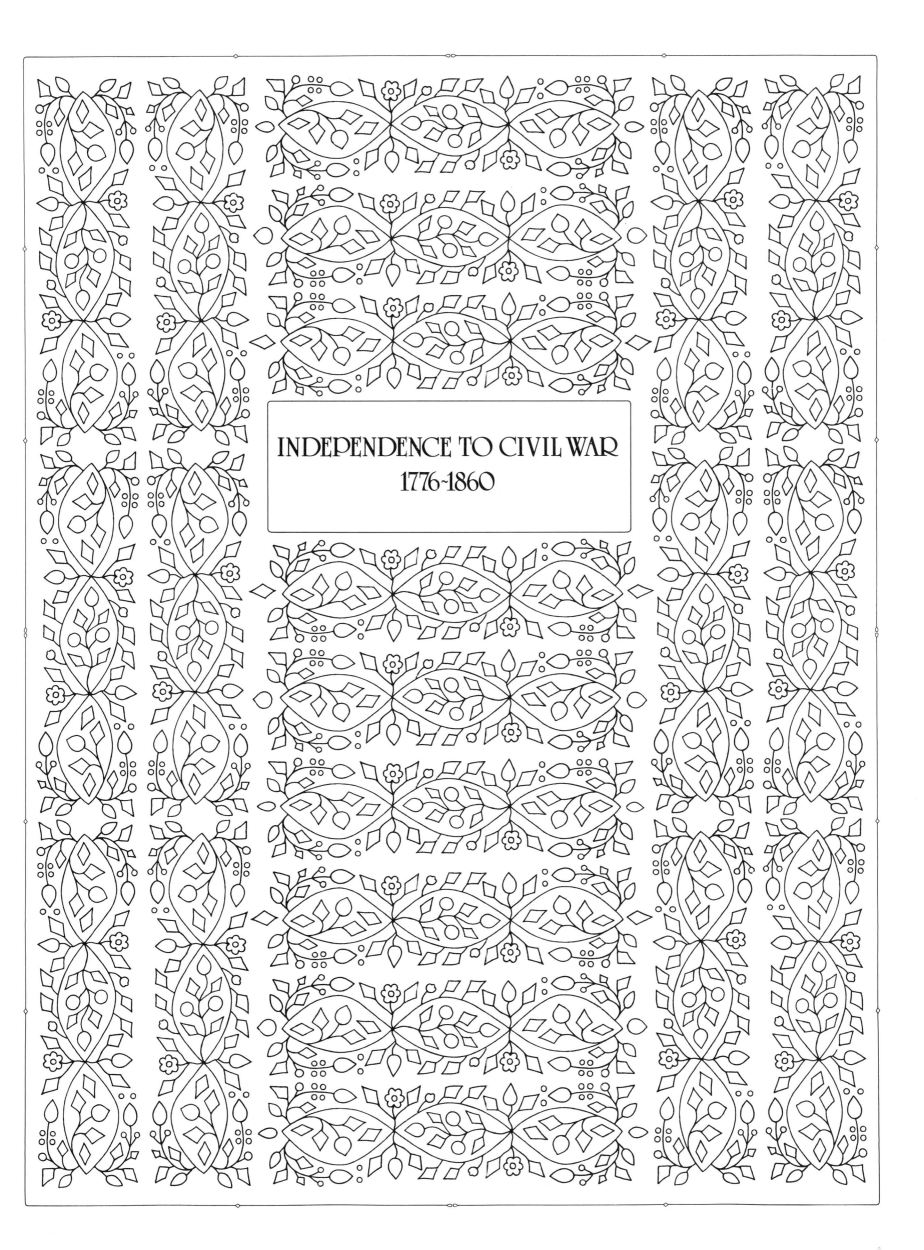

INDEPENDENCE TO CIVIL WAR
1776-1860

lthough victory in the American War of Independence freed the colonists from England economically and politically, they still were indebted to British taste for many decades.

During the last decade of the eighteenth century, English books on the decorative arts continued to be the dominating influence on products created by America's best craftsmen. Furniture makers readily adapted the designs offered by George Hepplewhite in *The Cabinet-Maker and Upholsterer's Guide* (1788) and by Thomas Sheraton in his *Cabinet-Maker and Upholsterer's Drawing-Book* (1791–94). The decorative objects that were excavated at Herculaneum and Pompeii during the eighteenth century by French archaeologists also began to stimulate the American imagination. By 1800 richly carved, inlaid, and painted replicas of furnishings of the ancient world were replacing refined English-inspired designs in the United States.

Communications and transportation improved immensely in the early nineteenth century, bringing cosmopolitan taste to an ever-increasing rural population. Handcraftsmanship waned as technology expanded, making possible factory production of a great variety of decorative objects.

The first truly international exposition of the decorative arts, entitled The Industry of All Nations, was presented in 1851 in London at the Crystal Palace, an innovative metal-framed, glass building erected especially for the exhibition. America was roundly criticized for the poor design of nearly all the entries sent over for display. British critics, however, were nearly unanimous in their praise for American technological achievements and the nation's ability to manufacture machines that made other machines.

Two years later at The World of Science, Art, and Industry exposition, presented at the Crystal Palace in New York City (on the present site of the main branch of the New York Public Library), Yankee ingenuity prevailed. The lessons taught by the British critics had led to the development of fine furniture, glass, ceramics, and textiles, in a brilliant diversity of design and shape. These products vied successfully with European entries shipped for the display. With the stunning success at this industrial and decorative arts exposition, the United States became a leading export nation in the areas of furnishings and design.

The Federal Style in Republican America 1776-1837

The American War of Independence did not actually begin as a struggle for independence but as a demand by Americans for an active voice in their government. Fierce opposition to taxation without representation in Parliament was the main rallying point that led to the war and ensured sympathy and participation on the part of the majority of the colonists.

When the Declaration of Independence was signed on July 4, 1776, the war had been under way for well over a year. Paul Revere's moonlit ride on April 18, 1775, the battle of Bunker Hill fought on June 17, and Washington's appointment as commander of the army at Cambridge, Massachusetts, on July 3 were accomplished facts. In spite of nationalistic zeal, neither the Continental Congress nor the individual colonies had adequate political machinery to generate financial support for the long struggle that would ensue. There were no banks or other monetary institutions that could provide financing for the war. Manufacturing capabilities for goods, especially weapons and ammunition, were virtually nonexistent, as the British Parliament had prudently prohibited armament production in the colonies. Against all these odds the colonists fought on doggedly, defending themselves against British mercenary troops. Victory was finally achieved in 1781, when the French fleet bottled up General Charles Cornwallis at Yorktown. The British commander surrendered, and the fighting was over.

The new nation organized under the Articles of Confederation soon realized that a strong central government headed by an effective executive was mandatory if economic and political stability were to be established.

During the 1790s, the Constitution, which was drafted at the Constitutional Convention between May 25 and September 17, 1787, and ratified by 1790, provided a framework for government that became the law of the land. Attitudes toward Britain and France varied greatly and Americans formed two major political factions—the Federalists, led by Alexander Hamilton, and a Jeffersonian party, under the influence of Thomas Jefferson, which at first was called the Republicans and then the Democratic Republicans, later becoming known as the Democratic party. The Federalists were conservatives who favored a strong centralized government, development of industries, and attention to a well-ordered society; their members were drawn largely from the wealthy merchants and northern property owners. They supported reconciliation with Britain, whose industrial and financial interests were viewed as complementary to those of the new nation. The Jeffersonians, who were comprised of southern landowners and generally the less privileged, opposed tariffs and federal banks. They favored a closer political alliance with France, which led to an awareness of the French taste in the decorative arts.

During the revolutionary war, when Americans could not purchase British goods, infant industries such as munitions factories, fabric mills, and glass-works appeared wherever water power was easily harnessed and raw materials were abundant. These industries thrived and expanded in the postwar years and were the foundation of America's later industrial wealth.

Immediately following the Revolution, the American Federal style, inspired by English and French studies of antiquity, came into being. It flourished between 1785 and 1810 and was strongly influenced by design concepts and drawings in George Hepplewhite's *The Cabinet-Maker and Upholsterer's Guide,* published in London in 1788, and Thomas Sheraton's *Cabinet-Maker and Upholsterer's Drawing-Book,* published in the same city in 1791 (the second edition was issued with additional plates in 1794). In their publications Hepplewhite and Sheraton were refining the more extravagant neoclassic designs of the

146. Tambour desk. John Seymour (attr.). Boston, Massachusetts. 1795–1800. Mahogany with satinwood inlay, height 42¼". Greenfield Village and Henry Ford Museum, Dearborn, Michigan

Inlay again became fashionable around 1790, and the light furniture of the period such as this Federal-style desk is often embellished with this technique.

English architect Robert Adam. Hepplewhite was an obscure English cabinet-maker and furniture designer who died in 1786, before success was totally within his grasp. In fact it was not until two years after his death that his wife, Alice, published his manuscript. Hepplewhite showed a preference for fine inlay in many of the plates that illustrated his book. In his influential guide he recommended that chairs in general should be constructed of mahogany, "with the bars and frame sunk in a hollow, or rising in a round projection, with a band or lift on the inner and outer edges. Many of these designs are enriched with ornaments proper to be carved in mahogany." Another quality he emphasized was the tapered leg, square in section. Typical of the American adaptations of Hepplewhite's designs are the tambour desk (plate 146), the shield-back side chair (plate 148), and the painted and decorated side chair (plate 149).

Thomas Sheraton, from Stockton-on-Tees in England, moved in 1790 to London, where he taught drawing and wrote books on design theory. Not a craftsman himself, he visited most of London's cabinetmaking shops and there

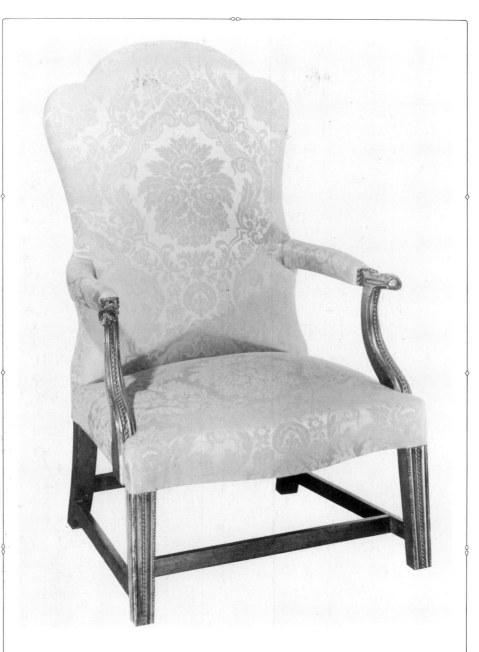

147. *Upholstered open armchair.*
Thomas Affleck. Philadelphia,
Pennsylvania. c. 1794. Mahogany,
height 51″. Greenfield Village
and Henry Ford Museum,
Dearborn, Michigan

This Hepplewhite chair, carved
by Affleck, is recorded as having
been used by the original Speaker of
the Supreme Court in
Philadelphia's Independence Hall.
The bead-and-reel carving on the
arms and legs is characteristic of
Affleck's style.

he found inspiration for many of the illustrations in his *Cabinet-Maker and Up-*
holsterer's Drawing-Book. His gift was an innate sense of proportion and style
and a natural approach to the current design. American variations of the Shera–

148. *Museum installation. Federal*
parlor. America. Third quarter of
eighteenth century. Greenfield
Village and Henry Ford Museum,
Dearborn, Michigan

This period room installation
features furniture in the
Hepplewhite style. The shield
shape on the back of the side chair
in the foreground is repeated on the
movable shields of the pair of pole
screens flanking the door with
windows. The large secretary-
bookcase has brass ball ornaments
as well as a brass eagle perched on
its cornice. The small two-drawer
table to the left of the secretary is
known as a worktable; when the
lower drawer is pulled out, the
hanging fabric bag comes with it.
These tables were used by women
to store their needlework projects.

149. Museum installation. Imlay Room. New Jersey. 1790. Henry Francis du Pont Winterthur Museum, Winterthur, Delaware

This room was part of a house built by John Imlay about 1790 in Allentown, New Jersey. The furniture is a blaze of painted decoration of rare refinement and style. The mantel, with plaster composition, was probably created by Robert Wellford. The fireplace opening is surrounded by Liverpool tiles imported from England.

ton style include chairs with square backs and various pieces of furniture with turned and reeded legs, such as the bed (plate 150) and the demilune commode (plate 152).

In the last decade of the eighteenth century and in much of the first half of the nineteenth, fine city-made furniture continued to utilize imported mahogany. The armchair from Independence Hall (plate 147), carved by the Philadelphia cabinetmaker Thomas Affleck, has tapering legs that anticipate the full acceptance of the American Hepplewhite style in later pieces. As with the Chippendale furniture that preceded it, it is of solid wood. Its decoration is in the form of beaded carving down the fronts of the arms and legs. Affleck, a Royalist banished from Philadelphia to Virginia in 1777, was commissioned by the citizens of Philadelphia to design the furniture for Congress Hall when he returned to the city after the war.

During the Federal period American cabinetmakers revived the use of veneer and inlay, a mode of furniture decoration that had passed out of fashion in the 1720s. The mahogany tambour desk (plate 146), attributed to the shop of John Seymour of Boston, is inlaid with light-hued satinwood. The delicate bellflower stringing on the sliding doors in the upper section, the bellflower motifs cascading down the tapered legs, and the string inlay on the case are fine examples of this revival. A comparison of the legs of the Hepplewhite chair (plate 147) with those of this desk made slightly later illustrates the rapid adaptation of Hepplewhite's style in America. Tambour desks must have been considered important pieces of furniture, for they were owned by many affluent families. In his will George Washington left to his compatriot Dr. Carik "my bureau, or, as the cabinetmakers call it, tambour-secretary, and the circular chair, an appendage of my study."

The Sheraton style flourished concurrently with the Hepplewhite style, and ingenious Americans borrowing from both design books produced a mingling that was quite individual. The furniture in the room interior (plate 148) is for the most part in the Hepplewhite style. Mahogany with inlaid decorative motifs prevails. The tall-case clock, a form associated with the colonial period, continued to be produced in large quantity. Surprising, considering their prevalence, clocks were costly and valuable possessions, and Robert Sutcliffe, an Englishman traveling through New York in 1805, was astonished by the quality of American timepieces he saw there: "The cabinet work of the case, as well as the engravings and paintings about it, and also the movements, although done in a beautiful and workmanlike manner, had all been executed by men, none of whom had served an apprenticeship to their respective lines of business. The mechanism was executed by the grandfather of the kind friend in whose house it stands. This family are remarkable for ingenuity, and have rendered essential services to this country."

Painted furniture was conspicuously popular well into the last decades of the eighteenth century. Painted and decorated furniture generally was placed in two distinct categories—expensive stylish pieces decorated by craftsmen who considered themselves artists and simple country furniture ornamented by rural decorators working for the middle class. The typical painted Baltimore furniture in the Imlay Room (plate 149) was purchased by John Imlay, a Philadelphia merchant who retired to Allentown, New Jersey, about 1790 and built a large house there. Delicate decoration plays an important part in the overall visual impact of these pieces. Somewhat more fragile is the decoration on the furnishings in the Gold and White Room (plate 150). Painted shells and seaweed decorate the center of the inlaid top of the demilune commode (plate 152) crafted by the Boston cabinetmaker Thomas Seymour for the daughter of a prominent merchant of Salem. The original bill from Seymour for the commode is in the Boston Museum of Fine Arts and it identifies John Ritto Penniman, a talented decorator from that city, as the painter of the "shels on Top." Penniman possessed a large collection of marine shells and at an auction of his effects in 1827 a sportsman's basket filled with them was offered for sale. Sheraton in *The Cabinet Dictionary* included a section on designs and techniques specifically for

OPPOSITE:

151. Settee. John and Hugh Finlay (attr.). Baltimore, Maryland. c. 1808. Painted wood, length 51". Baltimore Museum of Art, Baltimore, Maryland

John and Hugh Finlay, Irish immigrants working in Baltimore, advertised that their furniture could be decorated with "views adjacent to this city." The top rail of this Sheraton-style settee, which is painted black with polychrome and gilt decoration, illustrates this claim by picturing three well-known Baltimore buildings: (left to right) Homewood, a southern mansion now on the campus of Johns Hopkins University; the Bank Building of Baltimore; and Mount Clare, erected about 1760 by Charles Carroll. Two of the structures are still standing today.

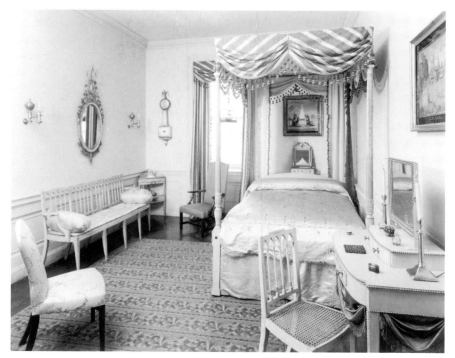

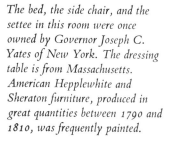

150. *Museum installation. Gold and White Room. New York and New England. Late eighteenth century. Henry Francis du Pont Winterthur Museum, Winterthur, Delaware*

The bed, the side chair, and the settee in this room were once owned by Governor Joseph C. Yates of New York. The dressing table is from Massachusetts. American Hepplewhite and Sheraton furniture, produced in great quantities between 1790 and 1810, was frequently painted.

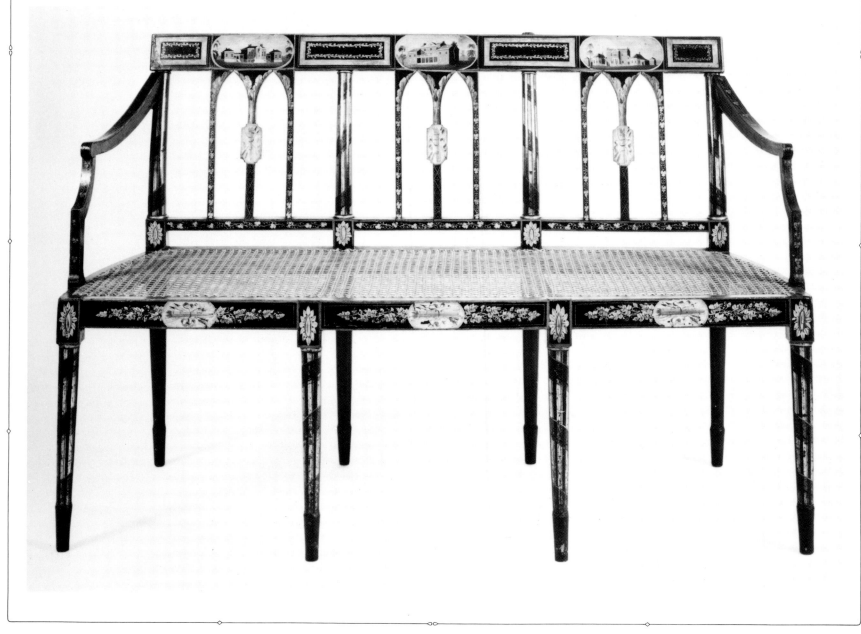

This commode in the Sheraton
style was crafted for Elizabeth
Derby, daughter of the prominent
merchant and shipowner Elias
Hasket Derby of Salem,
Massachusetts. An elegant piece,
with its light and dark veneer,
inlay, carving, and painted
decoration, it is equal in
sophistication to almost any
furniture of the period. The four
mahogany posts were probably
carved by Thomas Whitman and
are terminated with brass paw
feet, commonly used by Duncan
Phyfe and other New York
cabinetmakers of the period. The
bail pulls are of stamped brass.
The top consists of radiating strips
of veneer alternating between
satinwood and mahogany.

OPPOSITE:

153. Lady's cabinet and writing
table. Maker unknown.
Baltimore, Maryland. 1795–1810.
Mahogany, height 62⅛''. Henry
Francis du Pont Winterthur
Museum, Winterthur, Delaware

The design of this case piece,
which includes églomisé gilt
classical figures on a black
background, shows a close affinity
to a design appearing in Plate 50
in Sheraton's Drawing-Book.
The legs terminate with brass
casters, an innovation that became
increasingly common in the Federal
period. The sources for the figures
in the glass ovals are still
undiscovered.

painted and decorated furniture. Sheraton believed that what he referred to as varnish colors, although far more expensive, were considerably more effective than "common oil painting."

In the first decades of the nineteenth century Baltimore emerged as a major American city, and a visitor there during the War of 1812 commented that it had become one of the fairest urban centers in North America. Painted furniture was especially popular in this southern city, and the settee (plate 151) is believed to have been painted by John and Hugh Findlay, Irish craftsmen who came to Baltimore, where they advertised caned furniture decorated with realistic landscapes, flowers, trophies of music, and personifications of war, love, and other abstractions dear to the nineteenth-century Romantics. The left panel on the top rail of the settee executed by the Findlays shows Homewood, a gracious southern mansion built in 1808 and now part of the campus of Johns Hopkins University. When this plantation building was erected, it cost the

154. Banjo clock. Simon Willard. Massachusetts. 1815. Gilt case and bezel, height 40″. Seamen's Bank for Savings, New York City. Fine Arts Collection

This eight-day banjo clock with gilt case and bracket base has painted glass panels, the lower one depicting the 1812 sea victory of Isaac Hull, commander of the Constitution. The upper panel includes the figure of a woman, symbolizing Hope, standing on an anchor; above her is a classical urn with a floral bouquet.

155. Bracket clock. Case by Slover and Kortright, New York City; movement by Andrew Billings, Poughkeepsie, New York. Dated 1795. Mahogany with satinwood inlay and brass trim, height 24¾″. Greenfield Village and Henry Ford Museum, Dearborn, Michigan

Clockmakers generally obtained their cases from furniture makers. A brass plate with an oval insert tacked onto this Federal bracket clock is inscribed: "Made by Andᵂ Billings for C. D. Colden, 1795." Cadwallader Colden, namesake grandson of the learned royal governor of the colony of New York, was himself mayor of New York City.

156. Trade label. Joseph B. Barry; engraved by J. Akin. Philadelphia, Pennsylvania. 1804–10. Current whereabouts unknown

This label, drawn and engraved by Akin, advertises various objects designed by the cabinetmaker and upholsterer Joseph B. Barry, who moved to Philadelphia from London before 1790. During the Federal period, Philadelphia furniture more closely mirrored English forms than that from any other section of the United States.

staggering sum of forty thousand dollars. Known for their stylish pieces, the Findlays supplied furniture for the refurbishing of the White House for James Madison in 1809.

Dwellings like Homewood were furnished with remarkable pieces such as the lady's cabinet and writing table (plate 153) produced in Baltimore between 1795 and 1810. This mahogany and satinwood case piece is very similar to one of the illustrations in Sheraton's *Drawing-Book*. The sources of design for the

157. The Shop and Warehouse of Duncan Phyfe, 168–172 Fulton Street, New York City. Artist unknown. United States. Early nineteenth century. Pencil, ink, and watercolor on paper, $15\frac{3}{4} \times 18\frac{7}{8}''$. Metropolitan Museum of Art, New York City. Rogers Fund, 1922

Classical details abound on Phyfe's establishment on Fulton Street in New York City. The fanlights over the doorways to the house and shop, the classical columns and cornice on the shop, and the three urnlike finials on the workroom reflect Phyfe's reliance on the new Federal style.

158. Museum installation. Phyfe and
Lannuier furniture. New York City.
Nineteenth century. Greenfield Village
and Henry Ford Museum, Dearborn,
Michigan

This stylish room features pieces
associated with the New York City
cabinetmaking shops of Duncan Phyfe
and Charles Honoré Lannuier. The
récamier sofa in yellow silk, the sideboard,
and all of the chairs, with the exception
of the easy chair, are assigned to the
Phyfe workshop. The open card table
with winged birdlike figures and hairy
paw feet is attributed to the Lannuier
shop, one of Phyfe's toughest competitors.
Wooden blinds, much like those in
Independence Hall during the eighteenth
century, hang in this early-nineteenth-
century interior. The carved wooden
sconces, the glass chandelier, the painted
tole vases on the windowsills, and the
rug are all imports.

classical figures in the oval panels of églomisé, or reverse painting on glass, have still not been identified. Eglomisé, or verre églomisé, was named after the French frame maker and designer Jean-Baptiste Glomi. Not only were églomisé-painted panels often incorporated in the design of looking glasses, they also decorated large secretaries and secretary-bookcases.

Painted glass panels appeared on the handsome banjo clock (plate 154) fashioned by the noted American clockmaker Simon Willard. In 1802 Willard was granted a patent for his design for a wall clock in the banjo shape. His eight-day banjo clock, which he always referred to as an "Improved Patent Timepiece," was a refinement of the typical Massachusetts wall clock and earned for him immediate success for its accurate timekeeping abilities and for its fine proportions and beauty.

The bracket clock (plate 155) is an adaptation of a popular English form. The eight-day, hour-strike works were devised by Andrew Billings, and the delicately carved, inlaid, and painted case was produced by Slover and Kortright. American bracket clocks of this distinction are exceedingly rare.

By the end of the eighteenth century the bedroom became a place of splendor in the Federal home. The beautifully executed bed (plate 150), tastefully hung with the latest fabrics, and the veneered mahogany and satinwood commode (plate 152) were the kind of objects that would have been prominent features of the house in Newburyport, Massachusetts, described by Sarah Anna Emery in her 1879 memoir, *Reminiscences of a Nonagenarian,* derived mainly from her mother's recollections of the life and styles of the 1790s: "The best chamber was elegant with gay patch hangings to the high square post bedstead, and curtains of the same draped the windows. A toilet table tastily covered with white muslin, and ornamented by blue ribbon bows, stood between the front

159. The Tea Party. *Henry Sargent. Boston, Massachusetts. 1821–24. Oil on canvas, 64¼ × 52¼″. Museum of Fine Arts, Boston, Massachusetts. Gift of Mrs. Horatio Lamb*

Sargent's nineteenth-century paintings of Boston's upper class are splendid social documents of the era. This expensively carpeted and appointed interior is furnished with Empire armchairs sporting carved animal-form supports.

windows. The case of drawers was handsomely carved, the chairs matched those below, and there was a novelty, the first wash-stand I ever saw, a pretty triangular one of mahogany, a light graceful pattern to fit into a corner of a room."

Philadelphia Federal furniture more closely mirrors English taste than that from any of the other American cities. Johann David Schoepf in his *Travels in the Confederation, 1783–1784*, translated in 1911, described the Philadelphia

160. *Wardrobe. Charles Honoré Lannuier. New York City. c. 1815. Mahogany, height 100". New-York Historical Society, New York City*

This Empire wardrobe, which belonged to John Howard Abeel, has a broken-arch pediment centered by a classical bust with the signature "H. Lannuier New York" on the base. The rather simple chaste piece of furniture with beautiful proportions and fine inlay is enriched by the addition of brass hairy paw feet in front and brass moldings around the panels.

manner of living in the 1780s—elegant in style but apparently more practical and simpler than that of contemporary Europeans:

In the matter of interior decorations the English style is imitated here as throughout America. The furniture, tables, bureaux, bedsteads &c. are commonly of mahogany, at least in the best houses. Carpets, Scottish and Turkish, are much used, and indeed are necessities where the houses are so lightly built; stairs and rooms are laid with them. The houses are seldom without paper tapestries, the vestibule especially being so treated. The taste generally is for living in a cleanly and orderly manner, without the continual scrubbing of the Hollanders or the frippery and gilt of the French.

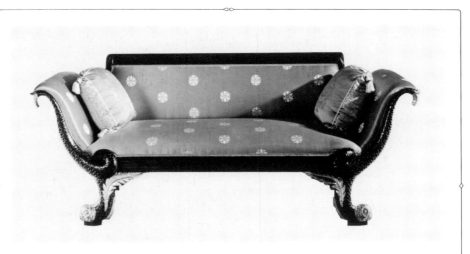

The carved dolphins forming the legs and arms on this Empire sofa are decorated with gilt.

Of the several new furniture forms that evolved in the late eighteenth century, none was as important as the sideboard, a form developed for the storage of flatware, table linens, and serving pieces which had a broad flat top designed to hold dishes of food that were to be served. It was derived from an English side table flanked by pedestal cupboards topped with knife boxes. The advertisement label of Joseph B. Barry, cabinetmaker and upholsterer who came to Philadelphia from London, is evidence of the direction taken by design ideas such as the sideboard (plate 156). In 1810 Barry was advertising furniture in the "Rich Egyptian and Gothic style."

Among Barry's chief competitors were two immigrant cabinetmakers working in New York: Scottish-born Duncan Phyfe and the French-born Charles Honoré Lannuier. Phyfe, who worked in Albany in 1783 or 1784 when he first immigrated to America, finally moved to New York City. He was originally listed in the New York City *Directory* for 1792 as "Fife, Joiner." By 1794 he shrewdly altered this to the more exotically spelled and prestigious-sounding entry "Duncan Phyfe, Cabinetmaker."

Duncan Phyfe's earliest furniture was predominantly in the Sheraton style, but in the span of his career the furniture produced by his firm represented all phases of the classical movement: Hepplewhite, Sheraton, Empire, and finally early Victorian. In many instances his furniture incorporated elements from all of them. His admiration for classical design and proportion is apparent in the watercolor painting of his shop and warehouse (plate 157), located on Fulton Street in New York City. Eventually Phyfe's name became nearly synonymous

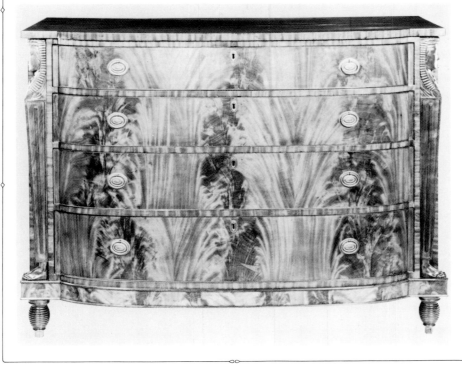

Barry appreciated the virtues of fine woods, and his skillful and consistent matching of the figured mahogany veneer is a hallmark of his style. The turned beehive feet on this Egyptian revival piece probably were once capped with brass terminals.

with the Federal style, and his predilections in this direction are reflected in the sideboard, the récamier sofa, and the curule-based chair in front of the harp in the museum installation (plate 158). Phyfe's large cabinetmaking shop employed many craftsmen; however, they appear to have worked on designs developed only by the master himself. His woodworking vocabulary was used extensively by other American furniture makers in cities like Boston, where wealthy residents filled their salons with richly carved and gilded furniture in the Empire style. *The Tea Party* (plate 159), a painting by Henry Sargent, is a vivid record of the way in which prominent citizens in the new democracy filled their homes with elegant furnishings in the French taste.

Beginning around 1800 the delicacy of the classically inspired Hepplewhite and Sheraton styles began to coarsen. In part this occurred because of the large influx of French cabinetmakers into America's major cities; they brought with them French enthusiasm for ornate reproductions and adaptations of early furniture forms. These designers also added elaborate decorative motifs that were

163. Piano. Joseph Hisky. Baltimore, Maryland. c. 1830. Mahogany with inlay, length 67". Greenfield Village and Henry Ford Museum, Dearborn, Michigan

A rich combination of stenciled and freehand decoration offsets the painted pastoral scene above the keyboard. Few Empire pieces of this type are as beautiful in design and decoration.

inspired by the design of household objects then being excavated at ancient sites such as Herculaneum and Pompeii.

Charles Honoré Lannuier advertised in a July 1803 edition of the *New York Evening Post* his expertise in constructing beds, chairs, and other pieces of furniture in the newest and latest French fashion. Lannuier noted that he had brought with him gilt and glass frames, borders of ornaments, and handsome safe locks, as well as numerous patterns with which to serve his New York clientele. The beautifully proportioned Empire wardrobe by Lannuier (plate 160) is graced with classical details. The broken-arch pediment topped with a carved figural bust, the doors flanked by flat Ionic columns, and the brass hairy paw feet are all details associated with designs from the ancient world.

Lannuier is also credited with crafting the card table with winged birdlike supports for the tabletop (plate 158). The handsome sofa with carved dolphins that comprise the legs and arms (plate 161) is also probably of New York origin. This masterpiece of cabinetmaking is another example of the fascination that animal forms held for tastemakers of the period.

After Napoleon's Egyptian campaign, from 1798 to 1802, Egyptian motifs were introduced into the area of the decorative arts. The French artist and museum official Dominique-Vivant Denon was staff archaeologist for Napoleon and in 1798–99 accompanied the French commander on his expedition to Egypt, sketching the monuments—often under the fire of the enemy. Baron Denon's sketches—published later, in 1802, in *Voyage dans la basse et la haute Egypte*—supplied French designers with new architectural and decorative ideas. These new conceptions filtered through to the cosmopolitan centers in America. Although the Egyptian revival movement in nineteenth-century America was never as dynamic or dramatic as other retrospective periods—that is, the Gothic, Renaissance, or rococo revival styles—craftsmen throughout the century borrowed from these exotic motifs. The drawers on Joseph Barry's finely matched mahogany veneer Egyptian revival chest (plate 162) are flanked by caryatids with realistic human feet, a human face, and a stylized Egyptian headdress.

164. Secretary-desk. Antoine-Gabriel Quervelle. Philadelphia, Pennsylvania. c. 1830. Mahogany, height 102". Munson-Williams-Proctor Institute, Utica, New York

This piece in the late Empire style bears the paper label of its maker. Applied fanlike convex panels decorate the base. The interior of the writing section is in bird's-eye maple. The bookcase section has semiengaged columns with carved capitals that lead the eye to a coved cornice.

Despite some of the restrictions in early colonial life against the gentler diversions such as singing and dancing and the reservations entertained by the Puritan leaders over secular music in general, this art form actually became an important part of the cultural life of the colonies. Early in the eighteenth century, public concerts were being arranged in the South as well as in New York and Philadelphia. Choral societies were initiated in New England towns, and various instruments—spinets, harpsichords, guitars, violins, and organs—were enjoyed during leisure hours throughout the century. George Washington piped out tunes on the flute, Thomas Jefferson was proficient on the cello, and Benjamin Franklin played an instrument made of various-toned glasses, which he may even have invented or perfected.

Enthusiasm for music as both an art and an amusing pastime mounted in the new Republic. In fact music rooms, designed especially to house instruments such as the handsome harp (plate 158) and the elaborately painted and stenciled piano (plate 163), became a refuge for the serious appreciation of the art. Even in relatively remote Bethlehem, Pennsylvania, Eliza Southgate Bowne, visiting the local homes and several schools in 1803, found that musical appreciation was a primary concern: "These Bethlehemites are all Germans, and retain many of the peculiarities of the country—such as their great fondness for music. It is delightful: there is scarcely a house in the place without a Piano-forte; the Post Master has an elegant grand. The Barber plays on almost every kind of music. Sunday afternoon we went to the Young Men's house to hear some sacred music. . . . We went to the Schools. . . . Here was a Piano-forte, and another sister teaching a little girl music. We went thro' all the different schoolrooms . . . and in every room was a Piano." Bowne's descriptions were included in selections from her voluminous letters published in 1887 in New York under the title *A Girl's Life Eighty Years Ago*.

During the 1820s and into the 1830s, a new prosperity resulting from the expanding economy produced a large middle class. For the first time there was a sizable group that could afford expensive furniture. In the popular taste that developed, richness of ornamentation often became confused with elegant and refined design.

Antoine-Gabriel Quervelle, a Paris-born cabinetmaker who worked in Philadelphia after 1817, produced splendid pieces like the secretary-desk (plate 164). This fine example of his work has a balance of design that he did not always maintain. The furniture Quervelle displayed in his cabinet and sofa manufactory on South Second Street, a few doors below Dock Street, often were coarse and excessive in their carved ornamentation and elaborately veneered surfaces. This inelegance notwithstanding, President Andrew Jackson acquired for the East Room of the White House two circular pedestal tables in 1829. Those tables were similar to the pedestal table in the Empire parlor (plate 165) from an Albany, New York, house erected about 1830. A high ceiling, long windows, and an Italian marble mantel flanked with carved caryatids provide an appropriate background for the late classical furniture. The doorways and window trim are formed of pilasters supporting classical entablatures, which might have been influenced by illustrations in such American publications as Minard Lafever's *Modern Builder's Guide*, printed in New York in 1833. Such an elaborate interior might have been described by that irascible English traveler to America, Mrs. Frances Trollope, whose general impression of life, particularly social manners, in the new nation was unfavorable. Her critical analysis of the country, published in London in 1832 as *Domestic Manners of the Americans*, did proffer a few favorable judgments, one of which was the observation that in New York "dwelling houses of the upper classes are extremely handsome and very richly furnished."

In the 1830s and 1840s a late classical, or pillar and scroll, style became the rage. In this style flat undecorated surfaces and S-scroll and C-scroll supports are the dominant design aspects. Furniture was most often constructed of pine or other inexpensive woods and veneered with rich matched-grain mahogany.

Among the leading New York manufacturers of pillar and scroll furniture were Joseph and Edward Meeks, whose company was later known as Joseph Meeks and Sons. The Meeks manufactory was one of the oldest and largest furniture-making firms in America. At the time of his death in 1868 at the ripe age of ninety-seven, Joseph Meeks had been in business for nearly eighty

165. Museum installation. Empire parlor. Thomas Hooker (attr.). Albany, New York. c. 1839. Henry Francis du Pont Winterthur Museum, Winterthur, Delaware

This parlor was constructed with woodwork from a house built by General Rufus King in Albany about 1839; the house possibly was designed by Thomas Hooker. Much of the Empire furniture is architectural in flavor. Several of the porcelains in the parlor are decorated with portraits of George Washington; a pair of pitchers on the pier table to the right of the fireplace are attributed to William Ellis Tucker of Philadelphia. The stencil-decorated worktable to the left of the window was crafted between 1834 and 1836 by Roswell A. Hubbard of New York. The window is hung with mull curtains embroidered with silver stars. The Aubusson carpet was imported.

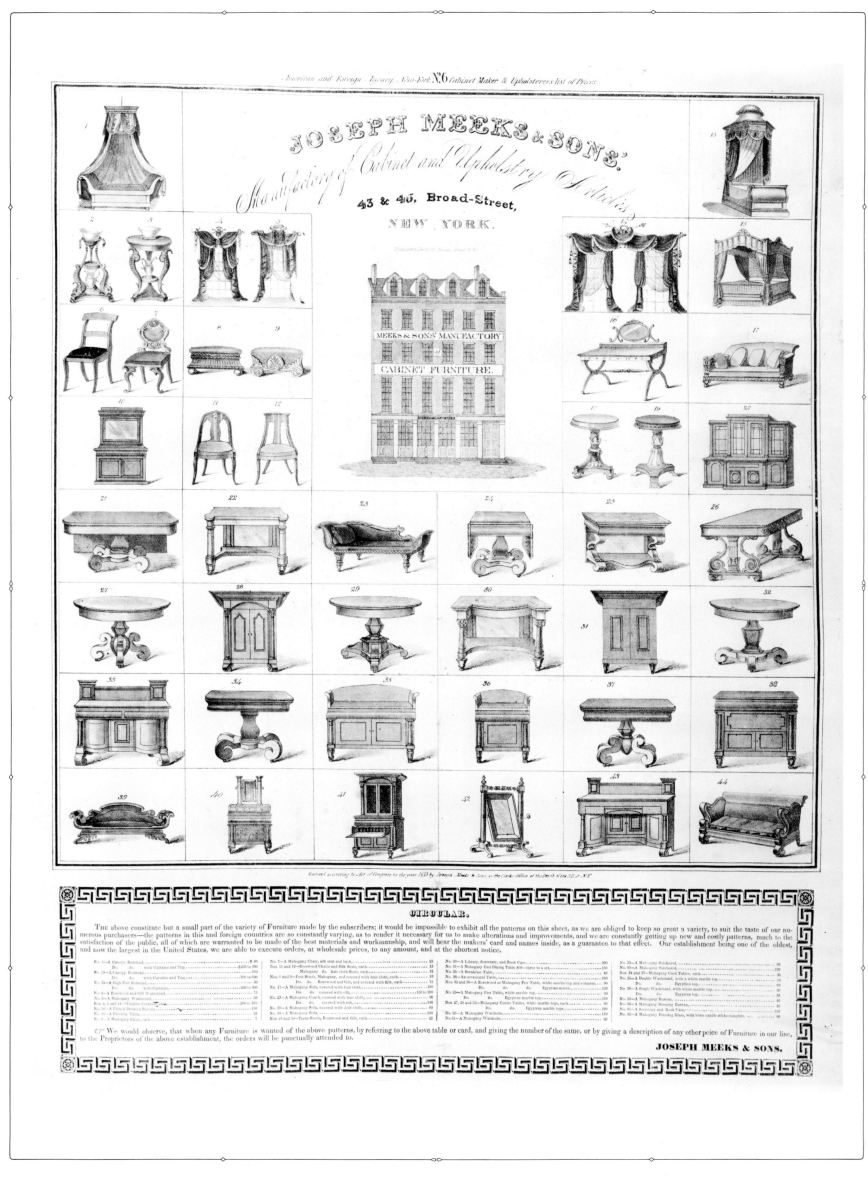

OPPOSITE:

*166. Broadside advertisement.
Joseph Meeks and Sons; published
by Endicott and Swett. New York
City. 1833. Lithograph, 21½ ×
17". Metropolitan Museum of
Art, New York City. Gift of
Mrs. R. W. Hyde, 1943*

*The furniture illustrated in this
broadside for the firm of Joseph
Meeks and Sons demonstrates
the full acceptance of the new
pillar and scroll style. Impressive
flat undecorated surfaces and
S-scroll and C-scroll supports
dominate the designs. The Meeks
broadside price list boasted forty-
one examples of furniture and two
sets of draperies.*

*167. Scrimshaw. Maker
unknown. New England. Early
nineteenth century. Whale tooth,
height 7½". Greenfield Village
and Henry Ford Museum,
Dearborn, Michigan*

*The carving of familiar designs
and motifs on ivory and whalebone
provided sailors with a link to
home. There is little doubt that
fancifully decorated scrimshaw
served a therapeutic purpose for
the sailors, by allowing them to
while away endless idle hours
aboard ship. This whale tooth
depicts the symbolic image of
Columbia, the Gem of the Ocean,
and several of the ships that
earned for New England the
sobriquet "America's queen
of the seas."*

years. As a major competitor of Duncan Phyfe, he had supplied far-flung
American markets across the expanding nation, from Boston to New Orleans,
and had family representatives as far away as Argentina and Brazil. Specializing
in elegant and durable cabinetwork, he also supplied furniture to the White
House. The Meeks broadside advertisement (plate 166) depicts the great variety
of forms available from their company in 1833. The leg shapes for the various
kinds of tables are striking examples of the pillar and scroll styles.

Pillar and scroll pieces were among the first mass-produced machine-made
furniture. During the early 1830s proprietors of small cabinetmaking shops,
who had specialized in handcrafted furniture, began to find competition with
the inexpensive, rich-looking products of the machine age difficult—and re-
luctantly, one by one, they closed up shop.

During the early years of the Republic, Americans were as obsessed with
oriental works of art as they had been in the William and Mary and Queen
Anne periods. By the early nineteenth century, trade with the East was responsible for the vast fortunes of New England's merchant princes. These merchants
dominated American trade, and their wealth provided an economic base for
building extraordinary homes filled with decorative accessories from all over
the world. Lacquer trays, paintings, reverse paintings on glass, porcelain, pottery, wallpaper, ivory carvings, and even children's toys were purchased in
Canton, the only Chinese port open to foreign trade until the Opium War of
1839–42. Goods were sold in hongs—factories or warehouses that lay between

168. Oriental Workshop. *Artist unknown. China. 1813. Watercolor, 11¾ × 15″. Benjamin Ginsburg, New York City*

This Chinese painting from a set of four depicts oriental craftsmen caning a daybed and crating furniture for export, the most important foreign markets at the time being those in the West.

169. Elijah Boardman. *Ralph Earl. United States. 1789. Oil on canvas, 83 × 51″. Metropolitan Museum of Art, New York City. Bequest of Susan W. Tyler, 1979*

Boardman was a prosperous textile merchant in New Milford, Connecticut. The bolts of fabric seen through an open door are similar to high-quality imported English and French cloth of the period.

170. Bed rug. Rachel Packard. Jericho, Vermont. 1805. Wool homespun, $93\frac{1}{2} \times 90''$. Greenfield Village and Henry Ford Museum, Dearborn, Michigan. Gift of Mrs. Delia Borgers

The background of this rug is worked in finely spun yarn, while the bright yarns used in the design are somewhat coarser in texture. Bed rugs appear in American inventories over an extended period. The earliest of them date from the seventeenth century and the latest from the middle of the nineteenth century.

171. Quilt. Sarah Furman Warner. Greenfield Hill, Connecticut. c. 1800. Cotton and homespun, $105 \times 84''$. Greenfield Village and Henry Ford Museum, Dearborn, Michigan

Accented with embroidery, this folk art masterpiece utilizing appliqué technique is wonderfully pictorial. It undoubtedly represents the buildings and the citizens of the small New England village in which it was created. The wide border composed of vines and birds and urns with flowers has been executed with unusual skill.

172. Pillow sham. Anne D. Miller. New England. 1832. Candlewick roving on homespun, 29½ × 61½". Collection Jay Johnson, New York City

A pillow sham functioned as a cover for the pillow when the bed was formally made, and its design usually repeated or otherwise was related to the bedcover. This is one of the finest extant candlewick pieces.

the walled city and the Canton River. Chinese workmen in the painting of an oriental furniture workshop (plate 168) are making Western-style furniture for export. Furniture specifically produced for the Western market was often ridiculed by affluent Chinese, for it was considered much inferior to the objects created for domestic use. In China ownership of finely crafted pieces of furniture was a status symbol. They were luxury items created for a highly discriminating minority consisting of nobility, scholars, wealthy merchants, and officials. The Chinese did not discard furniture when a style passed from favor, as was common practice in the West. The object was frequently adapted to suit the taste of a new owner or heir. The height would perhaps be altered or intricate carving added. Caned couches and settees like those being worked on in the painting are still found in the seacoast homes of New England, where returning captains sailed home with them for their clients and families.

Scrimshaw was made from the teeth and bone of whales by men aboard whaling and cargo ships. Whiling away long months at sea, these untrained artists ingeniously carved unusual gifts for friends and sweethearts at home.

173. Mrs. Reuben Humphreys and Her Child. Richard Brunton (attr.). East Granby, Connecticut. c. 1800. Oil on canvas, 44½ × 40½". Connecticut Historical Society, Hartford, Connecticut

In this painting Anna Humphreys, who bore twelve children during her lifetime, is shown with her infant daughter, Eliza. Paintings of early homes frequently illustrate contemporary furnishings and therefore provide valuable historical information on the decorative arts. Mrs. Humphreys is sitting in a Windsor chair, a Chippendale looking glass is supported on Battersea enamel knobs, and fashionable tea equipage is set out on the table.

The early-nineteenth-century whale tooth (plate 167) is engraved with a picture of the traditional figure of Columbia, the Gem of the Ocean, and several clipper ships.

Textiles were still being imported in large quantity even though Americans had been forced to establish small textile mills during the Revolution. In 1793 Samuel Slater, a mechanic who had emigrated from England, constructed textile machines at Pawtucket, Rhode Island. Because of his imaginative use of newly developed machinery made possible by the Industrial Revolution and by the systematic organization of his work force, he came to be known as the father of the factory system in America.

The portrait of Elijah Boardman (plate 169) painted by Ralph Earl shows bolts of prized fabrics through an open door to a stockroom. Although one can only surmise, the designs and quality indicate a type of cloth that would have been imported from England and France. From the appearance of Mr. Boardman, one can also surmise that dealing in fabrics was a congenial and lucrative business.

174. Covered tureen. William Ellis Tucker. Philadelphia, Pennsylvania. 1825–38. Porcelain, height 10⅝". Current whereabouts unknown

The Tucker products are characterized by gold decoration surrounding floral motifs. Although Tucker porcelain was produced for only a short time, there apparently was a rather large output since numerous examples are extant. The tureen bears the initials A T, for Anne Tucker, niece of the potter.

American women continued to ply their needles with great dexterity. The bed rug (plate 170) worked in 1805 by Rachel Packard in rural Jericho, Vermont, demonstrates that while such fancy goods as those in the Elijah Boardman portrait were available in cities, country women still found it necessary to produce for themselves much of what they used in the home. Probably the most beautiful of all American appliqué quilts is the famous bedcover (plate 171) executed by Sarah Furman Warner of Greenfield Hill, Connecticut. This folk masterpiece, its borders skillfully composed of vines, birds, and flower-filled urns, depicts the buildings and the citizens of the small New England village where the quilt was made.

Candlewicking is a type of bedcover often passed over or even ignored by historians of American decorative arts, since it was frequently undated and unsigned. There are two types of needlework known as candlewicking; one is embroidered by hand, the other is woven on a loom. The pillow sham (plate 172) was embroidered by Anne D. Miller in 1832. This gifted young embroidress chose the American eagle, in its characteristic pose as the symbol of the young nation, for the central motif on this pillow sham, or pillow cover. Woven candlewicking was produced as early as 1822 at the coverlet mill of Rutger Factory near Paterson, New Jersey. The decorative motifs on woven candlewick spreads tend to be geometric. Candlewicking derives its name from

175. Tea set. Paul Revere. Boston, Massachusetts. 1792–93. Silver and wood handle on teapot, height of teapot 6⅛". Minneapolis Institute of Arts, Minneapolis, Minnesota. Gift of James F. and Louise H. Bell

176. Punch pot. Simon Chaudron. Philadelphia, Pennsylvania. 1805–10. Silver, height 8⅞". Metropolitan Museum of Art, New York City. Gift of Mr. and Mrs. Marshall P. Blankarn, 1966

A delicate, restrained classicism, which was the influential style in silverware following the Revolution, is reflected in the elliptical shape of the teapot and tea caddy. Fluted sides, decorated with engraved swags and tassel drapery on the teapot and caddy, are also evident on the helmet-shaped cream pitcher and urn-shaped sugar bowl. The design of these chaste forms is further enhanced by stylized pineapple finials.

Animal forms, especially animal heads, were popular decorative arts motifs throughout the Empire period. This cylindrical-shaped punch pot, with rose finial, is in the French style. The double spouts, terminating in animal heads, form a symmetry characteristic of classical design. Chased leaves at the base of the spouts and the heads themselves are similar to leaf carving on innumerable pieces of Empire furniture.

an inexpensive, coarse twisted white cotton cord, or roving, resembling the wicks used by candlemakers.

When Mrs. Reuben Humphreys sat with her child for their portrait (plate 173) about 1800, the Connecticut artist Richard Brunton depicted her with a fashionable tea service of the sort that would have been imported. By the end of the eighteenth century several local potteries and ceramic manufacturers had begun operation. William Ellis Tucker became fascinated with the prospect of china production, and after working in his father's china store in Philadelphia

177. Chalice. Victor Rouquette. Detroit, Michigan. 1819. Silver gilt, height 10½″. Archdiocese of Detroit, Michigan

Rouquette made this silver gilt chalice for Saint Ann's Church in Detroit. The chalice must have been greatly treasured since the area was little more than a settlement in the wilderness when the object was crafted.

from 1816 to 1823, he began to experiment with various clays and formulas. By 1827 he had received a silver medal from the Franklin Institute for the best specimen of porcelain made in the state of Pennsylvania. The covered tureen (plate 174) was produced by Tucker between 1825 and 1838; it was originally owned by Anne Tucker, the niece of the potter, and bears her monogram.

In the early years of the new nation the design of American silver, as did that of furniture, changed abruptly. The remarkably beautiful tea set (plate 175) crafted in 1792–93 for John and Mehitable Templeman by Paul Revere was fashioned in the classical style. The covered sugar bowl is in the form of an urn,

and the cream pitcher is helmet-shaped; engraved swags and tassels ornament each piece of the hollow ware. All pieces in the service, with the exception of the tongs, have the initials J M T engraved on them. Although Revere is best known for his craftsmanship in the colonial period, he continued to produce exquisitely wrought silver pieces in the Federal period.

In the early nineteenth century the infant Empire style of furniture design, with its heavy reliance upon animal motifs and forms, extended to all of the decorative arts. The punch pot (plate 176) by Simon Chaudron of Philadelphia has double spouts terminating in animal heads. The striking symmetry of shape and the overall ornamentation are typical of the new classicism of the French style.

New technologies expanded the number of finishes available on metal objects. The chalice (plate 177) by Victor Roquette of Detroit, Michigan, was made of silver and then gilded to look like gold. Advanced technology also made it possible to have a wider choice of metals that could be worked with ease in the production of decorative objects for domestic use. The suite of astral mantel lamps (plate 178), cast in bronze and fitted with cut-glass shades and

prisms, was one result of the nation's incipient technical capabilities. Lighting improved substantially during the last years of the eighteenth and early part of the nineteenth centuries as new types of lamps with special burners were developed. The astral lamp was the result of a principle in oil-burning lighting devices developed in 1783 by Aimé Argand, a Swiss chemist. He fitted a hollow cylindrical wick between two metal tubes; the top extended down through and below the oil reservoir, allowing oxygen to reach the flame from both the

180. Covered goblet. New Bremen Glass Manufactory. Frederick County, Maryland. 1788. Blown glass, engraved, height 11¼". Metropolitan Museum of Art, New York City. Rogers Fund, 1928

Very few examples of American glass are as historic or as well documented. This goblet, known as the Bremen pokol, was blown and engraved by the glassworks of Frederick Amelung for his German backers, who came up with the capital to found his American factory.

interior and the exterior, thus producing a brighter and more smoke-free method of illumination. One of the most popular manufacturers of astral lamps in America was B. Gardiner of New York City. The brass andirons (plate 179) by Richard Wittingham of New York City also represent the kind of solid and handsomely designed utilitarian item that the new technology could produce.

The War of 1812 further stimulated the growth of a factory system in the United States, for trade with Britain was for the most part cut off. In spite of

America's enthusiasm for industrialization and the inexpensive goods that were its fruits, handcraftsmanship still prevailed in many areas.

By 1785 several new glass manufacturers had begun operation, but none was as successful as the German immigrant John Frederick Amelung, who founded the New Bremen Glass Manufactory in Frederick County, Maryland. Amelung was an experienced glassmaker who had managed a mirror and sheet-glass factory in his homeland. His glassworks produced useful and decorative wares; an engraved goblet known as the Bremen pokol (plate 180) is one of the earliest engraved presentation glasses manufactured in the United States. It is free-blown of nonlead glass and was made by Amelung for his German backers, who had provided ten thousand pounds to capitalize his factory. The wheel-engraved decoration displays the arms of the city of Bremen and the inscrip-

181. Decanter. Maker unknown. Pittsburgh, Pennsylvania. c. 1825. Blown and cut glass, height 11''. Wine glass. Probably Bakewell, Page and Bakewell. Pittsburgh, Pennsylvania. c. 1825. Cut glass, height approximately 4''. Compote. Probably Bakewell, Page and Bakewell. Pittsburgh, Pennsylvania. c. 1825. Cut glass, height approximately 10''. All private collection

The decanter, in the Anglo-Irish tradition, has a tooled triple-ringed neck and applied base. It is cut with panels and strawberry-diamond and fan design and has a star-cut and paneled hollow ball stopper with an applied neck. The wine glass is from a large set of matched water goblets, champagnes, and wines that are cut in the strawberry-diamond and fan pattern. The compote is paneled below the strawberry-diamond and fan cutting and the base is ray-cut. The heavy foot and the classical baluster on the compote are in the spirit of the Empire style.

tions read: "Old Bremen Success and the New Progress" and "New Bremen Glassmanufactory 1788 North America State of Maryland."

One of the earliest nineteenth-century glass manufacturers west of the Alleghenies was Benjamin Bakewell, who established a furnace in 1808 at the boom town of Pittsburgh, Pennsylvania. He produced clear glass of exceptional quality; much of it was cut and decorated with elegant designs such as the strawberry-diamond and fan pattern (plate 181). The strawberry-diamond and fan motif was introduced by English glass cutters about 1820, having been adapted from ancient molded-glass patterns. Bakewell's glass was of such distinguished sophistication that President James Monroe, visiting the plant in 1817, ordered a service engraved with the arms of the United States for use at the White House.

A French visitor to America in 1821 observed that nearly every American possessed a "mechanic in his soul." Although the description was sarcastic and may have been tinged with envy, mechanical ingenuity certainly did, in many respects, provide solutions for the ever-expanding, westward-moving nation. Some unknown enterprising glassblower developed a full-sized, multisectioned hinged mold that permitted increased production and a more standardized product at a decreased cost. The mold, into which a gather of glass had been blown, could be unfolded and removed, much as one would strip the peel from an orange. Blown-in-the-mold glass objects found acceptance with the American consumer because they could be purchased for much less than the cost of an imported or even a domestic cut-glass piece. Most glass plants adopted this timesaving technique. Designs were intricate, and a greater variety of patterns was practicable.

At about the same time, goblet bases and other small forms were shaped in a so-called lemon squeezer, or handpress. As an outgrowth of the hand-pressing process, by the early 1820s American glassmakers had perfected a way of mechanically pressing molten glass between two precisely made metal dies. For the first time mass production of glass was possible. Once the method proved technically and economically feasible, practically all glassworks incorporated pressed glass into their repertoire. Manufacturers discovered that most pressed glass lost its clarity when shaped in a metal mold, and they experimented to overcome this disadvantage. Lacy glass, with an overall pattern set against a stippled background (plate 182), solved the problem, and demonstrated again the potential of American ingenuity. Because lacy pressed glass was relatively inexpensive, it became extremely popular.

182. Lacy pressed-glass objects. Flint Glass Company, Keene, New Hampshire; Boston and Sandwich Glass Company, Sandwich, Massachusetts. 1828–40. Free-blown, mold-blown, and pressed glass, height of lamp 7½". Corning Museum of Glass, Corning, New York

The pressing process for glass was perfected between 1825 and 1830, and these three lacy pressed-glass pieces represent the earliest type of pressed-glass objects made. Although the opaque blue lamp has a pressed base, the font is blown because the technology had not been perfected sufficiently to produce pressed fonts at the time. For the same reason, the inkwell and sand shaker in the desk set are mold-blown rather than pressed. The sugar bowl is pressed opalescent glass.

With the introduction of the pressing process the American glass industry came of age. It could, at last, begin to satisfy the needs of a burgeoning population that demanded the amenities of a nascent industrial era. The Boston and Sandwich Glass Company at Sandwich, Massachusetts, employed 225 workmen and by 1829 their annual production was worth over $300,000. In time the mold designers and cutters gained a proficiency that enabled glassworks to manufacture products which exhibited a high degree of sophistication. Mechanically pressed glass virtually brought to an end the production of fine free-blown and blown-in-the-mold cut-decorated glass. Americans by this time did not have to be wealthy in order to own glassware.

When Queen Victoria began her reign in 1837, there was a resurgence of American dependence on England in matters of taste and style. There were many who still considered the native land of their ancestors somewhat nostalgically as their homeland as well. The Industrial Revolution, which actually began in the eighteenth century in England, brought about dramatic changes in the nineteenth in both nations. An agrarian handicraft economy was altering very rapidly to one dominated by industry. Similar technologies in the two countries, as well as a kindred spirit, led to a blending of American and English tastes.

Eclectic Design in an Eclectic World
1837-1860

Queen Victoria exerted a profound influence not only on life throughout the British empire but also on every aspect of American life during her reign, which from her coronation in 1837 to her death sixty-four years later in 1901 was the longest monarchic rule in English history. At the time of her coronation, American periodicals enthusiastically predicted a new prosperity and an era of peace in her reign. In the March 1838 issue of *Godey's Magazine and Lady's Book*—the woman's magazine par excellence—the editor adopted an exuberant moral stance typical of the age:

The "reign of intellect and feeling" should be ushered in by a woman. Victoria has come to the throne under many peculiar advantages. . . . She brings to her high station all the intelligence which the most careful education could bestow, to fit her for her duties. . . . She has also the inestimable privilege of living in an age when the moral power of right principles, of truth in its simplicity is, in a measure, understood.

Victoria ascended the throne in a period of agitated social and economic development. The traditional economy was rapidly being altered, and the effects of the Industrial Revolution became increasingly evident as the machine provided new capabilities. The organization of the work force into large units meant the beginnings of the factory system. Some areas of the old cottage system, particularly in textile production, moved to the new factories. Steam power, which furnished a means of transforming heat energy into mechanical energy, was one of the basic power sources of the new industrial society, and steam-driven tools had benefits for both architecture and furniture making. Mass production was employed extensively to yield both raw building materials and furniture, and machine-made furnishings supplied the requirements of a burgeoning middle class. The nineteenth century in general, while supplying more goods to more people, was marked by a departure from the old standards of craftsmanship.

The Victorian style cannot be easily categorized. It involved eclectic fashions based on revivals of older styles. There were many contradictions, such as massive simplicity and ornate decoration—both of which seemed to be a romantic harking back to Gothic forms and design.

Although American architecture at the beginning of the Victorian period was still emulating European fashions, it had begun to develop a style of its own. Benjamin Henry Latrobe, born in Yorkshire, England, is considered the first professional architect in the United States. Latrobe, who arrived in America in 1796 as a young man, expressed a strong predilection for the classical style in his important commissions—the Philadelphia Waterworks of 1801 and the reconstruction of the Capitol in Washington, D.C., after its destruction by fire in 1814. These classical buildings earned Latrobe a preeminent place in the annals of American architecture, and his inventive genius led to the erection of the first Gothic revival residence in America—Sedgeley, a country seat designed for the Philadelphia merchant William Crammond. Besides the various city residences he was engaged in constructing, Latrobe accomplished much monumental work and introduced Greek forms, an important element of the classic revival.

A second architect of great influence was Charles Bulfinch, a Harvard graduate who returned to his native New England from Europe in 1787. Bulfinch's Tontine Crescent in Boston and his numerous other city dwellings set new standards of convenience and flexibility of arrangement. His building designs were widely imitated. Bulfinch was one of the architects who through the years worked on completing the reconstruction of the Capitol; by 1827 he had built the first dome.

Asher Benjamin, a carpenter-builder, did more to influence early-nine-

183. Harold C. Brooks House. Jabez Fitch. Michigan. 1838. Marshall Historical Society, Marshall, Michigan

The successful and the affluent at the beginning of the Victorian era usually chose the Greek revival style when constructing their homes, such as the residence of Harold C. Brooks built at Marshall, Michigan, by Jabez Fitch. The grandeur of the style imparted a sense of elegant stability that appealed to the rising middle class across the nation.

teenth-century architecture than perhaps any of his contemporaries. His major influence was through his publications, which popularized the details of the late colonial style. Benjamin synthesized Latrobe's and Bulfinch's contributions in his book *The Country Builder's Assistant: Containing a Collection of New Designs of Carpentry and Architecture,* published at Greenfield, Massachusetts, in 1797. As a result of this pioneer publication, the first architectural guide originating in America, Benjamin received numerous commissions, which by 1803 enabled him to move from a small Massachusetts town to Boston. With the collaboration of Daniel Raynard, he was responsible for an even more influential book, *The American Builder's Companion: or a New System of Architecture Particularly Adapted to the Present Style of Building in the United States of America,* published in Boston in 1806. The second edition appeared in 1811 under Benjamin's name alone. The manual went into six editions through the years, an indication of its success and prestige.

Benjamin's books were used extensively as guides for the important structures being erected in new towns developing on the western frontier. Jabez Fitch, who was responsible for the imposing 1838 Greek revival residence (plate 183) at Marshall, Michigan, was most likely familiar with Benjamin's publications.

It is not surprising that when the noted architect Ithiel Town commissioned the landscape painter Thomas Cole, leader of the Hudson River school, to

OVERLEAF:

184. The Architect's Dream. Thomas Cole. New York. 1840. Oil on canvas, 54 × 84". Toledo Museum of Art, Toledo, Ohio. Gift of Edward Drummond Libbey

This painting reveals the prevailing eclectic taste in architecture at the beginning of the Victorian age. This canvas, painted for the architect Ithiel Town, offers a medley of Egyptian, Greek, Roman, Gothic, and Moorish styles. Many of these architectural styles were the basis for decorative arts design throughout the Victorian period.

PAINTED BY T. COLE
FOR I. TOWN ARCH.
1840.

185. Empire Parlor. *Alexander Jackson Davis. New York. 1845. Watercolor on paper, 13¼ × 18⅛". New-York Historical Society, New York City*

By the 1840s the taste for classically inspired designs and architectural furniture began to wane. Davis was captivated by the potential of the Gothic revival and much of his later work reflects that style. In this interior rendering, columns, friezes, and moldings, as well as the klismos-type chairs, the sofas, the lamps, and even the fire screen are suggestive of objects and styles from ancient Greece.

execute a large canvas, Cole chose a typically romantic title, *The Architect's Dream* (plate 184). This painting reflects the prevailing academic taste in architecture at the beginning of the Victorian period. Greek, Roman, Egyptian, and even Gothic details are incorporated into the array of styles represented in this eclectic assemblage.

The Greek revival style during the 1830s and 1840s was all-pervasive, and city homes in the East designed by America's most active architects relied heavily upon classical inspirations. Alexander Jackson Davis was one of the most famous of these eastern architects. Davis began his career as a junior partner of Ithiel Town and through Town's library developed his vivid imagination for historical styles. Davis influenced a generation of architects throughout the country and had a great effect on the decorative arts, since he customarily created not only the designs for the exteriors but also those for the interiors and the furnishings. His watercolor rendering of an Empire parlor (plate 185) incorporates columns, friezes, and moldings as well as klismos-type chairs, sofas, lamps, and even a fire screen—all reminiscent of ancient Greek furniture and household items.

186. *Museum installation. Parlor set. Duncan Phyfe. New York City. 1837. Mahogany, length of méridienne 72". Metropolitan Museum of Art, New York City. L. E. Katzenbach Fund, 1966*

The méridienne, curule stool, window bench, and gondola chair are part of a larger parlor set produced in the late classical style by Duncan Phyfe for the New York lawyer Samuel A. Foot. The pieces are covered in crimson linen and wool rep upholstery with woven gold medallions, which is a copy of the original fabric.

187A. Concert grand piano.
Jonas Chickering. Boston,
Massachusetts. c. 1840. Rosewood,
dimensions unavailable. Current
whereabouts unknown

Several decorative embellishments
which had first appeared in the
Empire style were used by the
maker of the piano case. The
legs are topped with a stylized
eagle carving and the foot-pedal
support is in the shape of a
classical lyre.

187B. Square piano. Robert Nunns and John Clark. New York City. 1853. Rosewood, width 88¼". Metropolitan Museum of Art,
New York City. Gift of George Lowther, 1906

Although many performers and collectors today would find the robust carving on this florid musical instrument rather extravagant, it was
considered the epitome of fine taste in the middle of the nineteenth century. The piano keys are mother-of-pearl and tortoiseshell. The music
rack is pierced in an extremely fine-carved pattern. Compared to the carving on the more classical Chickering grand (see plate 187A) of the
previous decade, Nunns and Clark's piano exhibits the ornateness of the full-blown rococo revival.

Pillar and scroll furniture, which had first come into vogue in the early 1830s, continued to be fashionable in the Greek-style palaces of the Victorian period. Duncan Phyfe, like all successful furniture designers at the time, adapted his styles to suit the prevailing taste. The pillar and scroll méridienne, or daybed, in the museum installation (plate 186)—as well as the other pieces, a gondola chair, a bench, and a curule stool—is part of a large suite of fourteen pieces produced at Phyfe's New York City workshop in 1837. According to a family tradition, the New York lawyer Samuel A. Foot purchased this mahogany furniture to furnish the parlor of his new home at 678 Broadway. Phyfe's competitors, who also studiously designed their wares to meet the demands of contemporary styles, included Charles A. Baudouine, Charles Klein, and Joseph and Edward Meeks of New York City, Ignatius Lutz of Philadelphia, and John Needles of Boston.

In 1840 John Hall, an English immigrant architect working in Baltimore, published his manual *The Cabinet Maker's Assistant,* illustrating various examples of pillar and scroll furniture that could be produced with a steam-driven band saw. The saw had the unique capability of cutting intricate curves and ornaments in many thicknesses of wood. Scrolled furniture, which was elegant and simple, easily constructed, and also modest in cost, continued in demand throughout the nineteenth century.

The nineteenth-century pulpit and press were highly critical of much of the local commercial entertainment such as vaudeville, minstrel shows, prize fights, melodramatic theater pieces, and Barnum's museum with its spectacle of acrobats, dwarfs, giants, and its waxworks. Spectators were frequently boisterous and rowdy, and the cause was not hard to find—the rank smell of whiskey permeated the auditoriums and theaters. Mrs. Trollope naturally had an easy target in the disorderly behavior of American audiences. Yet music—as a gentler, homespun pleasure—was acceptable to the moralists. In noticeable contrast to practices in Europe, the pianoforte could be found even in simple homes, and musical get-togethers became a trend in some of the more cultured cities. The grand piano (plate 187A), the very first concert grand by the American piano maker Jonas Chickering, was crafted from rosewood in 1840. Five years later, the enthusiastic travel writer and poet Nathaniel P. Willis (in the volume *The Prose Works of N. P. Willis,* published in Philadelphia) printed a paean to Chickering's abilities as a manufacturer:

Play to me ere I begin! Music is creative! What a benefactor to the world is John [sic] Chickering! How exquisitely balanced are those octaves, and how gloriously (with that touch) the rich instrument revels through the music! The builder of these caves of harmony has a poet's vocation. . . . He who writes a poem that is read and loved by a thousand hearths, links himself with an angel's round of delight and sympathy; and the builder of a thousand harmonious instruments follows in the same bright orbit of influence.

A comparison of the Chickering piano with the square piano (plate 187B) manufactured about 1853 by Robert Nunns and John Clark is a history lesson in the palpable stylistic changes that can occur over a brief period of not much more than a decade. The vigorous carving on the Nunns and Clark's highly decorated musical instrument—made of rosewood, similar to the piano of the previous decade—is the epitome of the newer rococo revival style.

With the new affluence of a rising middle class in the early Victorian period and the easy availability of goods resulting from the new factory system, Americans frequently became confused by the difference between tasteful furnishings and those that were merely expensive. They were interested in building their homes and furnishing them in a way that would prove the owner possessed an up-to-date perception of style. The acorn clock (plate 188) with its églomisé painted panels and brass trimmings is an unusual and exceedingly beautiful example of fine furnishings of the period. The proposal for Ravenswood (plate 189), lithographed circa 1845 by Nathaniel Currier after an original con-

OPPOSITE:

188. Acorn clock. Forestville Manufacturing Company. Bristol, Connecticut. c. 1850. Mahogany veneer, height 24¼". Greenfield Village and Henry Ford Museum, Dearborn, Michigan

The front of this clock is composed of two pieces of glass. The upper tablet is painted green with stenciled decoration. The lower one displays the Merchants Exchange in Philadelphia, a building in the classical style.

MERCHANTS' EXCHANGE
PHILADELPHIA.

189. Ravenswood. Nathaniel Currier (after design by Alexander Jackson Davis). New York. c. 1845. Lithograph, 17¾ × 50″. Museum of the City of New York, New York City. Harry T. Peters Collection

Alexander Jackson Davis created scores of designs that paraphrased medieval and ancient conceptions. His proposal for the Ravenswood development in Astoria, in the New York borough of Queens, reflected various contemporary obsessions, not only with medieval Gothic style but also with Tuscan, Greek, and Egyptian. His finest home is the Hudson River mansion Lyndhurst (see plate 190).

190. Lyndhurst. Alexander Jackson Davis. New York. 1838. Lyndhurst, National Trust for Historic Preservation, Tarrytown, New York

This Hudson River mansion, an outstanding example of American Gothic revival style, was designed in 1838 by Davis for William Paulding, mayor of New York from 1834 to 1851.

191. Brigham Young and His
Wife and Six Children. *William
Warner Major. Utah. c. 1847.
Oil on canvas, 28 × 36".*
Copyrighted by Corporation of the
President of the Church of Jesus
Christ of Latter-Day Saints,
Salt Lake City, Utah

*This idealized portrait of Brigham
Young and his family reflects the
pervasive interest in Gothic revival
throughout the nation in the second
quarter of the nineteenth century.
Gothic details are evident in the
woodwork. The chair appears to
be upholstered in velvet, and the
floor, either painted or covered
by a carpet, incorporates Gothic
designs.*

192. Museum installation. Parlor
from Colonel Robert J. Milligan
House. Saratoga Springs, New
York. 1853. Brooklyn Museum,
Brooklyn, New York. Gift of
Sarah Milligan Rand, Kate
Milligan Brill, and the Dick S.
Ramsay Fund

This richly ornate parlor
installation at the Brooklyn
Museum was originally part of
the Milligan residence at Saratoga
Springs. A striking example of the
rococo revival style, the room
features chairs by Galusha Brothers
of Troy, New York.

ceptual design by Alexander Jackson Davis, is a clear indication of the medley of styles acceptable to even one of America's most respected designers. Gothic, Tuscan, Greek, and Egyptian architectural styles are all represented in this scheme. In the same year this lithograph was published Solon Robinson in the April issue of *Cultivator* magazine described prefabricated homes on the western

193. Turtle-top table. Joseph Meeks and Sons (attr.). New York City. c. 1850. Laminated rosewood with marble top, height 30¾". Greenfield Village and Henry Ford Museum, Dearborn, Michigan

This rococo revival table was part of a suite of parlor furniture formerly in Abraham Lincoln's home in Springfield, Illinois.

prairies, a mode of construction which today is generally associated with twentieth-century practices: "As we rise upon the 25 miles wide prairie, which our road lies across, we see five miles ahead, a most enormous frame house, which was built (all but putting together) in Rhode Island."

The Gothic revival style in the United States was a conscious attempt to evoke a romantic image. It was based upon a continuation of an English medieval strain that had even in the seventeenth century been acknowledged by American architects and craftsmen. For example, Saint Luke's, a tiny brick church built in 1632 at Smithfield, Virginia, contained buttresses and pointed-arch windows. By the middle of the nineteenth century Gothic revival was widespread, and a freer attitude replaced the formal restraint evident in the neoclassic structures of the turn of the century. Andrew Jackson Downing, horticulturist, architect, and landscape gardener, wrote many popular and valuable treatises in all three fields; these works directly influenced the Gothic revival. His *Cottage Residences,* which pointed the way to improvement in rural homes, was published in New York and London in 1842. It was an instant best-seller and led to an unrestrained use of the exotic Gothic revival for exteriors, interiors, and for every imaginable decorative accessory, whether or not it was appropriate.

Asymmetrical designs created by Alexander Jackson Davis and his contemporaries emphasized a poetic style of architecture. Characteristic of this romantic leaning were picturesque villas and cottages undulating with crockets, cusps, oriel windows, pointed arches, towers, trellises, and turrets. The mode became such a craze that earlier houses were "modernized" by the gaudy application of Gothic motifs and gingerbread ornamentation. There are two notable instances of this updating. One is a farmhouse at Kennebunk, Maine, in which the foursquare brick house was encased in Gothic tracery and has come to be

194. Cabinet-bookcase. Brooks Cabinet Warehouse. Brooklyn, New York. 1850. Rosewood, height 72". Museum of the City of New York, New York City. Gift of Arthur S. Vernay

The twisted columns on this dramatic Elizabethan revival case piece, which was presented to Jenny Lind by members of the New York City fire department, were considered by most Victorians to be an Elizabethan feature. As in much Victorian furniture, a hodgepodge of revival styles makes an imposing design.

known as the Wedding Cake House. The other is Sunnyside, an old Dutch farmhouse at Tarrytown, New York, in which Gothic motifs were lavished on the simple structure when it was renovated by Washington Irving—who in his writings inspired by the Hudson River environs showed a similar predilection for Gothic details.

One of the most impressive of all American Gothic revival edifices is Lyndhurst (plate 190). The mansion was designed in 1838 by Davis for William

A considerably restrained interpretation of the Gothic revival is evident in the portrait of Brigham Young and his family (plate 191) painted about 1847 by William Warner Major, who was born in England, joined the Church of Jesus Christ of Latter-Day Saints there in 1842 and immigrated to America in 1844. He accompanied the Mormon trek from Illinois to Utah in 1846–48 and executed this idealized version of the Young family on that trip. The nineteenth-century admiration for a mix of historical styles from the past embraced furniture as well as architecture. During the 1850s and 1860s the Elizabethan revival style, with its rope and bobbin turnings, embellished

both fine city furniture, such as the rosewood cabinet-bookcase (plate 194), and inexpensive mass-produced bedroom suites crafted from pine and decorated with bright paint and floral patterns. Elizabethan revival, which developed early in the Victorian period and bore a resemblance to the Cromwellian forms of the 1600s, enjoyed its greatest influence in the United States, especially with mass-produced cottage furniture. The cabinet-bookcase, made by the Brooks Cabinet Warehouse in Brooklyn, New York, has twisted columns associated with the Elizabethan revival style. This handsome rosewood piece was given by the New York City firemen to Jenny Lind, the Swedish Nightingale. The ornately carved crest rail and the undulating feet are in the rococo revival

Guest and autograph books—such as this guest book with its sentimental title characteristic of the age, The Token, or Affection's Gift—appealed to the Victorian taste for collecting sentimental memorabilia. Papier mâché generally was not incorporated into furniture design in America.

197. Book cover. Maker unknown. *United States, 1857. Papier mâché inlaid with mother-of-pearl, 8 × 5¼". Collection Mr. and Mrs. Charles V. Hagler*

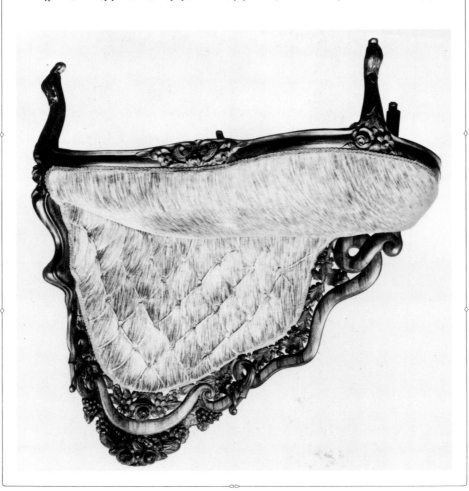

Henry Austin built this Italianate villa for Ruggles Sylvester Morse. The villa was furnished with many pieces in the rococo revival style, which remained in vogue during the 1850s and well into the 1860s.

196. *Victoria Mansion, Henry Austin, Portland, Maine, 1859.*
Victoria Society of Maine Women, Portland, Maine

Paulding, mayor of New York, and his son Philip R. Paulding, Lyndhurst, the great pointed and crocketed pile of stone, was erected at Tarrytown in the years 1838–41 and was remodeled and expanded in 1864–65 for George Merritt. This imposing residence overlooking the Hudson was later purchased by the railroad speculator Jay Gould and remained in the family until 1964, when it was left to the National Trust.

A *méridienne*, a type of settee-couch, was deemed an essential item in every well-furnished mid-Victorian parlor. Although *méridiennes* were amply upholstered, coil springs were not commonly utilized in them.

195. *Méridienne, John Henry Belter (attr.). New York City, c. 1850. Rosewood, length 52″.*
Collection Richard and Eileen Dubrow Antiques, Bayside, New York

198. Ewer. Samuel Kirk and Son. Baltimore, Maryland. c. 1850. Silver, height 15½". Fortunoff, New York City

Mid-century rococo revival reached its fullest expression in furniture and silver. The Kirk firm is best known for its elaborate repoussé ornamented objects. This exquisite example has deeply embossed foliage designs on the foot, the body, and the graceful handle.

199. Cream jug. Gelston and Company. New York City. 1835–40. Silver, height 5¾". Private collection

The chinoiserie decoration on this Victorian jug includes engraved exotic birds, Chinese men, and pagodas.

200. Catalog advertisement.
Gorham and Company.
Providence, Rhode Island. 1850–
60. Private collection

The excesses of Victorian taste
are amply evident in Gorham's
advertisement, which includes
many conventional forms that
feature such exaggerated
ornamentation they border
on the grotesque.

mode and a carved shell, reminiscent of the Queen Anne and Chippendale periods, centers the skirt.

The rococo revival style, popular from about 1850 to the early 1900s, achieved its most impressive flowering in the products manufactured in the New York City shop of John Henry Belter (plate 195). Belter was a German immigrant who had served his apprenticeship in Württemberg at a time when the revival of French rococo was having an impact on decoration in Germany. He opened a shop in New York in the 1840s, and in 1856 he applied for a patent to protect a process of laminating thin sheets of wood and, through the use of steam, molding them into the desired shape. The resulting plywoodlike boards were especially strong and, because of their relative thickness, could be pierced with overall ornate carving in naturalistic designs.

Belter's patents were almost immediately infringed upon. The French-born cabinetmaker Charles A. Baudouine, a New York City competitor, circumvented the patent laws by manufacturing chairs of laminated wood with a center seam in the back.

In 1859 Ignatius Lutz at his Eleventh Street establishment in Philadelphia utilized an ingenious method to prevent the natural tendency of carved mahogany to break. In working on carved chairs, he divided the mahogany pieces into several lateral parts and glued them together in such a way that the grain of the wood ran in different directions. By this method the strength of the wood was increased in proportion to the number of times it was divided. In the manufacture of large objects, such as sofas and armchairs, the advantages were partic-

201. Side chairs and cabinet.
Leon Marcotte. New York City.
c. 1860. Ebonized maple and
fruitwood, height of chair 39".
Metropolitan Museum of Art,
New York City. Gift of Mrs. D.
Chester Noyes, 1968

202. Mantel clock. American
Clock Company. New York City.
c. 1850. Cast iron and wood,
height 21⅝". Greenfield Village
and Henry Ford Museum,
Dearborn, Michigan

These items in the Louis XVI
revival style are from a suite
consisting of two sofas, a pair of
small cabinets, a large cabinet, six
side chairs, two lyre-back chairs,
two armchairs, and a fire screen.

As with all screen clocks, the
painted facade conceals a plain,
rectangular box that holds the
mechanism.

ularly apparent. Whereas Belter's firm—one of the largest in America—employed several hundred workers at its zenith, Lutz employed only fifty, but he supplied furniture for some of the finest homes in Philadelphia.

The opulent yet elegant parlor (plate 192) from the Colonel Robert J. Milligan House, built at Saratoga Springs, New York, in 1855, is an exemplary statement of the rococo revival style. The marble fireplace, the grand mirror above it, the marble-topped center table, and the robust chandelier and ceiling ornamentation are vivid expressions of the rich taste of the period.

The turtle-top center table (plate 193), attributed to Joseph Meeks and Sons, is from a suite of parlor furniture at one time gracing Abraham Lincoln's home in Springfield, Illinois. It indicates the richness of the fully developed rococo revival manner. This generally florid and extravagant style of design is reflected in many of the objects adorning the rooms of the Italianate Victoria Mansion (plate 196) built in 1859 at Portland, Maine, for Ruggles Sylvester Morse. This structure is perhaps one of the most beautiful examples of Italianate architecture in America. The building, which cost nearly $400,000 to erect, a

203. Calling-card case. Tifft and Whiting. North Attleboro, Massachusetts. 1840–66. Silver, height 4¾″. Collection Gray D. Boone

The obverse of the case is stamped with an impression of the U.S. Capitol building while the reverse is embellished with floral decorations. Anyone considering a visit, whether formal or merely friendly, in the Victorian era would not have ventured out without engraved calling cards, which were carried in cases of this type.

huge sum for that time, was modeled after Osborne House, a favorite residence of Queen Victoria located on the Isle of Wight.

The Italianate style continued in vogue throughout the nation for many years. In 1872 Sarah Wood Kane, a traveler to Provo, Utah, visited

a villa built in that American-Italian style which Downing characterizes as indicating "varied enjoyments, and a life of refined leisure." On its broad piazza our hostess stood ready to greet us. . . .

She conducted me over her house afterward, with a justifiable pride in its exquisite neatness and the well-planned convenience of its arrangements. She showed me its porte-cochere for stormy weather, its covered ways to barn and wood-shed, and the never-failing stream of running water that was conducted through the kitchen and dairy. I noticed the plump feather-beds in the sleeping-rooms, the shining blackness of the stoves (each with its teakettle of boiling water), that no speck dimmed her mirrors, and not a stray thread littered her carpets.

The charming impressions of Mormon households by Mrs. Kane, wife of Colonel Thomas L. Kane who was an old friend of Brigham Young, were published in 1874 in Philadelphia as *Twelve Mormon Homes Visited in Succession on a Journey*.

English products frequently influenced American interior decorating and furnishings, especially after the 1851 exhibition at the Crystal Palace in London. The so-called Day Dreamer, a papier-mâché easy chair with buttoned upholstery, designed by H. Fitz Cook and produced by the London–Birmingham firm of Jennings and Bettridge, was enthusiastically received by many critics when it was exhibited at the Crystal Palace. The *Illustrated Catalogue: The Industry of All Nations,* published in London as a special *Art-Journal* supplement the same year as the exhibition, gave the process of creating this light molding material a positive review:

The manufacture of Papier-Mâché into a great variety of useful articles of large size is the result of the efforts made, within a comparatively recent period, by the various artisans who have devoted their attention to this important branch of the industrial arts. It is not many years since the limits of the trade were circumscribed to a tea-tray, but now we find articles of furniture not only of a slight and ornamental character, such as ladies' work-tables or boxes, but of a more substantial kind, in chairs and sofas for the drawing-room or the entire castings of pianofortes . . . and our pages testify to their beauty.

204. Sewing machine. George B. Sloat and Company. United States. c. 1858. Cast iron and walnut, height 37½". Greenfield Village and Henry Ford Museum, Dearborn, Michigan

The development of the sewing machine dramatically altered women's lives throughout the world, allowing a freedom for pursuits in other handiwork, including the fine arts. In America the most expensive machines were enclosed in elaborate veneered and decorated case pieces. The less expensive versions stood on cast-iron bases.

Lightweight papier-mâché furniture, persistently popular throughout the reign of Queen Victoria, was rarely produced in America. Some clock manufacturers, however, placed their best works in brightly painted papier-mâché cases, and book covers (plate 197) were decorated with multicolored lacquers and inlaid with mother-of-pearl. By the 1840s American appreciation for books was well established, and in 1841 the Library of Congress contained an impressive thirty-five thousand volumes. The sum of five thousand dollars was annually appropriated by Congress for the purchase of new books. Some citizens were a little wary about the appropriation and issued various complaints.

205. Woven coverlet. Maker unknown. United States. c. 1850. Wool, 90 × 78″. Collection Mr. and Mrs. Foster McCarl, Jr., Beaver Falls, Pennsylvania

This very elaborate coverlet, produced on a Jacquard loom, is replete with attractive motifs, including vases of flowers, birds feeding their young, and a "Christian and Heathen" border.

For instance, Augustus James Pleasonton—in a manuscript diary for the years 1838–44 which is now in the Historical Society of Pennsylvania in Philadelphia —set down his cavil that the books in the Library of Congress were "much injured by the members of Congress and their families who take them to their lodgings and amuse their children with them. Books of prints of the most costly price have been plentifully smeared with honey, sweetmeats, and butter by these juvenile amateurs."

During the first half of the nineteenth century the latest technology simplified the metalsmith's task. Rolled sheets of thin silver could be more easily shaped into hollow ware. Die-stamped ornamental bandings replaced time-consuming decorative hand engraving. By the 1820s it was evident that some upper-class urban Americans were dining in luxury if not outright ostentation. James Gregg, author of *The American Chesterfield* which was published in Philadelphia in 1828, offered a veritable litany on the proper use of dining utensils, at the time often referred to as dining furniture:

Every person at the table should be provided with knife and fork, plate, bread, etc.; and before every meat dish, a carving knife, fork and spoon; and a spoon before every dish of vegetables. At the corners of the table, spoons, a salt cellar, and small spoon for the salt; and, if pickles are there placed, a small knife and fork. If the table is large, the furniture of the corners should likewise be placed at short and convenient intervals. It has lately become common, in our Atlantic towns, and particularly at tables where light wines are used with water as a long drink, to place, at convenient distances around the table, bottles of Sauterne, Claret or other light wine . . . and goblets of water. This is found, by experience, to be an admirable arrangement for convenience, and gives the waiters more time to attend, among other duties, to the frequent changes of plates which modern refinement has now introduced. On the sideboard should be arranged, in order, all those articles of furniture which are necessary for the table. These are, the great sup-

206. Quilt. Maker unknown.
Shippensburg, Pennsylvania.
Dated 1844. Cotton with chintz
cutouts, 93 × 112″. Thos. K.
Woodard, American Antiques and
Quilts, New York City

This beautiful appliqué floral quilt
is enhanced by a small fabric
portrait of the young Queen
Victoria framed in the center.

207. American Institute Fair at Niblo's Garden. *B. J. Harrison. United States. c. 1845. Watercolor on paper, $20\frac{1}{4} \times 27\frac{1}{2}''$. Museum of the City of New York, New York City*

The American Institute was founded in the late 1820s to promote advancements in agriculture, commerce, manufactured goods, and the fine arts. Its annual fair in New York City, where displays of domestic goods brought many of the contemporary machine-made furnishings to the attention of the public, included exhibitors from across the nation.

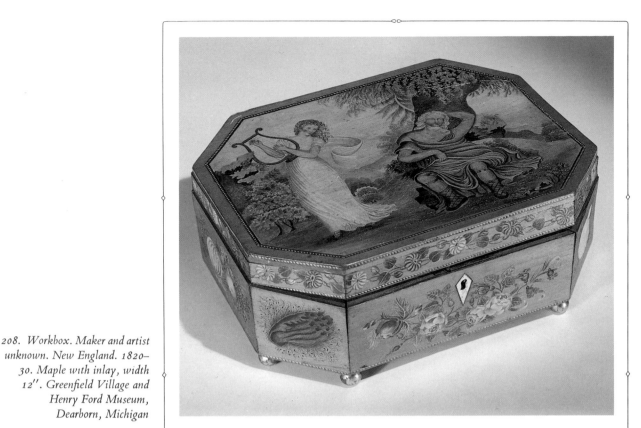

208. Workbox. Maker and artist unknown. New England. 1820–30. Maple with inlay, width 12″. Greenfield Village and Henry Ford Museum, Dearborn, Michigan

Boxes like this one were decorated by young women in academies, where patterns and pictures in drawing books provided the models for the decorative motifs. Often these boxes were embellished with mythological and biblical scenes as well as with romantic landscapes inspired by current best-selling novels.

plies of knives and forks, plates of different sizes, spoons, bread, etc.; but, in a particular manner, the castors. These should always consist of five bottles, at least; viz; cayenne pepper, black pepper, mustard, vinegar and sweet oil. Let the castors be FILLED—not half filled—with condiments of good quality, that is, the sweet oil not rancid, nor the vinegar SWEET nor the pepper in grains like hailstones, nor the mustard stale; and one word more, madame, before we dismiss the castors—A LITTLE SPOON FOR THE MUSTARD,—AND—REMEMBER THE SALT SPOONS.

Making one's way through such a maze of knives, forks, and dishes suitable to each course could be a daring feat to tax any but the most experienced in the stratagems of nineteenth-century etiquette. Victorian silversmiths contributed to the bewilderment by the specialized forms they invented—fish forks and knives, ice cream forks, and ladles and serving dishes shaped for specific uses.

The silver industry flourished in America at that time, the designs often influenced by prevailing furniture designs. Silver forms and decoration became more elaborate as the century progressed, and by mid-century there developed a noticeable fondness for ornate silver pieces such as the rococo ewer (plate 198) by Samuel Kirk and Son of Baltimore and the silver cream jug (plate 199) by Gelston and Company of New York. The numerous pieces in the advertisement for Gorham and Company (plate 200) indicate the dismaying tendency of grandiose conceptions to lapse into gaudy taste.

New furniture styles were introduced at an astonishing rate. Besides the previously mentioned Renaissance and Elizabethan revival styles that came into prominence at mid-century the so-called Louis XVI style appeared in what were often considered strict reproductions of neoclassic articles of the previous century. Sometimes Louis XVI elements were merged with those of Renaissance revival furnishings. Leon Marcotte of New York City crafted his Louis XVI chair and pedestal (plate 201) around 1860. These ebonized maple and fruitwood revival pieces are embellished with applied gilt and bronze decoration. Marcotte, a French immigrant, listed himself in New York business directories during the 1840s and early 1850s as an architect; later he altered this listing while in partnership with his father-in-law, Ringuet LePrince, to furniture dealer—in the best sense of the term. He was finally listed in partnership with Detlef Lienau. Marcotte moved in the best social circles and by the 1860s was recognized as one of New York City's most celebrated decorators.

OPPOSITE:

209. Seated Indian. Charles J. Dodge (attr.). New York City. c. 1858. Wood, height 66¼″. Long Island Historical Society, Brooklyn, New York

There are very few accounts of carved figures associated with American tobacco shops in the eighteenth century, but when cigar smoking became the rage by the middle of the next century, the Indian—native cultivator of the tobacco plant—stood proudly displaying his wares in front of smoke shops in practically every American city and town.

210. Distribution of the American Art-Union Prizes. *T. H. Mattison. United States. c. 1848. Lithograph, 15⅞ × 20⅞". Private collection*

Paintings by many American artists became widely known through the engravings copied from them and sold or otherwise distributed throughout the nation and abroad. Although some of the reproductions were engraved in Europe, most were done in the United States, which had many experts in this field. There were several agencies for distribution, of which the American Art-Union is the best known.

211. The Greek Slave. *Hiram Powers. United States. 1847. Marble, height 65½". Newark Museum, Newark, New Jersey. Gift of Franklin Murphy, Jr., 1926*

This is one of six replicas made by Powers of his most famous sculpture, depicting in the neoclassical style a nude woman bound and chained after her capture by Turks. The original, sculpted in 1843, is in the Corcoran Gallery of Art in Washington, D.C.

Metal mounts for furniture like those on Marcotte's French revival pieces had become fashionable in France in the eighteenth century during the rococo period. When French craftsmen came to America in large numbers in the early 1800s, they brought their predilection for this style with them. They continued to employ imported precast metal embellishments in spite of the fact that many Americans considered the metal treacherous to the clothing and cold and harsh to the skin.

Metal was also used—more felicitously—by the American Clock Company of New York City in 1855 for the case of the highly stylized mantel clock (plate 202). It is known as a screen clock, in which a cast-iron facade conceals a plain rectangular box containing the mechanism.

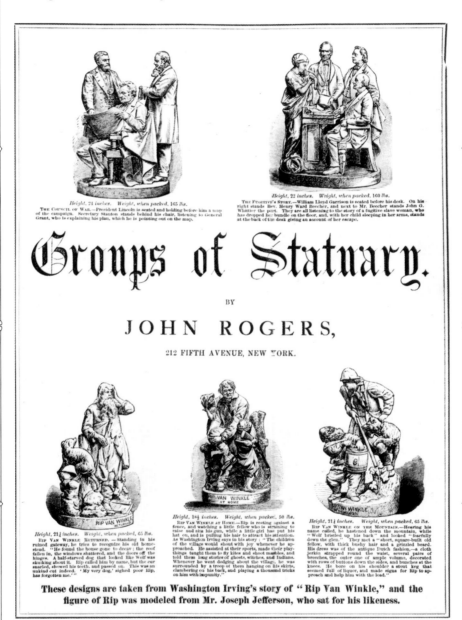

212. Broadside advertisement. John Rogers. New York City. c. 1880. Lithograph, 8 × 11". Greenfield Village and Henry Ford Museum, Dearborn, Michigan

John Rogers catered to Victorian sentimentality, and his three-dimensional plaster groups became a fad. He first worked a group in clay and then usually cast it in bronze, from which seemingly endless plaster copies were produced. This advertising leaflet was issued by Williams and Everett, sole agents for the sale of Rogers Groups in Boston.

The sophisticated urban centers produced a number of elegantly designed pieces that revealed a preoccupation with the obligations of social decorum. For example, the U.S. Capitol building is skillfully worked into the design of one side of the silver calling-card case (plate 203) devised by Tifft and Whiting of North Attleboro, Massachusetts. Floral rococo motifs also abound on this richly ornamented personal accessory without which no gentleman or lady of fashion would have considered venturing into the daily routines of Victorian society.

The innumerable textile manufacturing mills springing up wherever waterpower could be easily harnessed and cast-iron sewing machines like the one produced by George B. Sloat and Company around 1858 (plate 204) drastically altered the habits of the American woman. The spinning and weaving of cloth, and sewing it by hand into garments or home furnishings, would no longer occupy her days. New inventions and machine-made fabrics and furnishings allowed many middle-class women the leisure time to pursue other activities, particularly the finer arts. The coverlet (plate 205), woven circa 1850 on a Jacquard loom, is typical of bedcovers produced by professional artisans rather than by women working in the home. The French weaver Joseph Jacquard had invented a very sophisticated type of loom, operated by hand with a flying shuttle. It was introduced into America about 1820. The Jacquard attachment could be added to the looms already in use for double-weave coverlets, thus further improving the mechanization of weaving. Jacquard's invention consisted of a series of cards with large and small punched holes, resembling music rolls for a player piano, that activated the harnesses of the loom and created the pattern. The Jacquard loom made it possible for weavers to create large unseamed coverlets with handsome and complicated patterns.

Since the production of textiles such as quilts was not considered a worthy endeavor for well-to-do women, working-class women in cities and rural homemakers were responsible for handmade needlework in the nineteenth century. The appliquéd quilt with chintz cutouts (plate 206) was made in 1844 at Shippensburg, Pennsylvania. This strikingly beautiful quilt is adorned with a sensitive fabric portrait of the young Queen Victoria framed in the center. *Godey's Magazine and Lady's Book,* which attempted to elevate American taste after the 1830s, when it was first published, contained patterns and suggestions for the needlework arts. Perhaps some of the quilts hanging on the walls at one of the fairs of the American Institute at Niblo's Garden in New York City (plate 207) were inspired by patterns suggested by the editors of *Godey's Lady's Book.* In 1829 the institute organized what became an annual fair in New York to display some of the current machine-made furnishings. Though these furnishings lacked the individual refinements of handcraftsmanship, they were serviceable and they were less expensive, thus providing the average citizen with domestic comforts and conveniences previously unavailable.

Finishing schools, where needlework, painting (plate 208), and the polite arts were fostered, flourished in every town of any size. In the August 1851 issue of *The Horticulturist* an article about the Franklin Institute made a surprisingly strong case for the promotion of women in the mechanical arts. This was one of the first recorded references in the Victorian era suggesting that women could actually earn a living from artistic endeavors, a field previously dominated by men:

This truly benevolent institution is a branch of the "Franklin Institute for the promotion of the Mechanic Arts," at Philadelphia, and its design is to furnish woman another source of maintenance by preparing her to enter upon the lucrative business of engraving, designing, &c. It was commenced in November, 1848, by Mrs. Peters, whose benevolent heart had been pained for years, by seeing so large and increasing a number of deserving women, exposed to deprivation and suffering, for want of a wider scope in which to exercise their abilities for the maintenance of themselves and their children. . . .

The pupils are principally engaged in devising and sketching patterns or designs for calicos, delains [sic], oil-cloths, carpets, wall paper, table covers, hearth rugs, &c., though a large number are engaged in wood engraving, for magazines, and cuts representing machinery, &c. in sculpture, and indeed in designing, coloring or staining, painting, enameling, burnishing or carving household goods and utensils of every description. . . .

As soon as the knowledge of drawing is acquired, the pupil, if skillful, can commence to earn rapidly, while at the same time improving herself. The occupation is so light and delicate, and so lucrative, that with skill, a young woman can seldom, if ever, do so well for herself in any other way.

Despite the entry of women into the arts, the execution of carousel and show figures, circus wagons, woodcarvings for shop signs, and figureheads for ships remained predominantly the domain of men. The seated Indian figure (plate 209) attributed to Charles J. Dodge was intended as a sign for a tobacco

213. Vase with cover. New England Glass Company. Cambridge, Massachusetts. c. 1845. Cut glass, height 29¾". Toledo Museum of Art, Toledo, Ohio. Gift of Frank W. Gunsaulus

This dazzling cut-glass vase with cover has ruby flashing over clear glass.

214. *Flasks. Various makers. Eastern United States. First half of nineteenth century. Blown-in-the-mold glass, height of lyre bottle 8⅝". Greenfield Village and Henry Ford Museum, Dearborn, Michigan*

Flasks were produced in great quantities, and since they were intended to be discarded after using, little care was taken in their production or preservation. Because they were blown in the mold, there are many duplicates of most known patterns. The clear heavy pint flask with sunburst in an oval panel on obverse and reverse was made by the Keene Marlboro Street Glass Works in New Hampshire. The pale citron half-pint "Corn for the World" bottle was molded at the Baltimore Glass Works. The yellow green concentric eagle bottle also comes out of the Keene Marlboro Street Glass Works, while the deep aquamarine Jenny Lind lyre bottle was probably produced in Charleston, West Virginia.

shop and stood in front of a business on Montague Street in Brooklyn in 1862. By the last half of the nineteenth century, cigar store Indians reflected the taste and success of tobacconists. Tribes of figures of all sizes invaded every city until the 1890s, when ordinances required that the brightly painted obstructions be confined to the inside of the shops. The death knell for the cigar store Indian tolled when skillful marketing practices by chain stores caused the independent tobacconist to close his doors.

The American Art-Union, founded in the second quarter of the nineteenth century, sparked an appreciation for the arts in America. The organization purchased historical and genre paintings from living artists and issued lithographs to its member subscribers. Started as the Apollo Association in 1839 by a minor artist named James Herring, the Art-Union, as it was called after 1844, was based on a highly successful Scottish scheme that blended enjoyment of the arts with the charms of a lottery—a combination that also proved irresistible to Americans. By mid-century the Art-Union boasted 20,000 members paying five dollars a year; the membership was spread across the country as well as Canada and Europe and even relatively remote areas such as Brazil and New Zealand. Each member annually received a large lithograph duplicating a

215. *Decanters, vase, and compotes. Boston and Sandwich Glass Company. Sandwich, Massachusetts. 1858. Cut glass, height of vase 9". Greenfield Village and Henry Ford Museum, Dearborn, Michigan*

These five pieces of glass were especially cut for Deming Jarves and presented to him upon his retirement from the Boston and Sandwich Glass Company in 1858.

216. *Sinumbra lamp. Maker unknown. United States. 1840–45. Brass with glass globe, height 25½". Greenfield Village and Henry Ford Museum, Dearborn, Michigan*

The frosted shade of this sinumbra, or astral, lamp is beautifully decorated. This type of lamp, originating in France, was in demand in America because the design of the burner allowed improved combustion.

chosen American work, and a numbered ticket, which, if drawn at the annual meeting in December (plate 210), won the holder the original work of art the lithograph had been based on. From the beginning the lottery aspect of the Art-Union troubled the Victorian conscience, and in 1849 Thomas Whitley, a disgruntled artist, attacked the organization through the pages of the *New York Herald*. The newspaper picked up the cause, and the case eventually reached the New York Supreme Court. The lottery was declared illegal in 1852, and the union was forced to disband in 1853, but by that time it had generated a widespread interest in American art.

During its existence, the Art-Union distributed not only thousands of engravings to its members but also approximately 2,500 paintings and pieces of sculpture to fortunate winners both in the United States and abroad. The con-

217. *Lamp. Boston and Sandwich Glass Company. Sandwich, Massachusetts. 1850–60. Opalescent pressed glass, height 11". Greenfield Village and Henry Ford Museum, Dearborn, Michigan*

Lamps of this type were usually fitted with a burning-fluid burner. Because these lamps were not particularly safe and many of them blew up, few have survived.

cept inspired similar organizations to spring up in a number of other cities. The result was a convincing indication that the arts in America were not simply for the elite and wealthy but for everyone.

The trend toward neoclassicism in sculpture during the Victorian era was reflected in the works of the three most noted sculptors of the time—Horatio Greenough, Thomas Crawford, and Hiram Powers. The dominant academic European influence on American art may be partly explained by the grand tour, that essential climax to every young person's education. Greenough and Crawford both studied in Rome, and Powers eventually settled in Florence, where he spent the rest of his life. The extravagant conceptions in much mid-nineteenth-century sculpture are implicit in Greenough's toga- and sandal-clad statue of George Washington in the Smithsonian Institution—the attitude and attendant symbols are based on classical Greek sculptural conceptions of the Olympian Zeus.

Powers's *The Greek Slave* (plate 211), a more restful image that also harks back to a classical theme and attitude, was one of the most famous pieces of its kind in the nineteenth century. By today's standards, it would be classed as a smashing box-office success. After the completion of this work of sculpture in 1843, Powers arranged for an American tour during which the statue earned over $23,000 in admissions. The October 1847 issue of *The Union Magazine*

218. Candlesticks. Probably Boston and Sandwich Glass Company. Sandwich, Massachusetts. 1840–50. Pressed glass, height $10\frac{3}{8}''$. Greenfield Village and Henry Ford Museum, Dearborn, Michigan

Beginning in the late 1700s the dolphin was a familiar form in household decoration. Used extensively on furniture such as the Empire sofa (see plate 161), the motif continued to be popular throughout the nineteenth century.

reported that it was "curious to observe the effect produced upon visitors. They enter gaily or with an air of curiosity; they look at the beauteous figure and the whole manner undergoes a change. . . . all conversation is in a hushed tone, and everybody looks serious on departing." The sculpture was also the focus of the American exhibit at the 1851 Great Exhibition in the Crystal Palace in London (plate 225).

The popularization of fine art in the Victorian age was responsible for a trend that has continued unabated in the twentieth century. Many craftsmen found it profitable to sell plaster casts of famous people and sentimental scenes.

In *City Cries: Or, A Peep at Scenes in Town,* published in Philadelphia in 1849, an "observer" attempts to prove how these objects, first hawked on the streets, could form the basis of a profitable industry and an early retirement:

The itinerant seller of plaster casts is a regular street figure in all our great cities. By means of a few worn-out moulds which he has brought from Italy, the poor man makes a stock of casts, and mounting them on a board, cries them about the streets. He is not at all particular about prices. . . .

219. Catalog advertisement. Dietz, Brother and Company. New York City. c. 1845. Private collection

Dietz, Brother and Company, located at 62 Fulton Street in Brooklyn and 13 John Street in Manhattan, produced nearly every type of lighting device fashionable at the time.

When he has followed this street traffic for a few years, he has amassed money enough to begin business on a larger scale; and accordingly he hires a shop, and commences the making and selling of all sorts of plaster casts. He will model your bust, giving a very formidable likeness; or cast you a leaden Venus and Apollo to place on pedestals in your garden; or copy a pair of Canova's Nymphs to place in your hall. Instead of carrying a small shop on his head through the streets, he now sends forth a little army of his compatriots, poor expatriated Romans or Tuscans, regretting the glorius [sic] skies of Italy, while they are selling busts of the glorius heroes of America. When our seller of casts has made his fortune, he will go home and purchase a villa on the delightful shores of Lake Como; and tell his descendents what a wretched country is America.

No merchandiser of three-dimensional art was as successful as the sculptor John Rogers. His mass-produced plaster pieces are to formal sculpture what Currier and Ives prints are to painting. He first worked a group in clay and then usually cast it in bronze, from which seemingly endless plaster copies issued forth. One of the popular plaster groupings featured in Rogers's advertisement (plate 212) is *The Council of War,* a highly successful depiction of President Abraham Lincoln, Secretary of War Edwin M. Stanton, and General Ulysses S. Grant plotting a campaign.

The process of molding also affected the glassmaker's art. Improved technology meant that the number of shapes and designs could be increased sub-

220. Hexagonal pitcher. American Pottery Company (attr.). Jersey City, New Jersey. c. 1845. Transfer-printed earthenware, height 8½". Platter. Edwin Bennett Pottery Company (attr.). Baltimore, Maryland. Late 1800s. Transfer-printed earthenware, length 13". Both Greenfield Village and Henry Ford Museum, Dearborn, Michigan

The printed decoration on the pitcher includes crossed American flags under the lip and a view of Castle Garden with the inscription: "Landing of Gen. Lafayette / at Castle Garden, New York / 16th August 1825." The platter was transfer-printed in blue with a view of George E. Pickett's charge at Gettysburg, Pennsylvania, and an acorn-and-oak-leaf border enclosing medallions with portraits of the generals Winfield Scott Hancock, James Longstreet, Robert E. Lee, and George G. Meade.

221. Parian ware. Various makers. United States. 1845–58. Porcelain, height of center vase 10½". Greenfield Village and Henry Ford Museum, Dearborn, Michigan

The white pitcher decorated with roses and foliage was created by Christopher W. Fenton of Bennington, Vermont. The water lily pitcher was made by the United States Pottery Company, also in Bennington. The producers of the remaining items—including the one-of-a-pair blue and white vase with portrait medallion, the eagle vase, the figure of a girl lacing her shoe, and the blue and white pitcher in cherub and grape pattern—are all unknown.

222. Cup and saucer. Charles Cartlidge and Company. Greenpoint, New York. c. 1850. Porcelain, diameter of saucer 7". Brooklyn Museum, Brooklyn, New York. Gift of Mrs. Henry W. Patten

Realistic flowers framed by a gold arcade reflect the prevailing rococo revival style. American designs in this manner were generally less fussy than those on similar items in Europe.

224. The Crystal Palace.
*Dickenson Brothers. London,
England. 1854. Hand-colored
lithograph, 16 × 23". Greenfield
Village and Henry Ford Museum,
Dearborn, Michigan*

*The Crystal Palace—prefabricated,
easily assembled and capable of
being somewhat quickly disassembled
and put together again—was one
of the earliest structures completely
fashioned of iron and glass. It
housed the first international
exposition, mounted in London
in 1851.*

OPPOSITE:

223. Abraham Lincoln.
*Alexander Gardner. Washington,
D.C. 1863. Ferrotype, 5½ ×
7½". Greenfield Village and
Henry Ford Museum, Dearborn,
Michigan*

*The armchair in which Lincoln
sits for his portrait study was
produced by Bembe and Kimmel
of New York City, and it was
one of the chairs constructed in
1857 specifically for the House of
Representatives. In 1859 the
chairs were sold at public auction
and at least three were purchased
as props for the photographic
studios of Mathew Brady and
Alexander Gardner. The
ferrotype, commonly called the
tintype, was introduced in the
1850s, and because of advantages
such as durability quickly replaced
the daguerreotype.*

stantially. Blown-in-the-mold flasks (plate 214) were disposable liquor containers. Bottles and flasks became an important branch of glass production and collectors today admire them for their shapes and beautiful colors.

The exquisite cut-glass vase with cover (plate 213), fashioned about 1845 at the New England Glass Company in Cambridge, Massachusetts, is particularly striking for its ruby flashing over clear glass. Ruby glass was also made by the Boston and Sandwich Glass Company at Sandwich, Massachusetts. When Deming Jarves, founder of the Boston and Sandwich Glass Company, retired in 1858, he was presented with five pieces of clear cut glass produced by his firm (plate 215).

During the Victorian period, glass objects played an important part in the development of American lighting fixtures, as evidenced by the sinumbra lamp (plate 216), the whale oil lamp (plate 217), and dolphin candlesticks (plate

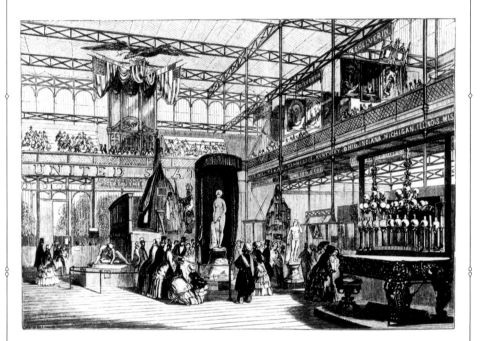

225. The Crystal Palace. *Artist unknown. England. 1851. Illustration from* The Art-Journal's *special supplement* Illustrated Catalogue: The Industry of All Nations *(London, 1851). Private collection*

This view of the American display at the Great Exhibition in the Crystal Palace in London appeared in the official exhibition catalog. Hiram Powers's famous neoclassic sculpture The Greek Slave, *presented under a canopy, was a focal point of the exhibit (see plate 211).*

218). The sinumbra, or astral, lamp, first developed in France, was perhaps the most popular version of the Argand lamp in America during the 1830s and 1840s. Aimé Argand, a Swiss chemist and inventor, first marketed his innovative lighting device around 1783. The novel design of the burner allowed air to circulate to both the inner and outer surfaces of the tubular wick. Glass chimneys improved combustion, thus providing a quantity and quality of light previously unobtainable.

In the first half of the nineteenth century, oil lamps created a market that gave new impetus to the whaling industry. Whale oil became one of the most favored lighting fuels in America and was used in lamps made of tin, pewter, brass, silver, and glass. All were fitted with metal wick tubes that projected about one-quarter of an inch above the lamp and extended approximately one inch into the font. Nearly all lamps fitted with whale oil burners could also utilize any other lighting fuel, and in Europe, where whale oil was extremely expensive, vegetable oils were a common substitute. The advertisment of Dietz, Brother and Company of New York (plate 219) illustrates the variety of lighting devices obtainable from many lamp shops by mid-century.

Early-nineteenth-century American pottery and porcelain had a tendency to be conservative in design. Profiles were often reminiscent of Greek and Roman prototypes fashionable during the classical revival that began around 1790. By the middle of the century pottery makers were introducing naturalistic details into their products. This is evident in the output of the Jersey Porcelain and Glass Company and in the fine pottery (plate 220) manufactured by its successor, the American Pottery Company, which operated from 1825 to

1845 at Jersey City, New Jersey. These companies always faced sharp competition from foreign manufacturers.

In 1847 Christopher W. Fenton of Bennington, Vermont, introduced Parian (plate 221), a new type of porcelain that had been developed a few years earlier in England. His interest in naturalism is expressed in statuary and in the undulating designs of ornamental household articles and curios that anticipated the rococo revival of the 1850s and 1860s.

Fenton entered into several partnerships. In 1849 he commenced operation of a new plant at Bennington, and by 1853 his products were marketed under the United States Pottery Company trade name. Although much of this firm's merchandise was reminiscent of European prototypes, some was distinctly American and catered to domestic taste.

In an attempt to attract potential customers, Fenton in 1853 displayed porcelain, flintware, and various other products at the Crystal Palace international exhibition in New York. A reporter from *Gleason's Pictorial Drawing-Room Companion* summarized the success of his efforts, attributing it both to his location near excellent sources of materials and to Fenton's perseverance:

The neighborhood of Bennington, Vermont, is one well adapted for the establishment of a pottery manufacture, as there is a considerable deposit of plastic clay, which is met with in large quantities, and of a great purity, in at least a dozen other places in Vermont. Indeed, there is no State in the Union better adapted for manufacturing porcelain and other earthen wares, containing all the mineral elements, and also ores of iron and manganese. These, however, in themselves, constitute but a portion of the success of any branch of manufacture, and it is to the untiring industry and skill of Mr. C. W. Fenton that this country is indebted for the establishment of this art, at Bennington. . . . At the sacrifice of time and health he has also succeeded in introducing the manufacture of Parian Ware in this country; produced the Flint Enamel Ware, for which he has secured a patent; and is engaged in extension of porcelain manufacture—which has been followed by other establishments in this country, but by no means to the same satisfactory development as by him.

Although Americans were willing to admire the fine European porcelain exhibited at the Crystal Palace in New York, their most enthusiastic praise was reserved for domestic wares. Charles Cartlidge and his partner, Herbert Q. Ferguson, operating as Charles Cartlidge and Company in 1848, took a prize for the fine quality of their products manufactured at Greenpoint, New York. The Cartlidge firm is noted for its colorful pieces such as the cup and saucer with an arrangement of delicate flowers (plate 222).

A keen interest in photography during the Victorian era was one of the reasons that portrait painting and the cutting of silhouettes declined sharply. The daguerreotype, developed by the French painter and physicist Louis Daguerre, was the first truly practical process of photography. It represented such a novelty to Americans that in 1839 the editor of the New York periodical *The Knickerbocker* exclaimed enthusiastically:

We have seen the views taken in Paris by the "Daguerreotype" and have no hesitation in avowing that they are the most remarkable objects of curiosity and admiration, in the arts, that we ever beheld. Their exquisite perfection almost transcends the bounds of sober belief. Let us endeavor to convey to the reader an impression of their character. Let him suppose himself standing in the middle of Broadway with a looking glass held perpendicularly in his hand, in which is reflected the street, with all that therein is, for two or three miles, taking in the haziest distance. Then let him take the glass into the house, and find the impression of the entire view, in the softest light and shade, vividly retained upon its surface. This is the Daguerreotype! . . . There is not an object, even the most minute, embraced in that wide scope, which was not in the original; and it is impossible that one should have been omitted. Think of that!

The daguerreotype looked like the image reflected in a mirror, which prompted its being called a "mirror with a memory." Because the plate was so fragile, it required very careful mounting. Actually an exact image, reflected on a silvered sheet of copper, was produced through the medium of the camera obscura. The principal shortcoming of the daguerreotype was its inefficiency in producing an image intended for wide distribution.

Photographic technology improved with time. The ambrotype and the tintype, both quite different from the daguerreotype, were easily distinguishable from their predecessor. The ambrotype—a glass photograph introduced in England by Frederick Scott Archer in 1851—represented a more permanent type of image. Not only was it easier to make but it could also be produced more cheaply than the daguerreotype. That and the paper photograph, already in an advanced stage in Europe, hastened the downfall of the American daguerreotype.

Ferrotypes, more commonly known as tintypes (plate 223), were introduced in 1856, and by 1860 the end of the daguerreotype was in sight. The

226. Buffet. Bulkley and Herter. New York City. 1853. Oak, dimensions unknown. Illustration from The World of Science, Art, and Industry, Illustrated from Examples in the New-York Exhibition, 1853–1854 (New York, 1854). Private collection

This catalog illustration portrays an enormous buffet exhibited by Bulkley and Herter of New York. The designs for the decorations were created by Herter and were executed by E. Plassman. Crafted of American oak, it was extolled in the catalog as the "best specimen of the art it exemplifies." Such praise squandered on a monstrosity of this kind reveals the gaudy extravagance of the fully mature Victorian style.

great advantage of these pictures was their durability. The tintype could also be trimmed with shears to fit into round or oval lockets and watchcases. Because it could be produced in multiples for as little as fifty cents a dozen, it came to be known as the "picture for millions."

After it received a French patent in 1854, the carte-de-visite, or visiting card, achieved immense popularity in the United States. The average size of the visiting card was $2\frac{1}{4}$ by $3\frac{1}{2}$ inches, and it was produced on a glass negative using a multiple lens camera. A contact print comprising four to eight pictures could be made on photographic paper, and the pictures were cut apart and mounted on cardboard as individual photographs. At the peak of their popularity, from about 1860 to the middle of the 1880s, millions of visiting cards were manufactured.

Between 1867 and the turn of the century the cabinet photograph became the favorite type of portrait picture. Cabinet photographs, essentially the same as the visiting card, came in a slightly larger size. Advanced lighting techniques and the use of elaborate backdrops now enabled photographers to create an attractive, as well as accurate, record of their customers' images.

With the advent of the new photographic process, mass production and the dissemination of photographic prints were possible. These new visual documents of personal and public history altered man's perceptions of the world. The concept of privacy and the sense of what was suitable for observation were radically revised. By the last quarter of the nineteenth century most households had accumulated their own photographic collections, particularly the family album.

Because of the Victorians' passion for novelty and their curiosity about the world, the international exposition became almost commonplace in the second half of the nineteenth century. The Crystal Palace saga is one of the most remarkable success stories of mid-century. Prince Albert, Victoria's husband and president of the Society of Arts, and his friend Henry Cole were elated by the success of the society's exhibition in England in 1847. In 1849 Cole visited the Paris Quinquennial, the last of the French national fairs, generally held every five years, in which the focus was on commercial and economic progress in that country. On his return from that industrial exhibition in Paris, Cole convinced Prince Albert that England should stage the first truly international exposition, which occurred in 1851. The Crystal Palace in London (plates 224, 225), one of the most dazzling and novel architectural structures ever erected, was designed to house the gigantic international Industry of All Nations exposition, commonly known as the Great Exhibition. The structure, designed by Joseph Paxton and made of iron and glass, was the largest prefabricated edifice ever constructed anywhere in the world. It was not only demountable but also remountable. *The Illustrated Exhibitor* waxed enthusiastic in its first issue of June 7, 1851: "Other triumphs have been won, and other victories celebrated, but none greater or more glorious than this."

Not everyone was quite as enthralled. Ralph Nicholson Wornum noted in an essay for the *Illustrated Catalogue: The Industry of All Nations*, published in London in 1851:

Style in ornament is analogous to hand in writing. . . . There are, of course, many varieties of every great style; but so long as the chief characteristics remain unchanged, the style is the same. From this point of view, therefore, the styles become comparatively few. We shall find that nine will comprise the whole number of the great characteristic developments which have had any influence on European civilisation: namely—three ancient, the Egyptian, the Greek, and the Roman; three middle-age, the Byzantine, the Saracenic, and the Gothic; and three modern, the Renaissance, the Cinquecento, and the Louis Quatorze. . . . That there is nothing new in the Exhibition in ornamental design; not a scheme, not a detail that has not been treated over and over again in ages that are gone; that the taste of the producers generally is uneducated, and that in nearly all cases where this is not so, the influence of France is paramount in the European productions; bearing exclusively in the two most popular traditional styles of that country—the Renaissance and the Louis Quinze—with more or less variation in the treatment of detail.

Two years later an American Crystal Palace was mounted in New York City. It housed a trend-setting international exposition, entitled The World of Science, Art, and Industry. In the two years that separated the London display and its American counterpart, American manufacturers had absorbed the lessons of the earlier exposition. Large handcrafted specimens of ornamental furniture such as the buffet (plate 226)—monstrosities by present-day standards of functionalism—were praised at the time for masterly carving and boldness of the material utilized. Both handcrafted and mass-produced decorative arts exhibited at the New York exposition were now offered competitively in the international marketplace.

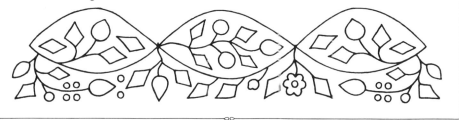

Country Styles
1776~1860

By the time the Constitution of the United States was signed in 1787, America was still a dual society. Although there was a concentration of dwellers in the coastal cities along the eastern seaboard, most of the population resided in rural areas and enjoyed a simple, modest way of life. While the sophistication of the prevailing European styles had a strong influence on urban-oriented designs for the affluent homes of the middle class, tastemakers in the remoter areas of the new nation relied on the less elaborate forms and designs of country furniture, in the nineteenth century often referred to as cottage furniture. But remoteness, both culturally and socially, from the cosmopolitan centers did not necessarily mean there was a lack of interest in color and basic decoration.

Within the folk idiom there were countless manifestations of a search for the beautiful. This quest led to a great flowering of American folk art, which began in the late eighteenth century and lasted until the 1860s. The work, generally produced by artists without formal training, represented a wide range of handcrafted items—shop and tavern signs (plate 227), ship figureheads and other rough-hewn figures (plate 267), house decorations (plate 230), children's toys, weathervanes (plate 265), carousel animals, and the legion of naive paintings (plates 232, 247, 254) imbued with a spontaneous, charmingly awkward quality frequently admired and imitated by sophisticated artists and craftsmen. Folk art represented a strong artistic undercurrent, and professional and semi-professional itinerant artists in rural communities traveled from town to town

227. Tavern sign (detail). Maker unknown. Guilford, New York. c. 1827. Wood, overall width 46½". Collection Alice M. Kaplan

This splendid portrayal of the angel Gabriel, one of the masterpieces of American folk sculpture, was hung under the portico of the Angel Tavern at Guilford. The tavern was built by Captain Elihu Murray for his son Dauphin. The congealed paint and weathering actually enhances its poetic beauty.

228. Candlestand. Maker unknown. Boston or Salem, Massachusetts. 1800–10. Mahogany with satinwood and ivory inlay, height 30''. Candlestand. Maker unknown. New England. Early nineteenth century. Maple, height 27½''. Both Greenfield Village and Henry Ford Museum, Dearborn, Michigan

The tripod tilt-top Federal stand on the left is an example of exquisite urban cabinetmaking. The graceful spider legs terminate in spade feet, the simple top has been embellished with sensitively balanced and meticulously worked inlay, and the vase section of the pedestal is stop-fluted and inlaid with bone. This masterpiece overshadows the craftsmanship of the Federal candlestand on the right; decorated to imitate mahogany graining and augmented with painted inlay and cross-banding on the maple top, it is a rural interpretation of its companion.

and farmhouse to farmhouse taking likenesses. Folk portraits (plates 234, 238, 248) added a dash of color to otherwise modest homes.

When modest country furnishings are compared to city productions of the same period, the influence of the urban cabinetmaker on the rural craftsman is clearly evident. Native woods such as hickory, pine, and maple took precedence over expensive imported materials, and simple adaptations of more ornate Victorian furniture designs, with an emphasis on both lightness and durability, were appropriate to the needs of rural America. The two tilt-top candlestands (plate 228) illustrate how a cosmopolitan style might be interpreted and adapted by a country artisan. The stand on the left, produced in an urban shop, was crafted of mahogany with figured wood and bone inlay. That on the right is of maple, a less expensive wood that was native to the area of production, and was painted and grained to simulate more costly, imported materials. The Federal chest of drawers (plate 229) is a simple rural case piece, crafted in 1814 in Livermore, Maine, by E. Morse. It is constructed of pine, one of the most modest of furniture woods, and again paint has been so skillfully applied that the decoration resembles expensive fine-grained wood as well as delicate inlay bordering the top edge and the four drawers.

Paint was also ingeniously employed in the art of stenciling. Stencils were cut and utilized by the craftsman who decorated the parlor of the Stencil House (plate 230) to create brilliant floral and geometric designs. The impression of exquisite expensive carpets was often created through the use of these geometric devices. Delightful landscapes and other primitive scenes were executed on woodwork and plaster and wood walls with the aid of stencils as well as the application of freehand painting. Journeymen painters traveling from town to town and door to door were responsible for much of this special kind of folk art.

The typical eighteenth-century Windsor armchair in the parlor of the

Stencil House contrasts dramatically with the nineteenth-century arrowback Windsor included in William Sidney Mount's 1835 painting *The Sportsman's Last Visit* (plate 231). Mount, known for his good-natured genre paintings, spent his childhood and later life in Stony Brook, New York, on Long Island, the locale of many of his rural paintings. He has sensitively captured the conflict between the well-mannered gentleman and his rural counterpart, who are both obviously vying for the attention of the young beauty.

While fashion-conscious residents of means on the East Coast sought out and commissioned the latest building styles and consulted publications like the extremely popular builders' manuals by the architect Asher Benjamin, the simple unadorned dwellings in the mid-nineteenth-century folk painting *Twenty-two Houses and a Church* (plate 232) expressed the typical styles in the hinterland

229. Chest of drawers. E. Morse. Livermore, Maine. 1814. Pine, width 36⅝". Greenfield Village and Henry Ford Museum, Dearborn, Michigan

As with the candlestand (see plate 228), paint has been utilized in decorating a simple rural form to simulate the quality and material of fine city furniture. Graining, which emulates mahogany, and trompe l'oeil inlays have been masterfully created with paint.

on the western frontier. Bishop Morris, an itinerant preacher and son of a western pioneer, had carefully observed the mode of living in the western states for forty years, and in the May 1846 issue of *The Ladies' Repository and Gatherings of the West,* he offers a description of the "modern style" and then recalls in unselfconscious detail the way of the previous generation:

When a young married couple commenced housekeeping, from thirty to forty years ago, a very small outfit sufficed, not only to render them comfortable, but to place them on an equality with their friends and neighbors. They needed a log cabin, covered with clapboards, and floored with wooden slabs. . . . Usually, one room answered for parlor, sitting-room, dining-room, kitchen, and dormitory. . . . As to furniture, they needed a stationary corner cupboard, formed of upright and transverse pieces of boards, arranged so as to contain upper, lower, and middle shelf, to hold the table ware and eatables. In order for comfort and convenience, it was requisite, also, to have the following articles: one poplar slab table, two poplar or oak rail bedsteads, supplied with suitable bedding, and covered with cross-barred counterpanes of homemade, one of which was for the accommodation of visitors; six split-bottomed chairs, one long bench, and a few three-legged stools were amply sufficient for themselves and friends; a half a dozen pewter plates, as many knives and forks, tin cups, and pewter spoons for ordinary use, and the

The wall patterns were stenciled
in bright colors against a soft green
background. The house was built
at the end of the eighteenth century
in Columbus, New York, but was
moved to Shelburne, Vermont, in
the middle of the twentieth century
and reconstructed on the museum
grounds. The stencil decoration of
the parlor was applied about 1820.

same number of delft plates, cups, and saucers for special occasions; also, one dish, large
enough to hold a piece of pork. bear meat, or venison with the turneps [sic], hommony,
or stewed pumpkin. All this table ware was kept in the corner cupboard, and so adjusted as
to show off to the best advantage, and indicated that the family were well fixed for comfortable living. When the weather was too cold to leave the door or the window open,
sufficient light to answer the purpose came down the broad chimney, and saved the ex-

Mount, one of America's foremost
genre painters, chose farm scenes
with landscape and figures, as well
as other rural themes, as his
favorite subjects. The appointments
of this sparse interior would tend
to prove that the dazzling beauty
was indeed a country girl. The
fireplace mantel is a simple
handcrafted affair, and the curtain
at the window is certainly
unpretentious. The yellow-painted
arrow-back Windsor chair was a
familiar form in virtually every
chairmaking shop in the country.
The brass candlestick was probably
one of the most treasured items in
this home.

This simple folk painting is a masterpiece of primitive design. Bold in conception, it transcends the artist's technical limitations. The layout and depiction of the houses are so specific that it would appear that this is not an idealized landscape but a portrait of a real town—much like those that were springing up in the developing nation.

pense of glass lights; and as for andirons, two large stones served as a good substitute. The whole being kept clean and sweet, presented an air of comfort to the contented and happy inmates.

Rural artisans frequently catered to the special interests of the people who ordered or utilized their wares. The pine sea chest (plate 233), with the painted full-sail ship on the top and the dolphins and knotted rope on the front, might well have been the property of the unidentified sea captain painted by Sturtevant J. Hamblen (plate 234).

With the exception of Windsors, no type of seating furniture in the nineteenth century was as commonplace as the Hitchcock-style chair (plate 235). Lambert Hitchcock, popularizer of painted chairs that were a combination of both Windsor and fancy chairs, mass-produced a vast quantity of pieces that served as prototypes for virtually every country craftsman. The chair had a rectangular back, a wide crest rail, one or more horizontal slats, and a square seat. The vogue of the Hitchcock type of chair and settee reached its height between 1825 and 1850. A well-constructed example, handsomely painted and decorated, could be purchased in 1829 for $1.50. More expensive Hitchcock chairs had rush or cane seats; the least expensive, plank. It is believed that Hitchcock first manufactured his chairs in 1818, when he shipped knocked-down parts to both the Midwest and the South for assembly. The original Hitchcock manufactory operated from the mid-1820s into the 1850s. In 1826 he built a large factory at what is now Riverton, Connecticut, and until 1829 chairs fabricated there were marked: "L. Hitchcock. Hitchcocks-ville, Conn. Warranted." Suffering financial reverses in 1829, Hitchcock was forced to take on a partner, and chairs from then until 1843 were marked: "Hitchcock. Alford. Co. Hitchcocks-ville, Conn. Warranted." In 1843 Hitchcock moved to Unionville and continued the production of chairs until his death. For the modern collector the presence of a Hitchcock factory mark increases a chair's value over an unmarked one.

Another familiar, unpretentious chair form of the middle of the nineteenth century was the Boston rocker (plate 236) with its broad, scrolled plank seat. Literally hundreds of firms specialized in the production of rockers. Like the Hitchcocks and the country Windsors, they were grained and often decorated with stenciled floral motifs, leaves, vines, and baskets of fruit.

Some decorators of country furniture preferred to work in an abstract style. The cannonball bed (plate 237) shows the results that could be achieved

233. Chest. Maker unknown.
Probably Massachusetts. 1800–35.
Pine, width 44¾". Greenfield
Village and Henry Ford Museum,
Dearborn, Michigan

The painted patterns on this
chest—ship, knotted rope, and
painted dolphins—are obvious
signs that this item would have
been the possession of a sailor
or officer at sea.

234. Sea Captain. Sturtevant J.
Hamblen. Maine. c. 1830. Oil
on canvas, 26 × 22". Private
collection

Much of Hamblen's work is
difficult to distinguish from that of
his more famous brother-in-law,
William Matthew Prior. A picture
nearly identical to this one is in
the Colby College Museum of
Art, Waterville, Maine. It is
believed that Hamblen sometimes
painted stock canvases during off
months, which he completed by
later painting in the head of the
sitter.

when an ambitious artisan, employing a freehand technique, put forth his best efforts.

There were numerous ways of graining woodwork. Frequently a solid dark color was first laid over the ground. After it dried, a lighter color was applied, and before the second was completely dried, parts of it were wiped away—frequently with a graining comb. Metal combs were fashioned so that the teeth were of varying widths, enabling the decorator to produce dramatic contrasts. For those who could not afford combs—which were usually imported —a corncob, a wadded-up piece of paper, or even a cork could create a similar effect. The doors in George Washington Mark's painting of a girl coming through double doors (plate 238) give the impression of traditional grained woodwork. The armoire (plate 251) from Louisville, Ohio, is an example of freehand graining.

The decorative arts of some of the religious and utopian socialistic communities, epidemic in America in the nineteenth century, have had a profound

235. Hitchcock-style chairs and a washstand. Makers unknown. Eastern United States. 1825–50. Maple, height of washstand 35″. Greenfield Village and Henry Ford Museum, Dearborn, Michigan

Furniture of this type was produced inexpensively during the second quarter of the nineteenth century, when technology had developed to the point that interchangeable sections could be crafted with the aid of machines. The decoration was generally a combination of freehand painting and stenciling. The washstand displays a flint enamel washbowl and pitcher.

and permanent effect on furniture, architecture, and even on the design of tools. In particular, the Shakers, who were dedicated to productive labor and a life of perfection, contributed a distinctive style of handicraft to American culture. The simple, functional, and honest craftsmanship of their meetinghouses, barns, household objects, and tools had a lasting influence on American design. The movement, which originated from a small branch of the English Quakers, was named the United Society of Believers in Christ's Second Appearing but became popularly known as Shakers or Shaking Quakers because of their meetings in which ritual expressions of spiritual faith were manifested by seizures of shaking, shouting, whirling, and singing in tongues. Conversion was the only method of increasing membership in a society whose members pledged themselves to celibacy and adhered to strictures against marriage as laid down by their Millennial Laws.

Ann Lee, a young textile worker of Manchester, was converted in 1758 and became the leader of this sect. Mother Ann, who was illiterate and from a poverty-stricken background, received a series of mystic revelations and came to regard herself—and was accepted by her followers—as the female aspect of God's dual nature, or the daughter of God. With eight disciples, she arrived in New York in 1774 and in the following year founded the first Shaker community at Watervliet, New York. By the time of the Civil War, American membership in the sect had increased from the original eight to nearly six thousand brothers and sisters living in eighteen communities from Maine to Ohio. Members

236. Boston rocker. Maker
unknown. Boston, Massachusetts.
1840–60. Maple and pine,
height 45". Greenfield Village
and Henry Ford Museum,
Dearborn, Michigan

The typical Boston rocker was
ornately painted, grained, and
stenciled. The cost to the
purchaser was determined to some
extent by the elaborateness of the
decoration.

237. Cannonball bed. Maker
unknown. Eastern Connecticut.
1835–40. Maple, length 84".
Private collection

The boldness of the turned posts
and the beauty of the painting
make this a masterful example of
the country style.

were required to relinquish their worldly goods and participate in a communal life that recognized equality of the sexes and encouraged common ownership of possessions.

Shaker architecture, furniture, and utensils reflect a basic belief that creativity and work were forms of worship and praise of God. Strict doctrines governed the manufacture of furniture and accessories (plates 239, 240). Only meetinghouses could be painted white, only movable furniture could be varnished, and only oval boxes—known as nice boxes—could be stained with a reddish or yellow hue. A purity of design was stressed, untainted by embellished superfluities, which the Shakers fervently believed added neither to an object's goodness nor its durability.

The Shaker community was made up of a well-built, organized village surrounded by cultivated vineyards, orchards, and farmland. Garden seeds and processed and prepared foods, including sweet corn, lima beans, tomatoes, and various preserved fruit, were widely distributed beyond the community. These products were packaged with colorful, handsomely designed labels (plate 241). Hard goods like furniture, fabrics, baskets, and objects made of leather were also marketed to the outside world.

The Germans who settled in rural farming communities in Pennsylvania in the seventeenth and eighteenth centuries clung to their cultural traditions throughout the nineteenth century and even into the twentieth. Centuries-old forms and picturesque peasant designs from their European homeland were preserved by these settlers. The Fraktur Room (plate 242), ablaze with color and rich in texture, is an excellent example of a nineteenth-century Pennsylvania country room. The walls are hung with frakturs, or illuminated pictorial writings, a descendant of medieval German manuscript illumination, which ornamented baptismal certificates, bookplates, and house blessings. The paneling of the room comes from the second story of a large stone farmhouse built in 1783 near Kutztown, Berks County, Pennsylvania, by David Hottenstein. This country room retains its original mottled blue paint on the woodwork, the bold dentil cornice, and the projecting chimney breast. On the sawbuck table are several illuminated hymnals as well as school exercise books. A typical wainscot chair from Chester County and a red and blue painted secretary-desk illustrate the German-American willingness to combine Philadelphia Chippendale forms with traditional European folk decoration. Slipware pottery on the mantel shelf, on the windowsills, and on tables throughout the room exhibits the inherited German taste for richly glazed and decorated ceramics.

The Pennsylvania Germans traditionally were noted for their decorative motifs, an example being the hex sign on barns. The amount of painting on a particular object is often very extensive. The whole surface of a bed, chair, chest, or wardrobe (plate 243) might be covered. Walls and beams were commonly decorated with geometric and floral designs, and occasionally biblical scenes (plate 244) were depicted. The slip- and sgraffito-decorated redware (plate 246) and the tole coffeepot (plate 245) are further indications of the German American delight in vivid colors and traditional forms.

One of the best-known Pennsylvania artists was Edward Hicks, who was born in 1780 in the village of Attleboro, Bucks County. At the age of thirteen young Hicks entered into apprenticeship with a coachmaker. Soon after the turn of the century he became a partner in a Milford coach-making and painting business, and there he painted street as well as shop and tavern signs. A jack-of-all-trades, Hicks also executed decorative paintings on furniture, fireboards, and clock faces. He was a deeply religious Quaker who was accepted into the ministry of the Society of Friends, traveling extensively and delivering devout sermons to large gatherings. A completely untrained primitive artist, Hicks devoted a great deal of his time painting historical and religious scenes inspired by European engravings and illustrations in the Bible. He often repeated versions of a composition if it sanctified an edifying moral that appealed to his devout Quaker beliefs, being particularly struck by the prophecy in Isaiah (11:6) that the beasts of the jungle shall live peacefully with the gentler creatures

OPPOSITE:

238. Girl Coming Through a Doorway. *George Washington Mark. Greenfield, Massachusetts. c. 1845. Oil on canvas, 71½ × 56⅜". Greenfield Village and Henry Ford Museum, Dearborn, Michigan*

The doors in this life-size picture have been painted to simulate the grained decoration in vogue at the time. An ingrain carpet covers the floor.

239. Shaker furniture. Mount Lebanon, New York, and other Shaker communities. Nineteenth century. Maple and pine, approximate height of armchair 35″. Private collection

Modern designers and collectors have frequently expressed enthusiasm for the beautiful spare furniture and household utensils created by the Shakers. Objects made for exclusive use of the communal society include the table with a single drop leaf and the large red-stained carrier on the floor. The Shakers also crafted furniture for sale outside of their villages, represented here by the armchair—one of a pair, produced in the community at Mount Lebanon—the sewing basket with handle, and the oval fingered boxes on the table. The room was designed in 1980 for a New York City apartment.

240. Oval boxes. Unknown Shaker artisan. New England. Nineteenth century. Maple and pine with brass tacks, length of largest box 13¼″. Museum of American Folk Art, New York City. Promised anonymous gift

These simple boxes, elegant by present-day standards, were made for use in the Shaker community as well as for sale to customers on the outside.

OPPOSITE:

241. Dried Green Sweet Corn. Artist unknown. New York. c. 1880. Reverse painting on glass, 33 × 27″. New York State Museum, Albany, New York

The Shakers were famous for their fine-quality seeds and were among the first communities to create a thriving business from preserved foods and dried seeds.

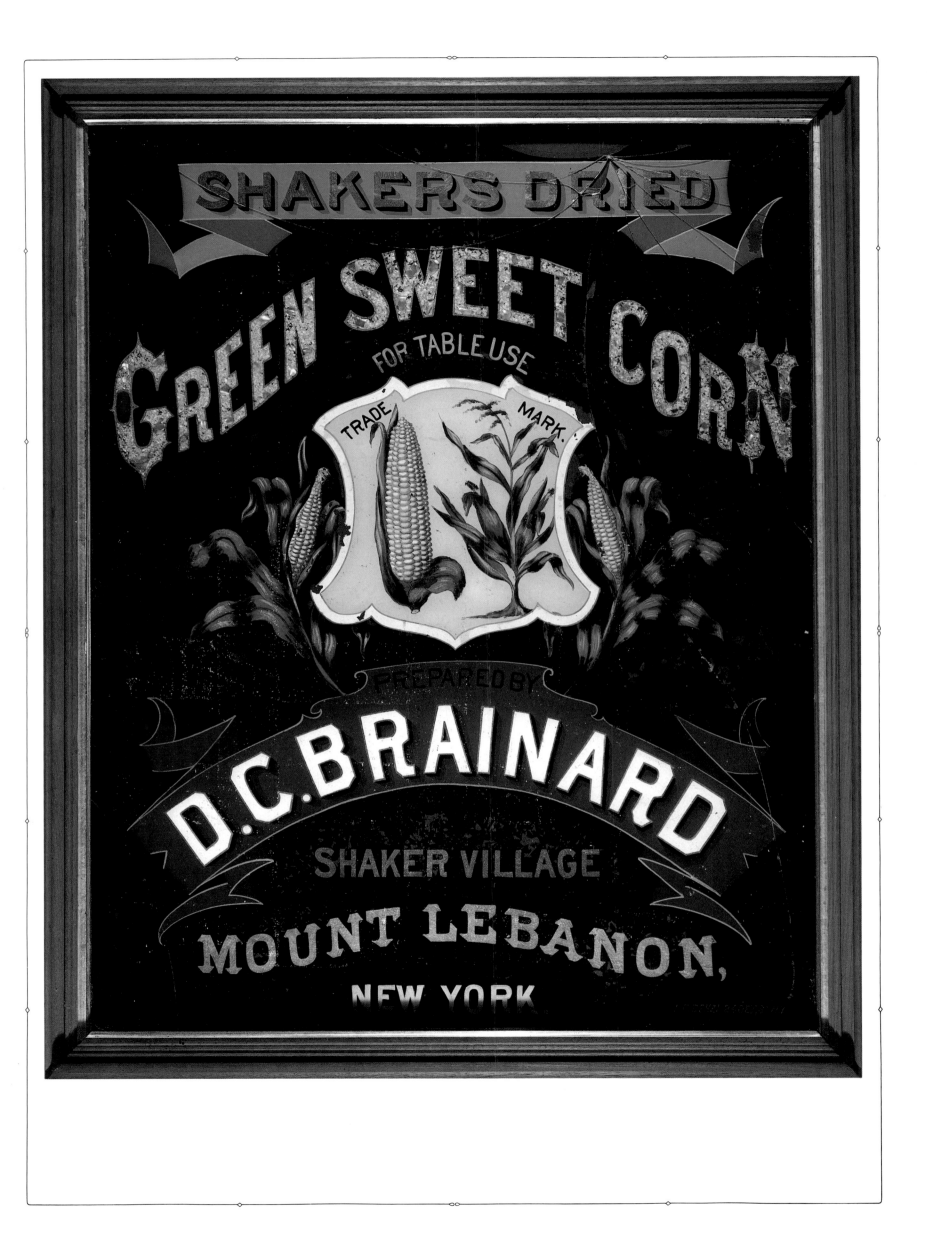

242. Museum installation.
Fraktur Room. Pennsylvania.
1783. Henry Francis du Pont
Winterthur Museum,
Winterthur, Delaware

The installation features
Pennsylvania German woodwork
from David Hottenstein's stone
farmhouse built in 1783 near
Kutztown, Berks County,
Pennsylvania. The furnishings
include painted chests, a secretary-
desk, walnut chairs, and a sawbuck
table. The walls are decorated
with frakturs, or illuminated
manuscripts, and pictures that
reflect a tradition originating in
medieval German monasteries. The
floor is covered with a handwoven rag carpet worked in
narrow strips and stitched together.

OPPOSITE:

243. Wardrobe. Maker unknown.
Lancaster County, Pennsylvania.
c. 1790. Pine, width 88".
Greenfield Village and Henry
Ford Museum, Dearborn,
Michigan

The upper section of this wardrobe
—also known by its German
equivalent, schrank—has two
cupboard doors that are hung on
rat-tail hinges. The lower section
contains five drawers painted and
grained to simulate marble. The
decorator of this polychrome piece
emphasized the rich blue green of
the background with an acid-hued
red outlining the raised floral-
motif panels.

244. Album illustration. Ludwig Denig. Chambersburg, Pennsylvania. 1784. Ink and watercolor, each page 6½ × 8½". Collection Mr. and Mrs. Samuel Schwartz

This unique fraktur book of biblical scenes contains 59 pictures, 114 pages of script, and several pages of music.

245. Coffeepot. James Fulivier. Eastern Pennsylvania. c. 1825. Tin, height 10½". Greenfield Village and Henry Ford Museum, Dearborn, Michigan

Collectors today prefer the brightly painted Pennsylvania tole to utensils with black or mat backgrounds. This handsome pot is inscribed on the bottom: "James Fulivier, 75 CTS is the price of this" and "Jared H. Young."

OPPOSITE:

246. Ceramic display. Various makers. United States. Eighteenth and nineteenth centuries. Redware, various dimensions. Private collection

Pennsylvania furniture was often gaily painted and decorated with traditional motifs such as hearts, tulips, distelfinks (stylized birds), and parrots, but this eighteenth-century cupboard with its simple gray grained paint provides an appropriate background for a rich collection of slip- and sgraffito-decorated redware. Sgraffito, or incised decorated slipware, is one of the most treasured forms of American ceramic. The cupboard sits on shoe feet, a design feature frequently found in Pennsylvania German furniture.

247. The Peaceable Kingdom.
Edward Hicks. Newtown,
Pennsylvania. c. 1847. Oil on
canvas, 26 × 29½″. Private
collection

This charming painting, one of
the many variations on the theme
made famous by Hicks, portrays
in the left background William
Penn in friendly dialogue with the
Indians. The painting is an
ingratiating and literal
interpretation of the prophecy in
Isaiah (11:6): "The wolf also
shall dwell with the lamb, and the
leopard shall lie down with the
kid; and the calf and the young
lion and the fatling together; and
a little child shall lead them."

248. Portrait of John Thomas Avery. *Artist unknown. United States. 1839. Watercolor on paper, height 15½″. Collection Mr. and Mrs. Samuel Schwartz*

By the beginning of the Victorian period the tall-case clock like the one in the Avery household, long the precious sentry of the home, was being replaced by smaller, more easily transportable timepieces.

of God's kingdom, with a child leading them. Hicks seems never to have tired of his vision that the wild beast and civilized man could peacefully coexist in God's world. He painted nearly one hundred known versions of the subject, titling the compositions *The Peaceable Kingdom* (plate 247), twenty-five of which are extant.

The westward movement throughout the nineteenth century showed a significant migration of population. The frontier had shifted from New England and the eastern seaboard to the South and beyond the Appalachian Mountains. Many Germans moved west with the frontier, and Sir Charles Lyell, leading geologist of Victorian England, in his 1845 study of geologic formations and fossil remains in North America, *Travels in North America, in the Years 1841–1842*, recorded his encounter with German immigrants in their westward migrations: "In our passage over the Alleghenies, we now followed what is called the National Road to Cumberland and Frostburg. . . . We passed many waggons of emigrants from Pennsylvania, of German origin, each encumbered with a huge heavy mahogany press, or 'schrank,' which had once, perhaps, come from Westphalia. These antique pieces of furniture might well contain the penates of these poor people, or be themselves their household gods, as they seem to be as religiously preserved."

A tall-case clock, much like the one included in the portrait of John Thomas Avery (plate 248), and the marbleized and painted wardrobe (plate 243) might have been among the furnishings accompanying the westward drive of the German settlers, who were continually in quest of rich new farmland.

Hunters and trappers (plate 249) were not always happy to see the farmers arrive, for they cleared the virgin forests, tilled the land where game had been plentiful, and opened roads that brought in settlers in ever-increasing numbers. When the handsome brick dwelling (plate 250) with its several outlying farm buildings and mill was constructed on the Ohio River at the turn of the century, the Northwest Territory was undeveloped. In 1803 Ohio became the first area within the territory to be admitted as a state. By 1825 the National Road had extended across Ohio and into Indiana. In the same year the Erie Canal was completed to Buffalo. Yet the canals were not seriously extended in the area, because the railroad (plate 266) eclipsed their purpose. The railroad provided better transportation and brought in both land speculators and commercial investors. Goods could now be transported more economically. With the railroad came numerous local industries, which in time mushroomed into major manufacturing concerns that encouraged the building of large cities.

Although the strong French influence in the midwestern portion of the country had dissipated substantially after the French and Indian Wars when Britain obtained Canada and the Old Northwest, isolated pockets of early settlers continued to use the traditional French designs for the construction of their furniture. The painted and grained poplar armoire (plate 251) may be considered a French provincial piece. Although poplar was typically an American wood, there were similar large wardrobes produced in Normandy in the previous century, and this particular example was made in a French settlement that existed in Louisville, Ohio, from about 1820 to 1840.

As the American frontier expanded in the nineteenth century, the traditions of Freemasonry, a secret fraternal and patriotic order, moved westward as well. The order was especially strong in the eighteenth century, and many of the leaders of the Revolution were active members, including Thomas Jefferson, Paul Revere, and the French general Lafayette. George Washington was the first president of one of the branches but he was never very actively involved in Masonic activities. Benjamin Franklin was, but he opposed the tradition of hereditary membership through the eldest son as contrary to republican principles. An elaborate catalog of design motifs in the Federal period was derived from Masonic symbols. The all-seeing eye of God, which adorns the dollar bill, was merely one of these motifs given currency in the decorative arts. John Luker, a German craftsman working in Ohio, painted the decoration on his Worshipful Master's Chair (plate 252), part of the furnishings of a Masonic lodge hall located at Mount Pleasant.

E. Hall, another Ohio craftsman, who came from Newton Township, Tuscarawas County, fashioned in 1858 the stoneware jug (plate 253) decorated with incised patterns, applied motifs, and blue glaze, an example of the lively designs employed by country artisans of the time. Stoneware jugs were ideal storage vessels for general household use and for spirits as well. A similar stoneware jug would have held the libations passed about at the spirited husking bee described by a correspondent in the September 24, 1836, issue of *The Penny Magazine of the Society for the Diffusion of Useful Knowledge*. The husking bee was intended as "a sort of frolic"; mostly young persons of both sexes had been invited, and an hour or two after dark the business of husking began:

The "huskers" squat promiscuously among the bundles, and dexterously stripping off the leaves or "husks" which envelope the corn-ears, sever them from the stalks and deposit them in baskets placed for that purpose; while the un-eared stalks are cast to the common pile of "corn-fodder." The business of "husking" is not carried on in total darkness, for to every little group of five or six "huskers" a lantern, lending a "dim and dubious light," is commonly allotted. If the "cider season" has commenced (which commonly is the case), new cider is freely distributed, and the "whiskey-jug" is passed joyously around, "from mouth to mouth," for it is the custom to drink from the neck of the bottle. About midnight they are regaled with hot coffee, with sundry cakes and sweetmeats; while fun and frolic, merriment and glee, reign uncontrolled, until some one announces that it is time to re-commence "husking." During the whole night "songs are sung and tales are told," and it is at "husking bees" that "matrimonial engagements" are frequently made up. Whiskey and cider continue to circulate as the night advances; and by the time that day begins to dawn, the "huskers" will adjourn to the interior of the barn, and join in a country dance, to the popular and national air of "YANKEE DOODLE." The whisky-jug is then once more passed round, and the whole party,

somewhat drowsy and weary, depart for their respective places of abode, with the understanding that they are to assemble, a night or two hence, to have another "husking-frolic" at the house of some other farmer.

The South produced its own variety of folk art and its own regional customs. The painting *The Plantation* (plate 255) illustrates how a well-organized southern farm or plantation operated. The plantation owner and his family lived in the handsome manor house or mansion, which when possible was built on a rise so that they could view the entire expanse of the farm. Below were slave quarters and the overseers' houses and there was generally a storage or

251. *Armoire. Maker unknown. Louisville, Ohio. 1820–40. Poplar, height 78". Greenfield Village and Henry Ford Museum, Dearborn, Michigan*

The style of this large wardrobe, which was painted and grained freehand, is similar to eighteenth-century examples from Normandy; however, the wood and hardware are typically American. The wardrobe was produced in the French settlement that existed at Louisville, Ohio, from about 1820 to 1840.

warehouse set close to the water so that the products of the land could be easily shipped to distant markets. Frequently a lumber mill also was part of the plantation. This view by an unidentified artist working around 1825 includes a mill in the lower right-hand corner.

Throughout the Shenandoah Valley region, which extended from Pennsylvania through Maryland and West Virginia into Virginia, pottery makers like John Bell worked at their craft. The redware lion (plate 254) is nearly identical to two other known examples made by Bell in the middle of the nineteenth century. He used a typical creamware glaze for the body and a brown glaze for the coleslaw mane, beard, and tip of the tail.

Although the Spanish were the first Europeans who aggressively explored and attempted to set up colonies in North America in the sixteenth century, it was not until the next century that they established permanent colonies in Mexico and the southwestern areas of the United States. When the colonists in Mexico made their forays into the American Southwest in search of legendary cities of fabulous wealth, they found only humble Indian pueblos. Yet they decided to set up a northern outpost of their sprawling empire, bringing with them their crusading Roman Catholic faith. Spanish traditions have remained an important part of the culture of the area, particularly the art and artifacts of a deeply religious people. The santo, a representation of Christ or other holy figure, was fashioned for churches and private homes by itinerant craftsmen much like the folk painters on the East Coast who traveled from town to town in search of commissions. There were two types of santos—the bulto and the

252. Worshipful Master's Chair. John Luker. Ohio. Nineteenth century. Pine and maple, height 72". Collection Mr. and Mrs. Charles V. Hagler

Every midwestern community of any size had a Masonic lodge in which fraternal meetings were held. Painted on a blue ground are various Masonic symbols as well as the names of the manufacturer, John Luker, and Worshipful Master J. H. M. Houston, for whom the chair was made.

retablo. The bulto is a freestanding carved sculptural figure; whereas the retablo, or altarpiece, is a flat two-dimensional picture, either carved or pierced. The bulto of the Madonna with Child (plate 256) and the painted retablo entitled *La Huida a Egipto* (plate 257) reveal the simplicity and pious quality of these objects. Although the nineteenth century represents the heyday of santo art in the Southwest, many craftsmen today continue to utilize design customs that have been passed down from the heads of families to their children. The Spanish intermarried with the Indians, and nineteenth-century furniture of the Southwest (plate 258) is a delicate blend of traditional Spanish and native American designs.

Although rugs had been rare in colonial America—whether local handcrafted ones or expensive imported types—some households in the eighteenth century were using rugs as table covers. By the nineteenth century imported examples frequently adorned the floors of the well-to-do on the East Coast,

253. Jug. E. Hall. Newton Township, Tuscarawas County, Ohio. 1858. Stoneware, height 17½". Greenfield Village and Henry Ford Museum, Dearborn, Michigan

Hall decorated this stoneware jug with applied and incised motifs painted blue—clasped hands, a running horse, and a flowering plant growing out of a heart. On one side is impressed "Fountain of Health, R. Seaers"; on the other, "Made by E. Hall / Ohio" appears three times.

254. Figure of a lion. John Bell. Waynesboro, Pennsylvania. Middle of nineteenth century. Redware with cream glaze, height 7½". Private collection

Three nearly identical lions are known to have been created by Bell. The toothy grin provides an air of humor for this piece, which is physically small but monumental in presence.

255. The Plantation. *Artist unknown. Southern United States. c. 1825. Oil on wood, 19⅛ × 29½". Metropolitan Museum of Art, New York City. Gift of Edgar William and Bernice Chrysler Garbisch, 1963*

Nearly every aspect of southern plantation life is evident in this striking and famous painting. The manor house at the top of the hill would have been maintained by the slaves and overseers who occupied the auxiliary buildings. A mill powered by a waterwheel is in the lower right-hand corner of the painting. Imported goods were delivered by ship to the waterfront warehouse.

256. Nuestra Señora la Reina de los Cielos. *Artist unknown. New Mexico. Late eighteenth century. Cottonwood and painted canvas, height 33″. Collection Mr. and Mrs. James O. Keene*

In this bulto representing Our Lady Queen of the Heavens the figure wears a silver crown. The skirt is put together from fabric stretched over wooden staves. A sculptural piece of this type was often a significant image in a devotional corner or private altarpiece in Spanish homes of the Southwest.

while hooked rugs were common floor coverings in rural homes. The parlor from the Luther Burbank House (plate 260), built at Lancaster, Massachusetts, about 1800, includes a handsome hooked rug that combines geometrics and floral motifs. Although not as complex as the famed Caswell carpet (plate 259), it is distinctive nonetheless. The Caswell carpet is one of the great examples of American textiles and was embroidered by Zeruah Higley Guernsey Caswell in Vermont between 1832 and 1835. Caswell sheared the wool from her father's sheep, spun it into yarn, dyed it with homemade dyes, and, using a chainstitch, embroidered coarse homespun squares, each of a different design. It was two years before the squares were sewn together and the rug completed just in time for her anticipated marriage, which is represented pictorially in the rug.

Painted floor cloths served as colorful and inexpensive floor coverings. The spinning and weaving was also usually done by the woman at home and then the completed fabric nailed to the side of a barn or a garret floor so that she could more easily apply the painted patterns. Factory-produced floor cloths were introduced during the first half of the century, and these cheap substitutes for handcrafted carpets were instantly popular since they were affordable by even those of the most modest means.

In 1854 manufactured floor cloths were disapprovingly described by Sir Joseph Whitworth and George Wallis in their historical guide *The Industry of the United States in Machinery, Manufactures, and Useful and Ornamental Arts*, published in London:

257. La Huida a Egipto. *Artist unknown. Northern New Mexico. Nineteenth century. Tempera and gesso on pine panel, height 30″. Spanish Colonial Arts Society, Inc. Collection on loan to Museum of New Mexico, Museum of International Folk Art, Santa Fe, New Mexico*

The theme of the flight into Egypt was a favorite of traveling santeros—the local artisans in the Southwest who created the popular carved holy objects (santos)—and numerous versions are known.

258. Trastero. *Maker unknown. Northern New Mexico. c. 1830. Pine, height 88″. School of American Research Collections, Museum of New Mexico, Museum of International Folk Art, Santa Fe, New Mexico*

This simple cupboard, known as a trastero in Spanish, with panels painted and decorated in tempera and gesso is topped with an ornate crest. The interior panels are also painted with floral motifs.

259. Caswell carpet. Zeruah
Higley Guernsey Caswell.
Castleton, Vermont. 1832–35.
Wool embroidered on wool,
160 × 147″. Metropolitan
Museum of Art, New York City.
Gift of Katherine Keyes, 1938,
in memory of her father, Homer
Eaton Keyes

Caswell spun, dyed, and wove
the wool that she herself had
sheared from the family sheep.
The carpet consists of richly
designed embroidered squares, each
of a different pattern.

260. *Parlor of Luther Burbank House. Lancaster, Massachusetts. c. 1800. Greenfield Village and Henry Ford Museum, Dearborn, Michigan*

Country furniture—including the Salem rocker, arrow-back Windsors, and a fall-front desk— furnish this simple interior. The clock, with its two painted tablets flanking a mirror, is an unusual type. The cradle was handcrafted for the infant Luther Burbank by his father. The large hooked rug combines geometric and floral designs.

The manufacture of floor-cloths appears to be one in which, ultimately, the Americans will succeed, so far, at least, as the use of the materials is concerned; the dry character of the atmosphere being very favorable to the rapid drying of the work.

They have a few admirably printed specimens, but, with few exceptions, they are as thoroughly wrong in design, and as antagonistic to everything like the true principles of floor decoration, as the generality of such things in this country. For instance, one specimen has its surface ornamented with a portrait of Washington, and a view of Mount Vernon alternating in panels, surrounded by a wreath of flowers and the American Eagle! Yet this is intended for a floor covering, and of course to be walked upon!

261. *Bedcover. Maker unknown. American. First half of nineteenth century. Embroidery on black wool, 96 × 80". Greenfield Village and Henry Ford Museum, Dearborn, Michigan*

This dazzling piece of needlework art would turn any bed into a delicate flower garden.

262. Memorial picture. Artist unknown. New England. c. 1830. Ink and watercolor on paper, 28 × 32″. Private collection

This striking memorial picture for Sylvia W. Proctor, who died at the young age of twenty-one, includes a severed willow tree representing the cutting off of life. The figure of the mourning woman resembles a watercolor silhouette.

As technology improved and mass-produced substitutes were readily available, hand-loomed coverlets and embroidered bedspreads (plate 261) were no longer so fashionable. Many women used their new free time to enjoy more artistic pursuits. The art known as Chinese, or theorem, painting was studied by young women in the seminaries. Stencils, cut from oiled paper, were combined in an infinite number of ways to create a finished picture, or theorem. High-waisted bowls overflowing with flowers and fruit, exotic fauna, and

263. Unidentified Child. William Matthew Prior. Portland, Maine. 1830–35. Oil on canvas, 27½ × 22″. Private collection

This painting is a large version of Prior's inexpensive "without shade" pictures and possibly cost the sitter's parents about ten dollars, considerably more than the flat likenesses measuring approximately 10 by 13 inches for which the artist charged $1.25.

264. Doll's cradle. Jacob Turnerly. Connecticut. Dated 1853. Wood with whalebone inlay, length 22". Private collection

Turnerly's daughter Sarah was born four years before he carved and assembled the cradle, and her name is inlaid with whalebone on the cradle's bonnet. Nineteenth-century doll cradles were seldom as lovingly crafted as this delicately designed and decorated example.

265. Spotted hen weathervane. Maker unknown. New England. 1850–60. Pine, height 16½". Private collection

Few nineteenth-century vanes are as compelling as this plump full-bodied hen, assembled from five pieces of wood that have been nailed together.

flamboyant birds were highly favored subjects that seemed to express some of the sentimental yearnings of early-nineteenth-century America. The memorial picture (plate 262) also became popular early in the century when the European romantic movement was imbuing death with a poetic quality.

The painting of the bald doll-like baby (plate 263) by William Matthew Prior might also be a memorial picture, with the truncated stump and drooping vine symbolic perhaps of a withered life or one cut off too early. Prior also executed reverse paintings on glass and is known for his portraits in this medium of prominent Americans like George and Martha Washington. Eventually he developed a technical proficiency that enabled him to execute fine, fully representational portraits and well-composed landscapes.

At mid-century, handcraftsmanship was still employed for special objects— a gift for a well-loved child, for example. Whalebone inlay embellishes the distinctive doll cradle (plate 264) that Jacob Turnerly put together in 1853 for his

266. Tray. Maker unknown. United States. c. 1850. Tin, length 24¼". Greenfield Village and Henry Ford Museum, Dearborn, Michigan

Simple utilitarian pieces such as this brightly painted and decorated tray are often excellent indicators of the events that fascinated people in a particular period. In many areas of rural America at mid-century the train was still a novelty.

daughter. Turnerly, a ship's barrel maker, plied his trade aboard the *Sarah Sheate* and the bark *Oriole* during the 1850s. His daughter Sarah was born in 1849 near Clinton, Connecticut, and her name is inscribed on the whalebone facing of the cradle's bonnet.

Weathervanes, too, continued to be made by hand at mid-century. The spotted hen (plate 265) was crafted in New England between 1850 and 1860. This plump, full-bodied vane is assembled from several pieces of wood that have been nailed together. In just a few years factory-produced metal vanes would replace most handcrafted versions.

As technology improved and machines were perfected, handcraftsmanship like that exhibited on the hen weathervane, the painted and decorated tray (plate 266), and the carving of the fierce-looking *Miss Liberty* (plate 267) all but disappeared from the American scene. Mid-nineteenth-century factory processes practically drove out handcraftsmanship from the ancient trades and obliterated the techniques of producing by hand fine utilitarian objects. Later in the century, as a reaction to the growth of industrialism, the English arts and crafts movement and that of the European-oriented art nouveau sought a return to the work methods and techniques and the splendid decorative arts of the Middle Ages. William Morris initiated the arts and crafts movement in England in order to revivify applied design in the field of the decorative arts. This new emphasis on hand fabrication had a tremendous influence in America, and in the twentieth century an enthusiastic reevaluation of the nation's past caused a resurgent interest in handcrafted objects.

OPPOSITE:

267. Miss Liberty. Artist unknown. Tilton, New Hampshire. 1850–60. Wood, height 25¾". Barenholtz Collection

Although many representations of the symbolic figure of Liberty are depicted as strident defenders of America, there are few that convey such a sense of fierceness and determination as this one. The carving originally came from a boathouse at Tuftonborough, New Hampshire.

269. Card room of LeGrand
Lockwood Château. Herter
Brothers. Norwalk, Connecticut.
1869. Lockwood-Mathews
Mansion Museum, Norwalk,
Connecticut

This sumptuously decorated room
with bird's-eye maple woodwork,
inlaid with boxwood and ebony,
was created by Herter Brothers,
perhaps the most successful interior
design firm at mid-century. It is
one of sixty rooms in the mansion
(see plate 268).

In their response to technological improvements many American manufacturers had successfully produced inexpensive and accurate timepieces for the
average home. American Victorian shelf clocks and mantel clocks were as efficient and finely devised as those imported from England and France. They
failed to attract rich East Coast purchasers who preferred the most costly imported clocks because of the elaborate cases in which they were housed, especially if the decorative motifs harked back to ancient cultures.

Clarence Cook, the outrageously outspoken journalist and art critic, in his
1878 book *The House Beautiful* complained about the disadvantages of having
timekeepers anywhere in the contemporary home:

Hardly anything in the modern parlor is so uninteresting as the mantelpiece. . . . A
clock finds itself naturally at home on a mantelpiece, but it is a pity to give up so much
space in what ought to be the central opportunity of the room, to anything that is not
worth looking at for itself, apart from its merely utilitarian uses. It is very seldom worth
while to look at a clock to know what time it is, and, as a rule, it would be much better to
keep clocks out of our dining-room, though, for that matter it is hard to say where they
are not an impertinence. In the dining-room they are a constant rebuke to the people
who come down late to breakfast, and they give their moral support to the priggishness of
the punctual people, while they have, no doubt, to reproach themselves for a good share
in the one bad American habit of eating on time. In a drawing-room a clock plays a still
more ill-mannered part, for what can he do there but tell visitors when to go away, a

ings by P.-V. Galland symbolize music, painting, and poetry, and the ceiling canvases were aflutter with birds and floral motifs. The Lockwood mansion surpasses any house of its era for size, craftsmanship, and lavishness. The cost of construction at the time amounted to two million dollars, an extraordinary sum for almost any period.

One-of-a-kind cabinet pieces for such homes were often handcrafted. The Renaissance revival pier table with display cabinets (plate 271) is rich in detail and quite probably came from an East Coast shop catering to men of great wealth like Lockwood. The Renaissance revival was characterized by scrolls, brackets, and plaques made more prominent by incised line decoration. Mahogany, rosewood, ebony, and other precious imported woods on the pier table are enhanced with rich carvings and delicate inlays. Of special interest are the Egyptian heads incorporated into the design of the freestanding front legs. Leigh Hunt, the English poet, essayist, critic, and influential tastemaker of the early Victorian period, firmly criticized decorative motifs of this type in his delightful *Table-Talk,* a collection of conversational newspaper pieces published in London in 1851:

268. *LeGrand Lockwood Château. Detlef Lienau. Norwalk, Connecticut. 1869. Lockwood-Mathews Mansion Museum, Norwalk, Connecticut*

This French Renaissance-style château was designed for the wealthy industrialist and financial broker LeGrand Lockwood. In addition to lavish living quarters, the dwelling was a small estate in itself with a bowling alley, theater, library, art gallery, fourteen bathrooms, two billiard rooms, and was equipped with every convenience imaginable at the time, including a dry-cell burglar alarm system.

Among the customs at table which deserve to be abolished is that of serving up dishes that retain a look of "life in death"—codfish with their staring eyes, hares with their hollow countenances, &c. It is in bad taste, an incongruity, an anomaly; to say nothing of its effect on morbid imaginations.

Even furniture would be better without such inconsistencies. Claws, and hands, and human heads are not suited to the dead wood of goods and chattels. A chair should not seem as if it could walk off with us; nor a table look like a monstrous three-footed animal, with a great flat circular back, and no head. It is such furniture as the devil might have had in Pandemonium—"Gorgons, and hydras, and chimeras dire."

A lady sometimes makes tea out of a serpent's mouth; and a dragon serves her for a seat in a garden. This is making a witch of her, instead of a Venus or a Flora.

William S. Wooton of Indianapolis, Indiana, produced an exceptional line of secretaries and desks during the 1870s. This American manufacturer was so well known that in 1874 his firm created a presentation piece (plate 272) for Queen Victoria. Wooton, a Quaker minister who may have searched for the practical and efficient even in his designs, advertised that the office worker or the industrious homemaker seated at a Wooton desk could reach as many as 110 compartments without moving or swiveling the chair. A Wooton desk was usually locked with a single key and the lock was a patent bank-lock type. Nearly all of the Wooton pieces are of exceptional design and the quality of the construction elevates them above the products of his competitors.

Days of Abundance
1860-1876

Four candidates competed in the presidential race of 1860, with the problem of slavery the biggest issue. Abraham Lincoln, the Republican candidate, emerged victorious on an abolitionist platform. The nation split apart on the issue, and on December 20 South Carolina seceded from the Union soon to be followed by five other states, which formed the Confederacy. Jefferson Davis was elected its provisional president. The outbreak of hostilities was precipitated by the fall of Fort Sumter near Charleston on April 13, 1861, and the subsequent call to arms by Lincoln and Davis. The conflict raged for the next four years, fueling a boom economy in the North but wreaking economic and social devastation in the South. The war, often considered the first of the modern wars, was the most costly in American lives—until the sophisticated weaponry of World War II exceeded it—and required an industrial mobilization on both sides unprecedented at that time.

During the 1860s the North enjoyed a period of rapid expansion, and the newly wealthy industrialists built mansions that were unparalleled in their elaborate decoration and accessories. These luxurious homes were criticized as gaudy and ostentatious, but at their best they displayed a magnificence that reflected an increased awareness of the ability of the decorative arts to cater to one's personal comfort while buttressing self-esteem.

The Gothic revival style, which came into fashion in the 1830s, flourished throughout much of the nineteenth century. In 1864–65, when the mansion of Lyndhurst was substantially altered by architect Alexander Jackson Davis for its new owner, George Merritt, the dining room (plate 270), added at that time, became one of the finest American rooms in the Gothic revival style. Davis's obsession with the overall unity of a room dictated the design of all its furnishings—the furniture, carpets, chandeliers, candlesticks, fireplaces, and even the leaded-glass windows.

An equally impressive residence is the French Renaissance-style château (plate 268) built in 1868–69 at Norwalk, Connecticut, by LeGrand Lockwood, a prominent Wall Street broker and successful railroad magnate. This stylish dwelling, designed by Detlef Lienau, has a floor plan in the form of a Greek cross. The sixty-room house was replete with fourteen bathrooms, two billiard rooms, bowling alley, theater, library, music room, card room, art gallery, in addition to sumptuous living quarters, and was equipped with every convenience that ingenuity could devise or the most generous expenditure purchase, including a dry-cell burglar alarm system. Lockwood traveled throughout the world in search of priceless art treasures for his new mansion, which was decorated by the French-born Leon Marcotte, noted for handsome French-style furniture. Herter Brothers supplied the bird's-eye maple woodwork, inlaid with boxwood and ebony, for the card room (plate 269). The wall paint-

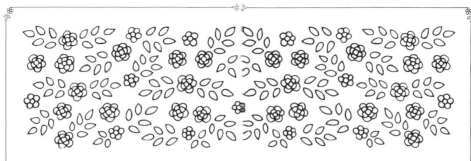

hen General Robert E. Lee surrendered at Appomattox on April 9, 1865, four years of civil war ended, and although the bitter struggle had been a shattering experience for the nation, Americans looked to the future with optimism. The country turned to the problem of reconstruction, changing the social and economic structure of the South, reorganizing currency, taxes, and banking, and embarking on an unprecedented development of its natural resources—coal, oil, gold, and silver. At the same time manufacturing of every conceivable product took a giant leap, while a network of railroads was built to carry resources and goods throughout the nation.

During the succeeding decades of rapid expansion, an upwardly mobile middle class became a substantial upper class whose wealth was based on sheer economic ability. This moneyed elite pursued splendor with a parvenu zeal. Although often criticized as excessive, the best furnishings from this period possess a sumptuous beauty that speaks of the age.

The Centennial International Exhibition mounted in Philadelphia in 1876 celebrated the achievements of the American nation in its first hundred years. It also focused on European cultures and the decorative arts associated with them. For the next several years, numerous fairs and expositions displayed the products of a rapidly advancing technology.

The ever-changing succession of styles during the second half of the nineteenth century—the mature Victorian period—had their inception in the fashionable decorating shops on the East Coast that set trends and dictated taste for the rest of the country. Many of these styles, made by machine for a little and sold for a lot, were aimed at the new mass market created by an ever-increasing agrarian population and the incessant flood of European immigrants to America's shores.

At the World's Columbian Exposition in Chicago in 1893 a completely electrified kitchen of the future, featuring a stove, hot water heater, lighting fixture, double boiler, and teakettle, captured the imagination of the American people and of the world. Imagine harnessing old Ben Franklin's lightning to do your cooking! The hymn to technology and its positive benefits for the modern world was chanted throughout the land.

In the early years of the twentieth century there came a reaction against too much technology too soon, and a strong conservative trend gained momentum, from which grew an appreciation for the quickly disappearing handcrafted products of simpler days. The relationship of technological advancement to handcraftsmanship became the preoccupation of social reformers throughout the world. The resulting arts and crafts movement, the art nouveau movement, and the mission style led directly to the international style, which began to emerge during World War I. At the same time the colonial revival, which had its beginnings prior to the Philadelphia Centennial, grew stronger and by the close of the war it dominated American popular taste and design.

THE MATURING NATION
1860~1914

270. Dining room of Lyndhurst. Andrew Jackson Davis. New York. 1864–65. Lyndhurst, National Trust for Historic Preservation, Tarrytown, New York

The dining room of the Lyndhurst mansion is one of the finest American interiors in the Gothic revival style. Lyndhurst (see plate 190) was built in 1838–41, and nearly twenty-five years later Andrew Jackson Davis, the original designer, supervised additions to the house for its second owner, George Merritt.

271. Pier table with display cabinets. Maker unknown. United States. 1865–75. Mahogany inlaid with walnut, maple, birch, and other exotic woods, height 104". Greenfield Village and Henry Ford Museum, Dearborn, Michigan

Because of its elaborateness, it has been suggested that this impressive architectural piece in the Renaissance revival style was formed in a major East Coast cabinetmaking shop. Yet it is very possible that it was crafted by European immigrants working in Grand Rapids, Michigan, which by this time had become a main center of American furniture making. The niches flanking the mirror would have displayed marble sculpture or ornate porcelains.

piece of information the well-bred man is in no need of, and which the ill-bred man never heeds. So that, if a clock must usurp the place of honor on a mantelpiece, it ought to have so good a form, or serve as the pedestal to such a bit of bronze, or such a vase, as to make us forget the burden of time-and-tide in the occasional contemplation of art eternities. We get this habit of clocks, with their flanking candlesticks or vases, on all our mantelpieces, from the French, who have no other way, from the palace to the bourgeois parlor. But they get rid of the main difficulty by either making sure that the clock does not keep good time,—the best French clocks being delightfully irresponsible in this particular,—or by having clocks without any insides to them, a comfortably common thing, as every one used to Paris "flats" knows. Ever since Sam Slick's day, America has been known as the land where cheap clocks abound. If we were a legend-making people, we should have our Henry IV, who would have said he wished every peasant might have a clock on his mantelpiece. But, though we have cheap clocks enough, we have no pretty ones, and we are therefore thrown back on those of French make, which are only to be endured when they are mere blocks of the marble they polish so finely, of which we can make a pedestal to support something we like to look at.

No area of criticism was immune to Cook's sharp pen. His carping at clock designs was mild compared to the attacks on contemporary artists in his spirited column for the *New York Tribune* in the 1860s, which were so brutal that a delegation of his victims protested en masse to the paper's bemused editor, Horace Greeley.

The mass production of shelf clocks had begun in Connecticut in 1807 when Eli Terry, a well-known clockmaker of the day, accepted an order for approximately four thousand wood movements. Shelf clocks, introduced in

272. *Wooton patent secretary.*
William S. Wooton. Indianapolis,
Indiana. 1874. Walnut, burl
walnut, and satinwood, height
72″. Collection Richard and
Eileen Dubrow Antiques,
Bayside, New York

This particular desk was made as
a presentation piece for Queen
Victoria, and a high quality of
craftsmanship was lavished on it.

Massachusetts in the decade 1760 to 1770, were probably the result of attempts to produce a timepiece less expensive than the tall-case clock, which relatively few families could afford. At first the works were made of wood. Since a more accurate device could be manufactured from brass, this metal was substituted as soon as it was technically feasible. Seth Thomas Sons and Company of Thomaston, Connecticut, was only one of the numerous producers who offered inexpensive as well as stylish shelf clocks. The cast-iron shelf clock (plate 273), by an anonymous maker in the 1870s, features a spring-driven brass movement.

Spindles, pistons and knobs, ship's wheels, club feet, and cogs—all are structural parts of the now-famous eclectic chairs made by German-born George Hunzinger. Defying specific classification—some historians consider them part of the Renaissance revival, others assign them to the influence of Charles L.

Eastlake, who espoused medieval and Jacobean forms—these extraordinary examples of chairmaking often give the general appearance of having folding capabilities, yet most are stationary. The chairs Hunzinger patented in 1861 and 1866 were so popular that for years he was kept busy manufacturing only seating pieces. The Asher and Adams *Commercial, Topographical, and Statistical Atlas and Gazetteer,* published in New York in 1876, praised Hunzinger's chairs for being "as strong as they are beautiful and as comfortable to sit in as they are graceful in appearance. . . . In this establishment the useful and ornamental are so thoroughly combined as to draw acknowledgement from all who examine them." The side chair (plate 274) retains its original upholstery. Like most Hunzinger pieces, it is signed under the seat with an impressed mark.

The Renaissance revival, which enjoyed great popularity throughout the nineteenth century, was often referred to as Louis XVI or Marie Antoinette. The handsome rosewood sofa (plate 275), originally from Jedediah Wilcox's forty-room Connecticut mansion, is a fine example of the best of this style. Modest manufactured objects, such as the secretary and the wall pocket in the midwestern interior of the anonymous watercolor *Victorian Family Group* (plate 278), were adaptations of expensive furniture in the voguish Renaissance revival. The family in the group portrait is obviously one of substance, for they are well attired and their home is furnished in middle-class comfort. Although the people remain anonymous, the man of the family has an aura of success, a quality much admired by Edward P. Hingston as defined in *The Genial Showman,* Hingston's 1870 reminiscences of the life of the popular humorist and inveterate punster Artemus Ward:

The adaptability of the American to any pursuit [is] a peculiarity which forms a national characteristic. Apprenticeship to any art or calling is not thought to be required in the United States. A Yankee learns a trade in six months to which an English youth is apprenticed for seven years. In professions, instead of a man waiting till he is middle-aged before he commences to practise, he gallops through all the sciences he has to learn, or makes a *coup-de-main* on all the art he has to acquire, and begins his profession and his manhood together. Should he commence as a doctor and not like his calling, he will probably turn to be a lawyer. If still dissatisfied, he will possibly try hotel-keeping, horse-dealing, or architecture. None of these suiting, he will attempt something else. Before he is forty he may have been a soldier, captain of a vessel, proprietor of a theatre, contractor, stonemerchant, and piano-forte manufacturer. By the time he attains his climacteric, he may have exhausted all the professions and tried every trade.

Fascination with oriental styles prevailed through the last third of the nineteenth century. Few American houses of this period equal Olana at Hudson, New York (plate 277), built in 1870–72 by the landscape painter Frederic Edwin Church. The artist, in his wide-ranging search for the exotic, toured Palestine and Syria, where he gathered art objects for the incredible dwelling that rejoices in a breathtaking view of the Hudson River. Its 327 acres were carefully planned by the eminent landscape architect Frederick Law Olmsted, whose most famous commission was New York City's Central Park. Olana, which means "Our Place on High" in Arabic, is a grand assemblage of Persian, Moorish, Saracen, Chinese, and Japanese motifs successfully blended to satisfy even the most extravagant Victorian taste for evocative, picturesque architecture.

Besides the exotic eclecticism peculiar to the age and the ornate characteristics of many prevailing styles, there were a number of American architects and interior designers in the 1870s who attempted to express a new realism, which tended toward a frank exposure of construction materials. Both the exterior (plate 276) and the interior of the William Watts Sherman House—designed by Henry Hobson Richardson and built in 1875 at Newport, Rhode Island—are examples of this tendency. Richardson, one of the most gifted American architects, studied civil engineering at Harvard, and in 1860 was accepted at the prestigious Ecole des Beaux-Arts in Paris, entering the atelier of Louis Jules André. His first architectural efforts in Paris were in the néo-Grec style, a design

273. Shelf clock. Maker
unknown. United States. c. 1875.
Cast iron with brass movement,
height 20¼". Private collection

The works of shelf clocks, which
were first introduced into America
in the 1760s, were wooden, but
metal was substituted as soon as
this was practical. This version,
from the following century, was
made with a brass eight-day
spring-driven movement.

274. Side chair. George
Hunzinger. New York City.
1869. Walnut, height 33".
Lyndhurst, National Trust for
Historic Preservation, Tarrytown,
New York

Hunzinger's seating pieces were
praised in the 1870s for their
comfort as much as for their
graceful beauty. This Victorian
chair retains its original upholstery.

275. Sofa. Maker unknown. New
York. c. 1870. Rosewood, length
76¾". Metropolitan Museum of
Art, New York City. Gift of
Josephine M. Fiala, 1968

This sofa is from a suite of
Renaissance revival furnishings
that originally adorned the sitting
room of the forty-room mansion
built by Jedediah Wilcox at
Meriden, Connecticut. Much
of the best Renaissance revival
furniture is embellished with
incised lines and carved urns
similar to those found on
this piece.

concept based upon borrowings from ancient Greece. By 1870 Richardson had returned to Boston and set up a very successful business. Trinity Church, one of his most important commissions at the time, brought him international fame. Although known primarily for his public buildings, Richardson's large domestic dwellings such as the Sherman House are primarily in the shingle style, a method of construction where the exteriors of large wood-frame structures were finished with shingles.

In an era of increasing sophistication, in which the decorative arts were willfully complex, there coexisted an enthusiastic appreciation for the rustic. Andrew Jackson Downing's 1842 guide, *Cottage Residences,* had expressed the opinion that simple rustic seats placed here and there in the right spots in gardens and on lawns would heighten the charm and encourage enjoyment of quiet yet beautiful places. Another naturalistic mode, the so-called organic

276. William Watts Sherman House. Henry Hobson Richardson. Newport, Rhode Island. 1875. Salve Regina College, Newport, Rhode Island (photograph Wayne Andrews)

This Newport structure by· Richardson expressed a new realism that competed with the clutter and ornateness of the late Victorian style. American architects by this time were consciously attempting to reveal their construction materials as part of the design idiom, a principle more fully developed later in the century by Louis Sullivan and the Chicago school of architecture.

style, concentrated on furnishings constructed from tree branches and roots. Also known as Adirondack furniture, these rough-hewn pieces were intended to give fashionable mountain resorts and hunting lodges an air of authenticity. The gardens of Lyndhurst, designed by Alexander Jackson Davis, a close friend of Downing's, included this type of furniture. Rustic architecture was not rare, but in general it was commissioned for simple but expensive vacation palaces catering to a moneyed clientele. The lobby of Old Faithful Inn (plate 279) was photographed by William Henry Jackson on a trip to the Upper Geyser Basin at Yellowstone National Park in the early decades of the twentieth century. The exposed woodwork—beams and balcony construction—were taken almost intact from tree trunks and limbs. A number of handsome American Indian rugs of the period adorn the floor of this impressive watering spot. Jackson, a pioneer photographer, recorded the scenic grandeur and historic sites of the American West, and his series on the Yellowstone region was instrumental in having the area set aside in 1872 as the first national park.

A contrast to the interior of the Old Faithful Inn, and an indication of the broad range of Victorian taste, is an advertisement (plate 280) for Thonet furniture manufactured by Thonet Brothers (Gebrüder Thonet), makers of Austrian bentwood furnishings. This aggressive Viennese firm, with sales outlets all over the world, maintained its primary depot for the United States at 808 Broadway in New York City, with a second facility in the Palmer House, Chicago's fashionable hotel. Thonet furniture was first produced about 1840. In 1851 it was shown at the Crystal Palace exhibition in London to a large international audience, which praised its neatness, lightness, and great strength. By the middle

277. Central hall and staircase of Olana. Frederic Edwin Church. New York. 1870-72. Olana State Historic Site, Taconic State Park Commission, New York State Office of Parks and Recreation, Hudson, New York

Construction of Frederic Edwin Church's "Persianized" mansion at Hudson began in 1870. The Church family moved in two years later, while the building was in progress, and it was completed in 1874. Few American homes can boast the dazzling exoticism of Olana. Even the location is impressive, with the structure perched on a hilltop overlooking the Hudson River. The magnificent spacious grounds were laid out by the landscape architect Frederick Law Olmsted.

period of the Victorian era American bentwood furniture, manufactured by firms like the Sheboygan Chair Company of Sheboygan, Wisconsin, was available in mahogany, walnut, ebony, and antique elm.

During the 1830s and 1840s it became fashionable to include sculpture, paintings, and prints in the furnishings of a house. Young American sculptors, bored with producing the standard portrait bust, began to model romanticized figures, which were then carved in marble by craftsmen in Italy. No well-furnished home was complete without its monumental sculptural decorations. By the middle of the century these idealized figures, which often expressed a fundamental pathos, gained such popularity that some of the artists were able to earn comfortable livings by specializing exclusively in their production. A few of them actually moved to Italy, focusing their attention on affluent Americans making the grand tour. Despite the attraction of the ideal or literary pieces, such as William Wetmore Story's *Cleopatra* (plate 283), most artists were finally faced with the unalterable fact that purely ideal subjects must go begging for clients. Portrait sculpture was the sculptor's mainstay.

The art of painting fared no better. Naturally there were some American artists who enjoyed international fame. For instance, the mammoth landscapes of Frederic Edwin Church, one of the most prominent members of the Hudson River school of painting, went for astonishingly high prices at the time. For the most part, however, the successful American painter was either a portrait painter—especially before the daguerreotype and other photographic forms were successfully exploited later in the century—or a furniture decorator. The decorator concentrated on fanciful floral and arabesque designs and striking landscapes such as the view of the Narrows on the Hudson River near West Point painted on the top of the wooden box (plate 281).

For those who could not afford a Church landscape or even a fine decorated item, a chromolithograph might satisfy the simple need to add a splash of color or a dash of sentimental charm to the parlor wall. *Little Bo-Peep* (plate 282), after a painting by John G. Brown, was published by L. Prang and Company of Boston in 1867. Louis Prang's firm was one of the first and most successful printing companies to utilize a four-color lithographic process, and it was producing fine color prints and greeting cards as early as the 1860s. Prang catered to popular taste and produced innumerable homespun pictures that many Americans felt were every bit as good as an oil painting—and they cost a good deal less.

By mid-century the progress of technology changed the look of building exteriors, making it possible to erect strong and handsome cast-iron storefronts and houses. Many foundries, including one owned by James Bogardus in New York City, specialized in this type of production, which became increasingly prevalent after the Crystal Palace—the gigantic exhibition building put up in 1853 at Forty-second Street and Sixth Avenue in New York City, just behind the present site of the New York Public Library—sparked the American imagination. A few years prior to the erection of this mammoth iron-and-glass structure, Peter Naylor of 13 Stone Street in New York already enjoyed a successful business based on the use of prefabricated iron. Naylor's notice in the March 31, 1849, edition of the *New York Tribune* summarized his faith in the practicality of putting up his structure anywhere in the country:

The galvanized iron houses constructed by me for California, having met with so much approval, I am thus induced to call the attention of those going to California to an examination of them. The iron is grooved in such a manner that all parts of the house, roof and sides, glide together, and a house 20 × 15 can be put up in less than a day. They are far cheaper than wood, are fireproof, and are much more comfortable than tents. A house of the above size can be shipped in two boxes . . . the freight on which would be about $14 to San Francisco. There will also be no trouble in removing from one part of the country to another, as the house can in a few hours be taken down and put up. By calling upon the subscriber a house of the above size can be seen.

Iron was also important in the construction of expensive buildings. The fashionable society architect Richard Morris Hunt, a conspicuous exponent of nineteenth-century eclecticism, erected a dazzling Moorish-style iron building in New York City which was illustrated in *The American Architect and Building News* for July 1876. Iron was also a serviceable material for picture frames, garden furniture, machinery, and heating stoves. The stylishly bustled woman in L. Prang and Company's lithograph of an interior of a manufactory of iron products (plate 284) is looking at the kinds of heating stoves available at the time. More up-to-date and modern than the cast-iron stoves was the handsome tile-covered heater (plate 285) designed especially for yachts by the Murdock Parlor Grate Company of Boston, Massachusetts.

The floral tiles that practically encase the Murdock stove are but one indication of American fascination with ceramics and ceramic art. One would surmise that the company used domestic tiles exclusively, since the general public held a very strong bias toward American goods. In fact a great stir was created when Abraham Lincoln ordered his official presidential china (plate 286) from France in 1861. There was vociferous agitation by public officials to "buy American," and consequently from then on most presidents were sensitive to this question and began to purchase their special dinnerware from American producers of china.

In this chauvinistic era even the importation of rare books by the serious collector generated a public outcry. The librarian's report in the *Proceedings of*

278. Victorian Family Group.
Artist unknown. United States.
c. 1875. Watercolor on cardboard,
14 × 17¼″. Greenfield Village
and Henry Ford Museum,
Dearborn, Michigan

The Renaissance revival style first
became fashionable in America
with expensive, elegant furniture.
By 1870 it had been adapted and
modified by small manufacturers
throughout the country, as
exemplified by the secretary and wall
pocket in this midwestern interior.

*279. Lobby of Old Faithful Inn.
Robert C. Reamer. Upper Geyser
Basin, Yellowstone National
Park, Wyoming. 1903–04.
William Henry Jackson
photograph private collection*

*In the last decades of the nineteenth
century and into the twentieth,
sophisticated architects and
designers looked to nature for
inspiration. In what was often
referred to as the organic style,
tables, chairs, benches, and even
the woodwork of room interiors
consisted of tree trunks and limbs.
This type of interior design was
especially popular for expensive
watering places such as the Old
Faithful Inn, still in operation at
Yellowstone National Park. The
photograph was taken in the early
twentieth century by William
Henry Jackson on one of his
many trips to the park.*

the American Antiquarian Society for April 1861, relating the heated discussion over the duty on imported books, reveals the philistine attitudes of some officials toward productions that were not homegrown:

When a member [Charles Sumner] of this Society, who holds a distinguished place in the Senate of the United States, proposed that books which had been printed more than thirty years should be admitted free of duty, *a senator from Oregon* expressed the opinion, that a new edition of a book (of Shakespeare, for example) is better than any old one, and that a man who is fool enough to pay a great price for what can be had for a small one ought to pay the duty. In this opinion *a senator from North Carolina* concurred; and not only advanced the theory, that, "if all the books one hundred years old were destroyed, no valuable knowledge would be lost," but declared that "there is nothing in an old book, of any value, that has not been republished in our own time." *A senator from Missouri* also was clear, that "if a work has been published thirty years, and has not been introduced into the United States, it is sufficient evidence that it is not fit to come here," and that, if introduced, "the reprint here is better than the original print in the foreign country;" adding some remarks not complimentary to the good sense of those who pay high prices for old manuscripts and original editions.

It is not surprising that old but venerable objects were denigrated in this heady time of new inventions and new processes that brought fine furnishings

280. Broadside advertisement. Gebrüder Thonet. Vienna. c. 1873. Lithograph, 29¼ × 19½". New-York Historical Society, New York City

The Viennese firm of Thonet Brothers manufactured and exported to American depots great quantities of bentwood furniture in a wide variety of forms. Usually the Thonet products were not assembled until they reached the depot showrooms.

The painted top depicts the Narrows on the Hudson River near West Point. The floral and arabesque motifs would have satisfied even the most demanding Victorian purchaser.

and accessories within the reach of many. The art of electroplating, or laying onto a base metal a series of silver washes, was perfected just after the Civil War. The Meriden Britannia Company of Meriden, Connecticut, between 1855 and 1901 specialized in the production of various items such as calling-card holders, water pitchers fitted with tumblers (plate 287), spoon holders, butter dishes, figural napkin rings, pickle jars, revolving casters, and assorted flatware. This vast outpouring of electroplated ware replaced the more costly, one-of-a-kind pieces like the unique trowel (plate 288) Mayor John T. Hoffman in 1867 used to lay the cornerstone for the new Tammany Hall building being put up in New York City. The coffee service (plate 289), also silver-plated, incorporated motifs of the Renaissance revival style—including the hoofed feet and engraved decoration—as the dominant design elements.

Renaissance revival was a significant influence in almost all areas of American decorative arts. The gold brooch and earrings (plate 290), probably crafted in New York City about 1860, are designed in this style. The elaborate jewelry cabinet (plate 291) designed by the architect Bruce Price to hold the European jewelry owned by his wife, also has prominent Renaissance revival features, but it does show the eclecticism dominant in the period. In fact it was during the Victorian period that most American women could first hope to possess more than a handful of personal adornments, since only the richest women, such as the wives of bankers or those few success stories of the Industrial Revolution, could have afforded these luxuries previously.

Lighting in the American home improved brilliantly during the 1860s. Gas, a viable substitute for candles and burning fluids, was first made available for public distribution in 1816 in Baltimore, and during the late 1820s numerous cities across the nation converted their streetlights to gas, a more easily regulated illuminant. Despite its frequent use in public places, gas was considered for a long time ill-suited for domestic lighting. In a delightfully opinionated essay, "Philosophy of Furniture"—published in 1840 in *Masterful Essays: Fanciful, Humorous, and Serious*—Edgar Allan Poe complained that he found gas "totally inadmissible within doors. Its harsh and unsteady light offends. No one having both brains and eyes will use it."

Not everyone agreed. Mrs. A. W. Smith's parlor in her Philadelphia boardinghouse in 1853 was lighted by a gas lamp that stood on a table with cast-iron supports similar to those on sewing machines. A rigid pipe projecting from the wall supplied the fuel for the lamp in this otherwise attractively furnished middle-class room. By the third quarter of the century gas had become possibly the single most important source of illumination. An unidentified "tastemaker" in *The Art-Journal* in 1877 was almost ecstatic about the progress that could be discerned in the design of gas fixtures:

Prang and Company was one of the first and most successful firms to exploit the chromolithographic four-color process and produced many sentimental prints based on commonplace themes. Prang's catalog at the time described this pretty scene as the picture of a "chubby little rogue who has no doubt just run away from his mother and is endeavoring to hide behind the red leaves of a sumach bush."

Probably there is nothing in the wide range of our American Art-industries which has been so rapidly developed during the last ten years as that of metal-work, and as evidence of it we take great pleasure in calling attention to the accompanying illustrations of gas-fixtures, which are after designs executed by Messrs. Mitchell, Vance and Co., of New York. . . . In the manufacture of gas-fixtures, perhaps, more than any other department of metal Art-work, the designs have become more and more skilful and elaborate until it would appear as if the genius of the designers was almost exhausted.

283. Cleopatra. William Wetmore Story. United States. Dated 1869. Marble, height 54½″. Metropolitan Museum of Art, New York City. Gift of John Taylor Johnston, 1888

Large monumental sculpture was an essential appointment in every well-furnished Victorian mansion. Contemporary homes and public buildings were copiously supplied with romanticized figures from the ancient world.

The author might well have been referring to the chandelier (plate 292) with its dazzling array of contemporary Victorian decorative motifs.

Although gas was common for both domestic and public facilities until the end of the century and even into the twentieth century, after the discovery in 1859 of rich petroleum deposits in western Pennsylvania kerosene came into use. For the first time clean, efficient, and inexpensive artificial lighting was generally available. Because it is a lightweight oil, kerosene was capable of quick absorption through a long wick. The initial American patent for a kerosene lamp was granted in 1859. The fact that an additional forty patents were processed the same year proves that the fuel was taken seriously by industrialists and engineers alike. Almost overnight the kerosene lamp became an integral part of the American home. During the 1860s kerosene-burning chandeliers and glass lamps (plate 293) and pottery lamps were manufactured in great numbers.

American glass products changed dramatically in this period, since new technology led to the development of an astonishing array of forms and designs for pressed glass. No design was more popular than the three-face pattern, which appears on the covered sugar bowl (plate 294). This delicate pressed-glass piece of about 1874 is assigned to George Duncan and Sons of Pittsburgh. The body is clear and the masks and the foot are frosted.

284. Tinsmith's Shop.
L. Prang and Company. Boston,
Massachusetts. 1874.
Chromolithograph, 14 × 21¾".
Greenfield Village and Henry
Ford Museum, Dearborn,
Michigan

This illustration shows the activity
of an iron-manufactory workroom
as well as a glimpse of a salesroom
that offered various finished
products—including stoves,
stovepipes, birdcages, and various-
sized pots, pans, and miscellaneous
cooking utensils.

Textiles produced in the home in the 1860s and 1870s were not much different from those of earlier periods. One particular form, the crazy quilt, became quite the rage during the Victorian era. Its overwrought style perfectly

285. Heater. Murdock Parlor
Grate Company. Boston,
Massachusetts. c. 1873. Metal
and tile, height 27". Greenfield
Village and Henry Ford Museum,
Dearborn, Michigan

The upright rectangular box-
shaped heater is covered on top,
front, and sides with floral-
decorated pottery tiles. Although
it was designed especially for
yachts, the stove was advertised as
desirable for domestic use as well.

286. China service. Haviland.
France. 1861. Porcelain, diameter
of plate 10''. Private collection

The service was made for
Abraham Lincoln for use at the
White House. Many American
presidents ordered their official
state china from Europe. After
both political and public agitation
had stressed "buy American"
policies, White House officials
usually commissioned American
firms to produce their special
orders.

287. Water pitcher on stand with tumbler. Meriden Britannia Company. Meriden, Connecticut. 1868. Silver-plated, height 20". Greenfield Village and Henry Ford Museum, Dearborn, Michigan

The plating on silver-plate items is frequently worn through, exposing the base metal, such as in this water pitcher. Modern collectors, who like to use their silver pieces, often have them replated.

288. Trowel. Francis W. Cooper. New York City. 1867. Silver with wood handle, length 14½". Greenfield Village and Henry Ford Museum, Dearborn, Michigan

This trowel was used by Mayor John T. Hoffman to lay the cornerstone for the new Tammany Hall building erected in New York City in the late 1860s. Hoffman was Grand Sachem of the Tammany Society.

289. Coffee service. Maker unknown. United States. c. 1870. Silver-plated, height of coffeepot 12¼″. Greenfield Village and Henry Ford Museum, Dearborn, Michigan

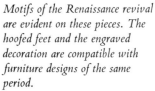

Motifs of the Renaissance revival are evident on these pieces. The hoofed feet and the engraved decoration are compatible with furniture designs of the same period.

suited the nineteenth-century devotion to the sentimental: treasured hair ribbons, bits of mother's wedding dress, and even men's neckties, bathing suits, and odd items of memorabilia were incorporated into the patterns. Elaborate cotton or silk embroidery fancied up a commonplace piece and made it fashionable.

Quilts were generally classified as two types: the whole cloth quilt—made from two large pieces of fabric, one forming the front and the other the back—and the patchwork quilt—either appliquéd or pieced. The appliqué technique involved sewing pieces of cut fabric on a background square. After the individual squares were sewn together, areas without a design were frequently quilted in a decorative pattern. Pieced quilts were made by sewing small straight-edged fabric pieces together to create an overall patterned top. Designs were contained within a square of fabric, or block, which could comprise as many as fifty or

290. Brooch and earrings. Maker unknown. New York City. c. 1860. Gold, length of earring 2″. Private collection

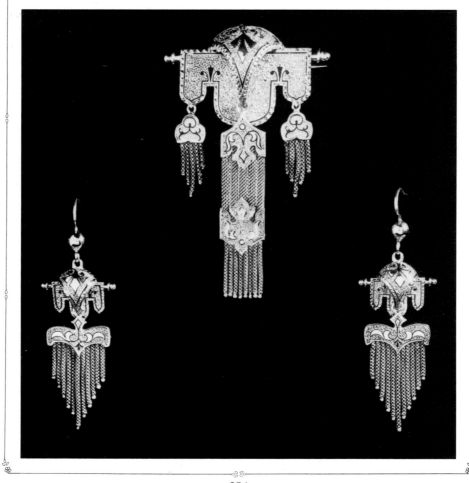

The Renaissance revival style was pervasive in the Victorian era, and it influenced every aspect of personal adornment as well.

291. Jewelry cabinet. Bruce Price. United States. 1872. Ebonized wood, height 69''. Museum of the City of New York, New York City. Gift of Mrs. Emily Price Post

This unusual piece of cabinetmaking shows a medley of styles, with elements of the Renaissance revival, the rococo, and the Moorish.

sixty small bits of cloth. The pieced blocks were then sewn to each other to form the quilt top. The pieced crazy quilt with brilliant silk yarn embroidery (plate 295), executed by Celestine Bacheller of Massachusetts, is without equal. It is astonishing that a sixteen-year-old girl could conceive and fashion such a remarkable design.

The hooked rug depicting an American eagle and shield (plate 296) was probably inspired by the vast outpouring of patriotic enthusiasm for the Philadelphia Centennial, the celebration of the first one hundred years of the found-

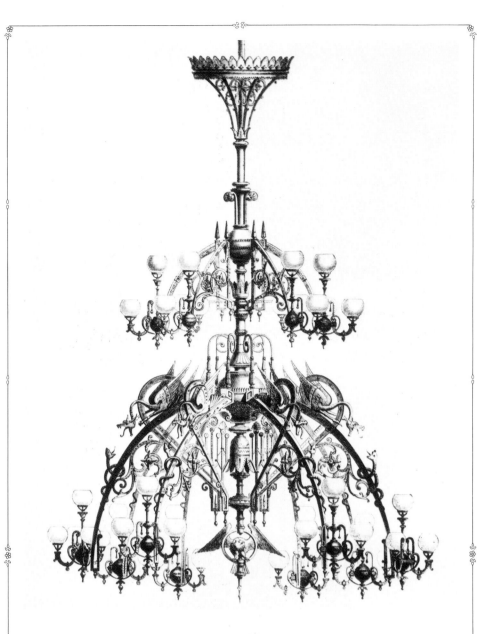

292. *Chandelier. Cornelius and Sons. Philadelphia, Pennsylvania. 1876. Cast and wrought iron with lacquer gilt, dimensions unknown. Illustration from* The Masterpieces of the Centennial International Exhibition *(Philadelphia, 1876, vol. 2). Private collection*

293. *Kerosene lamps. Makers unknown. United States. 1860–80. Glass, brass, and marble, height of center lamp 23". Greenfield Village and Henry Ford Museum, Dearborn, Michigan*

The style of this elaborate gilded chandelier with seventy-two lights was given the solemn appellation of Greco-medieval. Today the more likely classification would be Renaissance revival.

When rich petroleum deposits were discovered in 1859 in western Pennsylvania, kerosene became preferred as an efficient and inexpensive fuel. Attractively designed lamps and elaborate chandeliers were produced in great quantity to satisfy the demands for artificial light during the last third of the nineteenth century.

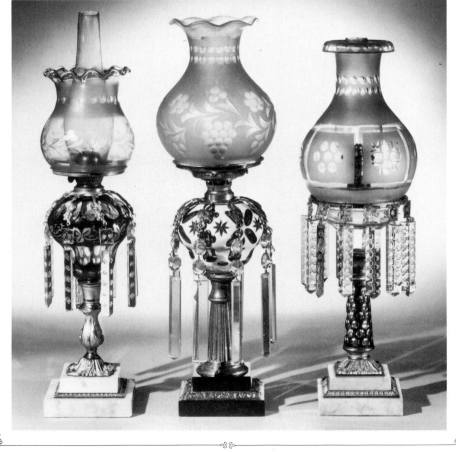

294. Covered sugar bowl. George Duncan and Sons. Pittsburgh, Pennsylvania. c. 1874. Pressed glass, height 9⅞". Greenfield Village and Henry Ford Museum, Dearborn, Michigan

This clear piece has a frosted three-face base and finial. As a result of the new forms and designs made possible by improved glass technology in the second half of the nineteenth century, pressed glass was very much in vogue with contemporary American homemakers.

ing of the United States. This rug was hooked on a pattern stenciled on burlap by Edward Sands Frost, a peddler from Biddeford, Maine, who traveled throughout the New England countryside in the 1860s. Observing the colorfully designed rugs in his customers' homes, Frost decided to find a quicker way of putting a design on the burlap backing. He made 750 zinc stencils that enabled him to produce more than 180 different patterns. This example of Yankee ingenuity in the field of textiles is but one of many areas in which the American self-made man achieved success during the years of rapid industrialization in the mid-Victorian era.

296. Hooked rug. Maker
unknown; stencil by Edward
Sands Frost. New England. Last
quarter of nineteenth century.
Wool, $31\frac{3}{4} \times 64\frac{3}{4}''$. Greenfield
Village and Henry Ford Museum,
Dearborn, Michigan

Edward Sands Frost, a Yankee
peddler, freely borrowed the
designs of the hooked rugs he saw
in the homes of his clients and
incorporated them into his own
rug patterns. This handsome item,
worked on a burlap stencil,
celebrates the American Centennial
at Philadelphia.

OPPOSITE:

295. Crazy quilt. Celestine
Bacheller. Wyoma, Massachusetts.
c. 1900. Linen, pieced and
embroidered, $73\frac{1}{2} \times 57''$.
Museum of Fine Arts, Boston,
Massachusetts. Gift of Mr. and
Mrs. Edward J. Healy

The fad of the crazy quilt reached
its peak during the Victorian
period. The scenes in this superb
embroidered linen quilt, conceived
and stitched together by a sixteen-
year-old girl, apparently represent
actual landscapes and houses near
Wyoma.

Fairs, Fairs, and More Fairs
1876-1914

There is no record of the number of Americans who journeyed to London to visit the Great Exhibition of The Industry of All Nations at the Crystal Palace in 1851. But one thing is certain: every publication in the United States reported in detail on the world's first international exposition. Enthusiasm for an international fair was so great that in 1853 a similar exhibition—The World of Science, Art, and Industry, presented at the New York Crystal Palace—attempted not only to duplicate but to expand on the achievements in London.

The general impression that an international fair brought to the attention of the world the best of each nation's industrial arts and design led to many other popular international expositions in the second half of the century. Perhaps the best attended of these extravaganzas was the Centennial International Exhibition at Philadelphia in 1876, which was mounted to celebrate the first one hundred years of the Declaration of Independence.

One of the jurors at the Centennial, Richard Morris Hunt—the highly successful architect serving the fashionable and the rich in the last decades of the nineteenth century—enthusiastically described in the *General Report of the Judges* the great diversity of the materials exhibited: "The display of building-materials at the Centennial Exhibition was remarkable rather for extent than for novelty. The great natural wealth of the United States was in this respect well represented. American labor-saving machinery, too, in building

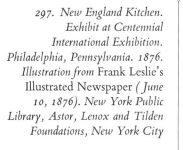

297. New England Kitchen. Exhibit at Centennial International Exhibition. Philadelphia, Pennsylvania. 1876. Illustration from Frank Leslie's Illustrated Newspaper *(June 10, 1876). New York Public Library, Astor, Lenox and Tilden Foundations, New York City*

INTERIOR OF THE NEW ENGLAND KITCHEN.

A prototype modern regional kitchen at the 1876 Centennial exhibition was furnished with antique objects from various periods. The public's new awareness of an indigenous colonial style of furniture and architecture was directly attributable to this extremely popular exhibit.

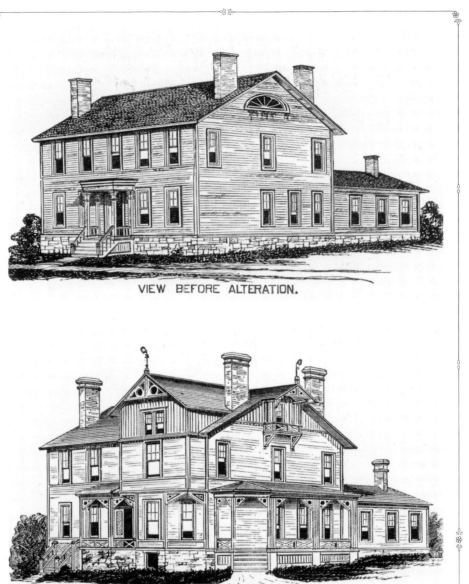

VIEW BEFORE ALTERATION.

VIEW AFTER ALTERATION.

298. *Proposed architectural renovation. A. J. Bicknell and Company. New York City. 1879. Published in* Specimen Book of One Hundred Architectural Designs *(New York, 1879). Private collection*

This before-and-after view of an architectural alteration offers the Victorian homeowner plans for turning what was then referred to as a colonial house into the more current so-called Queen Anne style. It seems a curious endeavor since many Americans in the 1870s had developed an appreciation for their colonial heritage and were modifying their homes to approximate the earlier forms.

appliances compared most favorably with that of other nations." A sense of chauvinism about American goods seemed a natural response at this birthday celebration. The public believed that everything exhibited at Philadelphia compared favorably with the products of other nations, especially machinery and industrial materials, and the popular press fervently heralded America's entry into the international marketplace.

Few exhibits at the Centennial were better attended than the New England Kitchen (plate 297), constructed with a beamed ceiling, leaded casement windows, and a great fireplace and furnished with objects dating from the seventeenth, eighteenth, and nineteenth centuries. This immensely popular presentation had far-reaching consequences. The ensuing craze for collecting and decorating in the colonial, or early American, style caused manufacturers—quick to sense the possibility of big profits—to turn their workmen from the production of French-inspired Victorian furniture to the crafting of modern "antiques," or reproductions of earlier period pieces.

Architecture during the last quarter of the nineteenth century was also affected by this obsession with previous styles. Many fashionable architectural firms issued plans for remodeling Victorian homes, often inaccurately labeling the renovations with the names of historical styles. One publishing house, A. J. Bicknell and Company, included in its specimen design book a before-and-after view (plate 298) that suggested an alteration from a contemporary structure into what was referred to as Queen Anne—a misnomer among architectural idioms since it was a revival in name only and bore no real relationship to the

299. Century Vase. Designed by Karl Mueller; manufactured by Union Porcelain Works. Greenpoint, New York. 1876. Hard-paste porcelain, height 22¼″. Brooklyn Museum, Brooklyn, New York. Gift of Carll and Franklin Chace in memory of their mother, Pastora Forest Smith Chace

Nearly every major manufacturer produced special exhibition pieces for the Centennial International Exhibition at Philadelphia, which celebrated the nation's first one hundred years of independence. The overglaze enamel vignettes to the left of Washington's head depict the stringing of telegraph wires in the West, to the right a potter jiggers a ceramic plate on a revolving mold, and below him the Brooklyn Bridge begins to take shape.

mature Queen Anne style of the previous century. The nineteenth-century Queen Anne architecture played on the contrast of materials. First floors were often exposed brick or stone, upper stories stucco, clapboard, or decorative shingles. Roofs were gabled, and there were second-story projections and corner turrets borrowed from the French château. The projecting bay front capped by a gable or pinnacle roof was a picturesque sight across the nation in the 1880s, from the grand summer cottages of Newport to the smaller residences of bankers and physicians of small-town America.

Many American companies created wares especially for exhibition at the Centennial. The Union Porcelain Works of Greenpoint, New York, exhibited a flamboyant hard-paste porcelain vase designed by Karl Mueller, called appropriately the Century Vase (plate 299). A relief profile of George Washington, a gilded eagle, and three-dimensional American buffaloes are emphatic reminders of patriotic themes. Events of American history are depicted in six biscuit panels at the bottom, and painted vignettes illustrate contemporary machines and processes that had contributed to the nation's dramatic progress in the industrial arts. Individual artisans also crafted objects that honored the patriotic celebration; the quilt (plate 300) by G. Knappenberger is a cheerful example that features Pennsylvania German motifs and large appliquéd letters that spell out "Centennial."

The rapture over American political values, natural resources, and innovative technology increased throughout the nineteenth century and extended to all areas of the decorative arts. The center table fashioned from animal horns (plate 301) by Wenzel Friedrich was awarded a gold medal at a later international exposition devoted specifically to the industrial arts, the New Orleans World's Industrial and Cotton Centennial Exposition of 1884–85. This unique item is composed of twenty steerhorns with the remainder of the framework horn-veneered.

While enthusiasm for American products dominated the central displays at the Centennial in Philadelphia, the public in general and the press in particular expressed interest in several specialized areas. The fine arts were singled out for their high quality and diversity. The main art exhibits were held in Memorial Hall, which was itself the featured image on a printed souvenir handkerchief (plate 302). The exhibits in the vestibule of the Rotunda and in the entranceway to the Western Pavilion (plate 303) concentrated on sculpture. For many Americans this was their first opportunity of viewing original fine art firsthand.

300. Appliqué quilt. G. Knappenberger. Possibly Pennsylvania. 1876. Cotton, 70 × 90″. Museum of American Folk Art, New York City. Gift of Rhea Goodman

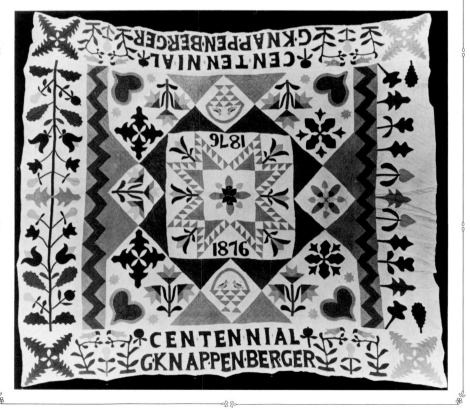

Traditional Pennsylvania German elements of design—hearts, paired birds, and tulips—abound on this needlework treasure honoring America's Centennial celebration.

OPPOSITE:

301. Center table. Wenzel Friedrich. San Antonio, Texas. 1880s. Steerhorn with horn veneer, height 29½". San Antonio Museum Association, San Antonio, Texas

The table contains twenty horns and the framework is horn-veneered. The horns at the corners have acorn tips turned from horn, and the pendent horns beneath the table are tipped with ball finials also made from horn. The feet have glass ball casters. An inlaid star centers the top as well as the skirt at each side of this extraordinary piece.

The arts joined in celebrating the first one hundred years of the United States as a political entity and the industrial and mechanical achievements attained in that short span of time. The painting commemorating the fast mail delivery of the Lake Shore and Michigan Southern (plate 304) is a kind of hymn to the early American railroad. The upper section of the painting depicts a man on horseback—a method of mail delivery made obsolete by modern technology.

Another form of art that enjoyed immense popularity at the Centennial was the manufactured art produced by American business. The Century Vase (plate 305), a monumental display piece exhibited by the Gorham Manufacturing Company, was crafted from solid silver after designs by George Wilkinson and Thomas J. Pairpoint. Like the elaborate porcelain souvenir vase (plate 299), it abounds with opulent symbolism that expressed the nation's extreme optimism in the last decades of the nineteenth century over its ostensible mission as the promised land.

Of the many foreign exhibitions at the Centennial, the Japanese building and its garden (plate 306) and the Chinese pavilion elicited the most interest. The Japanese display, constructed by a Japanese crew from over fifty carloads of building materials and display objects, intensified an already prevailing interest in oriental styles. Antique bronzes, wood and ivory carvings, lacquer work, pottery, and curious specimens of porcelain made a strong impression on the public. The American manufacturing community, picking up on this renewed interest in objects from the Far East, began to incorporate oriental motifs into the designs of their products.

During the late 1870s and throughout the 1880s another wave of exoticism enjoyed a special popularity with elite East Coast decorators and their clients. The Turkish corner—an alcove of a room, or the room itself, especially set aside for the purpose of creating an area with an exotic flavor—was crammed with authentic imported antiques, contemporary objects from remote, faraway lands, and domestic pieces approximating the Turkish style. The craze for Eastern and Near Eastern styles, all indiscriminately referred to at the time as oriental, extended to every aspect of home decoration. The Moorish smoking room (plates 308, 309) from the John D. Rockefeller House in New York City is filled with ebonized carved furniture. The mantels, painted and gilded ceilings, and carved and inlaid woodwork are combined with rich fabrics to create the kind of fin

302. Handkerchief. Maker unknown. United States. 1876. Cotton, 20 × 22". Collection Marjorie L. Plessinger

The Memorial Hall at the Philadelphia Centennial contained the Art Gallery, one of the most popular displays. This handkerchief souvenir is printed in red and blue on a white ground.

303. *The Art Gallery—Western
Pavilion. Philadelphia,
Pennsylvania. 1876. Illustration
from* The Masterpieces of the
Centennial International
Exhibition *(Philadelphia,
1876, vol. 3). Private collection*

*The vestibule of the Rotunda and
the entranceway to the Western
Pavilion, both with extensive
displays of sculpture, gave many
Americans at the Philadelphia
Centennial their first experience of
viewing the fine arts.*

OPPOSITE:

304. *The Flight of the Fast
Mail on the Lake Shore and
Michigan Southern Railway.
Artist unknown. United States.
1876. Oil on canvas, $76\frac{1}{2} \times
57''$. Greenfield Village and
Henry Ford Museum, Dearborn,
Michigan*

*This painting celebrates one of the
technological advances achieved in
the United States between the
years 1776 and 1876.*

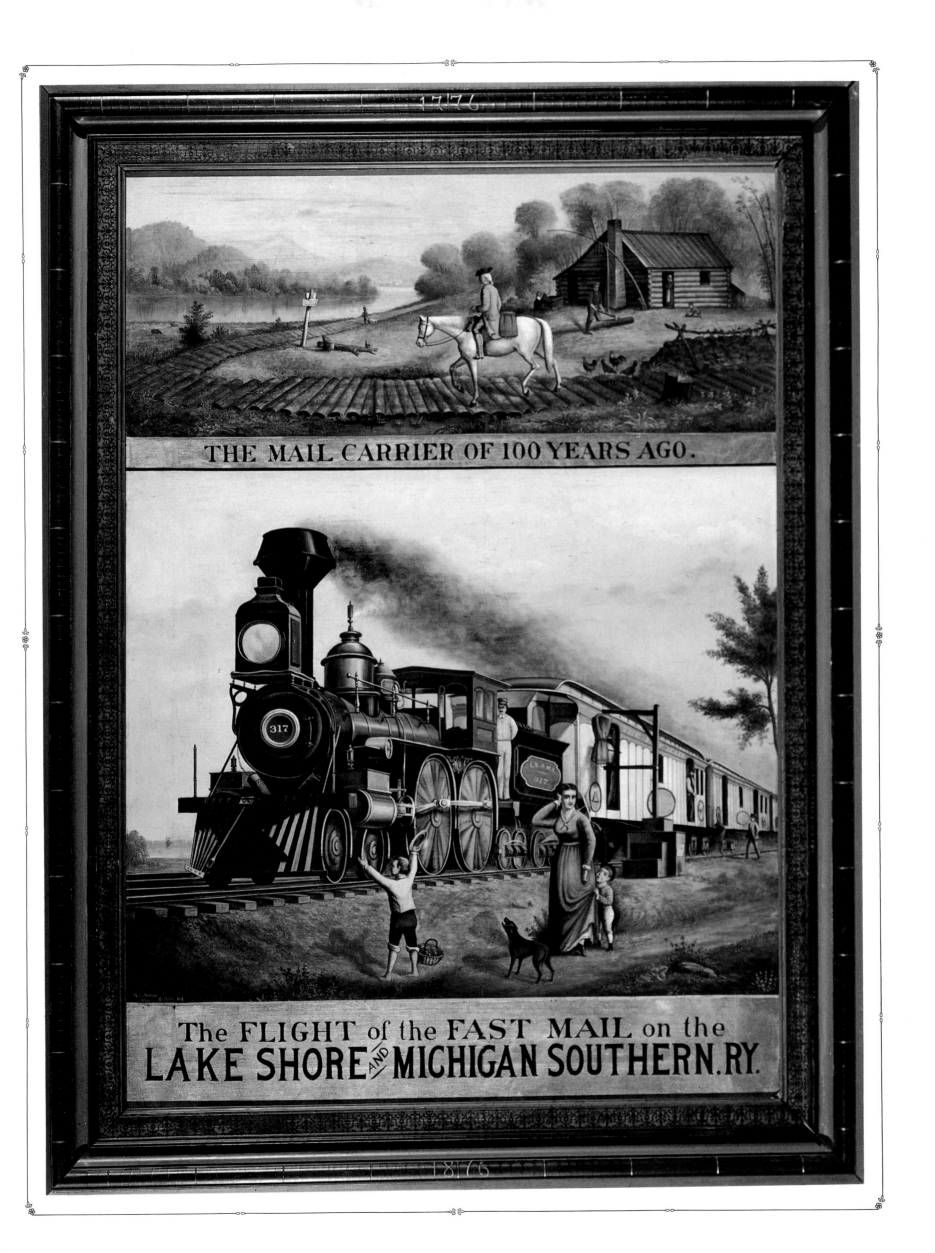

THE MAIL CARRIER OF 100 YEARS AGO.

The FLIGHT of the FAST MAIL on the
LAKE SHORE AND MICHIGAN SOUTHERN. RY.

Gorham produced this vase
especially for exhibition at the
Centennial. Although American
tastemakers of the time readily
admitted that ambitious designs
were often overloaded with
meretricious ornament, the
Century Vase was the hit of the
exhibition. Abundant symbolism,
including allegorical figures and
historical emblems, provoked
Godey's Magazine and Lady's
Book to complain: "No one
goes so far astray in elaborate
ornamentation."

de siècle splendor suitable for the urban mansion of a member of the new class
of American industrial barons. The Rockefeller House, erected in the 1860s
at 4 West Fifty-fourth Street, was remodeled for Arabella Worsham in the
1870s, prior to Rockefeller's ownership of the building in 1884. Arabella Duval
Worsham Huntington Huntington was a colorful mysterious woman whose
carefully guarded history was kept secret throughout her life. For many years
the unofficial wife of the railroad magnate Collis P. Huntington, she eventually
married him; later she became the wife of his nephew Henry E. Huntington.
Enormously wealthy, she was a patron of the arts on a grand scale and was also
a devotee of the latest fashions in late-nineteenth-century decorative arts.

Many practical appointments produced in the last decades of the century
reflected, at least in spirit, a wide range of the influence of foreign conceptions
in American decorative arts. Both the tall-case clock (plate 307), mounted in a
dazzling case in the new taste, and the brilliant tea set made in 1888 (plate 310)
were designed by Edward C. Moore, a partner and the chief designer at Tiffany and Company in New York. The Tiffany firm was one of the main forces
behind the appreciation of orientalia in the United States.

306. The Japanese Bazaar.
Exhibit at Centennial International
Exhibition. Philadelphia,
Pennsylvania. 1876. Illustration
from Frank H. Norton's
Illustrated Historical Register
of the Centennial Exhibition,
Philadelphia, 1876, and of the
Exposition Universelle, Paris,
1878 (New York, 1879). Library
of Congress, Washington, D.C.

The Japanese displays at the
Centennial caused more comment
than most of the other foreign
exhibits. They were largely
responsible for the widespread
American appreciation of oriental
motifs that was particularly keen
during the 1880s. The craze for
Japanese design lasted to the end
of the Victorian period.

307. Tall-case clock. Designed by Edward C. Moore; manufactured by Tiffany and Company. New York City. Patented November 7, 1882. Mahogany, height 105″. Metropolitan Museum of Art, New York City. Gift of Mary J. Kingsland, 1906

Edward C. Moore, the chief designer for Tiffany's, was influential in forwarding the appreciation of oriental design in the United States at the end of the nineteenth century.

Also somewhat exotic in feeling is the cherry secretary (plate 311) manufactured about 1877–82 by the prestigious decorating firm of Herter Brothers of New York City. Designers and decorators on a grand scale, Herter Brothers were influential figures after the Civil War when the so-called palaces of the pioneer millionaires were being erected, and anyone interested in furniture in the latest style and the best taste was obliged to visit their showrooms. The large secretary, part of a bedroom suite, was made with ebonized wood embellished with dramatic floral inlay. It displays the rectangular shape, honesty of construction, and flat surface decoration recommended by the English tastemaker Charles L.

308, 309. Museum installation. Moorish smoking room from John D. Rockefeller House. New York City. Late 1870s. Brooklyn Museum, Brooklyn, New York. Gift of John D. Rockefeller, Jr., and John D. Rockefeller III

Ebonized carved furniture, carved and inlaid woodwork and mantels, and painted and gilded ceilings combine with rich fabrics to create the exotic splendor favored by the nouveau riche of the late nineteenth century. The late Victorian obsession with what was then commonly known as oriental motifs, in this instance an eclecticism dominated by Moorish design, is also evident in the carved and inlaid woodwork on the door to the room.

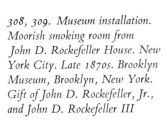

310. Tea set. Designed by
Edward C. Moore; manufactured
by Tiffany and Company. New
York City. c. 1888. Silver with
enamel, length of teapot 11".
Metropolitan Museum of Art,
New York City. Gift of a Friend
of the Museum, 1897

The oriental influence in American
decorative arts was prevalent
throughout the Victorian period
but was particularly acute in
the last quarter of the nineteenth
century. The items in this tea
service, an extremely fine example
of arabesque design, would have
been perfect accessories for Frederic
Edwin Church's exotic mansion,
Olana (see plate 277), of the
previous decade.

OPPOSITE:

311. Secretary. Herter Brothers.
New York City. c. 1877–82.
Cherry, ebonized, height 54".
Metropolitan Museum of Art,
New York City. Gift of Paul
Martini, 1969

In the second half of the nineteenth
century America produced some of
the most sophisticated furniture
influenced by the reform movement
begun earlier in the century by
Charles L. Eastlake. His emphasis
was on rectangular furniture forms
and flat surface decoration of
painting, marquetry, or low-
relief carving. Herter Brothers
manufactured this handsome
secretary as part of a bedroom
suite for one of the homes of
multimillionaire financier and
railroad magnate Jay Gould.

Eastlake in *Hints on Household Taste in Furniture, Upholstery, and Other Details,* printed in London in 1868. In this highly influential publication Eastlake expressed his desire to revitalize the principles of early handcraftsmanship. Eastlake noted in the fourth edition of his work, published in 1878, that his writings had great influence in the United States, but complained that he found American tradesmen continually advertising tasteless products they were pleased to call Eastlake furniture. He bitterly objected to the fact that these pieces with which he had nothing to do should be considered his responsibility. On the contrary, American craftsmen did produce some very fine Eastlake-influenced furniture. Eastlake, who was a reformer of furniture design more than an innovator, was a leading exponent of Gothic revival and Jacobean styles.

An exact definition of the American Eastlake style is difficult since during the 1870s and 1880s it represented something different to everyone. Scholars

312. *Picture gallery of Malden Public Library. Henry Hobson Richardson. Massachusetts. 1885. Malden Public Library, Malden, Massachusetts*

This early photograph reveals typical furnishings in a public room in the last quarter of the nineteenth century. The gallery includes a turned spindle bench similar to those illustrated in Charles L. Eastlake's Hints on Household Taste. *The original furniture from the gallery is now on loan to the Museum of Fine Arts in Boston.*

have recently associated the Gothic and Romanesque furniture and buildings of the American architect Henry Hobson Richardson with the spirit and intent of Eastlake. The spool and spindle turned and decorated pieces that Richardson designed in 1885 for the Malden Public Library (plate 312) in Massachusetts are definitely similar to illustrations in Eastlake's book.

Few American objects in the Eastlake style are as fully realized as the pool table (plate 315), designed and built at the Brunswick Balke Collander company in New York City. Complex in construction and embellished with sensitive carving and turnings, it is a tour de force of fine Renaissance revival design.

Oriental motifs also abound in the Pearl Room (plate 314) in William Henry Vanderbilt's mansion built in New York City in the early 1880s. The sumptuous Italian Renaissance structure was a block-long triple mansion between Fifty-first and Fifty-second streets on Fifth Avenue, the southern section occupied by Vanderbilt and the northern section by his daughters and their families. Christian Herter, head of the firm of Herter Brothers, served as architect, designer, and decorator of the Vanderbilt complex. Not only was he responsible for the exterior and interior plans, he also designed most of the furniture, textiles, mosaics, and carvings. One enthusiastic critic declared that this building was a "typical American residence, seized at the moment when the nation began to have a taste of its own, an architecture, a connoisseurship, and a choice in the appliances of luxury, society, culture."

William Henry Vanderbilt, son of a steamship and railroad magnate, was

313. Art gallery of Mrs. Potter Palmer House. Illinois. Late nineteenth century. Chicago Historical Society, Chicago, Illinois

The gallery in the Chicago home of Mrs. Potter Palmer is the epitome of Victorian eclecticism. Few of the furnishings match in this willfully cluttered interior. Mrs. Palmer had a fascination for small antique boxes. Some of the pieces from her very extensive collection are displayed on the stepped table in the foreground.

himself a successful financier and railroad promoter. Although he was noted for being relatively simple in his personal tastes, his enormous wealth was established at over $190 million in the 1880s and his mansion on Fifth Avenue was the talk of the nation. The Vanderbilt family commissioned many lavish homes on the eastern seaboard, every structure increasing in size and splendor. Richard Morris Hunt designed a number of notable residences for Vanderbilt's sons. Marble House in Newport, Rhode Island, was designed in 1888 by Hunt—

314. Pearl Room of William Henry Vanderbilt House. Christian Herter. New York City. 1881. Illustration from Edward Strahan's Mr. Vanderbilt's House and Collection (Boston, 1884, vol. 1). New York Public Library, Astor, Lenox and Tilden Foundations, New York City

Christian Herter utilized a medley of styles in the design and decoration of the drawing room in Vanderbilt's New York mansion, which formerly occupied the block between Fifty-first and Fifty-second streets on the west side of Fifth Avenue. Established New York society was content with modest brownstone dwellings, but the newly rich demanded palatial structures and ostentatious decor such as the massive gold-encrusted framed doorways and velvet-covered walls of Vanderbilt's drawing room. There was also a vast gallery in which his art collection, valued at $1.5 million, was hung. Vanderbilt spent over $800,000 decorating his mansion, a trifling sum for a man of his enormous wealth.

315. Pool table. Brunswick Balke
Collander. New York City.
c. 1882. Walnut marquetry,
length 108''. Sotheby Parke
Bernet, Inc., New York City

This table has many of the
characteristics of fine Renaissance
revival design, including inlaid
and painted decoration and delicate
incised lines emphasized with gilt.
In the late nineteenth century
music rooms and game rooms were
regular features in all fashionable
affluent homes.

OPPOSITE ABOVE:

316A. Amberina glassware. New
England Glass Works. Cambridge,
Massachusetts. c. 1886. Plated
glass, height of pitcher 7⅛''.
Bennington Museum, Bennington,
Vermont

The gold ruby of Amberina glass—
such as (left to right) this cruet
bottle, punch cup, tumbler, and
pitcher—was lined or plated with
an opalescent glass. After the piece
was finished, one edge was
reheated, causing that portion to
turn red. The pieces are usually
ribbed or pleated.

OPPOSITE BELOW:

316B. Peachblow glassware. J. H.
Hobbs, Brockunier and Company.
Wheeling, West Virginia.
c. 1883. Plated glass, height of
Chinese vase 10''. Bennington
Museum, Bennington, Vermont

Wheeling Peachblow is really an
Amberina glass, a type of plated
glassware lined or cased inside with
opaque, milk white, or opal glass.
These examples (left to right) are
a Wheeling copy of a famous
Chinese porcelain vase, a square-top
pitcher, and a stick vase. The copy
of the Chinese vase is known as
the Morgan Vase, after the
original owner, the widow of J.
Pierpont Morgan. The vase stands
on a five-footed gargoyle-shaped
pressed amber stand.

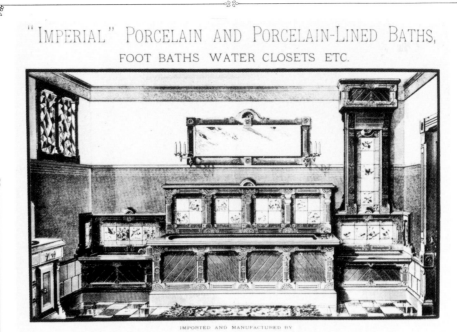

"IMPERIAL" PORCELAIN AND PORCELAIN-LINED BATHS,
FOOT BATHS WATER CLOSETS ETC.

IMPORTED AND MANUFACTURED BY
The J. L. Mott Iron Works, 88 & 90 Beekman Street, New York.
CATALOGUES OF ALL THEIR FINE GOODS FOR BATH ROOM USE SENT ON APPLICATION.

317. Magazine advertisement. J. L. Mott Iron Works. New York City. 1883. Private collection

This advertisement for porcelain bathtubs, sinks, and toilets, manufactured by the J. L. Mott Iron Works, shows the fancy elegance available in bathrooms at the end of the nineteenth century. After the Civil War most city homes included a completely equipped bathroom with running water, both hot and cold, and a dependable sewage system.

and completed in 1892—for William Kissam Vanderbilt. As with many of the great palatial homes in Newport, it is now owned by the Preservation Society of Newport County and run as a museum. A larger and even grander Hunt-designed mansion owned by the Preservation Society is The Breakers, constructed in 1893–95 for Cornelius Vanderbilt II. The most ambitious estate of all, Biltmore—a large château erected in 1890–95 for George Washington Vanderbilt III near Asheville, North Carolina, and also presently a museum—vied with the most sumptuous European palaces of the same period.

When Mrs. Potter Palmer, internationally famous Chicago socialite, built her turreted castle overlooking Lake Michigan, she included a room indispensable to every fine home of the time—an art gallery (plate 313). In the Potter Palmers' gallery the walls were hung chiefly with European paintings since few Americans believed that their countrymen could produce fine art of any significance.

The pervasive interest in works of art mirroring forms and motifs of the Orient steadily increased throughout the last decades of the nineteenth century. The oriental influence was apparently greater on glass objects and ceramics than on any other forms. In order to satisfy the demand, American firms conducted elaborate experiments that stretched technical skills and produced vast quantities of new decorative glass or art glass wares. At first the confusing array of evocative names such as Agata, Amberina (plate 316A), Burmese, Crown Milano, Peachblow (plate 316B), Royal Flemish, among others, perplexed all but the most dedicated collectors. Yet the gathering of art glass became very fashionable, and the specialty stores that offered the wares did a brisk business with collectors who wanted to demonstrate their superior knowledge. Most nineteenth-century glass manufactories were staffed by Europeans newly immigrated to America in search of greater opportunities. They brought with them a refined taste in decoration and a pride in craftsmanship, refreshing assets to the new methods of American mass production. One-of-a-kind free-blown specialty pieces created by the artist-craftsman caused popular critics to look upon art glass as the "fine summer of perfected art." Articles in the popular press as well as in trade publications added to the appreciation for these decorative wares.

Toward the end of the 1880s the J. H. Hobbs, Brockunier and Company at Wheeling, West Virginia, came out with a reproduction of a Chinese porcelain vase-on-stand which created a great sensation when it was auctioned in New York for a staggering price. The reproduction vase-on-stand was copied at lower and lower prices by other companies, until finally one New York

OPPOSITE:

318. Vase. Designed by Joseph Lycett; manufactured by Faience Manufacturing Company. Greenpoint, New York. 1889. Earthenware, height 26⅝″. Current whereabouts unknown

This vase, showing a typical Eastern influence in its design, was especially made for Edwin Atlee Barber, one of the first scholars to study American ceramic arts.

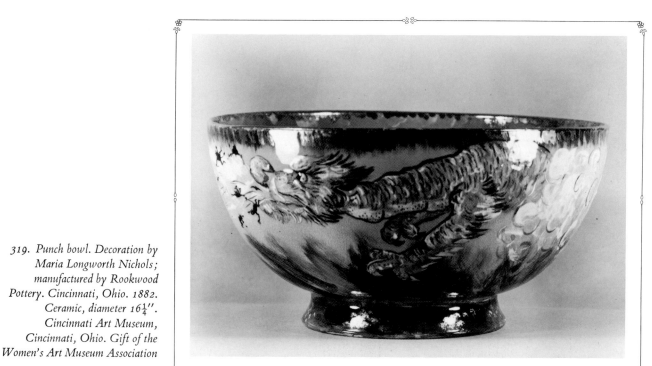

glassworks sold versions of it for ninety-eight cents. The Wheeling Peachblow vase (plate 316B, at left) is very similar to the original reproduction.

To satisfy the unabated demand for exotica, new ceramic factories sprang up all across the country. In 1879 John Gardner Low and his father, John Low, a civil engineer, opened a kiln at Chelsea, Massachusetts, for the manufacture of ceramic tiles. Their tiles might well have been used in the bathroom (plate 317) created by the J. L. Mott Iron Works of New York and advertised in their catalog for 1883. Both the urn (plate 318) by Joseph Lycett of the Faience Manufacturing Company at Greenpoint, New York, and the punch bowl (plate 319) decorated by Mrs. Maria Longworth Nichols for the Rookwood Pottery at Cincinnati, Ohio, have motifs evocative of oriental prototypes.

The Rookwood Pottery, founded in 1880, is probably the most noted American producer of ceramic art, and its pieces are the most sought after by serious collectors. This prestigious firm developed from modest beginnings—a class in china painting for women with leisure time, organized in 1874 in the home of a Cincinnati schoolteacher, Benn Pitman (brother of Sir Isaac Pitman, inventor of the shorthand system). Some of the women in this class decorated several pieces that were exhibited at the Centennial; the objects were praised, and

the women continued their artistic endeavors under the direction of M. Louise McLaughlin, who experimented with underglaze painting and developed a hard porcelain glazed at a comparatively low temperature. In 1879 McLaughlin founded the Pottery Club of Cincinnati. A member of the club and also a member of one of Cincinnati's most prominent families, Mrs. Maria Longworth Nichols (later Mrs. Bellamy Storer) began the Rookwood Pottery in 1880 and headed it until her retirement in 1890.

The Rookwood plant employed an impressive roster of decorators—Albert R. Valentien, William McDonald, Matthew A. Daly, and the Japanese artist Kataro Shirayamadani. Artus Van Briggle, who in 1900 founded his own art nouveau pottery at Colorado Springs, Colorado, also decorated for Rookwood during the 1890s. Rookwood wares were primarily ornamental and until 1900 were all hand-thrown. Because the form and decoration were of such high quality, the pottery was frequently as beautiful as authentic oriental pieces.

While the 1893 World's Columbian Exposition in Chicago did much to promote a revival of historical styles, it also served as a harbinger of the modern age of electricity, art glass, and—most revolutionary of all—women. Americans

321. Interior of Sarah Jordan Boardinghouse. Menlo Park, New Jersey. Electrified in 1879. Greenfield Village and Henry Ford Museum, Dearborn, Michigan

Many of Thomas Alva Edison's employees at Menlo Park resided in this dwelling, which Edison electrified in 1879. The ruby hobnail lamp, adapted for electricity, originally burned kerosene. The boardinghouse, in this instance gaily decorated for the Christmas holidays, is now installed at Greenfield Village.

looked upon "The City of Light" as the termination of the nation's youth. This exposition, with its many symbolic personifications of positive attributes (plate 320), seemed to reflect the general impression that America had come of age.

Fourteen years earlier, on New Year's Eve 1879, when Thomas Alva Edison gave a demonstration of practical electricity in Menlo Park, New Jersey, he brightened the way to a new age. Using his perfected incandescent lamp to illuminate the many buildings in his Menlo Park compound, he also electrified the boardinghouse, kept by Mrs. Sarah Jordan, in which several members of his staff lived. The hobnail hanging kerosene lamp (plate 321) in the center of the dining room was converted to electricity. Edison, a genius of technology, developed an extraordinary number of inventions, which resulted in his holding 1,093 important patents ranging from a practical stock ticker tape to the phonograph and a motion picture projector.

By the opening of the World's Columbian Exposition, a few cities had already installed electric streetlights, and the electric trolley was a not unfamiliar sight in the largest cities, but for most Americans electric light was something they had only read about in newspapers. Most of the exhibits relating to electricity were contained in the Electricity Building, which James W. Shepp and Daniel B. Shepp's 1893 catalog, *Shepp's World's Fair Photographed,* claimed was

322. Model Electric Kitchen. Exhibited at World's Columbian Exposition. Chicago, Illinois. 1893. Catalog illustration reproduced in Siegfried Giedion's Mechanization Takes Command (New York, 1948). New York Public Library, Astor, Lenox and Tilden Foundations, New York City

In this futuristic display at the 1893 fair every appliance—saucepan, water heater, broiler, and boiler—was connected to a separate outlet. It was not until the 1940s that kitchens were as extensively wired for electrical utensils. The electric range did not come into general use until about 1910.

"one of the richest looking structures on the grounds." The building was constructed to provide a dramatic display of electricity. Over 24,000 incandescent and nearly 4,000 arc lights were included in the combined exhibits of the United States and the other countries. The Electricity Building was also lighted on the outside, with 8,000 arc lamps of over 2,000 candlepower and about 130,000 incandescent bulbs of 16 candlepower. The greatest single spectacular effect seems to have been created by flashing lights in the tall towers on the grounds. The exterior took on a historical significance with a colossal statue of Benjamin Franklin, his face turned upward, his hand holding the key with which he drew electricity from the sky. An entry in the Shepps' catalog offered a descriptive tour of the Electricity Building:

We enter the building, and our first impression is of its vastness, for here are buildings, each of considerable size, within it. Before us is a Greek temple resembling the Erechtheum at Athens, guarded by two winged sphinxes, reminiscences of ancient Egypt. We

323. Colonial Parlor of the Woman's Building. Exhibited at World's Columbian Exposition. Chicago, Illinois. 1893. Photograph private collection

This interior was installed at the exposition by women from Kentucky, who favored a gold and white decorative scheme for the colonial revival extravaganza. The entire Woman's Building, and everything in it, was designed and created by women.

pass up the steps, and enter a cool hall, on the sides of which we see photographs of the principal telegraph buildings of the world; . . . fountains on either side lead us, for a moment, to forget that we are in one of the most remarkable buildings of the world. Before us spreads a long vista of machinery; to the left is an electric car, complete in all its appurtenances, and in the centre is a brilliantly-lighted revolving pavilion with a high tower, also crowned with a globe of light. The two ends of the structure are ornamented with great stars, plaques and shields, in electric lights that scintillate every moment, now faint and dim, now bright as the noonday sun. We know that everything here is for use, and that the dominating idea is a commercial one, yet all is beautiful; each machine seems to be tended lovingly by affectionate hands, and shines with gratification. What electricity cannot do would be easier to state than what it can do.

One of the most popular of all exhibits at the exposition was the Model Electric Kitchen (plate 322), since it both fascinated and intimidated the Victorian homemaker. For the very first time an electrified environment became the homemaker's assistant in preparing the daily meals: electric range, an electric boiler, and several electric kettles. To top it off, a spiderlike electric chandelier illuminated the new kitchen. By the end of the Victorian period few

324. Tablecloth. Maker unknown. Purchased at World's Columbian Exposition. Chicago, Illinois. 1894. Lace, 108 × 108". Private collection

The American Indian, sailing ships, locomotives, and other romantic subjects associated with nineteenth-century America are hidden among the intricate motifs in this dazzling example of the lacemaker's art, purchased in the second year of the exposition.

households had converted to electricity for heating and cooking. It was not until 1910 that the electric range was a common feature in kitchens. In the 1920s other electrical utensils came into general use.

Although contributions made by women were acknowledged at both the New York Crystal Palace exposition in 1853 and the Philadelphia Centennial International Exposition in 1876, it was not until 1893 at the World's Columbian Exposition that the exhibitions specifically designed for the Woman's Building drew attention to women's achievements in nearly every field of endeavor. Fourteen female architects submitted plans for the building, and those by Sophia G. Hayden of Boston were accepted. The Woman's Building, over 400 feet long and 200 feet deep, was built at a cost of $138,000, all of it raised by women. The ground floor of the two-story structure included a model hospital, a model kindergarten, a retrospective exhibit, and an area devoted to reform work and charity organizations. The second floor was set aside for ladies parlors, dressing rooms, committee rooms, a spacious assembly and club room, a model kitchen, refreshment rooms, and, as a special attraction, a library of books written by women. The acknowledged queen of the exposition, Mrs. Potter Palmer, was elected Lady President of the Fair.

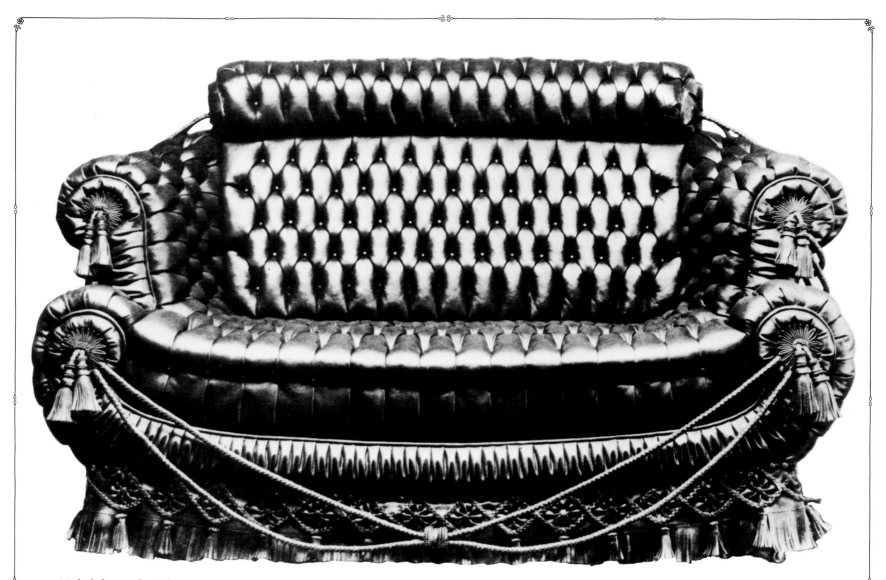

325. Turkish frame sofa. Maker unknown. Displayed at World's Columbian Exposition. Chicago, Illinois. 1893. Wood frame with metal springs, dimensions unknown. Whereabouts unknown. Photograph private collection

Metal coil springs were enclosed within a hidden frame in exotic pieces such as this Turkish sofa. They provided a degree of comfort previously unavailable.

OPPOSITE:

326. Shelf clock. E. N. Welch Company. Forestville, Connecticut. 1880s. Wooden case, height 26". Greenfield Village and Henry Ford Museum, Dearborn, Michigan

The gilt decoration on the glass door is typical of the designs on late-nineteenth-century clocks, books, and other small objects. The incised decoration on the hood is also typical of the period.

The studio, designed by Tiffany in conjunction with McKim, Mead and White in 1885, was part of his parents' home at Seventy-second Street and Madison Avenue in New York. The Tiffany mansion comprised three units on the site of present number 17–19, an apartment building erected in 1937.

Although the Woman's Building featured some European displays, the exclusively American exhibits were most popular. The Cincinnati Room, furnished as a model nineteenth-century drawing room, elicited the following comment in the Shepps' catalog: "The artistic work is all done by women. The design and execution of the frieze-work is by Miss Agnes Pitkin of Cincinnati, assisted by Miss Eva Stearnes and Miss Mary Tiwett. It is fully six feet wide; the tower design is a conventional scroll of buckeye in shaded reds. . . . There is also a large quantity of bric-a-brac, and some very fine china."

Women from Kentucky installed the Colonial Parlor (plate 323), a gold and white colonial revival extravaganza displaying historical records and souvenirs. The New York Room also inspired praise from the Shepps. Upon entering, "one soon becomes impressed with the culture and diverse intelligence of the American woman; no subject seems to have been too difficult for her to grapple; astronomy, art, science in every branch, even architecture and theology have not come amiss to her omnivorous genius."

Many of the exhibitions at the exposition showed objects that were greatly admired by many American women. The elaborate lace tablecloth (plate 324) with imagery of ships and locomotives, as well as a native American Indian, worked into the design must have delighted even the most sophisticated visitor to the fair. Women visiting the exposition would certainly have been pleased by the Turkish frame sofa (plate 325); this innovative piece, which reflected the prevailing American taste for anything hinting at the exotic or foreign, was constructed with metal coil springs tied together within an enclosed hidden frame. It provided comfort previously unknown in the American home.

The Ansonia Clock Company of Ansonia, Connecticut, set up a large, elegant display that featured timepieces in a multitude of styles. Attractive

328. View of Oyster Bay. *Tiffany Studios. New York City.*
c. 1905. Leaded glass, height 72¾". Morse Gallery of Art, Winter
Park, Florida. Courtesy the Charles Hosmer Morse Foundation

Tiffany's handsome stained-glass window was originally designed as
an interior window in the William Skinner House at 36 East Thirty-
ninth Street in New York. Through the wisteria on a trellis is a
distant view of Oyster Bay, a not unfamiliar sight from Tiffany's
large estate, Laurelton Hall, on the north shore of Long Island. The
huge loggia that was once the entrance to Laurelton Hall provides
the focal point for the new American Wing of the Metropolitan
Museum of Art in New York, where the View of Oyster Bay
window is also presently on view.

Captions for plates 329 through 332 are on page 294

329. Lamp. Louis Comfort Tiffany. New York. Late nineteenth or early twentieth century. Leaded glass and bronze, height 14⅝″. Metropolitan Museum of Art, New York City. Gift of Hugh J. Grant, 1974

The domical shade features cascading blooms and stems in a delightful raray of colors. The shade is supported by bronze stems rising from a cluster of small bronze flowers at the base.

330. Magnolia Vase. Tiffany and Company. New York City. 1893. Silver, enamel, gold, and opals, height 31″. Metropolitan Museum of Art, New York City. Gift of Mrs. Winthrop Atwell, 1899

Tiffany and Company created this elaborate vase for exhibition at the Chicago World's Columbian Exposition. Fine craftsmanship and opulent materials are combined in this extraordinary example of Victorian high style in America.

331. Peacock vase. Louis Comfort Tiffany. New York. Late nineteenth century. Glass, height 14¼″. Metropolitan Museum of Art, New York City. Gift of H. O. Havemeyer, 1896

The fan-shaped top of this beautiful favrile vase strengthens the visual image of a peacock's tail feathers. On December 8, 1896, Henry Osborn Havemeyer, one of the great benefactors of the Metropolitan Museum of Art, sent a letter to the museum's president offering the museum a collection of fifty-six objects "of rare beauty." "Since the Tiffany Glass Co. have been making favrile glass," Havemeyer noted, "Mr. Louis Tiffany has set aside the finest pieces of their production, which I have acquired for what I consider to be their artistic value."

332. Favrile glass objects. Tiffany Studios. New York. Late nineteenth or early twentieth century. Glass, height of tallest vase 18¾″. Metropolitan Museum of Art, New York City

Favrile glass has an iridescence—almost a golden mother-of-pearl surface—that was inspired by delicate partially decayed excavated Roman glass. Favrile objects were so popular that by 1898 Tiffany was forced to maintain an inventory of five thousand pieces in his storeroom.

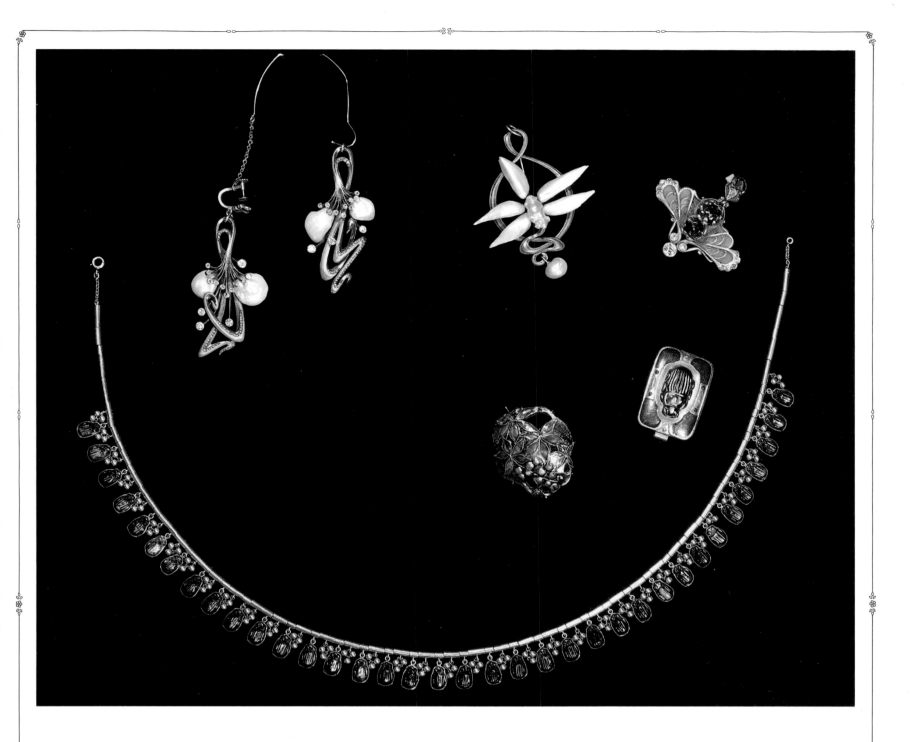

333. Jewelry. Various makers.
United States. Late nineteenth
and early twentieth century. Gold,
enamel, and precious and
semiprecious stones, length of
necklace 21″. Lillian Nassau,
Ltd., New York City

Many designers at the turn of the
century created jewelry using a
mixture of precious and
semiprecious stones and brilliant
enamelwork. Left to right:
jeweled and enameled earrings
attributed to Edward Colonna;
dragonfly pendant by Edward
Colonna; winged brooch by
Marcus and Company; gold and
enamel floral brooch by Tiffany
and Company; glass scarab in gold
pendant by Tiffany; necklace
made of scarabs set in gold by
Tiffany.

walnut shelf clocks, similar to the example with incised decoration and gilt-ornamented glass front (plate 326) made by the Connecticut firm of E. N. Welch Company, were one of the more common designs.

That magician of glass, Louis Comfort Tiffany, one of the best-known of all Victorian artists and businessmen, designed a modern Byzantine chapel for the exposition. Over a million minuscule bits of iridescent and opalescent glass, studded with semiprecious stones set in white and black marble, formed the chapel walls, ceiling, and floor. The chapel contained twelve stained-glass windows lighted by a sanctuary lamp made of glass set with jewels. This opulent installation and architect Louis Sullivan's golden door for the Transportation Building were two of the most impressive exhibits at the exposition.

Tiffany, noted for his imaginative designs and fresh forms, was one of the great forces in the art nouveau movement. He worked in a wide range of

334. French Pavilion. Exhibited at Louisiana Purchase Exposition. Saint Louis, Missouri. 1904. Library Picture Collection, Cooper-Hewitt Museum, Smithsonian Institution's National Museum of Design, New York City

At the international exposition in Saint Louis Americans were awed by what one art critic dubbed an "orgy of curvilinear woodwork" in the interior of the French Pavilion.

mediums, including painting, stained glass, art glass, ceramics, jewelry (plate 333), metalwork (plate 330), furniture, and the particularly dramatic but delicate leaded-glass lamps (plate 329) for which he is best known today. At the age of eighteen Tiffany became a student of the landscape painter George Inness and through him was exposed to a number of the leading artists of the day. A subsequent trip to Europe, where he studied briefly in the studio of the distinguished French artist Léon Bailly, and a jaunt to North Africa with the American artist Samuel Colman completed his formal training. Returning to America in 1870, Tiffany, then only twenty-two, opened his own studio. Although his European and African paintings received favorable criticism, his complex flamboyant personality required additional outlets for fulfillment. Following a second trip to France in 1875, he gave up painting for decorative work, because he was convinced that it was an area in which he could better express his creative genius.

Although many Americans in the second half of the nineteenth century experimented with glass windows, there are two notable artists who achieved unsurpassed aesthetic standards, Tiffany and John La Farge. Much of La Farge's best work, both mural paintings and stained-glass windows, was commissioned for churches; whereas Tiffany was particularly engaged in the decoration of secular buildings. Tiffany experimented with glass in the early 1870s. Through his studies in chemistry and many years of trial and error, Tiffany discovered means of avoiding the use of paints, and he etched—or burned—or otherwise treated the surface of the glass so that it became possible to produce figures in

335. Chair and desk. Designed by William Codman; manufactured by Gorham Silver Company. Providence, Rhode Island. c. 1904. Ebony and boxwood encrusted with silver and ivory inlay, height of chair 30". Gorham Silver Company, Providence, Rhode Island

These art nouveau pieces, which were awarded a grand prize when exhibited, were crafted especially for exhibition at the 1904 Saint Louis exposition.

glass in which even the flesh tones were not superficially treated but were built up with what he called genuine glass.

Tiffany perfected other techniques that ultimately enabled him to create a special line of innovative and artistic glassware. Experimenting with unique means of coloring for stained glass and mosaics, he developed a special glass, favrile (a neologism from the Latin word for craftsman, *faber*), which was iridescent and freely shaped and sometimes combined with bronzelike alloys and other metals. Favrile glass (plates 331, 332) represents the epitome of nineteenth-century handcraftsmanship. The Louis C. Tiffany and Company Associated Artists, primarily a decorating firm, began operation in 1879 with Samuel Colman, Lockwood DeForest, and Candace Wheeler joining Tiffany.

Samuel Bing, a French dealer in oriental art who visited the World's Columbian Exposition in 1893, opened his Salon de l'Art Nouveau in Paris in 1895. His shop became famous and provided the name for an emerging new style. He gave Tiffany's work prominent display space in his salon and ultimately became Tiffany's European agent. During the next several years Tiffany won major awards at virtually every important international exposition. Many elements of the art nouveau style were incorporated into Tiffany's studio (plate 327) in his parents' home on Seventy-second Street in New York City, which

336. Sofa. S. Karpen and Brothers. Chicago, Illinois. c. 1907. Wood, dimensions unknown. Engraving from sales catalog. Greenfield Village and Henry Ford Museum, Dearborn, Michigan

Karpen's 1907 sales catalog made the immodest claim that this "triumph of artists skilled in woodcraft" was "the most artistic and beautiful example of this school of decoration ever produced." A complete set of three pieces could be purchased for $660.

337. *Tumbler. Maker unknown.*
United States. 1904. Pressed
glass, height 5″. Collection
Patricia L. Coblentz

Ever since American pressed glass
began to be produced in large
quantities in the 1840s and 1850s,
it has remained popular. This
souvenir from the Louisiana
Purchase Exposition, held at Saint
Louis, Missouri, in 1904, depicts
several monuments in that city.

was designed in 1885. The fireplace is surrounded by hanging glass lighting devices and standing ceramic urns. The Tiffany Studios, established in 1900, employed hundreds of artisans, both men and women, who produced a variety of beautiful objects ranging from miniature ceramic trays to ornate bronze and glass electric lamps and stained-glass windows like the delicate *View of Oyster Bay* (plate 328) created about 1905 for the New York City home of William Skinner. Blue, Tiffany's favorite color, and wisteria, a recurring Tiffany floral motif, are dominant in this splendid leaded-glass work. One of Tiffany's largest commissions in this medium was the gargantuan, twenty-two-ton glass curtain for Mexico City's national theater, the Palacio de Bellas Artes. Although the work of Tiffany and his contemporaries passed from favor for a brief period, these examples of the decorative arts are avidly collected and greatly prized today.

Tiffany was not the only American art nouveau pace-setter. Edward Colonna, a naturalized citizen of German birth, worked in Dayton, Ohio, during the 1880s. Shortly before 1900 Colonna moved to Paris, where he designed for Bing sensitively balanced, finely proportioned furniture and jewelry in the new style (plate 333).

338. *Cigar lighter. Gorham*
Manufacturing Company.
Providence, Rhode Island.
c. 1900. Silver, height 3''.
Gorham Silver Company,
Providence, Rhode Island

Gorham produced an extra-fine
grade of silverware that was
marketed as Martelé, an indication
that the pieces were softer and
purer in grade than sterling.
Martelé was usually handcrafted
with tool marks left undisguised
on the plain surfaces.

When the French Pavilion (plate 334) was installed at the 1904 Louisiana Purchase Exposition at Saint Louis, Missouri, it gave Americans their first real exposure to authentic art nouveau furniture and architecture, which were characterized by linear designs of sinuous, floral forms. American manufacturers were not generally sensitive or responsive to the art nouveau style. The chair and desk (plate 335) designed by William Codman and manufactured by the Gorham Silver Company are fashioned from ebony and boxwood encrusted with silver and ivory inlays. While rich in detail, they lack the simplicity of the best French art nouveau furniture.

In 1907 the S. Karpen and Brothers furniture company of Chicago and New York published an extensive catalog of the pieces which their firm offered in the art nouveau style. The general outline and form of the settee (plate 336), from a suite of three pieces, are significantly heavier and cruder than French pieces produced in the same period. The undulating, sinuous figure at the center of the crest rail was inspired by the American dancer Loie Fuller, who was the toast of the international set in Paris. The Karpen firm produced some of the best American art nouveau furniture of the period. The company won a Grand Prix at the 1904 exposition in Saint Louis for three pieces in the Catillya l'Art Nouveau suite.

Although the art nouveau style was introduced at the Saint Louis exposition and there was genuine curiosity expressed for the undulating curves characteristic of the style, the public's enthusiasm for the more traditional forms of the time dominated popular taste in the years preceding World War I. Of particular interest is the pressed-glass tumbler (plate 337), a souvenir from the exposition. The tumbler commemorates several monuments in Saint Louis, and its eclectic designs combine the C-scrolls popular in earlier periods with the sinuous floral motifs of the art nouveau.

The bulk of furniture as well as other household items made in the United States around the turn of the century was mass-produced for a general public. Yet, as some of the best designers had demonstrated, there was a market for finely wrought furnishings in the progressive styles of the time. Perhaps some of the most successful items were the silverware marketed as Martelé, a high-grade ware introduced by Gorham in 1896. The idea behind Martelé, which clearly reflects art nouveau influence, was that the objects should be entirely handmade and designed in the modern style. Gorham produced Martelé from

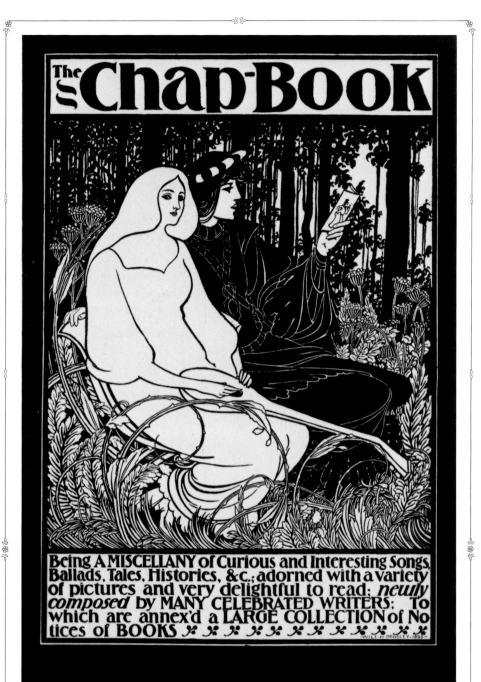

*The vines in this art nouveau
poster that advertised the Chicago
avant-garde magazine* The Chap-
Book *beautifully simulate the
curved form of the Thonet
bentwood chair, first produced in
the 1840s but very much the vogue
throughout the second half of the
nineteenth century.*

1896 through 1912 and perhaps as many as three thousand pieces were made in that sixteen-year period. The cigar lighter (plate 338) is an unusual form. More conventional were the designs for desk sets, penholders, lamps, bowls, and tiny silver boxes.

Will Bradley, a Boston-born designer who gained international recognition for his work in the new style, is perhaps the most important American art nouveau artist. Bradley, who acknowledged the strong influence on his work of Aubrey Beardsley, blended various styles of the 1890s into his own ingeniously eclectic designs. He became one of America's leading poster artists, and his illustrations and covers for popular magazines represent a high point in the American graphic arts, winning him a respected place in Samuel Bing's Salon de l'Art Nouveau. The 1895 poster advertising *The Chap-Book* (plate 339), one of the many little magazines of the nineties, shows medieval lovers in an idealized forest lounging on vinelike forms that seem to reflect the curved lines of Thonet bentwood chairs. This series of elegant advertisements appears to have sparked the American mania for collecting posters.

In ceramic work (plates 340A, 340B) the American art nouveau style reached its fullest expression. Ceramic objects were created by several manufac-

340A. *Art pottery. Various makers. United States. 1884–1906. Various glazes, height of tallest vase 12¾". Jordan-Volpe Gallery, New York City*

American art nouveau pottery is one of the most successful forms of expression in this style. In the front row (left to right): oatmeal and ocher speckled mat glaze vase, c. 1906, by Marblehead Pottery of Marblehead, Massachusetts; Sang-de-boeuf glaze vase, c. 1884, by Hugh C. Robertson for Chelsea Keramic Art Works of Chelsea, Massachusetts; yellow and green mat glaze vase, c. 1900, by Grueby Faience and Tile Company of Boston. In the back row: green mat glaze vase, c. 1905, by American Terra Cotta and Ceramic Company (Teco) of Terra Cotta, Illinois; pale blue green and rose mat glaze vase, c. 1900, by Newcomb College Pottery of New Orleans, Louisiana.

340B. *Art pottery. Various makers. United States. 1904–15. Favrile and various glazes, height of tallest vase 16¾". Jordan-Volpe Gallery, New York City*

Only recently have the art nouveau ceramics of the last quarter of the nineteenth century and the first decades of the twentieth received enthusiastic attention from collectors. In the front row (left to right): favrile pottery bowl, c. 1905, by Tiffany Studios of New York City; iris glaze vase, 1903, by Rookwood Pottery of Cincinnati, Ohio; iridescent glaze vase, c. 1904, by Jacques Sicard for S. A. Weller of Zanesville, Ohio. In the back row: two-handled copperdust and green flambé glaze vase, c. 1915, by Fulper Pottery Company of Flemington, New Jersey; turquoise, green, and mat glaze lilac vase, 1908–11, by Artus Van Briggle for Van Briggle Pottery Company of Colorado Springs, Colorado.

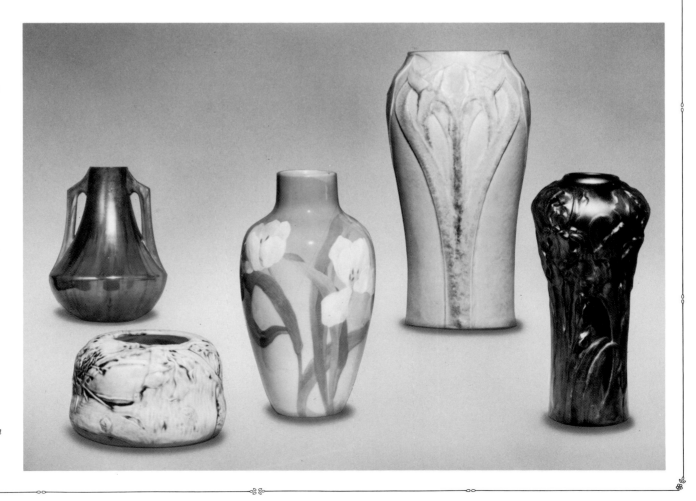

341. Isabella and the Pot of
Basil. *John White Alexander.
United States. 1897. Oil on
canvas, 75½ × 35¾″. Museum
of Fine Arts, Boston,
Massachusetts. Gift of Ernest
Wadsworth Longfellow*

*Both the delicate form of the
ceramic pot and the sinuous lines
of the woman's dress reveal the
influence of the late-nineteenth-
century art nouveau style in the
fine arts.*

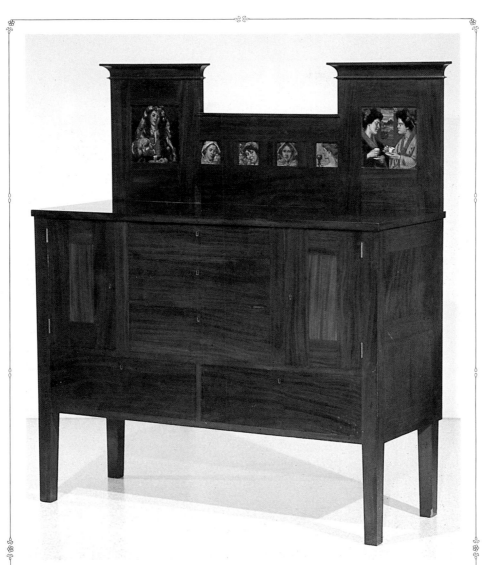

342. Sideboard. Sydney R.
Burleigh. Providence, Rhode
Island. c. 1900. Mahogany,
height 56⅛". Greenfield Village
and Henry Ford Museum,
Dearborn, Michigan

Burleigh, who both crafted and
decorated this sideboard in the
arts and crafts style, was a member
of the Art Workers Guild at
Providence and was one of the
leaders of the American arts and
crafts movement.

turers who operated on a very limited basis, by firms that mass-produced them
for the broad popular market, and by individuals who worked by themselves
forming objects for personal use. Fulper, Grueby, Newcomb, Ohr, Pewabic,
Rookwood, Roseville, Tiffany, Van Briggle, and Weller are among the most
important manufacturers, and while their products exhibit diversity in form
and decoration, at the same time they possess a definite stylistic kinship in these
two areas.

During the 1890s the exceptional art department at the H. Sophie Newcomb Memorial College, the women's division of Tulane University in New
Orleans, had in attendance students who were uncommonly talented. In 1895
Professor Ellsworth Woodward persuaded the trustees to institute a program
that would provide a commercial outlet for the hand-thrown, hand-decorated
pieces being created there. Newcomb pottery has a style all its own, reflecting
Woodward's strong—and enforced—belief that Newcomb women should
decorate their pieces only with motifs associated with the nearby bayou country.

The Grueby Faience Company, organized in South Boston in 1897 by William H. Grueby, produced quality pieces that are distinguished by green and
tan mat glazes. Grueby lamp bases were often fitted with Tiffany shades. At the
1901 Pan-American Exposition in Buffalo, New York, Grueby pottery was
exhibited with the mission-style furniture of United Crafts from Eastwood,
New York.

The Roseville Pottery, located eleven miles south of Zanesville, Ohio, prospered from its inception. It was incorporated in 1892 and within three years
it had purchased the William and McCoy Pottery at Zanesville and the Mid-
land Pottery at Kildow. In 1898 it moved to Zanesville, where it acquired the
Clark Stoneware Company, and in 1902 the Mosaic Tile Company became part

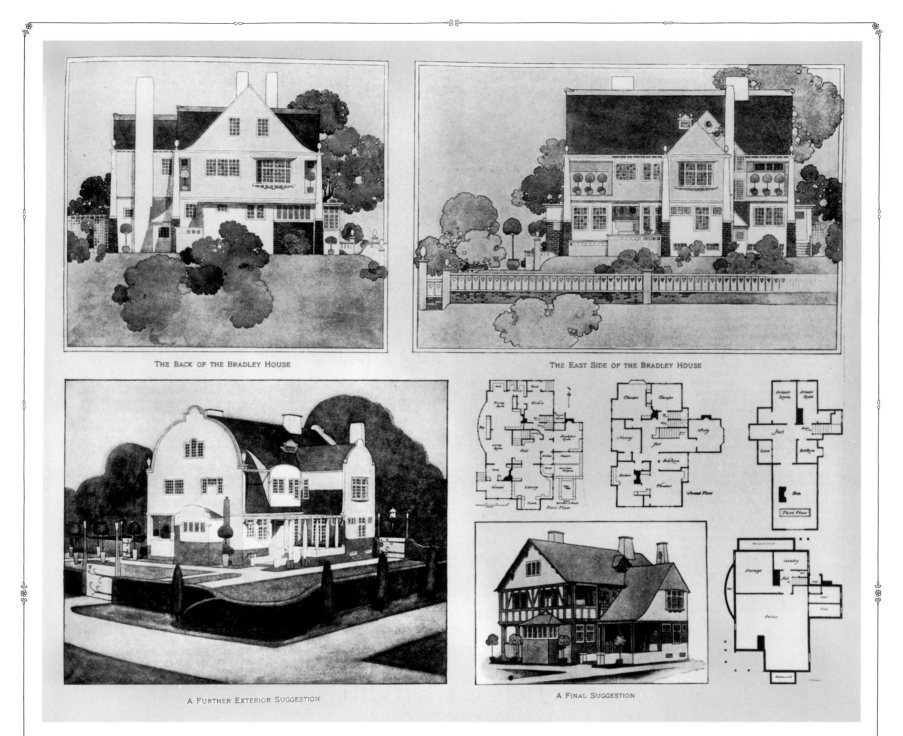

THE BACK OF THE BRADLEY HOUSE

THE EAST SIDE OF THE BRADLEY HOUSE

A FURTHER EXTERIOR SUGGESTION

A FINAL SUGGESTION

343. Designs for arts and crafts house. Will H. Bradley. United States. 1901. Published in The Ladies' Home Journal *(August 1902). Private collection*

Bradley was commissioned by the editor of The Ladies' Home Journal, *Edward Bok, to design houses, room interiors, and even furniture, and his work was a regular feature in the magazine. Between November 1901 and August 1902 the magazine published a series of exclusive designs for seven interiors and one exterior of a fourteen-room arts and crafts style house. The final installment in the series included suggestions of various possible exteriors around the same general layout. Bradley also was one of the main popularizers of the colonial revival style.*

344. Gallery installation. Display of mission furniture. United States. c. 1900. Jordan-Volpe Gallery, New York City

In the 1970s and 1980s there has been renewed enthusiasm for fine-grained mission-style oak pieces, illustrated by this 1980 installation in a New York gallery. The six-foot-long settle was created by Limbert Arts and Crafts Furniture Company of Grand Rapids, Michigan, the screen by Gustav Stickley of Eastwood, New York, and the Morris chair by L. and J. G. Stickley of Fayetteville, New York. The lamp on the small table is from Tiffany Studios of New York; its shade is in the acorn pattern.

of the vigorous conglomerate. Roseville is noted particularly for Rozane Royal, which was glaze-slip painted under a high glaze. Because ceramic artists moved from one plant to another in Ohio, which was the center of American ceramic production in the Midwest, it is often difficult to distinguish the early products of Weller, Rookwood, Owen, and Roseville unless they are clearly marked.

The manufacturer of the ceramic pot that was the model for the one depicted in John White Alexander's striking romantic painting *Isabella and the Pot of Basil* (plate 341) is no longer known, but the utensil itself is a crucial element in Alexander's theme. The lyrical picture, executed in 1897, is based upon a tale in Boccaccio's *Decameron,* popular with the brotherhood of English painters and poets known as Pre-Raphaelites. Isabella's peasant lover was murdered and buried in a wood outside Florence by her ambitious brothers, who were trying to force her to marry a nobleman. She unearthed her lover's body and, overcome with grief, severed the head and hid it in a garden pot, which she planted with sweet basil. The delicate curves of the pot and the undulating dress of Isabella suggest a pervasiveness of art nouveau attitudes in the fine arts.

In the second half of the nineteenth century the English arts and crafts movement represented the beginning of a new appreciation of the decorative arts throughout Europe; it was quickly taken up by the avant-garde designers in America. The English poet and designer William Morris was disturbed by the level to which style and craftsmanship had sunk in the wake of the Industrial Revolution and the advent of mass production. Morris was a follower of the Pre-Raphaelites of the previous generation, who rejected the growing materialism of industrialized England and through literary symbolism and imagery sought a refuge in the beauty and simplicity of the medieval world. This brotherhood of poets and painters was defended by the influential art critic and social theorist John Ruskin, who also bitterly criticized the waste of modern industry. Picking up on the social criticism of Ruskin and the aesthetic theories of the Pre-Raphaelites, Morris advocated technical and stylistic advances that he hoped would, when put into practice, bring about a reform of society.

As early as 1861 Morris had founded a firm of interior decorators and manufacturers devoted to the principles of the medieval craftsmen. His reforming zeal profoundly influenced many of the practitioners of the decorative arts, particularly the next generation of artists and designers in England and the United States. Early in the 1880s several English artists, furniture designers, and craftsmen, inspired by Morris, gathered in guildlike organizations where they were able to unite the fine and applied arts in the manufacture of furniture. This new generation of artists helped spread the ideas of the arts and crafts movement, which had a strong effect on American decorative arts. At Providence,

345. *Dining room design for Bradley House. Will H. Bradley. United States. c. 1905. Artist's letterpress proof, for* Moderne Bauformen *(vol. 5, 1906). Metropolitan Museum of Art, New York City. Gift of Fern Bradley Dufner, 1952*

The third installment in the exclusive series of Bradley designs for The Ladies' Home Journal *(see plate 343) was published in January 1902 and focused on the dining room.* *Some of the artist's color renditions were printed four years later in the elegant German magazine devoted to modern architecture,* Moderne Bauformen. *Perhaps because the* Journal *was restricted to black and white illustrations, elaborate directions for the color scheme were suggested. All the woodwork was to be golden oak, the frieze and the fireplace tiles blue delft, and the upholstered seats greenish-blue leather. The wall in the chimney nook would be hung in leather to match the seats and embossed in a darker tone.*

Rhode Island, the Art Workers Guild, led by Sydney R. Burleigh, Charles W. Stetson, and John G. Aldrich, handcrafted and painted furniture (plate 342) in a style that would have been acceptable to Morris. Their "craft pieces" were not unlike the designs of Will Bradley (plates 343, 345) commissioned in 1901–02 by the editor of *The Ladies' Home Journal,* Edward Bok.

The mission style, an American manifestation of late-nineteenth-century interest in the revival of sturdy native furniture, probably originated in 1894 when the Second Jerusalem Church was being built in San Francisco, California. Lacking funds to purchase furnishings, the congregation made several chairs themselves and used them in place of the usual pews. The decorator Dora Martin took note of the pieces and sent a model to Joseph McHugh, a furniture manufacturer in New York City. McHugh used fumed (smoked) ash for his

346. *Upright piano. J. P. Seeburg. Chicago, Illinois. c. 1910. Oak with stained glass, height 57″. Greenfield Village and Henry Ford Museum, Dearborn, Michigan*

By the time this mission-style piece, which Seeburg called an Electric Upright Grand Piano, was popular, manufacturers had borrowed freely from Tiffany's pace-setting stained-glass windows. Although the pictorial glasswork on this piano is handsome, it is simple, almost crude when compared to Tiffany's elaborately elegant productions.

347. Bedspread. Designed by
Emily Noyes Vanderpoel;
embroidered (in part) by Mary
Perkins Quincy. Connecticut.
1894. Homespun linen embroidered
in silk, 95 × 68″. Litchfield
Historical Society Museum,
Litchfield, Connecticut

During the late nineteenth century
a group of prominent socialites in
Litchfield, Connecticut, collected
and gathered early textiles for the
Litchfield Historical Society. This
bedspread was a commemorative
cover created by two members of
the group, who were expert
needlewomen.

348. Rocking chair. C. F.
Meislahn and Company.
Baltimore, Maryland. c. 1880.
Mahogany, height 35″.
Collection George McDonald

Manufacturers of colonial revival
furniture generally did not
attempt to make authentic
reproductions. They found it suited
their manufacturing techniques to
borrow freely from several styles
in order to create a form that
could be easily produced by the
machine. The Meislahn Company
labeled its pieces with the firm's
name and address plus a logo-type
sales pitch, "Fine Furniture,
Mantels & Artistic Decoration."

*349. Ballroom of The Breakers.
Richard Morris Hunt. Newport,
Rhode Island. 1893–95.
Preservation Society of Newport
County, Newport, Rhode Island*

*Hunt, who studied at the Ecole des
Beaux-Arts in Paris and had a
solid apprenticeship in Europe,
designed many magnificent
residences for the Vanderbilt
family. The Breakers was built at
Newport for Cornelius Vanderbilt
II, son of William Henry
Vanderbilt. Most rich Americans
at the turn of the century were
convinced that furniture in the
Louis XV style was the only
appropriate style for their domestic
palaces. They were, however, not
scrupulously discriminating and
seldom cared if the pieces were
authentic or only copies of the style.*

350. *Bedroom suite of Waldorf-
Astoria Hotel. New York City.
c. 1900. Museum of the City of
New York, New York City*

*The cluttered Victorian ambience
evident in this turn-of-the-century
photograph of a suite in the old
Waldorf-Astoria at Fifth Avenue
and Thirty-fourth Street in New
York is in marked contrast to a
streamlined modern hotel room
today.*

first pieces, but fumed oak later became the most popular material in the construction of mission furniture.

Gustav Stickley, a disciple of Morris and Ruskin, was the most influential and respected manufacturer of the mission style in the United States. Stickley

353. Baby buggy. Pioneer Manufacturing Company. Detroit, Michigan. c. 1905. Wicker, dimensions unavailable. Catalog illustration. Greenfield Village and Henry Ford Museum, Dearborn, Michigan

This baby carriage could be ordered upholstered in satin damask with a satin parasol and two ruffles for $33.

began work on his square-cut, hand-finished oak Craftsman line in 1898, and at the 1900 furniture exposition in Grand Rapids, Michigan, he first presented his pieces to the public. As editor and publisher of *The Craftsman,* a magazine started in 1901, he was an untiring campaigner for carefully designed and proportioned objects. It was through Stickley's proselytizing that mission furniture (plates 344, 346) became popular.

Stickley's rebellion against the Victorian "reign of marble tops and silk upholstery"—as well as his rejection of the sinuous curves of art nouveau—was immensely influential, and before the demise of his "empire" in 1915 he attracted not only countless followers but also numerous imitators. In the Craftsman heyday his activities were expanded to include the Craftsman Workshops near Syracuse, New York, the Craftsman Farms in New Jersey, and the Craftsman Building in New York City, where all forms of the decorative arts were displayed. Among the features at this Craftsman center were a home-builder's exhibit, a library, and a lecture hall.

Elbert Hubbard, working in East Aurora, New York, and the Limbert Arts and Crafts Furniture Company in Grand Rapids and Holland, Michigan, were the two other major producers of high-quality mission furniture. Hubbard, one of Stickley's most successful competitors, established a kind of commune at East Aurora, where young people could find "congenial employment, opportunity for healthy recreation, meeting places, and an outlook into the World of art and beauty." Craftsmen had the experience of working directly on *The Roycrofts,* a publication named after two seventeenth-century English printers, and on *The Philistine,* a second publication. In the numerous furniture shops the workers enjoyed the privilege of being exposed to the benign autocrat whose motto, "Not how cheap, but how good," disguised the fact that he was really a huckster at heart. Always with an eye toward the profit column on his

354. Frederick C. Robie House. Frank Lloyd Wright. Illinois. 1908–09. University of Chicago, Chicago, Illinois

This concrete and brick house on Chicago's South Side was designed by thirty-seven-year-old Wright as a town villa for the twenty-seven-year-old manufacturer Frederick C. Robie. There is no applied decoration or structural embellishment, mass and organic line being Wright's major concern. Siegfried Giedion noted in Space, Time, and Architecture (Cambridge, Mass., 1941) that it has had the "most far-reaching influence of all his works"; it was the building that shortly afterward introduced the new American architectural ideas to Europe. The Robie residence passed through many hands, and when one of its last owners, the Chicago Theological Seminary, wanted to raze it to put up a student dormitory, the University of Chicago acquired it and is in the process of restoring the landmark building.

355. Dining room of Frederick C. Robie House. Frank Lloyd Wright. Illinois. 1908–09. University of Chicago, Chicago, Illinois (photograph E. P. Dutton and Company)

The Robie House (see plate 354) was furnished with square-shaped, mission-inspired pieces. The oak dining table surrounded by six oak side chairs comprised Wright's most important furniture ensemble. The table and chairs are now on display at the University of Chicago's David and Alfred Smart Gallery.

356. Table lamp. Frank Lloyd
Wright. Illinois. 1903. Bronze
and leaded glass, height 14".
Susan Lawrence Dana House,
Springfield, Illinois (photograph
E. P. Dutton and Company)

*A comparison of Wright's lamp
with Tiffany's (see plate 329),
produced in the same era, clearly
shows that Wright's designs
were closer to the later
development of twentieth-century
decorative arts.*

monthly balance sheet, Hubbard managed to parlay his benevolent activities into
sizable earnings with astonishing adroitness.

English manufacturers of mission furniture often referred to their products
as quaint. The term also appeared in numerous advertisements placed during the
early 1900s by American department stores in *The Ladies' Home Journal* and
other national magazines with large circulations. In 1914 Bloomingdale's, the
New York department store, offered a white enamel tea table in the mission
style designed for a girl's room, but their ads contradicted the modern design
by describing it as "unusual and quaint."

Beginning with the Centennial celebration in Philadelphia, Americans
developed a keener interest in their history. This fascination with the past not
surprisingly gave rise to a colonial revival movement, which affected all aspects
of the decorative arts. In the late 1800s sewing groups were formed across
the country with the specific purpose of fashioning needlework that would
reflect the colonial heritage. The women who designed and embroidered the
homespun linen bedspread with silk embroidery (plate 347), created in 1894
in Litchfield, Connecticut, were probably members of such a group.

Colonial revival furniture design often followed early prototypes; however, it did not follow them slavishly, and the designs more likely than not
represented only a vague approximation of pieces from the past. Probably the
best-known manufacturer of colonial revival furniture was Wallace Nutting
of Framingham, Massachusetts. His faithful reproductions of forms from the
seventeenth and eighteenth centuries were based on authentic antiques in his
personal collection. Nutting's furniture sometimes carries an identifying paper
label; often, however, it is branded or stamped.

While Nutting painstakingly crafted thoughtful reproductions of furniture
based on earlier periods, firms like C. F. Meislahn and Company at Baltimore,
Maryland, produced pieces such as the rocking chair (plate 348), that were an
amalgam of styles. Traditional Chippendale motifs on this chair include a pierced
Gothic splat in the back, a seat rail centered by a shell, and cabriole front legs
with acanthus carving at the knee and claw-and-ball feet. The addition of the
rockers would be inappropriate on a Chippendale piece, and the basic proportions are definitely not on the same scale as those of chairs produced in the
eighteenth century.

While many Americans revered and repeated the taste and forms of their
own past, the nouveau riche frequently entertained the snobbish notion that
contemporary European designs were better. Elaborate fantasy buildings—
such as Richard Morris Hunt's design for The Breakers at Newport, Rhode

357. Fence section. Frank Lloyd
Wright. Illinois. 1895.
Wrought iron, height 98″. Art
Institute of Chicago, Chicago,
Illinois. Gift of the Graham
Foundation for Advanced
Studies in the Fine Arts

Wright was involved with the
design of his buildings as a whole.
He personally designed the
interiors, including furniture, as
well as exterior design elements,
such as this fence section from the
Francis Apartments in Chicago.

Island, and luxury hotels like the old Waldorf-Astoria at Thirty-fourth Street
and Fifth Avenue in New York City—were furnished with a jumble of pseudo-
French antique furniture that created a fashionable clutter (plates 349, 350).
The carved Renaissance revival side table (plate 351) from New York City's
landmark Hotel Chelsea on West Twenty-third Street reflects this late-Vic-
torian preference in America for elaborate European styles.

Sponsored by a group of artists who wanted studio accommodations, the
Chelsea was built in 1882–83 as a cooperative apartment house but became
a hotel in 1905. The hotel is now a slightly tarnished monument to vanished

grandeur, in the West Side district where it is located. Yet through the years its guest register reads like an artistic and literary biographical dictionary. Mark Twain stayed there on one of his national tours. John Sloan—a pioneer in the realistic tradition in American painting, for which he was dubbed a member of the Ash Can School, and an exhibitor at the sensational Armory Show in 1913—maintained a studio at the hotel. Other honored guests include O. Henry, Thomas Wolfe, James T. Farrell, Dylan Thomas, Brendan Behan, Jackson Pollock, and Virgil Thomson, who still resides in one of its apartment suites. The richly ornamented tier-upon-tier of iron balconies is the most remarkable feature of this picturesque Victorian Gothic edifice. The rooms of Henry Villard's Italianate Renaissance revival mansion complex between Fiftieth and Fifty-first streets on Madison Avenue, designed by McKim, Mead and White and erected between 1882 and 1886, also contained furniture similar in design to the Chelsea's extraordinary table. Once the offices of the Archdiocese of New York and later the Random House publishing offices, the Villard Houses are protected by landmark status, and some of the more fascinating rooms—particularly the music room—have been restored and are now public rooms of the new Helmsley Palace Hotel.

At the turn of the century there were distinct gradations in the decorative arts based upon taste, design, and cost. The better furniture was produced in limited quantities, and although it was not always fashioned completely by hand, it was made with great care. Much of the mass-produced furniture was inexpensive and quickly manufactured by machine. Rolltop desks (plate 352), round-top tables with claw-and-ball feet, and pressed-back chairs—typical massive oak forms—and wicker baby buggies (plate 353) were all aimed at the middle-class market, which continued to expand as the American population grew.

There was one giant among the architects and designers of the time. In his field no other American of the twentieth century has achieved the reputation enjoyed by Frank Lloyd Wright. The beginnings of the so-called modern movement in America are contemporaneous with the ascent of Wright's worldwide standing, and his methods have been adopted internationally. His radical innovations, in both structural and aesthetic terms, were particularly well expressed in a series of houses with low horizontal lines and dramatically projecting eaves; this type of design, which seemed to harmonize with the sweep of the surrounding landscape, was dubbed the prairie style. He was the first to break from the traditional closed volume and introduce open planning in interiors, achieving a fluidity of space by elimination of walls between rooms. By 1901 Wright was successful enough to be asked by editor Edward Bok to publish in *The Ladies' Home Journal* designs for a model prairie-style house with dining and living room areas that were defined within free-flowing space.

One of Wright's many great buildings was the Frederick C. Robie House (plate 354), planned in 1906 and erected on Chicago's South Side in 1908–09. The free-flowing interior spaces, overhanging roofs to shade windows and balconies, indoor recreation areas, and strong flowing lines of the Robie residence forecast trends in house design for the next fifty years. This concrete and brick structure was furnished with Wright's mission-inspired furniture (plate 355). Wright envisioned furniture as part of the whole scheme of a house and urged decorators to leave wood in its natural state, avoiding varnishes. He also hinted at his natural, almost casual approach to simplicity in design: "From the very beginning my T-square and triangle were easy media of expression for my geometric sense of things."

Wright's outstanding contribution to the decorative arts was the stripping away of the treasured ornamentation of the Victorian period. He designed objects that could be broken down into components easily produced by modern manufacturing techniques. Wright conceived his buildings as a whole and concerned himself with every detail—from the lighting (plate 356), the heating, and the furniture to the exterior ornamentation (plate 357).

Like Louis Comfort Tiffany, Wright was also interested in stained-glass windows. His 1912 windows for the Avery Coonley Playhouse (plate 358) at

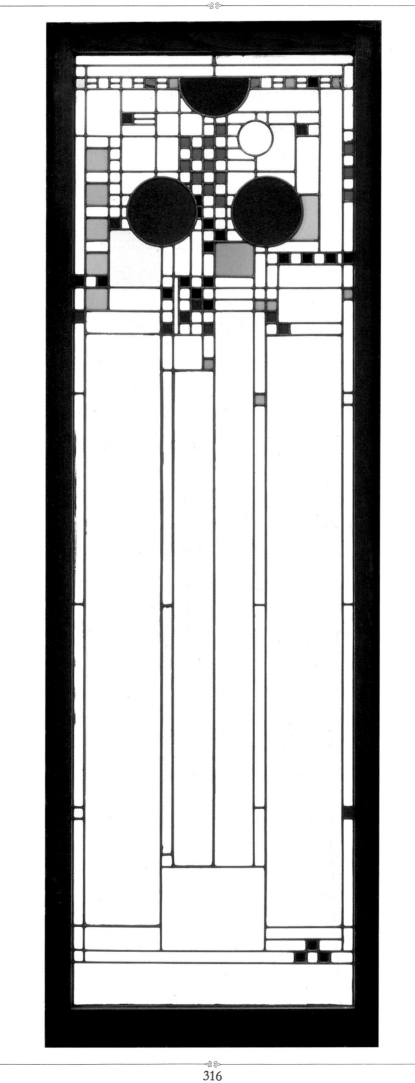

358. Window. Frank Lloyd
Wright. Illinois. 1912. Leaded
glass with wood frame, height
86¼″. Metropolitan Museum of
Art, New York City. Purchase,
Edward C. Moore, Jr.; gift of
Edgar J. Kaufmann Charitable
Foundation Fund, 1967

The trend away from the excessive
ornament of the Victorian period
already evident in Wright's 1903
lamp (see plate 356) is carried
further in these windows where
abstraction reigns. This is one of
the three windows Wright designed
for the Avery Coonley Playhouse
in Riverside, Illinois.

359. Dressing table. Designed by John E. Brower; manufactured by Sligh Furniture Company. Grand Rapids, Michigan. 1907. Gumwood, width 45″. Grand Rapids Public Museum, Grand Rapids, Michigan

Grand Rapids manufacturers were prominent among the American companies that exploited the modern style in furniture production.

Riverside, Illinois, would have startled his Victorian contemporaries, who were more comfortable with naturalistic depictions worked in colored glass. Wright's abstract windows heralded the international style of the period from 1920 to 1960, when large squares of glass held in place by steel frames would serve as exterior screens for mammoth office buildings and towers.

While Wright led the way in architecture, artists and designers such as Joseph E. Brower of Grand Rapids, Michigan, set the pace for furniture in the modern style. Grand Rapids was an important furniture-manufacturing center as early as the middle of the nineteenth century and was acknowledged as such when a bedroom suite of monumental proportions by Berkey and Gay Furniture Company was displayed in Philadelphia in 1876. Grand Rapids manufacturers later were apparently introduced to modern design by the great influx of immigrant craftsmen arriving from Austria in the early twentieth century. Brower's dressing table (plate 359), produced in 1907 by the Sligh Furniture Company, is from one of the first modern suites designed and produced in Grand Rapids and was crafted from solid gumwood, a material used extensively after the development of a kiln-drying process that prevented warping and checking. This new manufacturing technique and the design of the piece anticipate by almost twenty years the European moderne style of furniture first presented at the Exposition des Arts Décoratifs et Industriels Modernes held in Paris in 1925.

AMERICA THE BEAUTIFUL
1914~1980

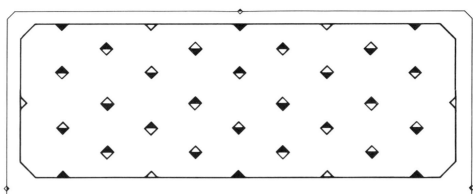

In the twentieth century, in a world where increased technology has permitted production of relatively inexpensive furnishings for the average citizen, reverence for machine-made products has flourished side by side with an appreciation for the hand-made. Purely functional furniture has enjoyed great popularity; it was initially handcrafted but ultimately was mass-produced and inexpensive to acquire.

Three main styles evolved in the first half of the century and still coexist: colonial revival, art moderne or art deco, and the so-called international style.

The colonial revival grew out of enthusiasm for American history as expressed at the celebration of the 1876 Centennial in Philadelphia as well as out of the rabid nationalism generated by the nation's entry into World War I. The movement became widespread during the first quarter of the twentieth century, and vestiges of the colonial revival can be discerned even today in stylish versions of rustic furniture.

Art moderne, or art deco as it was more commonly known after World War II, was perhaps the last of the great truly cohesive decorative arts styles. Art deco was initially defined as an expressive trend at the legendary Exposition des Arts Décoratifs et Industriels Modernes in Paris in 1925. The exposition served as a prototype for important furniture shows presented between 1925 and 1930 at leading department stores in America, and these provided credentials for the chrome-plated, tubular, enameled, and leather-upholstered furniture in the new taste.

America's gradual awareness of the emerging international style developed as innovative architects created highly personalized designs based on the principle of functionalism. Louis Sullivan was a precursor of the style, and his doctrine that outward form should faithfully express the function of a building became the inspiration for much of the century's designs after 1920. In the early years of the century, European architect-designers working in America also developed concepts of design that mercilessly removed unnecessary embellishment and excessive ornament. Their honest use of construction materials resulted in novel designs based on new aesthetic considerations of simplicity, clean lines, and pleasing proportions. The preference for geometric shapes and the new methods of production offered by the German workshops of the Bauhaus traveled to the United States after the dissolution of the Bauhaus in 1933, brought here by many of the most important Bauhaus teachers and students who came in search of political freedom and an economic future.

The concepts of interior design after World War II changed dramatically because of diminished living space. Rooms became smaller, houses and apartments more compact, creating a need for storage units that could be used in conjunction with the wall or as room dividers. Modular case pieces provided a new practicality. Modern technology—especially in the area of plywood, laminated wood, pressboard, metals, and plastics—revolutionized furniture manufacture. During the period 1950–1980 architect-designers, particularly those associated with the preeminent design firms of Knoll International and Herman Miller, developed pieces that earlier would have been technically impossible. The popularity of the high-tech style of the 1970s may be an indication that success in the decorative arts of the future will be derived from an unprecedented concentration upon technology and practical advances in science.

Reflections of the Past
◆ 1914~1980 ◆

World War I was touched off on June 28, 1914, with the assassination of Archduke Francis Ferdinand, heir to the Austrian throne, by a Serb nationalist. President Woodrow Wilson, seeking to maintain United States neutrality, advised Americans to be impartial in thought as well as in action. The neutrality presented new opportunities for the nation's businessmen, and between 1914 and 1916, with most of Europe embroiled in war, American exports actually doubled. Natural resources useful to the war effort were indeed a major part of this

360. Statue of Liberty. *Artist unknown. United States. c. 1914. Reverse painting on glass, height 18½″. Private collection*

The technique of reverse painting on glass extends back several centuries to the Orient. In this depiction of Liberty a cloud formation in the pale blue sky creates an image of the American flag. A submarine and a battleship are navigating New York harbor, a foreshadowing of U.S. involvement in the world war a few years after this painting was made. The frame, not hand-carved as in the eighteenth century, is decorated with a cast-plaster eagle, two cast-plaster flags, and a laurel wreath of victory.

burgeoning export activity; however, the decorative arts, especially the inexpensive but well-made furniture emanating from Grand Rapids, Michigan—that midwestern city of wood—represented a substantial portion as well.

The United States would probably have kept out of the European conflict if its declared neutrality had not been violated. In the early spring of 1917 German submarines sank several United States vessels, including the *Lusitania,* which cost the lives of many Americans. The United States joined France and Britain in the war and helped halt Germany's last great offensive in the spring of 1918.

During the United States participation in the war, nationalism reached a fevered pitch and a strident press enthusiastically supported architects and designers whose work had its roots in the nation's past. Nearly every manufacturer turned from the mission style as well as the so-called quaint style and produced their own interpretations of native antique furniture. The colonial revival was so entrenched by 1924 that when France invited the United States to participate in the Exposition des Arts Décoratifs et Industriels Modernes, to be held in Paris

361. The Gossips. *Artist unknown. United States. 1918. Oil on canvas, 24 × 36″. Private collection*

This early-twentieth-century painting bursts with enthusiasm for the disappearing rural way of life. The two aged women sit in what appear to be a Boston rocker and a Windsor side chair. Contemporary decorative items in the room include a crazy quilt slung over the back of the Boston rocker and a Queen Anne–Chippendale looking glass enriched with peacock feathers.

the following year, Secretary of Commerce Herbert Hoover regretfully declined the invitation with the excuse that there really was no modern decorative art movement in the United States.

The renewed interest in early American furniture modes, including a kind of ersatz colonial style, had its roots in the revivalistic tendencies of the late Victorian era. At the same time zeal for remote cultures, whether ancient or Far Eastern or even highly developed European, forced American designers to reconsider their own past and provided the impetus for the reuse of earlier styles.

Reverse paintings on glass, which had been in vogue in America at various times in the eighteenth and nineteenth centuries, reappeared in the early twentieth. The proud figure of the Statue of Liberty (plate 360), dominating what is now Liberty Island in New York Harbor, dates from the World War I period. During earlier periods the frame would have been hand-carved and the decoration either an integral part or carved separately and applied. By the time this piece was created, it was possible to simply cast the entire frame in plaster over a wood base.

Even though much of the population lived in large cosmopolitan cities like New York, which were fed by a vast industrial complex, the nation was still mainly agrarian and was nourished by the vitality of the land. The painting *The Gossips* (plate 361), which focuses on styles of the past in both furniture and dress, might well have been painted in mid-nineteenth century instead of 1918, a date visible on the almanac hanging from the Queen Anne–Chippendale look-

This opulent Venetian-style mansion built on Sarasota Bay in Florida for the world-famous circus promoter John Ringling and his wife, Mable, consists of thirty-two rooms stocked with elaborately carved furniture and objets d'art gathered by the owners in their travels around the world.

362. Ca'd'Zan. Dwight James Baum. Sarasota, Florida. 1925–26. Ringling Museums, Sarasota, Florida

363. Dining room of Ca'd'Zan. Dwight James Baum. Sarasota, Florida. 1925–26. Ringling Museums, Sarasota, Florida

The Ringlings, like many of their monied contemporaries, were convinced that it was more chic to collect authentic antiques, or reproductions of great period pieces, than to acquire the simpler and plainer styles being created by contemporary cabinetmakers. Acknowledgment of the important technological advances of the late nineteenth century are the hanging chandelier and the electrified sconces over the mantelpiece in the state dining room of the Ringlings' mansion (see plate 362).

364. American revival furniture. Century Furniture Company. Grand Rapids, Michigan. 1920s. Frontispiece from Furniture as Interpreted by the Century Furniture Company (Grand Rapids, 1926). Private collection

This catalog display features furniture based on vague historical precedents. The rope turning of the Cromwellian period, the tall cane back of the William and Mary chair, and the Queen Anne cabriole leg and pad foot were used indiscriminately on furniture evocative of the past.

365. Quilt. Maker unknown.
Ohio. 1938. Cotton percale and
threads, 79 × 91″. Collection
Mr. and Mrs. Hugh Lincoln Hoey

This appliquéd quilt, apparently
created to memorialize a treaty
with the Indians, is inscribed with
the dates 1788–1938 on the border.
The romantic depiction of an
historical event involving the
colonists and native Indians is not
unlike the background vignette in
Edward Hicks's Peaceable
Kingdom (see plate 247).

366. Colonial Flower Basket. Cybis Porcelains. New Jersey. 1976. Porcelain, height 11½". Cybis Porcelains, Trenton, New Jersey

ing glass dressed up with peacock feathers. Hand-me-down Boston rockers and Windsor chairs, such as the examples in this robust painting, were treasured as valuable relics from the ancestral past.

World War I had actually stimulated technological developments, and by the 1920s the automobile as well as radio and cinema were no longer novelties. It is not surprising that during this period the tastemakers in urban America would look upon the simple and unsophisticated furnishings of country farmhouses with disdain. For those of great wealth, European high culture was still the best model. When in 1925–26 the circus impresario John Ringling and his wife, Mable, built their sumptuous mansion (plate 362) on Sarasota Bay in Florida at a cost of $1.5 million, the architect, Dwight James Baum, based his design on the Doges' Palace in Venice. The thirty-two-room Ca'd'Zan ("House of John" in Venetian dialect) is filled with elaborately carved and painted furniture and works of art from all over the world. The marble swimming pool, Aeolian pipe organ, and gold-fixtured bathroom are modern appointments suitable to a millionaire who had entertained the nation with the "Greatest Show on Earth." The state dining room (plate 363) pays homage to the decorative and functional objects of Europe's past.

367. Birds of Peace. Edward Marshall Boehm, Inc. New Jersey. 1972. Porcelain, height including base 60½". Edward Marshall Boehm, Inc., Trenton, New Jersey

This monumental life-size composition, with a total weight of 350 pounds, was commissioned by President Richard M. Nixon as a gift to the People's Republic of China on his first state visit there in 1972.

Contemporary designers and collectors often attempt to re-create the spirit of the past by judiciously organizing their modern living spaces around authentic antiques. The accessories of this interior, such as silver by John Coney and Jacob Gerritse Lansing, delftware, and seventeenth-century candlesticks, are combined with Rhode Island and Massachusetts maple furniture to suggest the gracious style of the affluent homes of the colonial period.

Americans of more modest means had an immense fondness for objects created in the English neo-Adam style, especially when these included technological innovations as well. Electric coffeepots, chafing dishes, and other kitchen novelties, often finished with swags and panels reminiscent of the eighteenth-century designs of Robert Adam, were the rage, and the ad copy of nearly every issue of popular women's and home-oriented publications waxed enthusiastic over these echoes of the past in modern guise.

Design emphasis was on historical precedent, and the Century Furniture Company of Grand Rapids, in the forefront of this trend, issued a leather-bound limited edition in 1928, *Furniture as Interpreted by the Century Furniture Company*, which gave detailed information about traditional designs. At the end of the

This Chinese wedding room was designed by Palatinus as part of Bloomingdale's recent celebration of renewed American cultural ties with China. The room shows a sensitive means of combining traditional oriental forms with modern realities. The table and chairs are authentic antiques selected in China, but the wedding bed and armoires are contemporary pieces produced in the United States by Baker. The bed is queen-size and the armoires are constructed as separate units that open up and include a television set, stereo equipment, a bar setup, as well as general storage space.

370. Conoid side chairs.
George Nakashima. Pennsylvania.
1962. Persian walnut, height 35".
George Nakashima, New Hope,
Pennsylvania

Nakashima has combined oriental
motifs with early American forms,
producing a new look. These side
chairs have scooped seats much like
early Windsor chairs.

book a chronology of furniture listed styles in England, France, and America, and scattered throughout the publication were illustrations of the pieces currently in production by the Century company based on those styles. The frontispiece (plate 364) shows some of the colonial revival furniture being offered by Century. Today it seems surprising, especially in terms of authenticity, that the company did not consider it necessary to alter a piece structurally in order to market it as a different mode. In the frontispiece the highboy in front of the paneled wall might be painted red and embellished with red velvet and gold trim and sold as a Spanish style. Given a distressed white lacquer with gold accents, the same highboy was enthusiastically endorsed as French or French provincial. If it was japanned, it was labeled oriental, and in a natural finish it was sold as an American version of a Queen Anne highboy. This fudging on the question of genuineness is revealed in the sections of the catalog devoted to colonial American (1620–1795) and American empire (1795–1830) styles:

371. Side chairs and table.
Hitchcock Chair Company.
Connecticut. 1976. Wood, height
of chair 34". Hitchcock Chair
Company, Riverton, Connecticut

The form of the turtle-back
Hitchcock chair is identical to
pieces that were produced by the
forerunner of the firm in the middle
of the nineteenth century. The
painted and stenciled decoration
consisting of a silhouette of George
Washington and a view of Mount
Vernon is a present-day
acknowledgment of American
enthusiasm for the nation's first
president, especially in the
Bicentennial year when this
set was produced.

OPPOSITE:

372. Gallery installation. Knob Creek. North Carolina. 1980. Knob Creek, Inc., Morganton, North Carolina. Bucks County Collection

The pieces in this interior include a bench inspired by original Shaker furniture of the nineteenth century, a shoe-foot trestle table similar to eighteenth-century models, and four reproduction Windsor chairs. There are several case pieces, including a closed cupboard typical of Pennsylvania design and an open pewter cupboard based on a New England original. The modern rag rugs and tin chandelier are appropriate to this installation reminiscent of an earlier American decorative style. Some of the accessory items, such as the toy horse, are period antiques.

Although any consideration of Colonial styles in America must take us back to the Early Jacobean in England and the time prior to the reign of Louis XIV in France, it is quite proper to consider the Colonial styles last. Indeed, America during its early days became a veritable melting pot for furniture, even as it has since proved a melting pot for mankind. . . .

Colonial furniture is deservedly popular in America today. For modern use, it is somewhat lighter than original forms; but the style is charming, appeals because of its historical background, and is suited to modern requirements of beauty and usefulness. . . .

Modern manufacturers find a wealth of inspiration in early American forms; and many beautiful pieces have been built around motifs which predominated during the early years of this country as an independent nation. For the sake of proper classification, these styles are generally grouped under the head of Early American, and are not considered strictly Colonial styles.

It is clearly evident from the Century catalog that authentic reproductions were deemed by both the contemporary furniture makers and the buyer to be a waste of time; they thought of them as cumbersome to handle and uncomfortable at best. Although the purists could indeed point out the inherent contradiction, adaptation was the key word of the early-twentieth-century trend of exploiting the nation's heritage.

How much more specific in concept is the appliquéd quilt from Ohio (plate 365), sewn in 1938. This bedcovering apparently memorializes an early treaty made with the Indians on the banks of the Marietta River. The needleworker utilized her quilting technique expertly to depict cloud formations in the sky, tree bark, and foliage. Few twentieth-century needlework pieces are as sensitively executed.

While furnishings that reflected the past continued to be manufactured during the 1930s and 1940s, enthusiastic endorsement of the art moderne, or art deco, style substantially overshadowed the rampant revivalist tendencies. During the same period infant stirrings by modern architect-designers eventually led to the development of an elitist design group that created stark modern buildings and furnishings which had their foundation in utility and function as well as in machine production; this development is known as the international style. (These two movements, art deco and international style, will be analyzed in the last two chapters, respectively.)

It was not until the climax of the Bicentennial celebrations in 1976, enthusiastically endorsed by most Americans, that a keen interest was again revived in the nation's origins and the collecting of native antiques was regarded as a respectable pastime. The nationalistic fervor that the Bicentennial sparked has not yet diminished.

Just as fine porcelains were eagerly purchased by Americans throughout much of the country's history, particularly in the late 1600s and early 1700s,

373. Circus Parade. Kathy Jakobsen. Michigan. 1979. Oil on canvas, 24 × 36″. Museum of American Folk Art, New York City. Gift of the artist

During the nineteenth century the circus parade was an important event in small towns as well as major cities across the country, routinely attracting record-breaking crowds. Major efforts are being made by the National Trust for Historic Preservation and similar organizations to preserve the kind of architectural heritage represented by the small commercial buildings in this painting.

they were being seriously collected again in the 1960s and 1970s. Primary firms producing exceptional wares included Cybis Porcelains and Edward Marshall Boehm, Inc. They are still two of the most important porcelain manufacturers working today.

Cybis was founded by Boleslaw Cybis, a graduate of the Fine Arts Academy in Warsaw, Poland, who had gained a noted reputation in Europe for his paintings, sculpture, and "al fresco" murals created in France, Switzerland, and Germany, as well as in Poland and Russia. Cybis and his wife, Maja, also a distinguished artist, traveled to the United States in 1938 to execute murals commissioned by the Polish government for the Hall of Honor of the Polish Pavilion at the New York World's Fair, which opened the following year. Stranded in the United States at the outbreak of World War II, the Cybises founded a studio in Astoria, New York, to make porcelain sculpture. The studio was later moved to Trenton, New Jersey. The Cybis company, the oldest existing art porcelain studio in the United States, resembles European ateliers of an earlier period. Today many other artists, emulating the traditions established by Boleslaw Cybis, produce fine porcelain sculptures which are collected throughout the world.

The Colonial Flower Basket (plate 366) was issued in 1976 in a restricted edition of one hundred by the Cybis firm to celebrate the Fourth of July ceremonies held at Philadelphia during the Bicentennial year. The basket contains the state flowers from the original thirteen colonies. Among the earliest contributions of the colonists to the North American continent were seeds and flower slips carried over from the Old World. A few of these flowers and shrubs later were chosen as official flowers of the colonies: the lilac in New Hampshire, peach blossom in Delaware, jasmine in South Carolina, violets in Rhode Island and New Jersey, and a variation of the rose in Georgia and New York. Native plants also displayed in the basket include the mountain laurel of Pennsylvania and Connecticut and the trailing arbutus (called the mayflower by the colonists) of Massachusetts. Virginia and North Carolina honored the white dogwood and Maryland the black-eyed Susan.

One of the first native-born Americans to gain international attention for hard porcelain sculpture was Edward Marshall Boehm. He achieved many remarkable distinctions: he modeled pieces for five American presidents, and his works were purchased by museums throughout the world. Boehm began sculpting in hard porcelain in 1950, and even in his earliest efforts his respect for the traditional styles and methods was combined with a contemporary expression. A dedicated naturalist, he surrounded himself with wildlife, domesticated animals, and sea life; during the 1960s he established elaborately planned gardens as well as one of the greatest private collections in the United States of exotic birds. A careful study of Boehm porcelain sculpture reveals that he was concerned not only with the romantic and picturesque elements of nature but also with the more commonplace and smaller forms of life—beetles, snails, moths, butterflies, turtles, chameleons, and frogs. He was tenacious in his pursuit of beauty, and for him the world of nature was its source.

Following Boehm's death in 1969, the company continued the multiple production of porcelain sculpture under the direction of his widow, Helen Boehm. After she assumed responsibility for the company, the first major commission was from President Richard M. Nixon for his initial state visit, in 1972, to the People's Republic of China. The monumental composition Nixon ordered, *Birds of Peace* (plate 367), was a complex work of art that required nearly two years to complete. Before the original molds for the pair of life-size mute swans were destroyed, two additional examples were made, one presented to the White House and the other to the World Wildlife Fund, which later auctioned it in London to an anonymous American purchaser.

Fine porcelains are attractive accessories for traditional antique furniture, and collectors or designers who attempt to reproduce interiors from the past (plate 368) often include these brightly decorated wares. The interest in oriental objects and furniture, which developed in America as early as the middle of the seventeenth century, continued unabated into the twentieth. Black lacquer furniture, Chinese and Japanese screens, and teak and rosewood tables and chairs have been skillfully combined by many of America's finest decorators with the straight lines of contemporary glass and metal furniture. Traditional oriental rooms—such as Fred Palatinus's wedding room (plate 369) created in 1980 for Bloomingdale's immensely successful storewide promotional campaign, "China: The Dawn of a New Era"—have oriental-inspired furniture designed to compensate for the practical needs of the American life-style.

Many present-day artist-craftsmen have looked to the past for inspiration for their contemporary designs, particularly those who work in wood. With their special knowledge of tools and materials gathered from a profound study of traditional craftsmanship through the ages, many of these designers have managed to create new forms that please the aesthetic taste of the discriminating contemporary consumer and at the same time have taken inspiration from all historical modes. George Nakashima, one of America's foremost designer-artisans, has managed successfully to mingle the early American Windsor style

374. Sculptural outline of Benjamin Franklin House. Venturi and Rauch. Philadelphia, Pennsylvania. 1972. Steel, height 54' 6''. Venturi, Rauch and Scott Brown, Architects, Philadelphia, Pennsylvania (photograph © 1976 by Mark Cohn)

Present-day curiosity about America's past leaders and the world they lived in has created some anomalies. This outline of Benjamin Franklin's house, which once occupied the same site on Philadelphia's Franklin Court, is an imaginative contemporary effort at suggesting early American architecture. The firm of Venturi and Rauch conceived the idea in 1972, and the park was opened in 1976—the Bicentennial year—when interest in American cultural history was at its height.

with traditional oriental form in his side chairs (plate 370). Stylish in a truly modern sense, these chairs are also comfortable; they are fine examples of the best of contemporary American craftsmanship.

Nakashima, of Japanese descent, was born in Spokane, Washington. After architectural studies at the University of Washington and the Massachusetts Institute of Technology, he traveled to France, India, and Japan, working with numerous architects and woodworkers in an effort to learn the secrets of their respective trades. Returning to the United States in the early 1940s, he and his family were interned in a relocation center during World War II. Upon their release in 1943, they moved to New Hope, Pennsylvania, where Nakashima built a shop and home which have been the center of his artistic and creative life.

Nakashima—quoted in *Woodenworks,* the catalog for an exhibition of furniture objects by five contemporary craftsmen sponsored jointly in 1972 by the Renwick Gallery in Washington, D.C., and the Minnesota Museum of Art in Saint Paul—expressed enthusiasm for the material he works with and revealed a highly sensitive response to the use of that material:

We import logs from all over the world and ship them to a sawmill in Maryland where they are cut into lumber. This is very precise work and I like to be there to direct it. It's like cutting a diamond. Cut one way and you get something good, cut another and you lose it. The direction of cut, the thickness of cut, all of these things are very important. The growth lines of winter, when a tree is growing slowly, give the grain its bands of darker, harder wood. The summer growth is wider, lighter, softer. And because of all the strange twists inside even trees that look very straight, all these differences become exaggerated and beautiful in the cutting.

375. Barn interior. Raymond Waites. New York City. 1979. The Gear Barn, Erwinna, Pennsylvania (photograph Chris Mead)

The interior of this two-hundred-year-old Pennsylvania barn converted into a four-story living space is simple and represents a growing tendency to update country furnishings to a contemporary lifestyle. The project was designed by Raymond Waites, and the furnishings and fabrics were created by Gear Design, Inc. The geometric fabrics give a hint of the past and yet are less fanciful than most antique textiles. The ceiling of this part of the barn is enclosed with thermopane, and the building is heated with wood-burning stoves.

Nakashima is only one of many artist-craftsmen who have come to prominence in the past several years. Others of equal distinction who have produced fine furniture on a limited basis are Arthur Espenant Carpenter, Wendell Castle, Wharton Esherick, and Sam Maloof.

Not all designers and manufacturers were satisfied with the modern reworking of traditional forms, and several preferred to re-create the earlier pieces. The Hitchcock Chair Company after being abandoned for nearly a hundred years, restored the original manufactory at Riverton, Connecticut, in the 1940s and again began the production of Hitchcock chairs, which are frequently decorated with symbols from American history. The turtle-back Hitchcock chairs (plate 371), crafted in 1976, are decorated with a silhouette medallion portrait of George Washington centering the top rail and a view of Washington's beloved home, Mount Vernon, on the handsomely shaped center splat. To meet the public interest in recapturing its past, the Knob Creek furniture company in Morganton, North Carolina, began in 1980 to make reproductions of early American furniture, including typical Pennsylvania and New England pieces, Windsor chairs, and objects inspired by Shaker designs (plate 372).

Beginning in the 1960s designers with a new sense of self-assurance turned to the synthetic materials that technological advances in the chemical and engineering industries had made available. There was a renewed focus on comfort, and overstuffed seating pieces—seductively advertised as "superstuffed and fabulously comfortable"—were displayed in every department store and furniture showroom across the country. New materials such as urethane and polyurethane foam, polyester fiber, and cast rigid urethane—which eliminated the need for an inner structural frame—were used to create a radically different type of lounging piece, including the overstuffed chair, ottoman, and recliner.

A great number of contemporary primitive artists have concentrated on the cultural styles and traditions of previous eras. The best of these naive painters—such as Kathy Jakobsen, Tella Kitchen, Rose Labrie, and Mattie Lou O'Kelley—reveal a fanciful and fresh approach in their interpretations of the past while dealing with themes and images typical of the genre.

The youthful Kathy Jakobsen paints Michigan landscapes and genre pictures in watercolor as well as in oil. Preservationists have fought both strident personal and costly legal battles to save the kinds of architecture depicted in Jakobsen's *Circus Parade* (plate 373). In 1977, when her agent, Jay Johnson, queried

376. Bentwood furniture. Added Oomph. North Carolina. 1980. Willow, width of table 38". Added Oomph, High Point, North Carolina

The complete Added Oomph line, expressive of the recent trend toward a rustic, folksy look in American decorative arts, includes such diverse pieces as a chaise longue, an étagère, and a twig bed. All of the seating pieces are intended to be fitted with cushions and pillows that coordinate with a specific interior.

her about her original interest in painting, Jakobsen included a charming explanation in her answering letter: "When I was very young I decided that when I grew up I was going to be a boy, an artist, or a horse trainer. Well, I stayed a tomboy for as long as I could and eventually traded my horses for boyfriends, but I've never changed my mind about painting." Her art is based on a genuine interest in calligraphy, and her modern illuminations and frakturs are without precedent among contemporary naive art.

Even contemporary American architects, concerned with rigorous problems of functionalism, have been caught up by the zeal to preserve American history and furnishings. None have been as inventive as Robert Venturi, known especially for his stark iconoclastic structures. Discussing his work in his 1966 book *Complexity and Contradiction in Architecture,* this dramatic artist reels off a litany of values of incongruity that actually inspire him: "I like elements that are hybrid rather than 'pure,' compromising rather than 'clean,' distorted rather than 'straightforward,' ambiguous rather than 'articulated,' perverse as well as impersonal, boring as well as 'interesting,' conventional rather than 'designed,' accommodating rather than excluding, redundant rather than simple, vestigial as well as innovating, inconsistent and equivocal rather than direct and clear. I am for messy vitality over obvious unity. I include the non sequitur and proclaim the duality."

One of the most inventive instances of an attempt to re-create the past in modern times was begun by Venturi and Rauch in Philadelphia in 1972 when the architectural firm erected an outline of Benjamin Franklin's home (plate

374), which originally stood on the same site as the Franklin Court addition to the Independence National Historical Park. Franklin Court, the culmination of more than twenty-five years of research, is a national memorial honoring Benjamin Franklin's achievements as one of America's important statesmen and scientists. It blends historic restoration, interpretive exhibits, an historical shrine, and public open space characteristic of the eighteenth century. Pebblestone, flagstone, and brick surfaces suggest the carriage court and walkways of Franklin's time. Flower, hedge, and arbor plantings, as well as modern interpretations of colonial benches, recall the charm of a garden in that era. The open steel frame in the center approximates the profile of Franklin's three-story mansion and gives a sense of its presence in the garden. The floor plan of the house is delineated by white marble set in a black slate field.

In spite of the abundance of data accumulated during the site dig, scholars were unable to provide enough detail for an accurate reconstruction of the mansion. This design of what may be dubbed a ghost house avoids being a false replica while evoking a spatial impression of Franklin's house. Punctuating the paving are openings through which the visitor can view in situ the subterranean remains of the house foundations. Inscribed on the slate floor are excerpts from correspondence between Franklin and his wife, Deborah, during the construction of the house from 1763 to 1787, when Franklin was directing much of the work from England and France. A vivid sense of the interior as well as of the uses and appearance of the rooms emerges from these quotations. A mulberry tree, like the one under which Franklin habitually sat to enjoy his garden and receive visitors during the last years of his life, has been planted behind the mansion frame. Also in the courtyard, between the Market Street houses and the frame, is another steel ghost, representing the print shop, which included a type foundry and book bindery, built by Franklin for his grandson.

This design was created in response to the National Park Service's goals: to set up a museum explaining the range of Franklin's activities; to display the archaeological remains of his house; to preserve the remains of the rental houses he built and to reconstruct their facades accurately; and, above all, to create a monument to Franklin and the way he lived appropriate to the site of his home in Philadelphia.

Creative, daring, and thoughtful, Venturi has led American architects and designers in a new direction which will undoubtedly reach its culmination many years from now.

Numerous popular home-oriented magazines, such as *Better Homes and Gardens, House Beautiful, House and Garden,* and *Family Circle,* have promoted the country look with great intensity, emphasizing American homegrown styles and forms of the past. Simple antique objects—including stoneware jugs, redware plates, carved decoys, weather vanes, and rocking horses—have been blended with modern pieces of unsurpassed functionalism and utility in interiors that range from converted backwoods cabins and rural farmhouses to city apartments and urban row houses. The enthusiasm for country style expressed in the adaptation of a barn to contemporary living space (plate 375) is also evident in penthouse apartments in Manhattan high rises. The nostalgic bentwood tables and chairs (plate 376) produced by Added Oomph of High Point, North Carolina, are present-day versions of the self-consciously twiggy Adirondack furniture of the nineteenth century. Frequently these charming reminders of the past adorn the porches and interiors of weekend hideaways, but occasionally they add a homey touch to urban town houses.

The amalgamation of rustic and modern styles proved to be an expressive mode of interior decoration during the 1970s. A more flamboyant mixture of what at first would appear to be mutually exclusive idioms—American native forms and folk art, oriental and European period antiques, twentieth-century streamlined furniture—was first given serious treatment in Mary Emmerling's 1980 trend-setting *American Country*. This tendency in the American decorative arts—an eclectic movement that recently was awarded the catchy label of high-country style—is emerging as a dominant design vogue of the 1980s.

The Moderne-Deco Style
◆ 1925-1980 ◆

In the United States art deco is a relatively recent term for what was originally called art moderne, or simply moderne. In the 1960s it gained currency as a term for a movement in the decorative arts and architecture that originated in the 1920s and developed into a dominant style in the 1930s. The name is derived from the mammoth forward-looking Exposition des Arts Décoratifs et Industriels Modernes in Paris in 1925, where household utensils, furniture, and other decorative objects in this style were first exhibited. The formative influences on the moderne–deco manner were art nouveau, the Bauhaus, Diaghilev's Ballets Russes, and cubism, and one of its basic goals was to adapt design to the conditions of mass production.

In essence it was a reaction against the fantasy and exaggerated curves of art nouveau. This protest was instigated in the late nineteenth century by the Scottish designer Charles Rennie Mackintosh and the Glasgow school. Mackintosh attempted to establish a linear sense of design, simpler and more austere than the sinuous sweetness of French art nouveau design. Another important influence in the use of the straight line and geometric forms was revealed in the work of the Viennese architect-designer Josef Hoffmann. In 1903 Hoffmann participated in the founding of the Wiener Werkstätte, or Vienna Workshops, and was that craft studio's most prolific designer throughout its three decades of existence. He continued to refine Scottish attempts to simplify art nouveau. Hoffmann had studied under Otto Wagner—generally held to be the founder and leader of the modern movement in European architecture—and in 1899 joined in the founding of the Wiener Sezession, which was influenced by the forms and design of art nouveau but was more modernist than Wagner's approach. Hoffmann's furnishings reflect his mastery of geometric shaping and his delight in creature comforts, and he has been unofficially credited as the originator of art deco.

While Hoffmann and his associates dominated Viennese design, a similar group, the Deutsche Werkbund, was formed in Munich. The Werkbund's extremely well-made furniture, adventurous use of materials, strong colors, and coordinated style were the result of a conscious attempt to create an art that was new and contemporary. It aimed at bringing the artist back into the arena of industrial production. The group's awareness of present-day needs laid the groundwork for the modern spatial concepts of the Bauhaus at Weimar.

In spite of design developments at Vienna and Munich in the early years of the century, it was the Paris theater and dance world that gave rise to the first full flowering of the moderne style, which led to the deco style. Sergei Diaghilev brought his company of Russian dancers, including the legendary Vaslav Nijinsky, Tamara Karsavina, and Anna Pavlova, to Paris, and in 1909 his Ballets Russes made its debut there. This eccentric, highly gifted impresario employed

Léon Bakst, whose striking colors and astonishing costumes were immediately noted by critics and artists, and several other brilliant stage and costume designers, such as Pablo Picasso, Georges Braque, Juan Gris, Henri Matisse, Marie Laurencin, and André Derain. These artists worked with vibrant exotic colors

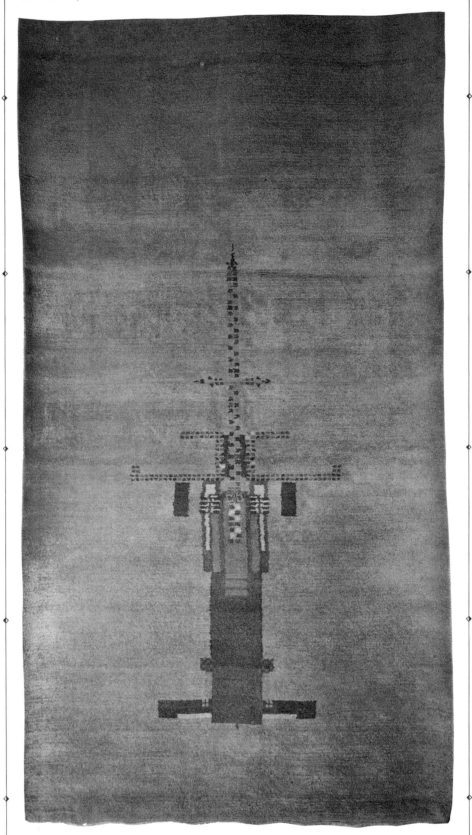

377. Rug. Frank Lloyd Wright. United States. 1916. Wool, 76½ × 142¾". Collection Mr. and Mrs. Robert R. Elsner, Jr. Courtesy Prairie Archives, Milwaukee Art Center, Milwaukee, Wisconsin (photograph E. P. Dutton and Company)

This textile was designed for the F. C. Bogk House in Milwaukee. Its geometric conception shows an obvious relationship to many of the other home furnishings Wright was designing for his affluent clients.

in Egyptian and oriental art styles, and also were part of the experiments of the various avant-garde movements that kept Paris abuzz with excitement in those years. The Ballets Russes's efforts, which initiated the public into expressionism, fauvism, futurism and cubism by way of the theater, were exceedingly popular and exerted a great influence on many of the leading contemporary artists and craftsmen working in the decorative arts.

With the outbreak of World War I the foundations from which art deco

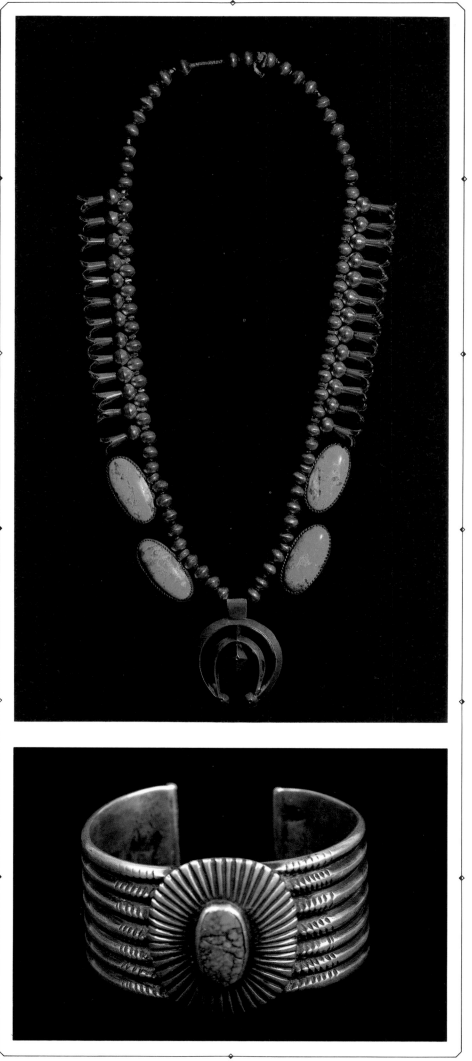

378. Bracelet and squash blossom
necklace. Navajo Indian. New
Mexico or Arizona. 1920–30.
Silver with turquoise, width of
bracelet 1¼", length of necklace
16". Museum of New Mexico,
Santa Fe, New Mexico

When the deco style became firmly
established in the United States,
fashion-conscious Americans sought
to find historical precedents for it in
their own country. Native
silverwork—an important part of
southwestern Indian creative
traditions—was not seriously
collected until the second half of the
nineteenth century. From about
1900 to 1920 a flourishing tourist
trade was responsible for the
creation of some extraordinary
pieces.

evolved were well in place. Geometric and rectilinear shapes were beginning to replace the graceful curvilinear designs and the asymmetrical excesses of the nouveau style. Art deco consisted of an austere purity exemplified by the use of industrial materials such as steel, concrete, glass bricks, plastics and bakelite, and was a challenge to the traditional barriers between art and technology. The French decorative impulse of the moment favored simplification.

By the end of the war deco had become a conscious style, and its rapid development brought to preeminence many of the outstanding avant-garde designers in various areas of the decorative arts. Emile-Jacques Ruhlmann produced custom furniture and designed interiors. René Lalique created beautiful glass, his favorite being a luminous, mat-surfaced, clear glass of faint bluish or

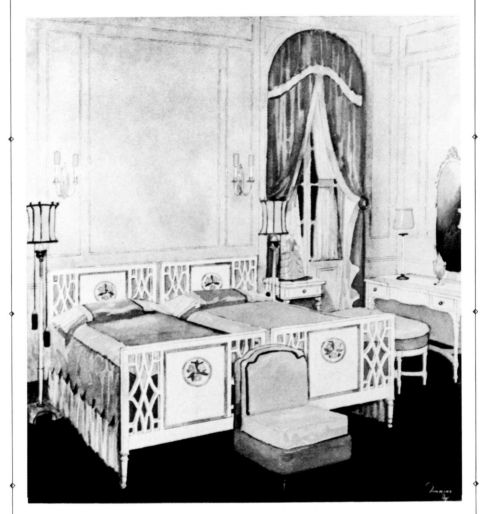

379. Bedroom suite. Simmons Company. United States. Early 1920s. Advertisement from Good Furniture Magazine *(December 1922). Private collection*

The pieces in the Simmons magazine ad show an early interpretation in America of the spare, rectilinear characteristics identifying the moderne–deco style. The bedspreads, pillow covers, chairs, and draperies were color-coordinated, creating a harmonious design effect.

oyster tint. Jean Puiforcat skillfully fashioned masterpieces of silver, and Raymond Templier designed decorative jewelry for the international set. The fashion styles of Paul Poiret and Erté were fanciful, yet their artful clothing designs were based on genuine aesthetic values.

The European moderne and deco styles in the 1920s frequently show the influence of the work of teachers and students at the Staatliches Bauhaus founded at Weimar in 1919 by the architect Walter Gropius. This German school of design—whose precepts had their origins in the late-nineteenth-century arts and crafts movement and the ideals of William Morris as well as in the reaction of critics John Ruskin and Henri van de Velde to what they viewed as the malignant materialism of the Industrial Revolution—was dedicated to a new unity of art and technology. Bauhaus designers at first had difficulty breaking with Jugendstil, the German equivalent of art nouveau; however, they came to believe that standardization, and only standardization, would lead to the development of a self-confident taste.

Between 1915 and 1930 several new design concepts were introduced into the growing deco movement. Motifs first developed by artists exploring the

tenets of cubism were freely adapted (plate 377). The discovery of Tutankh-
amen's tomb in Egypt in 1922 further strengthened contemporary efforts to graft
onto the deco style sensuous Egyptian motifs, while a reawakening of interest
in American Indian design (plate 378), particularly Aztec and Navajo, gave it
a new vitality.

Although the moderne style enjoyed its greatest popularity in France, the
United States was not without its sophisticated collectors and patrons who

*380. Diamond disc phonograph.
Thomas A. Edison, Inc. West
Orange, New Jersey. c. 1920.
Oak, height 50½". Greenfield
Village and Henry Ford Museum,
Dearborn, Michigan*

*Edison's first successful experiment
in reproducing recorded sound
was in 1877, but by the time he
established his own company he
had introduced a line of
phonographs sophisticated in
design and distinguished for
tonal quality. The pierced fretwork
panel of this phonograph could
be construed as either moderne or
colonial revival in style.*

could afford to indulge their fantasies by acquiring extravagant forms and designs and who enthusiastically adopted the latest international styles. In the
United States art deco as a full-blown style came to maturity after reverbera-
tions from the 1925 Paris exhibition reached the tastemakers in the major American design centers. In the few years preceding that date there were hints that
some American designers were already aware of the fervent activity in the
centers in Europe.

The room interior (plate 379) from an advertisement in the December 1922

381. *Vase. Maker unknown. United States. c. 1928. Pottery, height 5¾". Private collection*

The similarities of the motifs on this vase and on the California deco house (see plate 392) and the costume pictures (see plate 388) manifest a prevailing interest in the 1920s and 1930s in adaptations of Spanish motifs, which were known as Fiesta designs.

issue of *Good Furniture Magazine,* published in Grand Rapids, includes painted and decorated beds, a bedside stand, and dressing table as well as lamps and decorative accessories that already show an awareness of the moderne style. There

382. *Fashion photograph. Edward Steichen. New York City. 1925. Illustration from* Vogue *(June 1, 1925). Condé Nast Publications, Inc., New York City. Copyright © 1925; renewed 1953*

Edward Steichen, a pioneer in fashion photography and bold portrait studies of famous men and women, demonstrated his special sensitivity to shape and pattern in this handsome illustration. The model's shawl exhibits the fashion hallmarks—geometric shapes and vibrant colors—of the new deco style heralded by the decorative and industrial arts exposition held in Paris in 1925.

*383. Cocktail tray. Manufacturer
unknown. United States.
c. 1930. Chromium and glass,
18 × 12''. Collection Robert Heide
and John Gilman*

*Although this tray was
unquestionably mass-produced to
appeal to a broad popular market, it
is distinctive for both its utilitarian
aspects and its innovative decoration.
The reverse painting on glass on
the tray's flat surface reveals a
vivid and bold pattern known as
jazz moderne.*

384. Fruit bowl. Whiting
Manufacturing Company.
Providence, Rhode Island. 1922.
Silver, diameter 9¾". Private
collection

While serial production was
enthusiastically embraced by many
American manufacturers in the
1920s and 1930s, several
continued to produce handcrafted
pieces of distinction and beauty. A
silversmith at the Whiting
company created this piece by
raising it from a sheet of flat
silver, using a small malletlike
hammer. The feet were probably
cast and attached after the body of
the bowl had been formed.

is at the same time, however, as with much American furniture of this period, an acknowledgment of the nation's historical styles. The piercing in the headboards and footboards is reminiscent of the backs of Chippendale chairs or the balustrades on the facades of Georgian and Federal homes. These panels, as well, are not dissimilar to the colonial revival manner, which was still in vogue as late as the 1920s. The cabinet for the Edison manual-wind phonograph (plate 380), manufactured about 1920, is also in the moderne style. It was crafted from oak and indicates a continuing interest in the decorative possibilities of this much-admired wood, which dominated American furniture production during the late nineteenth century and the first two decades of the twentieth.

These pieces, while more modest than the elegant, flamboyant European moderne furnishings, were still considered "top of the line." This is evident when one compares them to the furnishings in the room interior (plate 385) from the publication *Adapting Quaint Furniture to American Needs,* issued in 1925 by Stickley Brothers Company of Grand Rapids. The furniture in this interior, obvious copies of the earlier Windsor style, relies upon turned members for its decorative quality. The window shades have painted or embroidered moderne-type medallions not unlike those that appear on the Simmons beds (plate 379). The rug in this Windsor interior, however, does have a strong resemblance to fabrics then being designed in Europe in a more cubist version of the style.

385. Parlor interior. Stickley
Brothers Company. Grand Rapids,
Michigan. 1920s. Illustration from
Adapting Quaint Furniture to
American Needs (Grand Rapids,
1925). Private collection

During the early 1920s,
production in Grand Rapids, one
of the major furniture-
manufacturing centers of the world,
emphasized a neocolonial style
exemplified by the Windsor-
influenced pieces in this interior.
The only acknowledgments of the
contemporaneous European
moderne–deco style are the
medallions on the window shades
and the rug on the floor, influenced
by the geometric shapes of cubism.

386. Main hall of New Art Exhibit. Joseph Urban. United States. 1922. Illustration from Good Furniture Magazine (December 1922). Private collection

This is one of the illustrations that accompanied a review of the deco presentation mounted by Joseph Urban at the Art Institute of Chicago. The cubist-influenced rectilinear motif of the chairs is repeated in most of the other accessories in the room.

By the end of the first quarter of the twentieth century, American designers, craftsmen, and manufacturers producing textiles (plates 377, 382), ceramics (plate 381), metals (plates 383, 384), and glass had to some degree assimilated the European deco style. Their appreciation of deco architecture and furniture, nevertheless, was not fully realized until the next decade.

William Laurel Harris, discussing in the December 1922 issue of *Good*

387. Deco illustration. Gordon Conway. United States. 1929. Cover for Eve: The Lady's Pictorial (January 9, 1929). American Institute of Architects Foundation, Washington, D.C.

The original chair that served as the model for this sophisticated magazine cover is now in the Conway archives of the Octagon House, which is an outstanding example of the Federal style in Washington and now a national landmark open to the public as a museum. Conway's moderne chair is a twentieth-century adaptation of an easy—or upholstered wing—chair, a furniture form first created in the late 1600s.

Furniture Magazine how styles had changed drastically in the period of a hundred years, analyzed the striking differences of two current exhibits of house furnishings, one at the Metropolitan Museum of Art in New York devoted to Duncan Phyfe, whose work seemed original a hundred years previously, and the other mounted by Joseph Urban at the Art Institute of Chicago, which included several aspects of the moderne–deco style (plate 386) that would have appeared novel even to the most avant-garde collector. Urban maintained a shop on Fifth Avenue in New York and was intimately familiar with European moderne. He included in the trailblazing exhibition objects that reflected the achievements of designers of the Viennese school as well as other important European centers and supplemented their works with pieces selected from New York showrooms. Harris was enthusiastic about the Urban installations, noting that they would "not appeal to conservative people of established tastes and fashion, but rather to progressive leaders in present-day ideas who feel that in our times there must be progress and perpetual change in decorative arts even as there are in all the arts and sciences." He came to the conclusion that the United States would take a leading role in the development of the modern style:

The great patrons of the new arts have usually been men who have recently made large fortunes, and this was especially true of pre-war Austria. The development of this movement, which began about twenty years ago, was due to the intelligent patronage by the *nouveau riche,* of the work of Viennese artists, especially that pertaining to the varied arts of interior decorating. Today the art patrons of Austria are reduced to abject poverty and further development of this movement is expected to take place in the United States.

The success of the "New Art" movement in the twentieth century starting in Vienna, is international in character, whereas Duncan Phyfe was more or less a provincial imitator of the new art of his day. The "New Art" exhibition in Chicago is almost entirely made up of individual works of art. It is a revolt against the historic styles as shown in our museums, on the one hand, and against factory-made products fabricated in quantity, on the other.

The question now is what this new life and new vitality shown in the Art Institute Exhibition portends, and how far it will lead to more satisfactory achievements in the realm of industrial art. No doubt there were many discussions concerning the changes in furniture making which were initiated by Duncan Phyfe a hundred years ago. There will be, no doubt, even greater discussions and wider differences of opinion concerning the future of the applied arts in the United States today. However, we have an immensely enlarged horizon and tremendously increased resources which offer us endless opportunities for decorative achievements.

In America the art deco style caught the popular imagination during the late 1920s, perhaps because, on a superficial level, the characteristic motifs of sumptuous female nudes, stylishly frolicking gazelles and antelope, and stylized foliage, sun rays, and rainbows uniquely reflected the optimism of the national sense of prosperity and frivolity. Only nine months before the stock market crash, the cover of the January 1929 issue of *Eve: The Lady's Pictorial* (plate 387) was created by American fashion illustrator Gordon Conway, renowned for her design work in many areas. Conway, born into a Texas family of substantial means, received "finishing" in Italy and was the toast of the social season in London at the beginning of World War I. From 1915 to 1920 she worked for Condé Nast, the publisher of *Vogue.* Conway maintained studios in both London and Paris and frequently executed commissions for American manufacturers and designers, pursuing modernism with a vengeance. Conway's cover for *Eve* depicts a serenely sophisticated siren of the period, lounging in a tall-back chair covered in a blazing red fabric.

Vibrant colors, which were typical of objects like that in Conway's cover illustration, made strong decorative statements and were the order of the day. More popular forms, such as deco costume pictures (plate 388), also emphasized a strong but graceful use of color. These items, which were more ephemeral

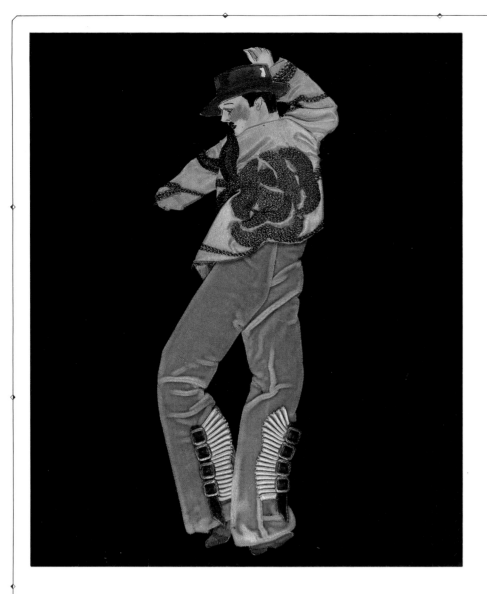

388. Costume pictures. Maker
unknown. United States. 1930–
1935. Paper and velvet, each 16 ×
12". Collection Patricia L.
Coblentz

Costume pictures were introduced
into America from England in the
late seventeenth and early
eighteenth centuries. The earlier
pictures were made by cutting prints
apart and dressing the figures in
fashionable clothes of the day.
During the 1920s and 1930s
young American women in their
idle time created countless similar
pictorial extravaganzas, such as
these Spanish dancers dressed in
pieces of sumptuous fabrics.

389. Buffet. Designed by Eliel Saarinen; manufactured by Tor Berglund. Michigan. 1930. Walnut, ebony, and maple veneer, length 60''. Cranbrook Academy of Art/Museum, Bloomfield Hills, Michigan

This simple but stylish two-door horizontal cabinet on legs, designed for the Saarinen House at Cranbrook, is decorated with geometric designs of inlaid wood.

than other household furnishings, are taken seriously by present-day collectors of art deco.

Many of the best American designers worked within the deco style, and some of the most memorable furniture items, particularly lamps and case pieces, were created by Eliel Saarinen (plates 389, 390), his son Eero, and Paul Theodore Frankl (plate 391). John Vassos, Lynd Ward, and Rockwell Kent were admired for their dynamic book illustrations as were Frankl and Donald Deskey for their stepped skyscraper furniture. Deskey designed that dazzling grand palace of deco—Radio City Music Hall, the crown jewel of Rockefeller Center in New York City. The influence of art deco on American luxury liners and architecture was particularly notable. Another impressive structure in New York that has become synonymous with the style is the Chrysler Building with its tapering geometric design. The new styles also influenced domestic architecture, and numerous deco residences, for the most part grandiose and expensive, but occasionally small (plate 392), were built in this trend-setting mode. The spare, rectilinear lines, sometimes executed as stepped layerings, adorned personal and household accessories—even radios and refrigerators. The decorations on low-slung furniture frequently combined precious ivory, ebony, and lacquer; in addition to man-made materials, exotic design elements utilizing jade, obsidian, and onyx were also fashionable.

Frankl, writing in *Form and Re-Form,* published in New York in 1930, commented on the modern style which had emerged by 1929, observing that new materials demanded new forms and that the values of the twentieth century—"ethical, aesthetical or merely hygienic"—could not be appropriately expressed in a meaningless masquerade of outworn conventions. "No longer do we dress in the stilted styles of the 'nineties. From our houses and our apartments we have banished red-plush ottomans and all dirt-catching fringes. We scorn the dishonesty of architectural styles based on a past which is alien to our country. . . . We are no longer preoccupied with our past. We are piercing the future. . . . Contemporary expression in the decorative arts is the logical and necessary outcome of a new spirit manifest in every phase of American life. This spirit finds expression in skyscrapers, motor-cars, airplanes, in new ocean liners, in department stores and great industrial plants. Speed, compression, directness

390. Floor lamp. Designed by
Eliel Saarinen; manufactured by
Nessen of New York. United
States. c. 1932. Aluminum,
height 67¾". Cranbrook Academy
of Art/Museum, Bloomfield
Hills, Michigan

The visual unity of a purely
functional object is seldom more
satisfying than in Saarinen's
elegant lamp. Made for the
Kingswood School at Cranbrook,
it has three cones flaring outward,
producing a soft, warm glow
of light.

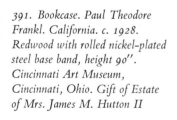

391. Bookcase. Paul Theodore
Frankl. California. c. 1928.
Redwood with rolled nickel-plated
steel base band, height 90".
Cincinnati Art Museum,
Cincinnati, Ohio. Gift of Estate
of Mrs. James M. Hutton II

This skyscraper bookcase, one of
a pair, was illustrated in Frankl's
seminal book on modern decorative
arts, New Dimensions, published
in New York in 1928. He
succinctly summed up the
contemporary trend in his chapter
on furniture: "Meaningless
ornaments should be avoided as
much as possible. Restraint is a
very important factor in modern
design."

392. Deco-style house. Architect unknown. San Francisco, California. c. 1928. Photograph private collection

Few architects have used art deco designs on small residences with such stunning success.

393. Man's den. Joseph Urban. United States. 1929. Installation from The Architect and the Industrial Arts exhibition. Metropolitan Museum of Art, New York City

Reviewing the current exhibition of American contemporary design in the March 1929 issue of the Metropolitan Museum of Art Bulletin, Charles R. Richards described this installation by Joseph Urban in glowing terms: "The fine proportions and severe and strongly articulated wood surfaces of wall cabinet and bookcase, desk and chairs give this small alcove rare distinction and character."

394. Man's study for a country house. Robert T. Walker. United States. 1929. Installation from The Architect and the Industrial Arts exhibition. Metropolitan Museum of Art, New York City

Walker's interior, with its furnishings, was favored by critics because it effectively created the impression of an elegant but sturdy environment. The upper part of the legs of both the chair and the stool incorporates the skyscraper motif, popular at the time. Elegant burled woods and a rich textured carpet add distinction to this fashionable exercise in masculine taste.

395. Room for a Lady. Eliel Saarinen. United States. 1934. Installation from Contemporary American Industrial Art exhibition. Metropolitan Museum of Art, New York City

While most of the furniture in this installation is, to contemporary eyes, unattractive, it was actually a softening of the type of art deco style shown at the Metropolitan in 1929. Comparison between the simplicity of this interior and the complex ornamentation of the earlier exhibition (see plate 393) indicates a growing trend in the early 1930s toward less decoration.

396. Dining room. Donald Deskey. United States. 1934. Installation from Contemporary American Industrial Art exhibition. Metropolitan Museum of Art, New York City

Deskey's dining room features a wall of glass block. First developed at the beginning of the century, glass blocks were not commonly utilized in construction until the 1930s.

397. Candy dish. Designed by
W. M. Mounts; manufactured by
International Silver Company and
Wilcox Silver Plate Company.
Meriden, Connecticut. c. 1928.
Silver-plated, height 3½". Private
collection

There were many variations
within the deco style. Although
beautifully designed and similar to
fine limited-edition objects that
continued to be commissioned or
purchased by affluent collectors,
this candy, or sweeetmeat, dish
was probably mass-produced for
the general market.

—these are its attributes. Freedom, frankness, freshness—these are its fruits."

Frankl also dealt with the development of the steel industry in the United
States and wrote forcefully of the country's greatest contribution to contemporary architecture—the steel skyscraper. He was fascinated with advanced
technology, which would provide a rapid transit system and functional yet
beautiful factories and grain elevators. Frankl realized that he was living in a
machine age and that beauty in furniture and furnishings was now being created
en série (plates 383, 390), a design concept popularized earlier in the century by
Frank Lloyd Wright. Frankl and his contemporaries such as Jacques Darcy,
Donald Deskey, Hunt Diederich, Pola and Wolfgang Hoffmann, Raymond
M. Hood, Ilonka Karasz, A. D. Pickett, Henry Varnum Poor, Winold Reiss,
Gilbert Rohde, Eugene Schoen, and Kem Weber thoroughly absorbed the
European deco style and struck out in bold directions—directions that would
be substantially altered by the devastating effects of financial crisis. The Wall
Street stock market crash on October 24, 1929, seriously curtailed the deco
style in its most sophisticated aspects as practiced by elite architects and interior
designers. Many design firms found economic survival difficult, if not impossible, during the Depression years. At the same time some artists who objected
to ostentation and excess in decoration confused their desire for elegant simplicity with an absolute rejection of decoration.

Throughout the 1920s the museum community carefully watched the new

398. Coffee service. Designed by
W. M. Mounts; manufactured by
International Silver Company and
Wilcox Silver Plate Company.
Meriden, Connecticut. c. 1928.
Silver-plated, overall width 13½".
Private collection

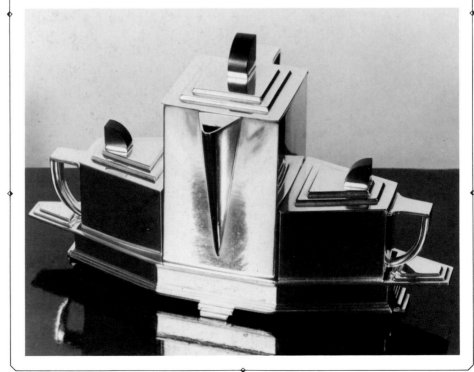

The geometric aspects of the design
of the coffeepot, cream pitcher, and
sugar bowl are especially decorative
and relate to many of the design
precepts being utilized by leading
architects in their new skyscraper
buildings. The finials on this
service are of bakelite, one of the
many man-made materials that came
into vogue in the late 1920s and
early 1930s.

The stylized eagle decorative motif on the bowl of the wine glass is typical of Egyptian-derived designs that were frequently associated with the art deco movement.

style unfold. In 1929 the Metropolitan Museum of Art mounted a special exhibition in their series devoted to contemporary American design and industrial art. This particular exhibition—entitled The Architect and the Industrial Arts—was under the general direction of Finnish architect Eliel Saarinen. Nine architects, preeminent for their exterior and interior designs, were invited to contribute not only the general layout of the galleries but also the interiors (plates 393, 394). Concerned with the most minuscule detail, they were responsible for a total concept in their projects. The museum asked over one hundred fifty companies to furnish objects for the exhibition, which, according to Richard F. Bach who wrote the introduction to the catalog, proved to be a unique stylistic presentation, "favoring no foreign national models, assuring correct use of known materials and logical interpretation of new ones, and serving no gods but those of cooperation between designer and producer, sincere individuality in expression, and reason in design."

In 1934, when the Metropolitan Museum of Art organized another exhibition in the series, under the simple title Contemporary American Industrial Art, it included installations (plates 395, 396) by twenty of America's leading architectural and industrial designers as well as household furnishings manufactured by two hundred companies and individual designers. Many of the objects were grouped to create separate room settings. H. E. Winlock, director of the museum, stated in an introductory note to the accompanying catalog that through a series of exhibitions the Metropolitan hoped to "aid the modern style in arriving at a more definite formulation of principles." He also noted that the contrast between the present exhibition and that of 1929 was the result of stringent economic pressures of the time: "One has only to compare the social and

400. Poster. Nembhard N. Culin. New York City. 1937. Lithograph, 20 × 30″. Nembhard N. Culin, Designer, Vineyard Haven, Massachusetts

The trylon and perisphere, symbols of the 1939 New York World's Fair, dominate this poster—itself an elegant exercise in late deco design—and served as the models for a vast array of trinkets and souvenirs ranging from spoons and plates to paperweights and salt and pepper shakers.

economic picture of 1934 with that of 1929 to understand essential differences in the general character and design of the objects shown. And yet, despite present difficulties, the continuing public interest in contemporary design inspires a steadily increasing number of firms to favor modern expression for objects produced in large volume."

The catalog's main text for the 1934 exhibition, again supplied by Richard F. Bach, further strengthened Winlock's notions about the uses and function of modern design: "Freedom of expression is essential to the growth of style, but even freedom must bow to good sense and good manners. . . . The good sense—that is, the strength and reason—of modernism in design is fully demonstrated, and the promise of good manners—which is its grace and culture—has been kept faithfully and without bluster."

The catalog to this exhibition of industrial art further dealt with quantity production, a term that by this time had come to mean mass production. Quantity production, anticipated by Paul Frankl and even earlier by Frank Lloyd Wright, signified an economic point of view based on the notion that a series of objects derived from a single design had the advantages of lower prices, uniformity, precision, quick delivery, and wide availability. A single object and its duplicate would mean that both objects would cost about the same. The continuation of serial reproduction of a pattern enabled the producer to anticipate and budget his costs and the movement and time entailed in production. Serial manufacture implied a specialized organization not only for the process of design but also for the marketing of it.

The 1934 exhibition assisted in the general acceptance of mass production, for the popular press throughout the nation illustrated objects from the show and wrote extensively about the installations and their contents. These new attitudes toward mass manufacture were part of the reason that design and marketing firms such as Herman Miller, Inc., and Hans Knoll Associates and its subsequent subsidiaries were highly successful in the third and fourth quarters of the century.

In spite of such attitudes, and the proselytizing for the advantages of volume production, handcraftsmanship continued to be demanded by the monied elite. The silver-plate candy dish (plate 397) and coffee service (plate 398) might well be a blending of machine technology carefully finished by artist-craftsmen who specialized in one-of-a-kind or limited-edition products.

The deco style in the United States at its best lasted into the 1940s, when high-quality decorative pieces of glass (plate 399) and metal were being produced for an ever-increasing appreciative market of buyers and collectors. The Libbey Glass Company, always a leader in the field, produced some of the very best American art deco glass. Yet at this time deco-style souvenirs and trinkets that dominated the New York World's Fair in 1939 (plate 400) led to an unending profusion of poorly designed, poorly made, and had-for-cheap objects—all participants in a dime-store parade of functional but uncomely everyday furnishings and decorations. The World's Fair—with its forward-looking optimistic theme, The World of Tomorrow—was a fantasy city crammed with science fiction structures displaying recent technological advances that were promoted as satisfying the dreams of the future. Fair goers had their first glimpse of television on an RCA TRK-12. Enclosed in a gigantic case, this tiny screen could only hint at a technology that would drastically alter American life.

During the 1940s, department stores across the nation were stocked with audiovisual equipment—radios, phonographs, and pioneering television sets—whose designs showed some influence of the streamlined idiom of the previous decade; in the midst of the changing styles there were some genuine throwbacks more than reminiscent of high deco art. The hooked rug (plate 401), although it reflected the style of the 1930s, most likely dates from the 1940s.

From the late 1940s to 1965 the art deco style went out of fashion and was neither produced nor seriously collected. In the early 1960s, however, several international trend-setters began to collect memorabilia from the era between the two wars. Deco was again admired for its modernness—it was the first style that had been totally and successfully mass-produced and it did reveal a unique elegance. The first comprehensive retrospective exhibition of art deco in the

401. Hooked rug. Maker unknown. United States. c. 1935–45. Wool on burlap, 28 × 43." Collection Jay Johnson, New York City

Handmade, popular interpretations of the deco style are relatively rare, for dime stores were filled with inexpensive assembly-line goods that cost less to buy than to make by hand. Very few hooked rugs in the deco manner are known to have been created.

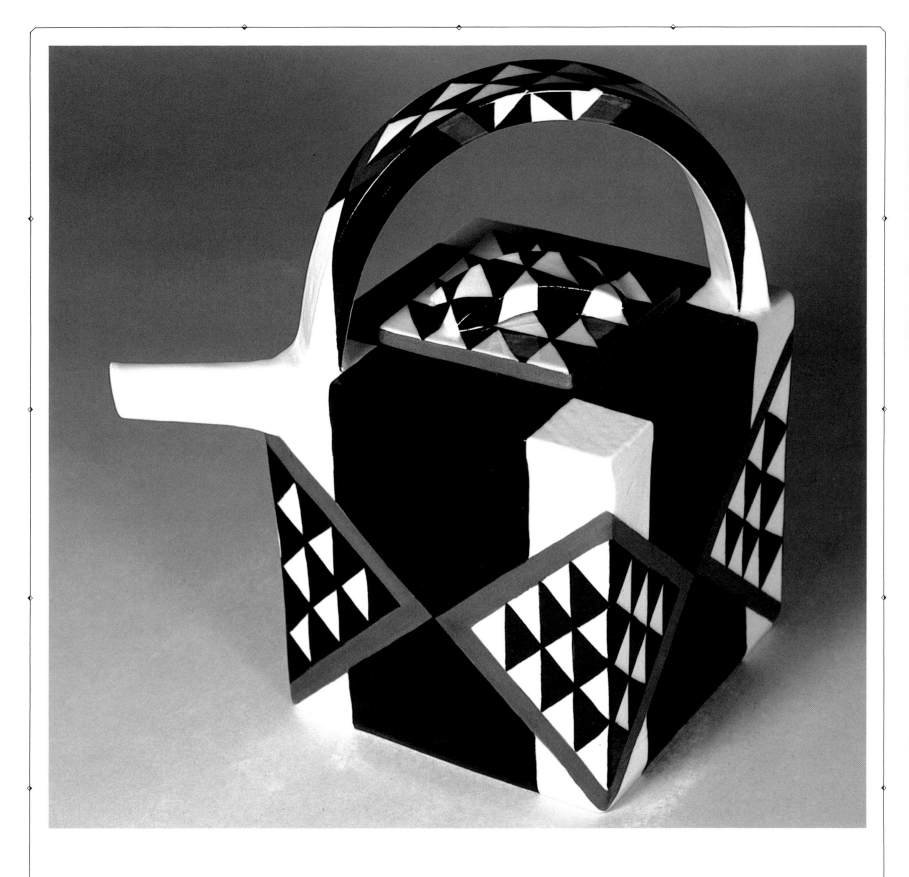

402. Tap Dance. *Kathryn
Sharbaugh. Michigan. 1978.
Porcelain, height 11″.
Private collection*

The form and design of this teapot
are obviously influenced by the
renewed interest in the 1960s and
1970s in decorative objects of the
1920s and 1930s. The designer's
amusing title for this item is also
reminiscent of the earlier era's
popular foot-stomping hits on
Broadway and lavish Hollywood
musicals.

403. *Townhouse facade. Michael Graves. New Jersey. 1978. Three-dimensional model, watercolor on paper, $5\frac{3}{4} \times 10 \times \frac{3}{4}''$ (detail shown). Michael Graves, Architect, Princeton, New Jersey*

Michael Graves has incorporated many elements of deco design, such as Aztec, Egyptian, and geometric motifs, in his proposal, commissioned by French and Company, for the renovation of a New York City townhouse facade. His achievement of sensitive balance is complemented by a subdued palette.

United States was held in 1970 at the Finch College Museum of Art in New York City. The exhibition provided the impetus for a self-conscious revival of deco throughout the 1970s.

Many American architects and designers during the 1970s and 1980s relied on deco prototypes. Plastic lamps in the shape of skyscrapers, bookcases in the shape of pyramids, and ornamental ironwork reminiscent of South American Indian temples were commonplace. Kathryn Sharbaugh's black and white teapot (plate 402) is a successful interpretation of deco created in 1978. Michael Graves's proposal for the renovation of a New York City townhouse facade (plate 403), produced in the same year, exploits many of the characteristic shapes and conceptions of the full-blown style. The pieced quilt (plate 404), assembled in 1980 by Nancy Crow, also borrows geometric and linear patterns from the earlier style. Crow is one of the most important textile artists working in the United States today and has spent considerable time mastering advanced weaving techniques, but she is also an accomplished ceramic artist as well.

The moderne–deco movement of the 1920s and 1930s had marked the end of traditional influences and the beginning of a new emphasis on the union of art and industry. There was a gradual acceptance of functional forms and the use of modern industrial materials, signaling the importance of the manufactured object in everyday life. The architects were not the leaders of the movement; rather the graphic designers, craftsmen, and fashion stylists were the ones concerned with decorative style and taste. The architectural phase of the modern movement found its expression in the austere framework slabs and the great glass curtains of the new international style.

404. Bittersweet III. *Nancy Crow. Ohio. 1980. Fabric, 39 × 39''. Nancy Crow, Baltimore, Ohio*

The artist's admiration for deco works is strongly expressed in this beautifully designed pieced quilt. Like so many artist-designers who create decorative accessories, Nancy Crow's background is in crafts.

The International Style
◆ 1930~1980 ◆

Although the moderne–deco style represents one aspect of modernism in terms of American design in the twentieth century, the rigid geometric eccentricities of this mode did not appeal to a large conservative population. Vague adaptations of historical styles, represented most notably by the colonial revival, provided a continuity with the past that was safe for those who, lacking the exposure to good design, were unable to form a critical evaluation of new trends. After World War I when communication among architects was reestablished, styles spread quickly from country to country and it was no longer pertinent to speak of national styles. There were two important principles of the new architecture. The first was the elimination of the bearing wall—a radical step made possible by the introduction of the structural steel skeleton. The second was the creation of style through the proportioning of solid form and space and by avoiding applied decoration.

Louis Sullivan, now considered the prophet of modern style in architecture, had an important influence on these two developments. His naturalistic decorative vocabulary and his identification with the aesthetics of early sky-scrapers presaged the huge concrete and glass buildings that became the epit-ome of the international style in the twentieth century. Sullivan's 1890 Wain-wright Building in Saint Louis, constructed of terra cotta and glass hung on an iron skeleton, was designed so as not to disguise its structural framework. Its

405. Barcelona chairs with matching stool and couch. Ludwig Mies van der Rohe. Germany. First introduced 1929–31. Stainless steel and leather, height of chair 30″. Knoll International, New York City

International-style furniture has always been popular with architects and designers. This interior from the glass house of the American architect Philip Johnson, built in 1949 in New Canaan, Connecticut, is furnished with Mies van der Rohe furniture. The Barcelona chair—introduced in 1929 at the International Exposition in Barcelona and now manufactured by Knoll International—is regarded as the most beautiful chair of the twentieth century. The matching stool was introduced in the same year, and the couch in 1931. The stainless steel has a polished finish and is upholstered with saddle leather straps that hold foam rubber cushions covered in top-grain leather. The foam rubber is a substitute for the original cotton, burlap, and horsehair fill.

406. Cesca side chair.
Designed by Marcel Breuer; first
manufactured by Gebrüder Thonet.
Germany. 1928. Polished-chrome
tubular steel with wood frame and
handwoven cane, height 31½".
Knoll International,
New York City

Breuer, a student at the Bauhaus
and later master of its furniture
workshop, considered the chair one
of the most important furniture
forms. The Cesca chair, a
cantilever chair, consisting of a
bent tubular steel frame and
caning, was designed by Breuer
soon after he left the Bauhaus.

407. Wassily lounge chair.
Designed by Marcel Breuer; first
manufactured by Standard-Möbel
or Gebrüder Thonet. Germany.
1925. Polished tubular steel
and canvas, height 22⅛".
Reclining chair. Designed by
Marcel Breuer; first manufactured
by Isokon Furniture Company.
England. 1935. Laminated beech
plywood with synthetic stretch
upholstery, height 31½".
Both Knoll International,
New York City

Breuer's work in both wood and
tubular steel demonstrates clarity
of structure and form. Knoll
International acquired the rights to
produce both chairs, along with the
Cesca chair (see plate 406), and
for several decades they were
among the company's most
successful offerings in America.
The club or lounge chair—
marketed as the Wassily chair
from about 1960 and named for
the Russian painter Wassily
Kandinsky—was Breuer's first
tubular-steel chair.

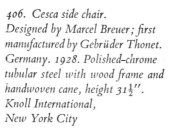

Rohde's conviction that people are more important than furniture and that furniture should not compete with an individual's activities has assured a continuing popularity of his innovative designs. His concern is not with trends and the exigencies of the marketplace but the basic needs within the home and business environments.

masterful relationship of form to function served as a criterion for later tall metal framed buildings hung with curtains of tinted glass.

Born in Boston, Sullivan studied at the Massachusetts Institute of Technology and the Ecole des Beaux-Arts in Paris; on his return to the United States he entered into partnership with the Chicago architect Dankmar Adler. In the final years of the nineteenth century there was a strong revival of traditional classicism led by C. F. McKim, which overshadowed Sullivan's advocacy of an architecture that would be functional and inherently American. Integrating romanticism with realism, Sullivan emancipated architectural thinking from hidebound convention. His Transportation Building at the 1893 World's Columbian Exposition, which was otherwise dominated by fin de siècle academicism, heralded a new viewpoint.

In the United States the visible concentration of austere framework slabs surrounded by an expanse of glass first occurred on Madison Avenue and Park

409. Marshmallow love seat. Designed by George Nelson; manufactured by Herman Miller, Inc. Michigan. 1956. Metal and foam, length 52". Herman Miller Archives, Zeeland, Michigan

Nelson, who built up a new image for Herman Miller through his involvement with corporate graphics and merchandising, also introduced many innovations in his own designs.

410. Dining and lounge chairs. Designed by Charles Eames; manufactured by Herman Miller, Inc. Michigan. 1946. Laminated molded plywood and steel, height 29½". Herman Miller Archives, Zeeland, Michigan

Throughout his career Eames was fascinated with the new possibilities for furniture design that have resulted from advanced technology.

Avenue in New York City, the cultural capital of the nation. Buildings erected in the international style, which has spread to nearly every other city and town throughout the country, rely upon simplicity and boldness of execution and have the added feature of being relatively inexpensive to construct.

While the work of Bauhaus teachers and students had great influence on late deco, it was also one of the fountainheads for the international style. The purpose of the educational process at the Bauhaus was to deny the nineteenth-century practice of isolating the artist from the technically expert craftsman and to train students to be equally effective in both areas. In April 1919 Walter Gropius issued a manifesto—included in *Bauhaus and Bauhaus People* edited in 1970 by Eckhard Neumann—in which he outlined many of the goals he hoped to achieve through the school:

Architects, sculptors, painters, we must all turn to the crafts! Art is not a "profession." There is no essential difference between the artist and the craftsman. The artist is an exalted craftsman. In rare moments of inspiration, moments beyond the control of his will, the grace of heaven may cause his work to blossom into art. But proficiency in his craft is essential to every artist. Therein lies a source of creative imagination.

Let us create a new guild of craftsmen, without the class distinctions which raise an arrogant barrier between craftsman and artist. Together let us conceive and create the new building of the future, which will embrace architecture and sculpture and painting in one unity and which will rise one day toward heaven from the hands of a million workers, like the crystal symbol of a new faith.

During their initial years Bauhaus workshops were taught by two instructors—a craftsman and an artist. As the school developed its own teachers, each

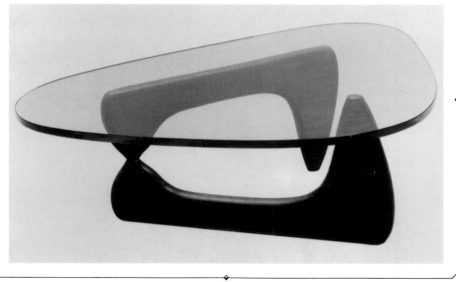

411. Coffee table. Designed by Isamu Noguchi; manufactured by Herman Miller, Inc. Michigan. 1950. Walnut and glass, diameter 50". Herman Miller Archives, Zeeland, Michigan

Noguchi's predilection for abstract forms in his sculpture is much in evidence in his textile and theater designs and it extended to furniture as well. This handsome wood and glass table is not only remarkable as a sculpture-for-use piece but also as a design to be produced commercially.

412. Action Office 2. Designed by Robert Propst and staff; manufactured by Herman Miller, Inc. Michigan. 1968. Metal, oak veneer, and plywood with plastic covering. Herman Miller Archives, Zeeland, Michigan

Much of the best furniture of the twentieth century has been created by architect-designers and was originally intended to be used in office buildings. Because it is so functional and beautiful, this furniture has found a significant place in the American home. Propst's Action Office has also been sold for domestic use.

workshop was led by only one trained artist-craftsman. Students completed a full three-year apprenticeship which consisted of a six-month preparatory course and then two and a half years in various training workshops where practical instruction was emphasized. The Bauhaus published its own books, pamphlets, and quarterly periodical. Many of these were translated into English; consequently their effect upon avant-garde American design was considerable.

The Bauhaus exerted an unprecedented influence in the fields of architecture and the industrial arts and gave the artist a definite position in the world of industrial production as designer and specialized technician. Bauhaus design tended toward nonobjective geometric art as practiced by the Dutch painter Piet Mondrian and his followers. In time the school became increasingly open to the influence of nearly every art movement flourishing at the time. Besides Gropius, the most important workers associated with the Bauhaus were the German architect Ludwig Mies van der Rohe, the German sculptor and painter Oskar Schlemmer, the Hungarian designer, typographer, and painter László Moholy-Nagy, and various artists who were noted primarily as painters, including Paul Klee from Switzerland, Lyonel Feininger from the United States, and Wassily Kandinsky from Russia. The Hungarian Marcel Breuer studied architecture, carpentry, and design at the school and upon graduation was appointed master of the furniture workshop.

The townspeople of Weimar failed to appreciate the work of the Bauhaus, and there were frequent attacks by the press and public. The state senate withdrew its support on the pretext that the school was socialistic and anarchistic,

413. Cabinet, oval table-desk, and lounge chair. Designed by Florence Knoll; manufactured by Knoll International. United States. Cabinet introduced in 1950, desk in 1961, chair in 1962. Wood and steel, length of cabinet 75⅜", length of desk 78", height of chair 30". Knoll International, New York City

Florence Knoll is admired for her ability to reduce furniture to its most elementary form and at the same time achieve luxurious comfort. The polished-steel base and rosewood veneer table-desk was originally conceived as an office piece; however, it has found a comfortable niche in American homes. The chair is made of parallel steel bars with handwoven wool upholstery, and the cabinet is walnut veneer with plastic laminate front panels.

414. *Pedestal chair. Designed by Eero Saarinen; manufactured by Knoll International. United States. 1956. Molded plastic with cast metal base, height 32¾". Knoll International, New York City*

The graceful plastic shells of Saarinen's pedestal chairs revolutionized American concepts of interior decoration when they were introduced in the 1950s. Saarinen's molded plastic pieces are frequently imitated today.

and it was dissolved in 1925 and reformed at Dessau, where innovative administrative, educational, and residential buildings were designed by Gropius. The Bauhaus quarters at Dessau, which were to make it famous, represented a culmination in the formation of the modern movement in architecture. Gropius resigned in 1928 and later, in 1930, was succeeded by Mies van der Rohe. The school was located in Dessau until 1932, when it was forced to shut down by the German National Socialist government because it was reputed to be a center of communist political activity. It moved to Berlin, but was closed permanently by the Nazis the following year.

Although the school produced fewer than five hundred graduates by the time of its closing in 1933, it was the wellspring of the progressive attitudes of modern design. The United States profited substantially from the closing of the Bauhaus when many of its leaders and students moved there to practice as architects and designers and teach at several important American universities and design institutes. Moholy-Nagy founded the New Bauhaus in Chicago, which later became the Institute of Design. Josef Albers became professor of art at Black Mountain College in North Carolina. Mies joined the staff of the Armour Institute (now known as the Illinois Institute of Technology) in Chicago. Gropius and Breuer were appointed to the School of Design at Harvard, their students including I. M. Pei and Paul Rudolph. Breuer's insistence that students not confine themselves to a specific traditional style but develop their own ideas had a great influence on a whole generation of American architects.

Mies van der Rohe's master plan for the Illinois Institute of Technology campus, the Cullinan Hall and Brown Pavilion at the Museum of Fine Arts in

The Bertoia collection, introduced by Knoll in 1952, included several innovative chairs that provided supreme comfort. While creating variations on his sculpture, Harry Bertoia realized they suggested new forms for chairs and new methods of manufacture. He has noted that when looking at his chairs, the viewer has the distinct impression that space passes through them—like his sculpture, they seem to be made of air. Working in his studio in Bally, Pennsylvania, Bertoia is surrounded by his sculpture and welded steel-wire chairs.

Houston, and the Seagram Building in New York City are monuments of modern design. Although best known for his office and commercial buildings, his apartment buildings at 860 and 880 Lake Shore Drive in Chicago have served as a model for residences designed by countless less innovative competitors.

One of the classic designs in modern furnishings is the Barcelona chair, an elegant metal and leather seating piece that Mies created as an original design for the German pavilion at the 1929 International Exposition in Barcelona. It represents a modern interpretation of the old Roman curule form. The distinguished American architect Philip Johnson chose furniture designed by Mies for his own home (plate 405), including the Barcelona chair and the couch of walnut, stainless steel, and leather upholstery, the latter introduced at the Berlin Building Exposition in 1931.

Breuer's work in both Europe and the United States had a considerable influence on American decorative arts and was celebrated in a 1981 retrospective exhibition at New York's Museum of Modern Art. He achieved fame for the Cesca side chair (plate 406) and particularly for the Wassily lounge chair (plate 407)—a tubular metal chair inspired by the handlebars of his bicycle. The Wassily chair, introduced in 1925, was the first chair made entirely of bent

Platner's tables range from a massive piece designed for dining, which has thicker steel rods than his other tables, to smaller ones with tops in walnut, teak, or rosewood. The bases on the coffee tables are finished with nickel or dark copper, and the tops can be purchased in plate glass, teak, rosewood, or walnut. The Platner concept of design—binding sheaves of metal together to form a base—has also been applied to side chairs, armchairs, stools, sofas, and settees.

417. *Chair. Sam Maloof. United States. 1950. Black walnut with leather seat, height 30½″. Collection Sam Maloof, Alta Loma, California*

The Danish modern furnishings created by Hans J. Wegner for Knoll International inspired many craftsmen, including Sam Maloof, who produces exquisitely honed furniture on a limited-production basis, such as this black walnut chair with sculptured back.

tubular steel, thus revolutionizing modern furniture design. Breuer left the Bauhaus in 1928, working first in Berlin and then moving to England, where the reclining chair (plate 407) was introduced in 1935 and manufactured by the Isokon Furniture Company. (This chair and other Breuer designs are now manufactured by Knoll International.) He is best known in America for his work done under the partnership of Marcel Breuer and Walter Gropius and then under Marcel Breuer and Associates. Breuer's furniture demonstrates clarity of structure, form, and visual balance. He believed that a piece of furniture is not an arbitrary item but a significant and necessary component of the environment. It takes on meaning only from the way it is used or as a part of a complete scheme. Breuer was not only a sensitive artist, but an author of substantial power, and his books and other writings have done much to disseminate information about modern design concepts.

Of the few firms preeminent in developing a modern consciousness of American decorative arts, that of Herman Miller was one of the most daring and innovative. The company was established in Zeeland, Michigan, in 1923 when Dirk Jan De Pree, Herman Miller, and a group of associates purchased the Michigan Star Furniture Company and renamed it Herman Miller Furniture Company. De Pree, a native of Michigan, was appointed manager, and under his skilled eye quality furniture in traditional styles was the primary stock-in-trade. With the crash of the stock market in 1929, many furniture companies folded. Sensing the practical implications of the European moderne–deco movement, De Pree hired the artist-designer Gilbert Rohde in 1931 to develop a new line that would satisfy consumers who wanted stylish multipurpose furniture—with added space-saving qualities—at modest prices.

De Pree's anticipation of future needs in the area of industrial arts led to intense innovation in both design and technology. At the 1933–34 Chicago

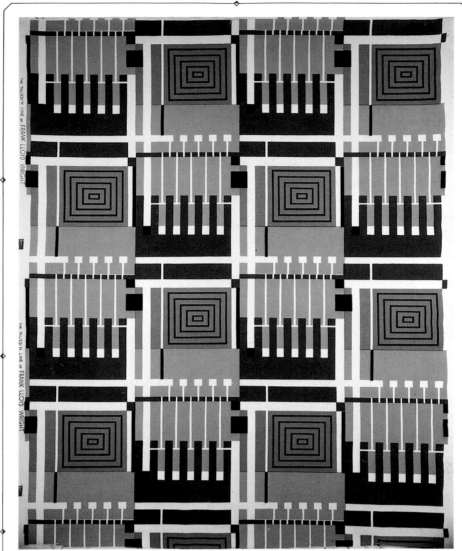

418. Fabric. Designed by Frank Lloyd Wright; manufactured by F. Schumacher and Company. New York. 1955. Linen, width 50″. F. Schumacher and Company, New York City (photograph E. P. Dutton and Company)

Wright's excursion into decorative arts design earmarked for mass production and distribution was not overly successful. His furniture for the North Carolina firm of Heritage-Henredon failed to meet the test of time, and because of its structural weaknesses little of it remains today. His Taliesin line of fabrics for Schumacher had a greater appeal.

World's Fair, entitled A Century of Progress, Herman Miller furniture, which was designed by Rohde and set up to approximate a model home, generated great excitement. By 1934 De Pree and Rohde knew that their design instincts were headed in the right direction, and they began to phase out the traditional styles that had previously been the mainstay of the company.

In *A Modern Consciousness*—published in 1975 on the occasion of an exhibition at the Renwick Gallery in Washington, D.C., celebrating the work of Florence Knoll and D. J. De Pree in gaining international acceptance for modern design in furniture—De Pree discussed the vision that he and Gilbert Rohde

419. Cow Wallpaper. Andy Warhol. New York. 1966. Silkscreen inks on wallpaper, image area 44 × 30″. Castelli Gallery, New York City (photograph O K Harris Works of Art)

Warhol followed his stunning gallery installation of Cow Wallpaper *seven years later with* Mao Wallpaper, *intended to serve as the background for an exhibition of Mao silkscreen paintings in the Castelli Gallery. The result was wall-to-wall Mao—1,951 times.*

420. Living–dining room area.
Robert Mayers and Michael Schiff.
New York City. 1969. Slogan
Residence, New York City
(photograph Norman McGrath)

Light plays an important part in
the overall design of this
cooperative apartment interior by
Mayers and Schiff, which was
created by removing several walls to
make a large room 60 by 20 feet.
All of the light in the room is in
the canopy and is controlled by
dimmers. The owners' living style
included extensive entertaining,
and they used neon light to create
an upbeat mood for their parties.
The Zographos chairs are chrome
and leather. The two squares
affixed to the wall are really
leaves, which can be removed and
used to extend the table.

421. Showroom installation.
Gary Gutterman. New York.
1980. Acrylic, length of consoletable
104″, height of chair 26″.
Gary Gutterman, Monmouth
Beach, New Jersey. Axius Design
Collection

Acrivue, a registered trademark,
is a highly developed acrylic of
great strength which is used to
create avant-garde furniture.
Gutterman's pieces are simple and
are modulated by the movement of
light.

422. Old Westbury House.
Richard Meier. New York.
1969–71. Richard Meier and
Associates, Architects, New York
City (photographs Ezra Stoller ©
ESTO)

Richard Meier's approach to
functional open space has earned
him an international reputation.
His complex buildings, such as the
Old Westbury steel frame house
with wood and glass skin, are
machines for living that give the
impression of ultimate simplicity.
The interplay of form and volume
within the interior takes place
within a rigidly organized
structural system in which the
columns are a constant rhythm.
With the vertical load distributed
to the steel framework, the outside
walls perform the simple function
of articulation and illumination.

423. Grouping of RLM lamps.
Original designer unknown.
United States. 1980. Porcelain
on metal, various dimensions.
Harry Gitlin, Inc., New
York City

RLM lighting fixtures, one of the
trademarks of the 1970s high-tech
style, are comfortable appointments
in large areas such as factories,
lofts, and spacious townhouses or
even in modest contemporary
apartments.

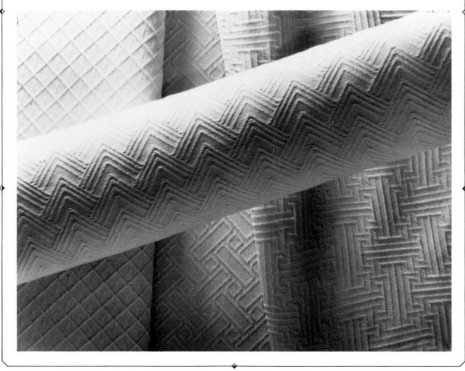

424. Upholstery textiles.
Stroheim and Romann. New
York. 1979. Cotton, width 54″.
Stroheim and Romann, New
York City

Since the 1950s, there has been a
consistent move toward simplicity
in textile design. The taste for
bold prints on upholstered furniture
has diminished substantially, and
fabrics with a distinct woven
pattern, created during
manufacture, are currently the most
popular.

shared in finding ways of improving the quality of contemporary life through
honesty of design and materials:

We came to believe that faddish styles and early obsolescence are forms of design immo-
rality, and that good design improves quality and reduces cost because it achieves long
life, which makes for repeatable manufacturing. By good design, I mean design that is
simple and honest. Materials should be used properly—wood should be treated as wood,
plastic as plastic, and metal as metal. Things should look like what they are, with no fak-
ery, no finishes to simulate the patina of age, and no surface embellishment other than
the material itself properly finished.

The Herman Miller company, featuring the first of many furniture systems
designed by Rohde, opened its Chicago showroom in the Merchandise Mart
in 1939. Consisting of desk tops, pedestals, and drawers that could be combined
in over 450 different ways, the designs were an immense success. Not only did
a great number of business executives purchase the system for office use, but
avant-garde decorators also adapted it to their most prestigious commissions
for home interiors. The senior executive desk (plate 408), introduced in 1940,
was constructed of walnut veneer.

Two years after Rohde's death in 1944, George Nelson, an architect noted
for his tenacious belief in integrity of design and technological innovation,

In the past several decades American artist-craftsmen have played an increasing role in home decoration. Their works of art often serve as decorative accessories. Ceramics in the abstract manner traditionally have been considered more suitable in starkly designed interiors.

joined the company as its leading designer (plate 409). Nelson brought the designs and textiles of Charles Eames, Alexander Girard, and Isamu Noguchi to Herman Miller. Nelson himself scored a big success for Herman Miller in 1958, when he introduced a comprehensive storage system—a series of shelves, work surfaces, and storage units that could be suspended from vertical aluminum poles. This forerunner of all pole-suspended furniture excited international interest, and creative designers throughout the world were attracted to the firm and its experimental work in the development of furniture systems.

No single Miller product has achieved the popular attention accorded the molded plywood chair of Charles Eames (plate 410)—aptly given the humor-

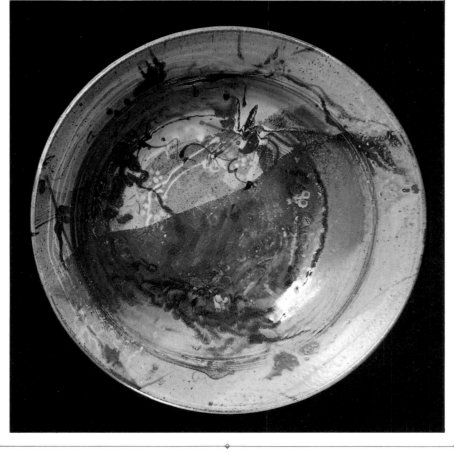

John Glick, at the Plum Tree Pottery in Farmington, Michigan, produces some of the most aesthetically appealing American ceramics today. This impressive piece is decorated with multiple slips and glazes in an abstract design.

ous appellation of potato chip chair—which was introduced in 1946. The concept for this piece may have originated during World War II while Eames was designing for the United States Navy special-support equipment for war-injured personnel. At the time he was experimenting with molded plywood techniques, which he would utilize throughout his career. He was also one of the first designers to use fiberglass and reinforced plastic for seating pieces.

Eames was a proverbial Renaissance man, an internationally recognized furniture designer, architect, teacher, filmmaker, and inventor. His experiments with materials led to many innovations in twentieth-century decorative arts. In 1961 he introduced a new method of cushioning reinforced plastic chairs by spraying foam-producing liquids directly over each chair's plastic shell and under its upholstery cover. This technique eliminated the need to build up layers of hand-applied padding and today is employed extensively by furniture manufacturers. Although Eames worked with Eero Saarinen and several other major architects, his design preference was furniture making. In an article on Charles Eames in *The Cranbrook Magazine* (Autumn 1971), Saul Pett quotes Eames's interesting analogies comparing filmmaking or writing to furniture design, which throws light on his decision to concentrate on design rather than on architecture: "I guess I'm a cop-out. Designing a whole building is just too demanding of attention to keep the basic concept from disintegrating. Builders, prices, materials, so many things work toward lousing it up. I've chosen to do things which one can attack and better control as an individual. Furniture design or a film, for example, is a small piece of architecture one man can handle. It's like the difference between a writer who takes something toward its logical conclusion and the poet who takes it to its ultimate conclusion."

The furniture in the Herman Miller Collection by the distinguished American sculptor and theater designer Isamu Noguchi shows the same characteristics as his other designs for industry—finely proportioned shapes that are logically planned for production. The large coffee table (plate 411) has complete stability so that the heavy plate glass top can be supported without any connectors.

By 1960 Herman Miller had expanded its research capabilities, and under the guidance of Robert Propst modern methods of creating entire furniture systems were developed. Units were designed with interchangeable components that could be arranged in numerous ways for maximum convenience to the user (plate 412). While furniture of this type was designed predominantly for offices, the efficiency of the Propst units applies to domestic use as well.

Primary among Herman Miller's competitors is Knoll International. Hans Knoll came to America from Germany in 1939 and established a furniture design firm under the name Knoll Associates. Florence Schust joined the staff in 1943 and a year later married Knoll. Schust, like De Pree, was born in Michigan, where she attended Cranbrook Academy of Art and worked under Eliel Saarinen; later she studied under Mies van der Rohe at the Illinois Institute of Technology.

Upon her marriage, Florence Knoll became a full partner in the company, and through her efforts the Knoll Planning Unit was established for the purpose of handling well-defined interior design operations. Her pieces were perhaps the most innovative of all modern furniture, for they were the simplest (plate 413). Relying on steel supporting parts, her minimal approach to functional furniture eliminated storage compartments and file drawers on executive desks. She felt that these appurtenances were unnecessary because the main activity of executives involved conferences and not the day-to-day close work of filing and other routine office chores. She pioneered the use of oval and round shapes—while also including rectangular desks—because curves are conducive to a more relaxed atmosphere.

Florence Knoll was instrumental in introducing many international architects and designers to the Knoll firm, including Eero Saarinen and Marcel Breuer and the artist Harry Bertoia, and she inspired them to create designs that showed a skillful balance between traditional styles and the more radical innovations of the international style. The designs of Mies, which have been of prime importance in twentieth-century decorative arts, were produced extensively by Knoll International almost since they were first conceived.

Saarinen, son of noted architect and designer Eliel Saarinen, was born in Finland and was brought to America as a teen-ager. He became a naturalized citizen in 1940. Some of his architectural and furniture projects were accomplished in conjunction with his father and with Charles Eames. Eero Saarinen is perhaps best known for his pedestal table and pedestal chair (plate 414), designed in 1956. Like all great furniture, the chair is structurally complete, support and seating section creating a visually harmonious and organic whole. Saarinen felt that he wanted to make the chair a complete unit once again, and the simple sculptural shape of the gracefully molded plastic shell of the chair is timeless in concept.

Bertoia is best known for his experimental furniture built upon welded steel wire and steel rod frames (plate 415). Born in Italy, he too went to America at an early age. He received his early training in painting, sculpture, mechanical drawing, and metalcraft in the School of Arts and Crafts at Detroit. After graduation, he attended Cranbrook Academy of Art, where he later taught painting and metalcraft. His affiliation with Knoll Associates began in 1950 when Hans and Florence Knoll persuaded him to establish a studio-barn in eastern Pennsylvania near one of the Knoll factories, and allowed him the freedom to do whatever he liked. Bertoia's attempt to combine technology and aesthetics is best summarized by his own words quoted in the catalog for an exhibition, Knoll au Louvre, held in 1972 at the Musée des Arts Décoratifs in Paris:

In the sculpture I am concerned primarily with space, form and the characteristics of metal. In the chairs many functional problems have to be satisfied first . . . but when you get right down to it, the chairs are studies in space, form and metal, too.

The sculpture is made up of a lot of little units, and these rectangles or hexagons or triangles are added together and produce one large rectangle or hexagonal sculpture. The same with the chairs. The chair has a lot of little diamond shapes in its wire cage, and they all add up to one very large diamond shape, and this is the shape of the whole chair. It is really an organic principle, like a cellular structure.

Everybody is a specialist now. I am trying to take in as much of the world as I can. . . . I try to find out as much as possible about anything I do . . . and sometimes the thing I think has no purpose at all, like my sculpture, turns out to be actually very useful.

My approach to design is to make the environment more pleasant and varied by merging the efforts of technology and the creative arts.

Hans Knoll died in an automobile accident in 1955, and Florence Knoll assumed the presidency of all three Knoll divisions—Knoll Associates, Knoll Textiles, and Knoll International. Her first order of business was to move forward with a continuing international expansion. While president, she utilized her superior knowledge of the design craft and became a perceptive leader and tastemaker. The direction of the company reflected her confidence as a designer and architect and indicated the richness of her personal aesthetic judgment. In 1959 she retired from primary leadership and became a design consultant for the firm after it was sold to Art Metal, Inc.

In 1967 Knoll International became a subsidiary of Walter E. Heller International, a Chicago financial firm. Yet the Knoll firm retained autonomy in all areas relating to manufacturing and design and continues to be a world leader through the work of its many American designers, such as Richard Schultz, Don Albinson, William Stephens, Andrew Morrison, Bruce Hannah, and Warren Platner.

Platner's work is daring in concept. His furniture is constructed on a steel wire frame and is often compared to the work of Bertoia. Platner's designs, however, are quite different because the parallel lines of the metalwork create a graphic picket fence illusion. During the development of his handsome chairs, tables, and stools, the designer visited several fabricators of steel wire. He experimented with tying wires like sheaves of wheat instead of meshing them as Bertoia did. The bases of Platner's tables (plate 416) are graceful concave

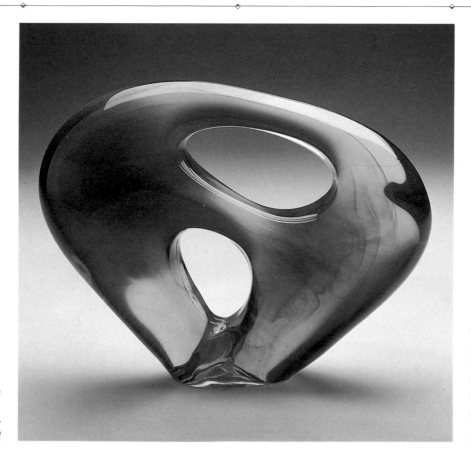

429. Spacial Movement.
Domenick Labino. Ohio. 1970.
Glass, width 8½". Cincinnati Art
Museum, Cincinnati, Ohio.
Jane Thomson Herschede
Memorial

The form of this hot-glass
sculpture is similar to the coffee
table designed by Isamu Noguchi
(see plate 411). While the fine
arts in the 1970s moved away
from abstraction, decorative artists
became increasingly fascinated by
the freedoms that it offered.

431. *Vase and bowl. Douglas Steakley. California. 1980. Silver-plated brass, height of vase 7½″; copper raised with oxide finish, height of bowl 4½″. Douglas Steakley, Carmel, California*

Artist-craftsmen today, resenting the sameness of mass-produced objects, have once again rebelled against machine technology. Douglas Steakley's handcrafted vase and bowl are sensitively shaped and beautifully proportioned works of art.

OPPOSITE:

430. *Vase and bowl. John Lewis. California. 1980. Blown glass, height of bowl 9″. John Lewis, Oakland, California*

In his Oakland studio Lewis creates brilliant blown-glass pieces that are technically the equal of the best of Tiffany favrile glass at the turn of the century.

432. *"Popsycle" table. Dan Droz. United States. 1981. Natural oak with glass top, height 27". Beylerian Limited, New York City*

Dan Droz's table—with its polyurethane-finish base comprising legs in the form of ice cream sticks—offers a glimpse of one trend that may dominate the 1980s: it is a handsome piece of furniture with a lighthearted, sophisticated touch. Since the base folds up compactly, the table is ideal for homes and apartments that have limited space. The glass top provides a clear view of the intricate pedestal.

cylinders of wire stalks. The spacing between each wire is a subtle innovation: the furniture visually contains all the space it defines and yet allows an open view of the entire structure.

Knoll's purchase of the Italian company Gavina in 1968 added to its already substantial leadership in the market. The most avant-garde modern furniture designs complement pieces first produced at the Weimar Bauhaus in the early 1930s which have become classics. Rights to the designs of the Danish craftsman Hans J. Wegner have also expanded and diversified the Knoll offerings.

During the 1940s and 1950s there was a great demand for furnishings in what became generally known as the Danish modern style. Danish design has exercised one of the greatest single influences on recent American interior furnishings. Yet the enthusiastic and uncritical acceptance in the United States of spare Danish forms seems to have been based on an aesthetic misunderstanding. In Denmark this extremely simple furniture was set against a cluttered background, producing a warm cozy atmosphere not unlike the self-conscious casual disorder of some Victorian interiors. Scandinavian furniture runs the gamut of materials from the Danish handmade wooden furniture of Wegner and Poul Cadovius to the industrialized products in metal and plastic of Verner Panton.

The most famous of Danish modern designs—Wegner's so-called round chair, introduced in 1949—was developed after Wegner spotted a Chinese child's chair on display in a Copenhagen museum. The round chair was first roughed by machine and then finished by skilled craftsmen using traditional cabinetmaking techniques, which limited the production to three a day. Wegner and the whole Danish modern movement inspired several American furniture makers to work in a similar manner—particularly the California designer-craftsman Sam Maloof, who, on a commission basis, fashions limited-production one-of-a-kind pieces for home and office. Although his subtle straight-lined chairs (plate 417) are totally original in concept, they have a quality reminiscent of the American Windsor. The purity of Maloof's designs and the great skill he demonstrates in their execution have earned him a deserved reputation as one of the leading American creators of fine handcrafted home furnishings.

During the 1930s and 1940s while Americans were being influenced substantially by European immigrants working in the Bauhaus and international styles, America's own creative genius, Frank Lloyd Wright—who had spent much of his early career producing designs for the decorative arts—had turned to architecture as his primary focus. He was an ardent opponent of the international style and wrote profusely in the cause of his own organic architecture. At mid-century, however, Wright again concerned himself with interior furnishings when he designed wallpaper and textiles (plate 418) for the New York firm of F. Schumacher and Company and furniture for the Heritage-Henredon Furniture Company in Morganton, North Carolina. The November 1955 issue of *House Beautiful* announced the Taliesin Ensemble with the enticing caption: "And now Frank Lloyd Wright designs home furnishings you can buy!" Through the years Wright had designed furnishings for the homes of his clients, but generally they were intended to be handcrafted on a limited-production basis. The Heritage-Henredon and Schumacher lines were his first major efforts in the mass market area. The furniture was an alternative to the typical commercial patterns available at the time. Wright's furnishings were not particularly well designed, yet they enjoyed a substantial vogue with those who were attracted to the famous name of the designer.

Many critics were not particularly enthusiastic about Wright's furniture for Heritage-Henredon. The author of an article in the October 18, 1955, issue of the *Chicago Daily News* felt that there was a confusion about his newest efforts:

We're not used to seeing velvet upholstery on modern furniture and Wright has used it on some occasional chairs. It reminds many people of the poorly designed velvet chair grandmother kept in her parlor, the one nobody dared use. You couldn't put Frank Lloyd Wright's furniture in a stark, sterile, "less is more" structure of glass and steel by Ludwig Mies van der Rohe. But you could put this rather sensuous furniture in any of the thousands of "ranch houses," bilevels and trilevels that have sprouted up since World War II. Wright's furniture would add something special to each.

Many of Wright's fabrics for Schumacher were designed to complement the new line of furniture. Several were brightly printed on Belgian linen, and obviously Wright hoped that they would provide a lively contrast to the earth tones of his furniture. The printed designs were conceived as two-dimensional surface patterns, acknowledging the flat nature of the material. Wallpapers that matched some of the fabrics were also produced by Schumacher.

Wallpaper design has attracted many artists during the twentieth century. Andy Warhol, one of America's most controversial artists, relied upon his obsession with the repeated single image when he designed *Cow Wallpaper* (plate 419) as a 1966 gallery installation at the Castelli Gallery in New York City. At the time the boldness of the design was unexpected even from a conceptual artist like Warhol. Yet in line with the precepts of pop, it is an instant product: it becomes art wherever it is used. The great strength of the imagery precludes the use of paintings or the textile wall hangings that are extremely popular in contemporary homes.

What appeared to be the exploitation of new materials and technological advances created some anachronisms. This became apparent in the 1950s and 1960s in the use of glass-block walls and partitions, particularly in the construction of industrial plants and public schools. Glass blocks, originally called glass lenses, were first developed at the beginning of the century and were utilized in architectural experiments. As a building material, however, they were not popular until the 1930s, when Le Corbusier (the pseudonym of Charles Edouard Jeanneret) and other architects of the international style found them useful for factories and commercial structures. Le Corbusier was influenced by the work of the French designer Pierre Chareau, who in 1928 designed Maison de Verre, a Parisian house sheathed in these blocks. Glass block, created by seaming together two identical molded pieces, has been manufactured in many sizes and styles since the 1930s. The glass block is admired by builders because it is sound-absorbent and at the same time insulating, It is resistant to impact and fire and can provide visual privacy while allowing light to enter.

OVERLEAF:

433. Loft apartment. Beyer, Blinder, Belle, Architects. New York City. 1979. David and Jane Walentas, New York City

Converted loft spaces often provide a comfortable oasis in the bustling industrial centers of large cosmopolitan areas. This New York loft features a charming arrangement of American antiques and folk art combined with the chaste forms of contemporary furnishings. Manhattan's SoHo district, where this loft is located, is noted for its landmark-quality cast-iron manufacturing buildings erected at the turn of the century, many of which have been converted to artists' lofts and elegant condominium apartments.

Throughout the 1960s and 1970s interior design has experienced an ongoing search for innovation. Every development in the field of technology has been incorporated into a parade of changing tastes, pursued by a nation eager to be different and ahead of fashion. Fluorescent lamps by the 1950s had created a bright new world with few shadows. Neon lights, usually associated with theater and cinema marquees and store-front advertising, had become sculpture in the hands of such noted artists as Dan Flavin. The neon light frequently used in the contemporary home was born in the physics laboratory at the end of the nineteenth century. At that time it was discovered that electric current passing through a tube filled with colorless neon gas would produce a brilliant reddish-orange glow. Other gases produced other colors, but the term "neon" became generic. The French physicist Georges Claude unveiled the first commercial neon sign in Paris in 1910. Between 1920 and 1950 many other types of signs were developed; however, neon reigned supreme.

By the 1960s commercial neon signs were beginning to be appreciated as authentic industrial folk art, and innovative architect-designers were introducing neon lights into domestic settings. Pop artists had also learned to work with neon in a very creative way, devising neon sculpture and other three-dimensional forms, and today it is possible to order neon custom-made for the home or office for $6 to $40 a running foot, depending on the complexity of the work. The neon lighting in the living–dining room area (plate 420) echoes the curved and angular lines of the tubular steel chairs. In the 1970s and 1980s many decorators have tested even bolder experiments in the play of light. Abstract psychedelic projections and other stroboscopic and cinematic effects have been used in exciting ways to highlight or complement steel-covered walls, lacquered ceilings, and metal sculptures.

Gary Gutterman, noted for a sculptural quality in his furniture, has created for the New York–based Swedlow Group an assortment of Acrivue pieces (plate 421) that reveal some of the provocative design possibilities of the new synthetics. Acrivue, a gemlike acrylic highly prized for its flawless clarity, is being exploited by Gutterman and other modern designers to create distinctive furnishings for today and the future. To facilitate a rigid degree of manufacturing control, Gutterman established his own company, which produces an artful array of functional pieces including chairs, sofas, tables, desks, consoles, and étagères.

In the field of architecture no one has utilized the international style for domestic commissions with more success than Richard Meier, who is known for his elegant, geometrically lucid houses based on cubist concepts and the early work of Le Corbusier. Meier demonstrates a highly developed sense of proportion, and in that respect may be compared with Mies van der Rohe. Meier, a native of Newark, New Jersey, studied architecture at Cornell. Before opening his own office in 1963, he worked with three New York architectural firms —Davis, Brody and Wisniewski; Skidmore, Owings and Merrill; and Marcel Breuer.

One of Meier's most important buildings is the house (plate 422) put up in 1969–71 in Old Westbury, New York. In this structure he has demonstrated a sound appreciation of the machine aesthetic—that is, many of the elements are contrived to look as if they were machine-made even though they are actually handcrafted. Meier favors all-white exteriors for his houses and frequently depends upon a system of architectural massing that directly reflects the cubist tradition. The house in Old Westbury has an unusual number of bedrooms and baths and an obvious need for controlled circulation. The organization of the plan is along a line of motion, and because of the size of the project the line is extended into the vertical dimension, ramps forming the vertical continuity.

Perhaps no single mode of interior decoration has been as successful in recent years as high-tech, first introduced in the 1970s. There are many familiar elements in the high-tech style—glass-block windows, industrial lamps, coffee shop shelving, and abundant stainless steel or brass furnishings. A no-nonsense functionalism recorded in 1978 in *High-Tech: The Industrial-Style Source Book for the Home* by Joan Kron and Suzanne Slesin produced a soundness of practical design at every price level. Designers of the high-tech style rely upon a universal light fixture—the RLM lamp (plate 423), a generic name for porcelain-on-steel incandescent light reflectors. The RLM was introduced by several manufacturers in the 1930s, when it was frequently employed in factories and warehouses. RLM is an acronym for Registered Luminaire Manufacturer Institute, a member of the Standards Institute Group, an organization of lighting manufacturers that controls the conformance of light fixtures to national electrical codes. Toward the end of the 1970s the blatant factorylike designs of high-tech began to soften. Marilyn Bethany, writing in the July 20, 1980, issue of the *New York Times,* enthusiastically endorsed the new style as it had gone glamorous, or, as she referred to it, "high gloss tech."

In an attempt to diversify Herman Miller's products, Alexander Girard, who joined the firm in 1951, began to develop wallpaper and fabrics. His first fabric lines, introduced in 1952, featured a repeating pattern of squares or round forms on the overall piece of cloth. His wallpaper collection, introduced in the same year, gave preeminence to architectural outlines against a plain background. Girard's later decorative materials are noticeably different from those produced by virtually every major manufacturer in the 1970s. Color has disappeared, and, in what would seem to be a hymn to chastity, white fabrics have become the fashion of the day. White-on-white in richly textured geometric weaves dominated showrooms that catered to designers and tastemakers.

Two of the leading producers of this type of fabric are Gretchen Bellinger, Inc., and Stroheim and Romann. The use of textured fabrics to upholster furniture and cover walls shows a trend evident throughout the 1970s toward clean-looking stark interiors with boldly upholstered luxurious seating arrangements. Bellinger, a graduate of the Cranbrook Academy of Design, assimilated many of the notions about modern textile design established by the Saarinens. The white-on-white upholstery fabric of Stroheim and Romann (plate 424) unites strength and beauty. The durable cloth is produced from an all-cotton fiber, and the textured geometric weave is styled for a classic look that is appropriate in a modern setting.

A profound interest in textile upholstery has resulted in raised platforms, upholstered cubes and squares, and large pillows covered with purely utilitarian fabrics (plate 425). Typical of fine upholstered pieces furnishing sparse modern living spaces is the Habana modular seating (plate 426) designed by Stanley Jay Friedman for Brueton Industries in New York. Overall upholstered modular seating pieces first appeared in the 1930s and reappeared in the 1970s with the revived interest in the deco style.

Traditionally few decorative accessories were added to the unencumbered, trim interiors designed for international-style furniture. Those that were added tended to be custom-made objects, not the mass-produced items associated with modern industrial techniques. Americans are once again appreciative of hand-crafted work at every level and are enthusiastically collecting one-of-a-kind pieces. In fact many of the best accessories are available only in design center showrooms established especially for this type of merchandise. Many of these objects, such as the ceramic form by Ka-Kwong Hui (plate 427), the ceramic bowl by John Glick (plate 428), the hot-glass sculpture by Domenick Labino (plate 429), the contemporary art glass vase and bowl by John Lewis (plate 430), and the silver-plated brass vase and copper bowl by Douglas Steakley (plate 431), have a freedom of form and a delicacy of execution that only the sensitive artist working with patience and skill could accomplish.

The home of the future appears to be diminishing in size. Smaller families, single buyers, energy consciousness, and the practical reality of a finite supply of land are some of the factors bringing dramatic change to the housing industry. In the large urban centers the scarcity and astronomical cost of apartments have forced many city dwellers to consider the advantages of studio living. The rise in utility costs is another serious factor in proving that a tiny apartment may be the economical answer for single people or couples without children. Suzanne Slesin, in an article in the April 2, 1981, edition of the *New York Times*, discussed the ways in which architects and interior designers have been asked to rethink their approaches to these spaces. Instead of taking down walls to open up a room, the restructuring of space would involve putting in architectural elements—such as partial-height and full-height walls, built-in storage and seating, and some platforms. Slesin's analysis of contemporary directions is couched in the latest aesthetic terminology: "It is an approach that might be called post-minimalist. Unlike post-modernism, in which architectural elements are often used purely for theatricality, this sparser style makes a space look as if it had been stripped bare, when actually many structural elements have been added to it."

Unquestionably manufacturing techniques and materials will dictate the look and the value of the decorative arts of the 1980s. Wood, a rare structural material in the 1970s, was replaced by pressed composition fibers finished with a photo-vinyl veneer, a reproduction of wood grain. At the Southern Furniture Market in High Point, North Carolina, in the fall of 1980 new distinctions were being established by America's foremost furniture-producing firms. The term "all wood" was used to refer to pieces made with pressed sawdust and finished with veneer, whereas "solid wood" was reserved for the products of a few manufacturers—such as Baker, Henredon, Kittinger, and Pennsylvania House—who continued to create furniture completely out of this quickly disappearing organic material. In the future, synthetics will undoubtedly dominate a world that has depleted much of its precious natural resources and that has even begun to show scant concern with honesty of materials.

As for future styles, High Point's Southern Furniture Market may have also offered several clues in the spring 1981 show. The cliché references to modern, casual, and contemporary seemed more interchangeable than ever, and some of the designers were denying that a revival style like art deco had peaked and were insisting that it was only beginning to penetrate the marketplace. Yet the real hits at the High Point exhibit were the borrowings of pop images and presentations, including wooden cutout Walt Disney accessories, such as Goofy holding a laundrybag, and references to commonplace throwaway objects such as Dan Droz's "Popsycle" table (plate 432), a table base made of wood units that look like ice cream sticks but pivot out to support a tabletop. The New York firm of Beylerian Limited, which offers the Droz table, also produces other fanciful items, such as a whimsical kite lamp designed by the noted graphics artist Milton Glaser. Based on the principle of the classic kite, the paper lamp hangs on a hook on the wall.

After World War II most major American cities lost a substantial part of their population to the suburbs. The search for private housing, better schools, and a more amiable way of life led to the development of enclaves of planned communities, where almost every aspect of daily life has been stringently governed by local protective legislation. During the late 1960s and early 1970s—as many small manufacturers joined this flight to the suburbs, deserting industrial buildings in the urban centers—artists seeking combined living quarters and large work areas began to fill the city vacancies.

The abandonment of industrial and light manufacturing lofts in downtown industrial centers in the 1970s led city dwellers faced with increasingly diminished living quarters to exploit these larger, more expansive spaces. The loft conversion (plate 433), designed in 1978 and completed in 1979, consists of multilevel free-flowing spaces. The high ceilings and large floorplan provide a feeling of openness not available in most other urban living spaces. A casual mix of decorative styles has been chosen for this loft. Modern furnishings, including contemporary upholstered seating pieces, have been effectively combined with simple objects—such as a lively menagerie of folk art animals—that are nostalgic reminders of the American past.

It is impossible to predict the future with certainty. The decorative arts have always existed on many levels, and this diversity is no doubt even more

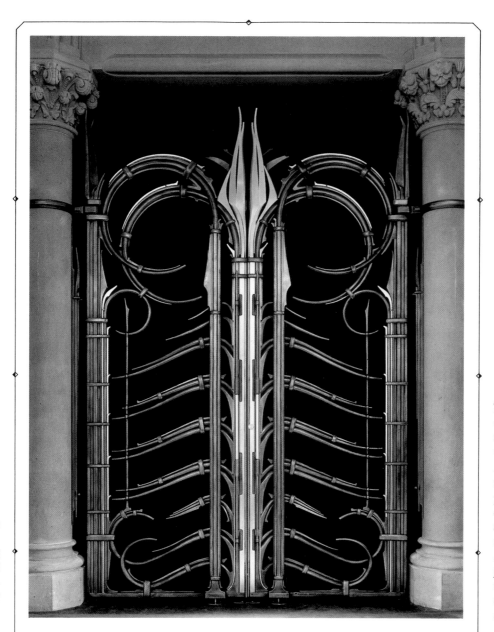

434. *Double-portal gate. Albert Paley. New York. 1980; installed 1981. Forged and fabricated mild steel, brass, and bronze, height 176". Senate Chamber, New York State Capitol Building, Albany, New York*

This massive double-portal gate is one of two sets installed before the antechambers of the Senate Chamber of the State Capitol Building in Albany. Paley's design is a bold contemporary statement, yet it unifies the nineteenth-century ornamental sensibilities evident in the existing architecture, designed in the 1870s by Henry Hobson Richardson. Despite their prodigious weight—each leaf weighs 3,000 pounds—the gates open and close at the touch of a hand.

widespread today. Although the majority of the population often appears to be conservative, more comfortable with the furnishings that reflect its cultural history, an elitist trend-setting group of architect-designers in each generation develops innovative ideas that interest the avant-garde. Albert Paley's double-portal gate (plate 434), combining the utilitarian with a sensitive ornamental design concept, is just such an indicator. Paley, who perhaps has had more exhibitions than any other artist-craftsman working in metal, has been offered many significant commissions, the most prestigious being the chalice for Pope Paul VI unveiled in 1976 at the forty-first International Eucharistic Congress in Philadelphia.

Paley's double-portal gate, commissioned for the New York State Capitol Building in Albany, was completed in 1980 and installed in the Senate Chamber in 1981. It is a fascinating synthesis of the past and future: the sinuous and organic qualities of art nouveau aesthetics—the last word in modern design at the beginning of the present century—are dramatically combined with elements suggesting the speed and upward thrust predictive of space age machinery of the twenty-first century. At the same time the gate is an elegant object rooted in sound workmanship, and it exemplifies the recurring bias of the American decorative artist and collector for stylish handcrafted one-of-a-kind objects. For more than three hundred sixty years such articles have taken pride of place among the best pieces of the nation's heritage. Brilliance of design, skill of execution, and imagination will certainly continue to dominate the American decorative arts of tomorrow.

◆ ◆ ◆

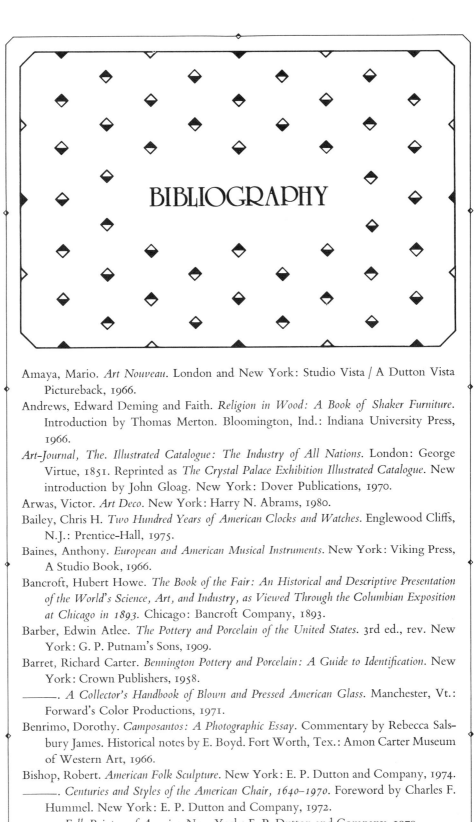

BIBLIOGRAPHY

Amaya, Mario. *Art Nouveau*. London and New York: Studio Vista / A Dutton Vista Pictureback, 1966.

Andrews, Edward Deming and Faith. *Religion in Wood: A Book of Shaker Furniture*. Introduction by Thomas Merton. Bloomington, Ind.: Indiana University Press, 1966.

Art-Journal, The. Illustrated Catalogue: The Industry of All Nations. London: George Virtue, 1851. Reprinted as *The Crystal Palace Exhibition Illustrated Catalogue*. New introduction by John Gloag. New York: Dover Publications, 1970.

Arwas, Victor. *Art Deco*. New York: Harry N. Abrams, 1980.

Bailey, Chris H. *Two Hundred Years of American Clocks and Watches*. Englewood Cliffs, N.J.: Prentice-Hall, 1975.

Baines, Anthony. *European and American Musical Instruments*. New York: Viking Press, A Studio Book, 1966.

Bancroft, Hubert Howe. *The Book of the Fair: An Historical and Descriptive Presentation of the World's Science, Art, and Industry, as Viewed Through the Columbian Exposition at Chicago in 1893*. Chicago: Bancroft Company, 1893.

Barber, Edwin Atlee. *The Pottery and Porcelain of the United States*. 3rd ed., rev. New York: G. P. Putnam's Sons, 1909.

Barret, Richard Carter. *Bennington Pottery and Porcelain: A Guide to Identification*. New York: Crown Publishers, 1958.

_____. *A Collector's Handbook of Blown and Pressed American Glass*. Manchester, Vt.: Forward's Color Productions, 1971.

Benrimo, Dorothy. *Camposantos: A Photographic Essay*. Commentary by Rebecca Salsbury James. Historical notes by E. Boyd. Fort Worth, Tex.: Amon Carter Museum of Western Art, 1966.

Bishop, Robert. *American Folk Sculpture*. New York: E. P. Dutton and Company, 1974.

_____. *Centuries and Styles of the American Chair, 1640–1970*. Foreword by Charles F. Hummel. New York: E. P. Dutton and Company, 1972.

_____. *Folk Painters of America*. New York: E. P. Dutton and Company, 1979.

_____. *How to Know American Antique Furniture*. New York: E. P. Dutton and Company, 1973.

Bishop, Robert, and Coblentz, Patricia. *Furniture 1: Prehistoric Through Rococo*. New York: Cooper-Hewitt Museum, Smithsonian Institution, 1979.

_____. *A Gallery of American Weathervanes and Whirligigs*. New York: E. P. Dutton and Company, 1981.

_____. *New Discoveries in American Quilts*. New York: E. P. Dutton and Company, 1975.

_____. *The World of Antiques, Art, and Architecture in Victorian America*. New York: E. P. Dutton and Company, 1979.

Bishop, Robert, and Safanda, Elizabeth. *A Gallery of Amish Quilts: Design Diversity from a Plain People*. New York: E. P. Dutton and Company, 1976.

Bohan, Peter J. *American Gold, 1700–1860*. New Haven, Conn.: Yale University Art Gallery, 1963.

Buhler, Kathryn C. *American Silver*. Cleveland: World Publishing Company, 1950.

————. *American Silver, 1655–1825, in the Museum of Fine Arts, Boston.* Boston: Museum of Fine Arts, 1972.

Champney, Freeman. *Art and Glory: The Story of Elbert Hubbard.* New York: Crown Publishers, 1968.

Charleston, Robert J. *Masterpieces of Glass: A World History from the Corning Museum of Glass.* Foreword by Thomas S. Buechner. New York: Harry N. Abrams, 1980.

Chase, Judith Wragg. *Afro-American Art and Craft.* New York: Van Nostrand Reinhold Company, 1971.

Christensen, Erwin O. *The Index of American Design.* Introduction by Holger Cahill. New York: Macmillan Company, 1960.

Clark, Robert Judson. *The Arts and Crafts Movement in America, 1876–1916.* Princeton, N.J.: Princeton University Press, 1972.

Clement, Arthur W. *The Pottery and Porcelain of New Jersey, 1688–1900.* Newark: Newark Museum Association, 1947.

Coffin, Margaret. *The History and Folklore of American Country Tinware, 1700–1900.* Camden, N.J.: Thomas Nelson, 1968.

Comstock, Helen. *American Furniture: Seventeenth, Eighteenth, and Nineteenth Century Styles.* New York: Viking Press, A Studio Book, 1962.

Connecticut Historical Society. *Morgan B. Brainard's Tavern Signs.* Hartford, Conn.: Connecticut Historical Society, 1958.

Cooper, Wendy A. *In Praise of America: American Decorative Arts, 1650–1830.* New York: Alfred A. Knopf, 1980.

Craven, Wayne. *Sculpture in America.* New York: Thomas Y. Crowell, 1968.

Cunnington, Phillis. *Costume in Pictures.* London and New York: Studio Vista / A Dutton Vista Pictureback, 1964.

Davenport, Millia. *The Book of Costume.* New York: Crown Publishers, 1948.

Davidson, Marshall B. *The American Heritage History of American Antiques from the Revolution to the Civil War.* New York: American Heritage Publishing Company, 1968.

————. *The American Heritage History of Antiques from the Civil War to World War I.* New York: American Heritage Publishing Company, *1969.*

————. *The American Heritage History of Colonial Antiques.* New York: American Heritage Publishing Company, 1967.

————. *The American Heritage History of Notable American Houses.* Biographical essays by Margot P. Brill. New York: American Heritage Publishing Company, 1971.

Davison, Mildred, and Mayer-Thurman, Christa C. *Coverlets: A Handbook on the Collection of Woven Coverlets in the Art Institute of Chicago.* Chicago: Art Institute of Chicago, 1973.

Distin, William H., and Bishop, Robert. *The American Clock: A Comprehensive Pictorial Survey, 1723–1900.* With a listing of 6,153 clockmakers. New York: E. P. Dutton and Company, 1976.

Downs, Joseph. *American Furniture in the Henry Francis du Pont Winterthur Museum: Queen Anne and Chippendale Periods.* Foreword by Henry Francis du Pont. New York: Macmillan Company, 1952.

————. *Pennsylvania German Arts and Crafts.* Rev. ed. New York: Metropolitan Museum of Art, 1949.

Durant, Mary. *The American Heritage Guide to Antiques.* New York: American Heritage Publishing Company, 1970.

Earnest, Adele. *The Art of the Decoy: American Bird Carvings.* New York: Clarkson N. Potter, 1965.

Eliot, Alexander. *Three Hundred Years of American Painting.* New York: Time Inc., 1957.

Emmerling, Mary Ellisor. *American Country: A Style and Source Book.* Foreword by Robert Bishop. New York: Clarkson N. Potter, 1980.

Fairbanks, Jonathan L., and Bates, Elizabeth Bidwell. *American Furniture: 1620 to the Present.* New York: Richard Marek Publishers, 1981.

Fales, Dean A., Jr. *American Painted Furniture, 1660–1880.* General Editor: Cyril I. Nelson. Illustrations and Design Editor: Robert Bishop. New York: E. P. Dutton and Company, 1972.

Fales, Martha Gandy. *American Silver in the Henry Francis du Pont Winterthur Museum.* Winterthur, Del.: Winterthur Museum, 1958.

Farrar, Estelle Sinclair, and Spillman, Jane Shadel. *The Complete Cut and Engraved Glass of Corning.* New York: Crown Publishers, 1979.

Feder, Norman. *American Indian Art.* New York: Harry N. Abrams, 1971.

————. *Two Hundred Years of North American Indian Art*. New York: Praeger Publishers, 1972.

Fitzgerald, Ken. *Weathervanes and Whirligigs*. New York: Clarkson N. Potter, 1967.

Freeman, John Crosby. *The Forgotten Rebel: Gustav Stickley and His Craftsman Mission Furniture*. Watkins Glen, N.Y.: Century House, 1966.

Fried, Frederick. *Artists in Wood: American Carvers of Cigar-Store Indians, Show Figures, and Circus Wagons*. New York: Clarkson N. Potter, 1970.

Gillon, Edmund V., Jr. *Early Illustrations and Views of American Architecture*. New York: Dover Publications, 1971.

Gould, Mary Earle. *Early American Wooden Ware and Other Kitchen Utensils*. Springfield, Mass.: Pond-Ekberg Company, 1942. Reprint. Rev. ed. Rutland, Vt.: Charles E. Tuttle, 1962.

Gowans, Alan. *Images of American Living: Four Centuries of Architecture and Furniture as Cultural Expression*. Philadelphia: J. B. Lippincott, 1964.

Grover, Ray and Lee. *Art Glass Nouveau*. Rutland, Vt.: Charles E. Tuttle, 1967.

Guilland, Harold F. *Early American Folk Pottery*. Philadelphia: Chilton Book Company, 1971.

Hanks, David A. *The Decorative Designs of Frank Lloyd Wright*. New York: E. P. Dutton and Company, 1979.

Hipkiss, Edwin J. *Eighteenth-Century American Arts: The M. and M. Karolik Collection of Paintings, Drawings, Engravings, Furniture, Silver, Needlework, and Incidental Objects Gathered to Illustrate the Achievements of American Artists and Craftsmen of the Period from 1720–1820*. Cambridge, Mass.: Harvard University Press, 1941.

Holstein, Jonathan. *American Pieced Quilts*. New York: Viking Press, A Studio Book, 1973.

Hood, Graham. *American Silver: A History of Style, 1650–1900*. New York: Praeger Publishers, 1971.

Hornor, William Macpherson, Jr. *Blue Book of Philadelphia Furniture: William Penn to George Washington with Special Reference to the Philadelphia-Chippendale School*. The author, 1935. Reprint. Rev. ed. Washington, D.C.: Highland House Publishers, 1977.

Hornung, Clarence. *Treasury of American Design: A Pictorial Survey of Popular Folk Arts Based upon Watercolor Renderings in the Index of American Design at the National Gallery of Art*. Foreword by J. Carter Brown. Introduction by Holger Cahill. 2 vols. New York: Harry N. Abrams, 1972.

Howat, John K., et al. *Nineteenth-Century America: Paintings and Sculpture*. New York: Metropolitan Museum of Art, 1970.

Innes, Lowell. *Early Glass of the Pittsburgh District, 1797–1890*. 2nd ed. Pittsburgh: Carnegie Museum, 1950.

Israel Sack, Inc. *American Antiques from Israel Sack Collection*. 6 vols. Washington, D.C.: Highland House Publishers, 1969–81.

Jacobs, Carl. *Guide to American Pewter*. New York: McBride Company, 1957.

Janis, Sidney. *They Taught Themselves: American Primitive Painters of the Twentieth Century*. Foreword by Alfred H. Barr, Jr. New York: Dial Press, 1942.

Johnson, Diane Chalmers. *American Art Nouveau*. New York: Harry N. Abrams, 1979.

Johnson, Marilynn; Schwartz, Marvin D.; and Boorsch, Suzanne. *Nineteenth-Century America: Furniture and Other Decorative Arts*. Introduction by Berry B. Tracy. New York: Metropolitan Museum of Art, 1970.

Jones, Harvey L. *Mathews: Masterpieces of the California Decorative Style*. Oakland, Calif.: Oakland Museum, 1972.

Kauffman, Henry J. *American Copper and Brass*. Camden, N.J.: Thomas Nelson, 1968.

————. *The American Pewterer: His Techniques and His Products*. Camden, N.J.: Thomas Nelson, 1970.

————. *Early American Ironware, Cast and Wrought*. Rutland, Vt.: Charles E. Tuttle, 1966.

Ketchum, William C., Jr. *Early Potters and Potteries of New York State*. New York: Funk and Wagnalls, 1970.

————. *Furniture 2: Neoclassic to the Present*. New York: Cooper-Hewitt Museum, Smithsonian Institution, 1981.

Kidney, Walter C. *The Architecture of Choice: Eclecticism in America, 1880–1930*. New York: George Braziller, 1974.

Kirk, John T. *Early American Furniture: How to Recognize, Evaluate, Buy, and Care for the Most Beautiful Pieces—High-Style, Country, Primitive, and Rustic*. New York: Alfred A. Knopf, 1970.

Knittle, Rhea Mansfield. *Early American Glass*. New York: Century Company, 1927.

————. *Early Ohio Silversmiths and Pewterers, 1787–1847*. Cleveland: Calvert-Hatch Company, 1943.

Kron, Joan, and Slesin, Suzanne. *High-Tech: The Industrial-Style Source Book for the Home*. Foreword by Emilio Ambasz. New York: Clarkson N. Potter, 1978.

Larrabee, Eric, and Vignelli, Massimo. *Knoll Design*. New York: Harry N. Abrams, 1981.

Lee, Ruth Webb. *Early American Pressed Glass*. Rev. ed. Northboro, Mass.: The author, 1946.

————. *Sandwich Glass: The History of the Boston and Sandwich Glass Company*. Framingham Centre, Mass.: The author, 1939. Reprint. Rev. ed. Wellesley Hills, Mass.: Lee Publications, 1947.

————. *Victorian Glass: Specialties of the Nineteenth Century*. Northboro, Mass.: The author, 1944.

Lipman, Jean, and Armstrong Tom, eds. *American Folk Painters of Three Centuries*. New York: Hudson Hills Press, 1980.

Lipman, Jean, and Winchester, Alice. *The Flowering of American Folk Art, 1776–1876*. New York: Viking Press, A Studio Book, 1974.

————, eds. *Primitive Painters in America, 1750–1950: An Anthology*. New York: Dodd, Mead and Company, 1950. Reprint. Freeport, N.Y.: Books for Libraries Press, 1971.

Little, Frances. *Early American Textiles*. Watkins Glen, N.Y.: Century Company, 1931.

Little, Nina Fletcher. *The Abby Aldrich Rockefeller Folk Art Collection: A Descriptive Catalogue*. Williamsburg, Va.: Colonial Williamsburg, 1957.

————. *American Decorative Wall Painting, 1700–1850*. Rev. ed. New York: E. P. Dutton and Company, A Dutton Paperback, 1972.

————. *Country Arts in Early American Homes*. Foreword by Wendell Garrett. New York: E. P. Dutton and Company, 1975.

————. *Floor Coverings in New England Before 1850*. Sturbridge, Mass.: Old Sturbridge Village, 1967.

————. *Neat and Tidy: Boxes and Their Contents in Early American Homes*. New York: E. P. Dutton and Company, 1980.

Lloyd, H. Alan. *The Collector's Dictionary of Clocks*. New York: A. S. Barnes and Company, 1964.

Maass, John. *The Gingerbread Age: A View of Victorian America*. New York: Bramhall House, 1957.

Mackey, William. *American Bird Decoys*. With a chapter on American decoys as folk art by Quintina Colio. New York: E. P. Dutton and Company, 1965.

Maher, James T. *The Twilight of Splendor: Chronicles of the Age of American Palaces*. Boston: Little, Brown and Company, 1975.

McClinton, Katharine Morrison. *American Glass*. Cleveland: World Publishing Company, 1950.

————. *Collecting American Nineteenth-Century Silver*. New York: Charles Scribner's Sons, 1968.

————. *Collecting American Victorian Antiques*. New York: Charles Scribner's Sons, 1966.

McKean, Hugh E. *The Lost Treasures of Louis Comfort Tiffany*. New York: Doubleday and Company, 1980.

McKearin, Helen and George S. *American Glass*. New York: Crown Publishers, 1948.

Meader, Robert F. W. *Illustrated Guide to Shaker Furniture*. Foreword by John Williams. New York: Dover Publications, 1972.

Mercer, Henry C. *The Bible in Iron*. Rev. ed. Doylestown, Pa.: Bucks County Historical Society, 1961.

Montgomery, Charles F. *American Furniture in the Henry Francis du Pont Winterthur Museum: The Federal Period*. Foreword by Henry Francis du Pont. New York: Viking Press, 1966.

Montgomery, Florence M. *Printed Textiles: English and American Cottons and Linens, 1700–1850*. New York: Viking Press, 1970.

Moody, Ella. *Modern Furniture*. New York: E. P. Dutton and Company, A Dutton Vista Pictureback, 1966.

Museum of Fine Arts, Boston. *M. and M. Karolik Collection of American Water Colors and Drawings, 1800–1875*. 2 vols. Boston: Museum of Fine Arts, 1962.

Museum of Fine Arts, Houston. *Southern Silver: An Exhibition of Silver Made in the South Prior to 1860*. Houston, Tex.: Museum of Fine Arts, 1968.

National Gallery of Art. *American Primitive Paintings from the Collection of Edgar William and Bernice Chrysler Garbisch*. 2 vols. Washington, D.C.: National Gallery of Art, 1954–57.

Naylor, Gillian. *The Bauhaus*. London and New York: Studio Vista / A Dutton Vista Pictureback, 1968.

Orlofsky, Patsy and Myron. *Quilts in America*. New York: McGraw-Hill Book Company, 1974.

Ormsbee, Thomas H. *Field Guide to American Victorian Furniture*. Boston: Little, Brown and Company, 1952.

Otto, Celia Jackson. *American Furniture of the Nineteenth Century*. New York: Viking Press, A Studio Book, 1965.

Palmer, Brooks. *The Book of American Clocks*. New York: Macmillan Company, 1950.

Peto, Florence. *American Quilts and Coverlets: A History of Charming Native Art Together with a Manual of Instruction*. New York: Chanticleer Press, 1949.

Rice, Alvin H., and Stoudt, John Baer. *The Shenandoah Pottery*. Introduction by Edwin LeFevre. Strasburg, Va.: Shenandoah Publishing House, 1959.

Rinhart, Floyd and Marion. *American Daguerreian Art*. New York: Clarkson N. Potter, 1967.

Rubin, Cynthia and Jerome. *Mission Furniture: Making It, Decorating with It, Its History and Place in the Antique Market*. San Francisco: Chronicle Books, 1980.

Rushlight Club. *Early Lighting: A Pictorial Guide*. Boston: Rushlight Club, 1972.

Safford, Carleton L., and Bishop, Robert. *America's Quilts and Coverlets*. New York: E. P. Dutton and Company, 1972.

Schiffer, Herbert F. and Peter B. *Miniature Antique Furniture*. Wynnewood, Pa.: Livingston Publishing Company, 1972.

Schwartz, Marvin D. *American Interiors, 1675–1885: A Guide to the American Period Rooms in the Brooklyn Museum*. Brooklyn, N.Y.: Brooklyn Museum, 1968.

Schwartz, Marvin D., and Wolfe, Richard. *A History of American Art Porcelain*. New York: Renaissance Editions, 1967.

Selz, Peter, and Constantine, Mildred, eds. *Art Nouveau: Art and Design at the Turn of the Century*. New York: Museum of Modern Art, 1959.

Shay, Felix. *Elbert Hubbard of East Aurora*. New York: W. H. Wise and Company, 1926.

Shelley, Donald A. *The Fraktur-Writings or Illuminated Manuscripts of the Pennsylvania Germans*. Allentown: Pennsylvania German Folklore Society, 1961.

Shepp, James W. and Daniel B. *Shepp's World's Fair Photographed*. Chicago: Globe Bible Publishing Company, 1893.

Silliman, Benjamin, and Goodrich, C. R., eds. *The World of Science, Art, and Industry, Illustrated from Examples in the New-York Exhibition, 1853–1854*. New York: G. P. Putnam and Company, 1854.

Sonn, Albert H. *Early American Wrought Iron*. 3 vols. New York: Charles Scribner's Sons, 1928.

Stillinger, Elizabeth. *The Antiques Guide to Decorative Arts in America, 1600–1875*. Introduction by Alice Winchester. New York: E. P. Dutton and Company, 1972.

Thwing, Leroy L. *Flickering Flames: A History of Domestic Lighting Through the Ages*. Rutland, Vt.: Charles E. Tuttle, 1958.

Tracy, Berry B., and Gerdts, William H. *Classical America, 1815–1845*. Newark, N.J.: Newark Museum Association, 1963.

Van Tassel, Valentine. *American Glass*. New York: Gramercy Publishing Company, 1950.

Varney, Almon C. *Our Homes and Their Adornments*. Rev. ed. Detroit, Mich.: J. C. Chilton, 1884.

Voss, Thomas M. *Antique American Country Furniture: A Field Guide*. Philadelphia: J. B. Lippincott, 1978.

Watkins, Lura Woodside. *Cambridge Glass, 1818 to 1888: The Story of the New England Glass Company*. Boston: Marshall Jones, 1930.

————. *Early New England Potters and Their Wares*. Cambridge, Mass.: Harvard University Press, 1950. Reprint. Hamden, Conn.: Archon Books, 1968.

Webster, Donald Blade. *Decorated Stoneware Pottery of North America*. Rutland, Vt.: Charles E. Tuttle, 1971.

Wilk, Christopher. *Thonet: One Hundred Fifty Years of Furniture*. Woodbury, N.Y.: Barron's Educational Series, 1980.

Wilson, Kenneth M. *New England Glass and Glassmaking*. New York: Thomas Y. Crowell, 1972.

◆ ◆ ◆

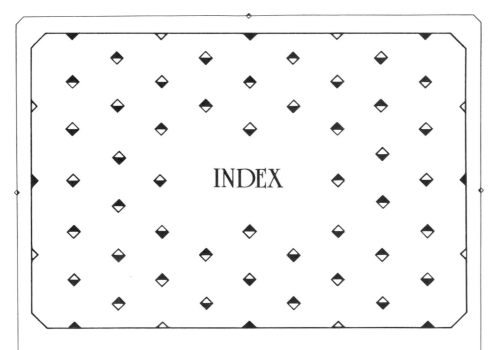

INDEX

Numbers in roman type refer to page numbers. Numbers in *italic* type indicate plate numbers. Asterisks* denote colorplates.

PHOTOGRAPH CREDITS

The authors and publisher wish to thank the museums, libraries, galleries, and private collectors for permitting the reproduction of objects in their collections. Photographs have been supplied by the owners or custodians of the works except for the following, whose courtesy is gratefully acknowledged. References are to plate numbers.

Albany Institute of History and Art, Albany, N.Y.: 73; Wayne Andrews, Grosse Point, Mich.: 276; *The Magazine Antiques:* 56; Douglas Armsden, Kittery Point, Maine: 39, 97; Gilbert Ask, Winterthur, Del.: 84, 128; William Edmund Barrett, Washington, D.C.: 387; E. Irving Blomstrann, New Britain, Conn.: 55; Will Brown, Philadelphia: 139; Geoffrey Clements, New York: 262, 334, 351; Mark Cohen, Pennsauken, N.J.: 374; H. Peter Curran, New York: 241; Charles d'Emery, Manugian Studio, South Norwalk, Conn.: 268; E. P. Dutton and Company, New York: 355, 356, 377, 418; Lee Fatherree, Berkeley, Calif.: 430; Bill Finney Photography, Concord, N.H.: 54; Dennis Flynn, Bayville, N.Y.: 195; Alexandre Georges, Pomona, N.Y.: 405; Kenneth M. Hay, Albany, N.Y.: 434; Helga Photo Studio, Upper Montclair, N.J.: 27, 199, 200, 383, 384; G. William Holland, Philadelphia: 370; David Huntington, Ann Arbor, Mich.: 277; Seth Joel, New York: 240, 373; Robert Koch, Norwalk, Conn.: 327; Gerald Kornblau Gallery, New York: 227; Robert Lorenz, Syracuse, N.Y.: 428; Herbert Matter, New York: 415, 416; Chris Mead, New York: 375; Allen Mewbourn, Houston: 53; Museum of Fine Arts, Boston: 312; National Geographic Society, Washington, D.C.: 161; O K Harris Works of Art, New York: 419; Herman S. Paris, Fair Lawn, N.J.: 244; Henry E. Peach, Sturbridge, Mass.: 129; David R. Phillips, Chicago Architectural Photo Company, Chicago: 354; Jonathan Pollock, Alta Loma, Calif.: 417; Rhode Island School of Design, Providence: 335; Sylvia Sarner, New York: 433; Mark Sexton, Salem, Mass.: 72; Chuck Sharbaugh, Holly, Mich.: 402; Smithsonian Institution, Washington, D.C.: 348; Ezra Stoller, Mamaroneck, N.Y.: 422; Joseph Szaszfai, New Haven, Conn.: 34; Keat Tan, Princeton, N.J.: 403; Richard Wurts, Litchfield, Conn.: 347.